LATINO
POLITICAL
POWER

LATINOS/AS:
EXPLORING DIVERSITY AND CHANGE

SERIES EDITORS
Edna Acosta-Belén, University at Albany, SUNY
Christine E. Bose, University at Albany, SUNY

EDITORIAL BOARD
Ginetta Candelario, Smith College
José E. Cruz, University at Albany, SUNY
Ramona Hernández, City College, CUNY
Cecilia Menjívar, University of Kansas, Lawrence
Clara Rodríguez, Fordham University at Lincoln Center
Vicki Ruiz, University of California at Irvine
Virginia Sánchez Korrol, Brooklyn College, CUNY

SECOND EDITION

LATINO POLITICAL POWER

Sharon A. Navarro
and Kim Geron

LYNNE
RIENNER
PUBLISHERS

BOULDER
LONDON

Published in the United States of America in 2023 by
Lynne Rienner Publishers, Inc.
1800 30th Street, Suite 314, Boulder, Colorado 80301
www.rienner.com

and in the United Kingdom by
Lynne Rienner Publishers, Inc.
Gray's Inn House, 127 Clerkenwell Road, London EC1 5DB
www.eurospanbookstore.com/rienner

© 2023 by Lynne Rienner Publishers, Inc. All rights reserved

Library of Congress Cataloging-in-Publication Data
Names: Navarro, Sharon Ann, author. | Geron, Kim, 1951– author.
Title: Latino political power / Sharon A. Navarro, Kim Geron.
Description: 2nd edition. | Boulder, Colorado : Lynne Rienner Publishers,
  Inc., 2023. | Includes bibliographical references and index. | Summary:
  "Maps the transformation of Latino political power from the 1960s to the
  present"— Provided by publisher.
Identifiers: LCCN 2022031918 (print) | LCCN 2022031919 (ebook) | ISBN
  9781955055819 (paperback) | ISBN 9781955055826 (ebook)
Subjects: LCSH: Hispanic Americans—Politics and government—20th century.
  | Hispanic Americans—Politics and government—21st century. | Power
  (Social sciences)—United States—History—20th century. | Power (Social
  sciences)—United States—History—21st century. | Political
  participation—United States—History—20th century. | Political
  participation—United States—History—21st century.
Classification: LCC E184.S75 N387 2023 (print) | LCC E184.S75 (ebook) |
  DDC 320.973/08968—dc23/eng/20221206
LC record available at https://lccn.loc.gov/2022031918
LC ebook record available at https://lccn.loc.gov/2022031919

British Cataloguing in Publication Data
A Cataloguing in Publication record for this book
is available from the British Library.

Printed and bound in the United States of America

 The paper used in this publication meets the requirements
of the American National Standard for Permanence of
Paper for Printed Library Materials Z39.48-1992.

5 4 3 2 1

Contents

List of Tables	vii
Acknowledgments	ix

1	Latino Politics: The Evolution of Inclusion	1
2	New Voices, New Contours of Political Power	19
3	The Struggle for Inclusion	43
4	Latino Politics in the Twenty-First Century	71
5	Participation and the Contours of Power	97
6	Political Power in the Sunbelt	129
7	Latinas: Political Activists and Leaders	167
8	Latino Political Power Today . . . and Tomorrow	195

References	209
Index	251
About the Book	269

Tables

1.1	Total Number of Latino Elected Officials, 2020	7
1.2	States with the Highest Number of LEOs	8
2.1	Chicano Electoral Representation, 1970	34
5.1	Latino Population in the Ten Largest Cities in 2020	101
5.2	Latino Voter Turnout	105
5.3	Analysis of Arizona Latino Voters, 2020	107
5.4	Analysis of Florida Latino Voters, 2020	108
5.5	Party Affiliation of Latino Voters by Ethnicity or Nationality Group	111
5.6	Latino Members of Congress	119
5.7	Latino Descriptive Representation	123
5.8	Latino Elected Officials, Education/School Boards	124
6.1	Miami-Dade County Population, 1960–2020	131
6.2	Exit Poll Results for Los Angeles Mayor in 2001	156
7.1	Latina US Representatives and Statewide Office	169

Acknowledgments

I cannot express enough the thanks and appreciation that I have for Kim Geron for allowing me to share in the completion of this project. He is an inspiring scholar, colleague, and friend.

It is also important that I thank my department and the College of Liberal and Fine Arts at the University of Texas at San Antonio for their financial support. Their assistance allowed us to complete this book.

The completion of the book could not have been accomplished without the support and patience of my family and loved ones. Thank you for understanding the importance of the book and for the sacrifices made to ensure its completion.

—*Sharon A. Navarro*

I want to express my sincere appreciation for the efforts of Sharon A. Navarro in taking on this project in the midst of the Covid-19 pandemic while juggling many other professional and personal responsibilities. Her insights and her knowledge of the complexities and nuances of the field of Latino politics have greatly enhanced this second edition. Many thanks, Sharon, for your many contributions and determined commitment to this new edition.

—*Kim Geron*

1

Latino Politics:
The Evolution of Inclusion

In 2021, in Salt Lake City, Utah, two Latinos were elected to the city council. Now four of the seven members are from racial and ethnic minorities, and there are now also four openly LGBTQ council members. Victoria Petro-Eschler and Alejandro Puy join council member Ana Valdermoros, making three Latinos on the council in a city that is 21 percent Latino and 63 percent White, with smaller percentages of Blacks, Asians, Pacific Islanders, and people of two or more races. In a conservative state politically, this election reflects the growing diversity in many communities across the United States.[1]

This book introduces the reader to the efforts of countless Latinos who have sought to fully participate in the US political system at its most basic level, as voters, political participants, candidates, and officeholders, among other forms of political inclusion at different levels of government. A largely untold story in American politics is the ascension of Latinos to elected office nationwide. In the early years of the twenty-first century, there are Latino elected officials (LEOs) at the local, state, and federal levels; many have achieved elected office fairly recently due to changing political structures and demographics, as well as Latinos' growing awareness of the importance of holding political power. Although there is uneven progress in the extent of officeholding from state to state and community to community, Latinos have established considerable influence statewide in several key Electoral College states, including Florida, Arizona, Nevada, and Texas. There are also enough Latino voters in other crucial states, like Wisconsin, Pennsylvania, and Michigan, to make a difference in closely contested elections.[2] Latinos are also the dominant influence in numerous large cities, such as Miami and San Antonio, and have growing influence in other cities, such as New York, Los Angeles, Chicago, and San Jose.

2   Latino Political Power

Yet Latinos in political office are not a new phenomenon in the United States. Spanish and Mexican settlers arrived in the late 1500s and established settlements and governed themselves in the northern New Mexico area beginning in the early 1600s under the sovereignty of Spain and Mexico.[3] After the United States annexed the northern half of Mexico in 1848, following the war between the United States and Mexico, the New Mexico region became a US territory. The Hispano descendants continued to govern themselves until New Mexico became a state in 1912. Mexicans who remained in the Southwest region of the United States following the annexation of northern Mexico became US citizens; over the next 100 years some of them were elected to political office, including city council member, mayor, US senator, US representatives, and governor. Outside New Mexico, however, only a handful of Latinos were elected to office; by and large Latinos remained marginalized in the US electoral arena. This began to change in the 1960s.

This book is a comparative analysis of the diversity of Latino politics in the United States. It explores the political struggles of Mexicans, Puerto Ricans, Cubans, Dominicans, Salvadorans, Colombians, and other Latinos in rural, suburban, and urban areas of the United States to transition from marginalized descendants of the Spanish conquest and indigenous peoples, to immigrants and political refugees, and to officeholders and decisionmakers. While the media have begun to focus on the growing significance of the Latino vote for presidential elections, the development of Latino political efforts at the state and local levels has not received much coverage. This book aims to explain one facet of a larger story of the Latino political experience: the efforts of Latinos to obtain political power, particularly at the local level, where the forces of opposition to their achievement of political equality have been most virulent.

The purpose of this book is twofold: (1) to describe the transition of Latinos from disenfranchised outsiders to political leaders and policymakers at the local level and, increasingly, at the statewide level, and (2) to observe their relationships with their ethnic communities as candidates and as elected officials. We examine to what degree Latino elected officials are sensitive to ethnic community concerns and whether they deliver policy benefits to their communities. This book highlights how Latinos have achieved political empowerment and how they have provided leadership in office. After obtaining elected office, not all Latinos act the same. Some are more responsive to ethnic community needs; others are more attentive to concerns of the larger communities they serve; still others straddle ethnic community needs and universal needs in their policymaking priorities. This chapter begins with a discussion of key terms used in the text, including the racialization process of Latinos; it then briefly reviews the underrepresentation of Latinos in politics. Next, an exploration of the growing impact of

Latinos on electoral power in the twenty-first century provides a look at contemporary Latino politics. A discussion of the concepts explored in the text, including representation and political incorporation, follows.

Labels

What is Latino politics? A discussion of the terms used in this text must by necessity begin with a definition of *politics*. Politics is the study of who gets what, when, and how. The *who* are the participants in politics, including voters, interest groups, political parties, and elected and appointed government officials. The *what* are the public policies produced by the political system in areas such as education, health care, and national defense. *When* and *how* refer to the dynamics of the political process, including campaigns for office and elections, implementation of legislation, and decisions made by the courts.[4]

In this book, the term *Latino* is used to refer to all individuals originally from Spanish-speaking regions of Latin America and the Caribbean. *Latino* does not refer to a specific race of people; rather it is inclusive of indigenous, White, Black, Asian, and mixed-race people. As Marcelo Suarez-Orozco and Mariela Paez note, "The Latino population is a highly heterogeneous population that defies easy generalizations."[5] The term *Latino politics* will be used to refer to the broad array of efforts by Latinos in politics, whether they are joint efforts by several national-origin groups working together in one group or political activity or the efforts simply of one national-origin group.

The term *Hispanic* is used by the US government, and by some who self-identify as such, to include anyone from a Spanish-speaking region, including Spain. This term will be used sparingly, except where it refers to a governmental designation or in those instances where it is the chosen self-designation. While *Hispanic* is controversial in some quarters, in a recent survey conducted by the Pew Hispanic Center, it was preferred over other such terms.[6]

Mexican American and *Chicano* are used to refer to people of Mexican descent raised in the United States. The term *Chicano* became popular among Mexican American political activists in the late 1960s as a means of political self-definition, and it retains popularity today. Others from a Spanish-origin population apply terms such as *Hispano, Spanish American*, and *Latin* to their heritage. *Tejano* and *Californio* are used to refer to Mexicans who lived in what is now the US Southwest before its annexation in 1848. Where possible, the word or term used in previous research or in a group or person's self-identification is used. *White* and *Anglo* are used to refer to non-Latino Caucasians, and *Black* and *African American* are used to refer to residents of the United States with an African heritage. People from the Caribbean islands

4   Latino Political Power

are referred to by their country of origin; similarly, persons from Central and South America are referred to by their country of origin.

Latinx has emerged in recent years as a new pan-ethnic term to describe the nation's diverse Hispanic population. It is increasingly being used in social media, where it is replacing earlier gender-neutral labels such as Latino/a or Latin@. The Latinx label has gained increasing use in higher education, where it is disrupting traditional notions of inclusion and shaping institutional understanding of intersectionality, particularly with people living gender-fluid and hybrid identities. When asked about their preferred pan-ethnic term to describe the Hispanic or Latino population, a majority of adults prefer other terms over Latinx. Only 3 percent preferred Latinx to describe the Hispanic or Latino population.[7]

Despite the diversity among Latinos, a common political legacy has been formed by their collective experiences and identity. This is not to say each distinct national-origin group does not have unique political as well as other characteristics, but the dominant US political system has racialized Spanish-speaking peoples from throughout the hemisphere into a broad category known by labels such as *Latinx, Latino, Hispanic,* and *Hispanic American.* In other circumstances, multiple national-origin groups of Latinos are racially lumped into one predominant group, such as Mexican, Puerto Rican, or Cuban, by those outside the Latino community, such as government agencies, the English-speaking media, and the public. In both instances, this has the effect of diluting national distinctions, and many Latinos find such dilution problematic.

Racialization is "the construction of racially unequal social hierarchies characterized by dominant and subordinate social relations between groups."[8] One form racialization takes is the US government's use of racial and ethnic categories for census enumeration and apportionment for political representation. After each ten-year census, federal, state, and local governments redivide political boundaries based in part on broad racial and group categories, including Hispanic. This process groups together all persons with origins in Spanish-speaking countries. The lumping of peoples from throughout the Americas into one category masks important political and social differences among Latinos, such as the influence of homeland politics, national-origin distinctions, party affiliation, citizenship status, and ideological beliefs. On the positive side, the commonality of a pan-ethnic designation has brought Latinos together to work for shared political goals, including civil rights, redistricting of electoral boundaries, support for bilingual education, and equal opportunity.

Still, despite efforts at cooperation among Latino ethnic groups and the growth of pan-ethnic organizations, at the time of this writing there is no political agenda adhered to by all Latinos. The heterogeneity of political views among the major ethnic groups, the lack of an identifiable national leader (or leaders) who could unite all Latinos around a common program, and a high percentage of new immigrants in the Latino community with strong ties to their countries of origin make political unity difficult in the short run. While Latinos tend to agree on some social issues, such as support for bilingual education, they are not united in their views on other issues, such as immigration—particularly illegal immigration. A 2013 survey indicated that over half—53 percent—of the Latinos believe undocumented immigrants have a positive impact on Latinos living in this country. A much heavier majority—75 percent—say they are helping rather than hurting the economy.[9] The presence of Democratic and Republican Latinos in Congress and in several state legislatures reflects political and more fundamental ideological differences and has resulted in distinct Latino caucuses based on party affiliation at the state and federal levels.

Nonetheless, as racial minorities in the United States, the majority of Latinos find themselves in barrios where local educational institutions are poorly funded, where crime and drugs are prevalent, and where politically they have been disenfranchised until very recently. This book makes the case that the Latino community in the twenty-first century—whether in Lawrence, Massachusetts; Orlando, Florida; Brownsville, Texas; Cicero, Illinois; Pueblo, Colorado; or Oakland, California—has developed common political experiences, and these similar experiences cross state lines and regional particularities. Today, a typical group experience of Latinos, whether they are American born or immigrant, involves participating in efforts to achieve political incorporation at the local level and beyond. In some instances, Latinos join together as Latinos, not simply as an alliance of national-origin Latinos. Other times there is a go-it-alone attitude, with an emphasis on national-origin compatriots. This is both a unique and not so unique experience: like African Americans and other racial minorities, Latinos have learned they need to join together to increase their opportunities for advancement; yet, at times there is only limited cooperation among Latino national-origin groups. Nevertheless, there is some evidence that a distinct brand of politics known as Latino politics has emerged in the United States. Time will tell whether it becomes established as a distinctive form of politics or becomes more similar to the political activities of other groups.

The Underrepresentation of Latinos

Historically, the domination of politics and economics by Anglos was almost universal in the United States. There were virtually no non-White elected officials until the 1950s, except in New Mexico and a few local areas. The emergence of the modern Latino civil rights and nationalist movements in the 1960s and 1970s forced the political process open for a

6   Latino Political Power

previously disenfranchised ethnic group.[10] Latinos used a variety of methods to gain entrance to institutions that had previously excluded them, "but underrepresentation remained the rule."[11] Inequalities in employment, unequal access to education, limited opportunities for social advancement, and a cultural bias that privileged the language, customs, and values of Whites were difficult to overcome. According to pluralist theory, an important theory in the study of US politics, power is dispersed in society somewhat equally among various groups and institutions; thus no one group dominates the full policy agenda in American politics. However, the experiences of racial minorities, including Latinos, reveal continuing major disparities between Whites and nonwhites in the political sphere and other aspects of society. Conventional pluralism is unable to explain why racial minorities have little power in our society despite the growth of interest groups focused on equality. The theory of two-tiered pluralism more accurately describes the system's formal political inclusion of minorities with Whites, while minorities remain marginalized with few avenues for full participation and equality.[12]

The political legacy of discrimination and marginalization of minority groups is manifested in underrepresentation in elected offices. According to one author, "When marginalized groups are chronically underrepresented in legislative bodies, citizens who are members of those groups are not fairly represented."[13] The extent of electoral empowerment of racial minorities can be viewed as a measure of whether the US political system can be categorized as just: "Equal access to decision making is therefore defined as an equal opportunity to influence the policy-making process. Such a situation has two elements: a realistic opportunity to participate on the basis of self-defined interests and a continuous opportunity to hold representatives accountable to community-based interests."[14]

To gain access to the electoral process, Latinos have used grassroots activism, legal challenges, and group protest.[15] The passage of the Voting Rights Act in 1965, the extension of voting rights legislation to linguistic minorities in 1975, the elimination of structural barriers to participation, and the creation of single-member districts eliminated many formal barriers to inclusion.

These legal and structural changes, combined with group mobilization efforts, have enabled Latinos to hold elected office in locations and in numbers not previously possible. In 1973, a few years after the passage of the Voting Rights Act, there were only 1,280 Spanish-surnamed officials in the six largest Latino-population states.[16] The growth of Latino political efforts in the post–civil rights era of the 1980s and 1990s is evident in the numbers of Latinos who hold elective office at all levels of government. As of 2020, there were 6,882 Latino elected officials, 39.1 percent of them Latinas (see Table 1.1).

Table 1.1 Total Number of Latino Elected Officials, 2020

Level of Office	Number of Males	Number of Females	Total
US senators	3	1	4
US representatives	27	12	39
State officials	11	6	17
State senators	43	45	88
State representatives	137	99	236
County officials	301	225	526
Municipal officials	1,493	749	2,242
Judicial law enforcement	565	338	903
Education school boards	1,436	1,156	2,592
Special districts	174	61	235
Total	4,190	2,692	6,882

Source: National Directory of Latino Elected Officials 2020.

Yet the total number of Latino elected officials is still woefully discrepant with Latinos' percentage of population. The 6,882 LEOs listed in Table 1.1 represented about 1.3 percent of the nation's 519,682 elected officials,[17] while the Latino population reached a record 62.1 million in 2020, up 930,000 over the previous year and up from 50.5 million in 2010.[18] By comparison, in 2019 the US Census Bureau estimated 48,221,139 African Americans (or 13.4 percent) in the United States, compared to 13 percent identifying as African American only in 2010.[19] The number of African American elected officials is on par (13 percent) with the share of the overall US population that is African American.[20] In addition, the number of African American elected officials is nearly double the number of LEOs for a comparable minority population. While the number of African American elected officials still falls short of their percentage of the population, their larger number relative to LEOs reflects several factors, including the long struggle to obtain the right to vote in the South and a high rate of US citizenship, which has enabled more African Americans to participate in the voting process and vote for an African American candidate.[21]

The imbalance in the number of LEOs relative to the Latino percentage of the population reflects a combination of factors, including the legacy of exclusion and structural barriers faced by Latino candidates for office, low participation rates in politics among Latino groups, and a high percentage of immigrants who are not yet engaged in politics. Latino elected officials are

8   *Latino Political Power*

concentrated in nine states, including three of the four largest-population states in the country (see Table 1.2). These nine states had 91.75 percent of the Latino elected and appointed officials in the United States and accounted for more than 20.10 percent of the total Latino population in 2019.[22] In California, New Mexico, and Texas, LEOs represented 74.3 percent of all Latinos elected in the United States.[23]

The Impact of Latinos in Recent Electoral Campaigns

Since the initial publication of this book, the power of the Latino vote during presidential seasons has found its footing. In the presidential election of 2008, Latinos voted for Democrats Barack H. Obama and Joseph R. Biden over Republicans John McCain and Sarah Palin by a margin of more than two to one, or 67 percent versus 31 percent,[24] with Latinos consisting of 9 percent of the electorate.[25] This was higher, by one percentage point, than the share in the 2004 national exit poll.[26]

Then again, in 2012, Latinos flexed their muscle at the polls and voted for President Barack Obama over Republican Mitt Romney by 71 to 27 percent, according to the Pew Hispanic Center.[27] Latinos made up 10 percent of the electorate, up from 9 percent in 2008 and 8 percent in 2004.[28] In 2016, the national exit poll showed that Hillary Clinton drew 65 percent of the Latino vote compared with 29 percent for Donald Trump.[29] Latinos made up 11 percent of the electorate in the 2016 presidential election.[30]

Table 1.2   States with the Highest Number of LEOs

State	Total
Texas	2,784
California	1,660
New Mexico	664
Arizona	383
Florida	202
New York	168
New Jersey	166
Colorado	157
Illinois	129
Total	6,313

Source: National Association of Latino Elected Officials (NALEO) Education Fund 2020.

According to the Pew Research Center, 16.6 million Latino voters cast a ballot in the 2020 presidential election nationally, comprising 13.3 percent of the electorate.[31] This represented a 30.9 percent increase, nearly double the nationwide 15.9 percent growth in ballots cast between the 2016 and 2020 presidential elections.[32] This was the single largest four-year increase in the Latino vote ever. Latino voters supported the Democratic candidate, Joe Biden, by very wide margins across the country.

Latino voters supported Biden over Trump by a nearly three-to-one margin in the counties that were analyzed in Arizona, California, Colorado, Illinois, New Mexico, Nevada, New York, Pennsylvania, and Wisconsin.[33] In Arizona, the size of the Latino electorate and its overwhelming support for Joe Biden flipped the state from Republican to Democratic for the first time since Bill Clinton ran in 1996.[34] Arizona showed just what Latinos acting as a concentrated voting bloc could achieve. In Wisconsin and Georgia, where Latinos make up less than 5 percent of registered voters combined, the Latino electorate helped tipped the results in favor of Biden, whose margin of victory was less than a single percentage point in each state.[35] Latino voters' strong support for Biden and growth in votes cast helped tip the state in favor of the Democratic candidate. In states like Georgia, a small but growing Latino electorate was part of a large, Black-led multiracial coalition that added to Democrats' winning. For years both Latino and Black voters felt as though they were left out of the conversation when it came to shaping policy and were seen as an afterthought when it came to elections. The 2020 presidential election changed that.

Latinos chose Biden over Trump by a margin of two or more to one in the counties analyzed in a study of Texas, Georgia, and Washington and in Florida outside Miami-Dade County.[36] In Florida, the Latino vote is diverse and unique from the rest of the nation. Latinos in Miami-Dade supported Trump by a two-to-one margin, but Latinos in the rest of the state preferred Biden two to one.[37]

Many observers said voting results in Miami-Dade County—where Trump got support from the majority of Latino voters—was evidence of a wider Latino swing toward Trump. Although the Miami-Dade result did help Trump win Florida, the Pew Research Center found in all Florida counties outside Miami-Dade, Latino voters favored Biden by a margin of two to one. And in every other state analyzed by Pew Research, Latinos voted for Biden by wide margins.

The power of the Latino electorate has also been measured by the many "firsts" in elected office. For example, in 2011, Susana Martinez became the first female governor of New Mexico and the first Latina female governor in the United States. In Nevada, Brian Sandoval became the first Latino governor of the state in 2011. In 2015, Evelyn Sanguinetti became the first Latina lieutenant governor in the United States. In 2017,

10   *Latino Political Power*

Nevada elected its first Latina Democratic US senator, Catherine Marie Cortez Masto. Prior to her rise to the US Senate, she served as the state's attorney general from 2007 to 2014. In 2019, Veronica Escobar and Sylvia Garcia became the first two Latinas ever elected to represent Texas in Congress. Escobar previously served as an El Paso County judge prior to her run for Beto O'Rourke's seat. Garcia previously served as a state representative prior to running for Congress. In 2019, Alexandria Ocasio-Cortez (D-NY) became the first Latina Democratic Socialist of America elected to serve in Congress. In 2020, Alex Padilla, a Los Angeles Democrat who once developed software for satellites but later rose through local and state political office to become California's secretary of state,[38] was chosen to take Vice President Kamala Harris's place in the US Senate. This appointment tears down barriers for Latinos that have stood for as long as California has been a state. Latinos can be a powerful political ally. They are youthful and diverse and projected to make up 27.5 percent of the American population by 2060.[39] This translates into immense political power as more of that population grows into the electorate.

Latinos and Representation in Government

Political representation has been the focus of the struggle for political equality by people of color, women, and others who are historically disadvantaged. *Political representation* refers to a prescribed relationship between elected officials and constituents. There are different dimensions of representation: formal, descriptive, symbolic, and substantive.[40] Formal representation refers to the institutional rules and regulations that precede and initiate representation. In *descriptive representation*, the race, ethnicity, or national origin of the representative matches that of his or her constituents.[41] As one author states, "Voters want to see someone who looks like them in office. Black voters tend to support black candidates and Hispanic voters tend to support Hispanic candidates."[42] The highest form of representation is *substantive representation*, where a representative acts in the interests of the represented, in a manner responsive to them.[43] The main component of substantive representation is policy responsiveness: "There should be meaningful connection between the representative and the represented."[44]

Descriptive representation, in which the representative reflects the social composition of the people he or she represents, is still an important goal for many Latino communities. Once elected, Latino officeholders need to bring both symbolic and material benefits to the Latino community.[45] *Symbolic representation* refers to the extent that representatives "stand for" the represented. This is important because Latino elected officials become role models for a community that has had few visible political leaders. Yet symbolism is not enough; the majority of Latinos remain impoverished, with many social problems that need to be addressed.

Economic resources are needed to provide affordable housing, expand youth services, improve the quality of education, and build recreational facilities. The structural inequalities in America severely limit what politicians can do to erase fundamental problems of inequality and poverty. Nevertheless, under certain circumstances some Latino officials have taken action to direct resources to address long-standing problems in the Latino community. Such actions need to be analyzed. Of course, Latino politicians do not exist in a vacuum; LEOs have also prioritized universal issues such as economic development, fiscal accountability, crime reduction, environmental cleanup, and traffic-congestion reduction. While these types of issues are concerns within Latino communities, the benefits of new policies are not specifically directed at the elected official's own community, although they may disproportionately impact the Latino community, particularly in low-income areas.

In a democracy there are limits to what an individual representative can accomplish for his or her constituents, since competing interests and priorities vie for the attention of lawmakers at all levels of government. Particularly for racial-minority legislators, ascending to elected office has not always substantively benefited the constituents who helped put them there.[46] Some argue minority legislators and executives have only begun to achieve political power after many years of exclusion; they are still a minority of the elected officials at the federal level and in state capitols and have limited resources at the local level to resolve basic inequalities.[47]

Latinos and Political Incorporation Theory

To move from disenfranchisement to political power, Latinos have used a variety of methods. To explain the process of achieving and retaining political power, we use political incorporation theory. According to researchers Rufus Browning, Dale Marshall, and David Tabb, *political incorporation* entails local "movements demanding the power of political equality and their ability to achieve it."[48] Political incorporation is a widely used measure of the extent to which group interests are effectively represented in policymaking in government.[49] At the lowest level, a group is not represented at all: there are no elected officials from the group, and the group does not participate in the governing coalition that controls political decisionmaking through its use of resources. At the next level, a group, such as a racial minority, has formal representation in a governing body, but the government body is dominated by a coalition resistant to racial minority group interests. In the highest form of incorporation, racial minorities have an

12 *Latino Political Power*

equal or a leading role in a dominant coalition that is strongly committed to racial minority group interests.

For Latinos, the achievement of political incorporation has been uneven; there is wide divergence in the levels of incorporation at the local, state, and national levels. Because the history of Latino political movements in achieving incorporation has unfolded differently in state and local contexts, patterns of mobilization have also evolved differently. In some situations, Latinos were until recently completely excluded from access to government. In other situations, they were partially included in a governing coalition as junior partners in a political party or on business-centered slates. Under certain circumstances, they achieved an equal or dominant role without the use of a biracial coalition; an example is the achievement of Cubans in Miami.[50]

Groups seek to obtain political objectives in several ways. They can petition or pressure government from the outside (the interest group strategy) or seek to achieve representation and a position of power or authority by electing members of the group to office (the electoral strategy). Each of these approaches is pursued depending on circumstances. The protest strategy is usually employed when a group has been excluded and seeks to use group pressure to win appointments to positions, funding for programs, and increased hiring of members of the group. The electoral strategy is used when a group is sufficiently large to win office by itself or with allies in a coalition.[51]

Pathways to Political Incorporation

We have modified these two forms of mobilization to include other pathways to incorporation. There are at least four distinct pathways to political incorporation: (1) demand/protest, (2) nonconfrontational political evolution, (3) legal challenges to structural barriers, and (4) coalition politics.

The first pathway, demand/protest, includes violent and nonviolent protests (sit-ins, demonstrations, boycotts) and also includes more traditional tactics, such as mass mobilization at city or school board meetings and direct exchanges with city officials.[52] A second pathway is a more gradual political evolution without demand and protest; instead, individuals in the Latino community are groomed by political elites to run for office, usually as pro-business candidates and as alternatives to more grassroots candidates. A third pathway is the use of legal challenges, usually voting rights lawsuits that challenge redistricting and reapportionment plans and lead to restructuring of the electoral system. Latinos have used the legal approach in many communities nationally to overturn discriminatory political structures and create single-member districts.

The fourth pathway is the use of coalition politics. Browning, Marshall, and Tabb discuss the critical importance of biracial coalitions of racial or ethnic minorities and liberal Whites to achieve political incorporation for minorities that do not comprise a majority of the local population. We view the coalition pathways as including other possibilities depending on the situation, such as the 2020 African American efforts in coalition with Latinos in cities such as Minneapolis, Miami, New York City, Los Angeles, and San Antonio to protest the murder of George Floyd and join the fight for racial justice.[53] These pathways are not mutually exclusive; each may include aspects of other pathways to achieve political incorporation. Latino political incorporation efforts have historically used all of them in small towns, medium-sized cities, major urban centers, and state houses of government.

What can reasonably be expected in a democratic society as a result of the incorporation of previously disenfranchised groups? One school of thought holds there are limits to what local officials can accomplish, given the fiscal limitations of local government in this era of global capital mobility and decreased federal and state assistance.[54] Others argue that while there are limits to what public bodies can accomplish in an era of globalization and fiscal conservatism, this does not mean that local government has no ability to redirect resources.[55] The general fund portion of any budget can be directed to address problems including social and economic inequalities; however, the level of resources will depend on the structural limitations of available funds. Furthermore, city leaders do not simply respond to a cost-benefit analysis of the prospect of economic advancement and political empowerment of racial groups. Poor and working-class people sometimes exercise power when they mobilize in mass defiance, breaking the rules that have restricted their participation in the institutions of a densely interdependent society.[56] At times resources are redirected to confront systemic problems. Many of the antipoverty programs of the 1960s arose in response to the riots in urban communities by racial minorities.

In addition to the structural arguments about achieving political power, there is the historical argument that the deeply embedded character of race relations and the history of racial antagonisms on an individual and institutional level have limited full participation by people of color in the economic, political, and cultural arenas of our society. The weight of this economic, political, and cultural domination has forced Latinos to try to overcome the legacy of exclusion by or condescension from Anglo politicians. The various outcomes of those efforts are important to document and compare.

As historical barriers to political inclusion have come down, Latino electoral efforts have blossomed; however, not enough is known about the consequences of these changes. Obviously, not all electoral efforts begin in the same way, seek to achieve the same objectives, or accomplish the same goals. These distinctions in the empowerment of Latinos reflect

14 *Latino Political Power*

basic differences in political conditions and the individual philosophies of candidates regarding the role of government. Both internal dynamics within ethnic communities and forces external to the Latino community influence its political development.

In short, this book examines Latina and Latino efforts to overcome discriminatory barriers, seek political office, and establish policy priorities once in elected office. It explores how LEOs address the challenges of limited resources and conflicting interests that confront all elected officials, while maintaining ties to the Latino community. In particular, this text explores the role of Latinas, immigrants, and ethnic-specific and pan-ethnic Latino politics.

Research and Data Sources

The research for this book is based on primary and secondary sources. Archival research, survey data, in-depth interviews, and ethnographic methods were used to gather materials from 2021 to 2022. We conducted semi-structured interviews with a cross section of community leaders and activists across the nation and observed firsthand how Latino politics operated in Latino-majority communities and in communities where Latinos numbered less than 2,000.

According to the 2020 National Directory of Latino Elected Officials, there are 2,692 Latina elected officeholders. We solicited a cross section of them over a period of several months. Follow-up emails and calls were made to ensure contact was made. However, the challenges of coordinating dates and times proved infeasible for many of them for the following reasons: a pressing national legislative agenda, participation in budgetary committees, states with year-round legislative sessions, primary mid-term election campaigns, campaigns for other state or local offices, and limited communication because of staff shortages (several staffers were multitasking and serving in more than one role, and scheduling interviews was not a priority). Interviews were conducted via Zoom and phone. We conducted archival research in public libraries, universities, and local governments in those areas. We also spoke with scholars and activists in many of the cities to draw on their insights regarding the operation of Latino politics in different contexts. Subsequently, we have continued to interview elected officials and study more recent political developments in several cities and counties.

Since we were a little over a year into the Covid-19 pandemic, it was impossible to attend national conferences and meetings of organizations involved with Latino politics, including the National Association of Latino Elected and Appointed Officials and the Southwest Voter Registration Education Project. A detailed review of articles, books, dissertations, and studies about Latino politics was completed as part of this research. This combination of research methodologies and sources has produced a study that combines the practical experiences of electoral politics with analytical observations about Latino politics.

Organization of the Book

This is an introductory text about Latinos in American politics. Its purpose is to provide an overview of historical and current efforts by Latinos to achieve political power. While many books have been written on the Latino experience, and several have been written on Latino politics, this book discusses in detail the strategies and methods Latinos have used to achieve political power. Furthermore, it tracks what happened once Latinos achieved political incorporation in various political contexts. The electoral arena is not the only, or even the main, vehicle that Latinos have used to achieve equal treatment under the law, end discrimination in schools, housing, and jobs, oppose racist stereotyping, and create positive images of themselves. Nevertheless, a study of the broad range of efforts by Latinos to influence and participate in the electoral system provides a means to explore the progress made to achieve representation. Latino politics is evolving within the larger American political system. It is our intent to study the evolving process of political inclusion, thereby creating a sense of agency and belonging.

We are now ready to explore the history and development of Latino politics and its contemporary features. Chapters 2 and 3 focus on the rise of Latinos in US politics, which began slowly in the late 1940s and the 1950s, increased markedly in the 1960s and 1970s, and progressed steadily to the beginning of the twenty-first century. Chapter 4 focuses on the first two decades of the twenty-first century and on the growing political clout of Latinos in several states and the continuing challenges facing Latinos around issues such as immigration policies, voting rights, and political representation. Chapter 5 provides an overview of the 2020s and Latino political behavior. Chapter 6 focuses on three large cities where Latinos play a major role in politics: Miami (and Miami-Dade County), Florida; San Antonio, Texas; and Los Angeles, California. Chapter 7 focuses on the history and growth of Latinas in politics and includes interviews with several elected officials. Chapter 8, the concluding chapter, focuses on strategies for electing Latinos in various local contexts.

This book does not explain all facets of Latino politics. An in-depth study of Latino grassroots efforts to influence the political process by opposing anti-immigrant laws, fighting discrimination in communities and workplaces, and

16   *Latino Political Power*

obtaining quality health care and education lies beyond the scope of this book. These struggles, many of them at the local level, produce the seeds of change that create community leaders. Some of these activists run for office, oftentimes successfully, other times not. *Latino Political Power* seeks to explain the history of political activism that has led to electoral empowerment efforts by Latinos. It is our intent to add to the understanding of Latino politics as part of the broader political process unfolding in the twenty-first century.

Notes

1. Canham 2021.
2. Narea 2020.
3. In 1680, a mass revolt by the Pueblo Indians forced the Spanish settlers to flee; it took more than a decade for Spain to reestablish its colonial outposts. See Gonzales 1999.
4. Dye 2001, 1.
5. Suárez-Orozco and Páez 2002.
6. Lopez, Krogstad, and Passel 2021.
7. Noe-Bustamante, Mora, and Lopez 2020. In a 2022 National Association of Latino Elected and Appointed Officials (NALEO) survey of Latino voters in Los Angeles conducted by BSP Research, 28 percent identified with the term *Latino*, 71 percent with the term *Hispanic*, and 1 percent with the term *Latinx*.
8. Marrable 2004.
9. Lilley 2013.
10. Jennings and Rivera 1984; Estrada et al. 1988; Torres and Velázquez 1998; Munoz 1989.
11. Gomez Quiñones 1990.
12. Hero 1992.
13. M. S. Williams 1998, 3.
14. Guinier 1995, 24.
15. Jennings and Rivera 1984; Regalado and Martinez 1991; A. Navarro 2000.
16. Lemus 1973.
17. NALEO Educational Fund. *2020 National Directory of Latino Elected and Appointed Officials*.
18. Noe-Bustamante, Lopez, and Krogstad, 2020.
19. Jones et al. 2021.
20. Brown and Atske 2021.
21. The situation is changing as the African diaspora draws immigrants to the United States; African and Caribbean immigrants of African descent cannot vote until they become US citizens. See Fears 2002.
22. NALEO 2020.
23. Ibid.
24. The analysis in this report is limited to nine states with sufficiently large Hispanic samples in state exit polls: Arizona, California, Colorado, Florida, Illinois, Nevada, New Jersey, New Mexico, and Texas. Voter survey results from the national and state exit polls were obtained from CNN's Election 2008 website on Friday, November 7, 2008.

25. Suro, Fry, and Passel 2005.
26. Ibid.
27. Lopez and Taylor 2012.
28. See CNN's Election 2012 at https://www.cnn.com/election/2012.
29. Gomez 2016.
30. Sonneland and Fleischner 2016.
31. Noe-Bustamante, Budiman, and Lopez 2021.
32. Ibid.
33. L. Mendez 2021.
34. Taladrid 2020.
35. Ibid.
36. Narea 2020.
37. Ibid.
38. Willon and McGreevy 2020.
39. Vespa, Armstrong, and Medina 2020.
40. Pitkin 1967, 11–12.
41. Swain 1993, 5.
42. Menifield 2001b.
43. Pitkin 1967, 209.
44. Whitby 1997, 7.
45. Geron 1998.
46. Reed 1995; R. Smith 1990b; Regalado 1998.
47. Matos Rodríguez 2003; Browning, Marshall, and Tabb 2003a, 377–378.
48. Browning, Marshall, and Tabb 1994.
49. Browning, Marshall, and Tabb 1997, 9.
50. Moreno 1996.
51. Browning, Marshall, and Tabb 1997, 10.
52. Browning, Marshall, and Tabb 1984, 78.
53. Murguia 2020.
54. Peterson 1981.
55. Fainstein et al. 1983; Stone and Saunders 1987; Stone 1989.
56. Piven and Cloward 1997.

2

New Voices, New Contours of Political Power

To understand the rise of Latino politics in the 1960s, it is necessary to recognize the context of world politics and global economics, which had a dramatic impact on the efforts of Latinos to achieve political power and political inclusion in the United States.[1] Following the end of World War II in 1945, the entire global political situation changed dramatically, and so did the fortunes of Latinos in the United States and Latin Americans throughout the hemisphere. The political behavior and demographic composition of the US Latino population were dramatically transformed. This transformation took place in the context of two global factors: competition between the United States and the Soviet Union for political domination and the expansion of economic globalization.

After the end of World War II and the defeat of German Nazism, Italian Fascism, and Japanese military aggression, a global conflict rapidly evolved between the two major economic and political blocs headed by the United States and the Soviet Union. The conflict between these "superpowers" overshadowed everything as both sides sought to gain political dominance throughout the world.[2] The struggle between the superpowers spilled into every nation, including in Latin America, and had a significant impact on US foreign policy.[3]

The international political conflict occurred just as economic globalization entered a new stage. Following World War II, the United States emerged with its industrial base intact and was unchallenged as the world's dominant economic power. Europe and Japan had to rebuild their infrastructures and reestablish their industrial capacities. Other nations, predominantly in the Southern Hemisphere, were economically devastated by the war and had limited economic development. By the 1960s, however, US-based companies faced greater competition overseas as transnational corporations challenged their economic control over resources and markets. Faced with declining profits and rising taxes to cover expanding social services, US companies began to relocate some of their activities, first to less developed regions within the United States—the South and Southwest, where wages and unionization rates were lower—and then overseas to less developed nations. The drive for greater profits also created an informal and formal conveyor belt of human capital from Mexico, Puerto Rico, and other nations in the Caribbean and Latin America as farmworkers and workers were recruited to centers of global capital such as the United States.

Globalization marked a new stage of the world economy. Capital investments from European and North American countries were already active in the less developed world, primarily in the extraction of raw materials. During the 1960s, international capital began to shift manufacturing to the developing countries, where wages were dramatically lower than in the developed world.[4] Developed countries began to experience deindustrialization as manufacturing industries moved to the poor countries with limited resources and as service industries in the United States expanded.[5] These two interrelated political and economic developments provided the external context for the rapid growth of Latino politics in this era. In the turmoil and conflict that erupted internationally, a window of opportunity emerged for Latinos in the United States in the 1960s as new immigrants and political refugees arrived at the same time as new social movements emerged and began to grow in influence there.

While this book focuses on the postwar period, the legacy of Latino political efforts in the United States before World War II is enormous. It includes the establishment of various settlements and community institutions in the Southwest, which began more than 200 years before the US government's annexation of northern Mexico with the end of the 1846–1848 Mexican-American War.[6] In the post-annexation period in the US Southwest, Mexican Americans, where they were allowed to fully participate, won elections for territorial, state, and federal government offices, such as in the territory and state of New Mexico. Where they were excluded, they mounted campaigns for inclusion and used many tactics to become equal participants in the political system. In most cases they were rebuffed, but they did not give up and by the 1940s were beginning to win electoral office in a few locations. In other places, they were starting to open up the closed and discriminatory political system. To win electoral office and retain these positions required organization, resources, a get-out-the-vote operation, and electable candidates. All were in short supply before World War II because of the closed racialized political environment of most local communities. Even in major cities in the North, Puerto Rican and Cuban immigrants were not able to fully participate in politics. In most cases, Latinos did not have the electoral numbers, and voters and candidates alike faced discriminatory barriers that prevented significant political advancement. Puerto Ricans and other Latinos who migrated to the United States were also limited in their efforts to achieve political incorporation. Yet these efforts were important building blocks in the decades-long struggle of Latinos to achieve political power in the United States.[7] These early efforts would not reap rewards beyond individual accomplishments until the 1960s.

Four distinct developments from the 1950s to the 1980s dramatically changed the landscape of Latino politics in the United States. Each of them was connected to the US government's foreign and domestic policies: (1) US involvement in the internal politics of Cuba and the Dominican Republic and subsequent agreements to accept large numbers of Caribbean-based Spanish-speaking political refugees; (2) a significant change in US immigration policy in 1965, with the passage of the Hart-Culler Act, which enabled large numbers of Latin Americans and peoples from the Caribbean islands to immigrate to the United States; (3) the rise of protest movements around the world, including in Latin America, which influenced the actions of US-based Latinos; and (4) the eruption of long-standing internal conflicts in Central America in the late 1970s and 1980s, with active intervention by the US government to support autocratic governing regimes, in turn leading to a new wave of political refugees and economic migrants fleeing to the United States to escape political violence and seek employment.

During this era, the United States stepped up its direct involvement in the affairs of other nations as US relations with the Soviet Union continued to produce conflicts. This included increasing political and economic influence in Latin America as Washington sought to dominate the region and blunt the Soviets' influence among revolutionary elements in numerous countries. The United States sought to do this in a variety of ways both publicly and covertly. Expanding globalization accelerated large numbers of low-wage workers seeking employment opportunities in the United States from Mexico, Central America, the Caribbean islands, and eventually South America.

The protest era of the 1960s was defined by the US war in Vietnam and Southeast Asia, the African American civil rights movement, other emerging social movements, such as the Chicano and Puerto Rican movements, and independence movements in the developing world, including the Cuban Revolution in 1960. The struggles of Latinos in this country for civil rights, quality education, and political power reflected the militant tenor of the times and helped create a rich resistance to domination and exploitation that would spread nationwide. Beginning in the 1950s and 1960s, Latinos began to pursue electoral office more forcefully in more locations in the Southwest and elsewhere. Their efforts to overcome discrimination and win elected office were aided by the street protests of the 1960s and 1970s mounted by young activists protesting the war in Vietnam, inferior education, abuses of farmworker rights, and restrictive immigration policies.

22   *Latino Political Power*

Political incorporation for Latinos was beginning to become a reality for a segment of the community. During this period, Latinos began to move from being perpetual outsiders in politics to enjoying symbolic and in some cases substantive representation.

The Start of Political Incorporation

After World War II ended, Latino politics grew and developed in the context of an international Cold War dynamic that influenced how politics were framed. As thousands of Mexican Americans and Puerto Ricans returned from the war, their contribution to the worldwide fight against fascism and for democracy came up against the economic and political reality of a segregated society. Mexican Americans continued to work in low-wage jobs and live in segregated housing in barrios throughout the Southwest and in growing numbers in the Midwest, where their labor was required in the postwar economic boom. As the only major industrial power to emerge from the war unscathed, the United States quickly rebounded and used the Bracero Program to keep wages low throughout the Southwest, particularly among farmworkers.[8] As one United Farm Workers of America (UFW) leader said, "When I got out of the Army, I went back into the fields. I had left for the Army from the labor camp near Los Baños and I was getting 85 cents an hour then. When I got back, the wage was down to 75 cents an hour, but the Braceros were getting 90 cents. That is when I led my first strike (1947). We didn't get very far."[9]

An incident in the late 1940s launched a grassroots effort among Mexican Americans and other Latinos to advocate for social justice. In 1949, a funeral home in Three Rivers, Texas, refused to provide wake services for Felix Longoria, a Mexican American WWII veteran, and offered only to bury him in the Mexican section of the local cemetery; Longoria had died in the Philippines in 1945, but the body was not returned home until four years later. In 1948 Hector Garcia and a group of concerned Mexican American veterans from Corpus Christi had founded the American GI Forum, a veterans' organization dedicated to combating discrimination and improving the status of Mexican Americans in Texas. A public campaign led by the GI Forum and the Mexican American community and supported by then Texas senator Lyndon B. Johnson exposed the racism of the town's refusal to hold a wake for a man of Mexican ancestry. Longoria was ultimately buried in Arlington Cemetery in Washington, DC.[10] By 1949, the GI Forum had established over 100 chapters in Texas. Although the organization was officially nonpartisan, members were encouraged to participate in politics. In the 1950s, when other groups were intimidated by anticommunist hysteria and Cold War politics, Forum leaders used patriotic symbols and its members' veteran status to combat charges that the organization was advocating radical politics, and they continued their advocacy and activism against discrimination in the coming decades.[11]

While middle-class Mexican Americans were beginning to develop their political influence, the plight of Mexican immigrants grew worse. The Cold War exacerbated anti-immigrant sentiments. The growth of the Bracero Program and increasing numbers of undocumented workers fueled a public backlash; one highly publicized action in 1954, Operation Wetback, led to the deportation of more than one million Mexicans, including many who were US citizens.[12] This was the second major mass deportation of Mexicans; during the 1930s, the US government had forcibly removed 400,000 to 500,000 Mexicans, many of them US citizens. The Cold War atmosphere also had a chilling effect on labor organizing efforts. Under the McCarren-Nixon Internal Security Act of 1950, immigrants found guilty of subversive activities could be deported; Mexican labor organizers were deported as part of this crackdown.[13] The massive deportation of Mexicans, combined with the Cold War view that any criticism of US government policies was inspired by communism, greatly affected the political climate for Mexican Americans in the 1950s. Nevertheless, Mexican Americans continued to struggle for equal rights and political empowerment.

One group that formed in 1960 openly admitted the political nature of its activities. The Mexican American Political Association (MAPA) was founded by 150 political activists who recognized the need for a statewide organization solely dedicated to advancing the political interests of Mexican Americans in California. They had lost faith in the Democratic Party's commitment to fight for the cause of Mexican Americans. When Edward Roybal ran for lieutenant governor of the state in 1954, he had received only token support from the Democratic Party. In 1958, when Henry Lopez ran for state treasurer, he also received little financial support from state Democratic Party leaders and went down to defeat in the midst of an otherwise strong Democratic landslide.[14] These and other actions prompted the formation of MAPA in 1960 at a convention in Fresno.[15] MAPA worked within the Democratic Party, but its emergence signaled a new, independent direction of militant political action by Mexican Americans who had grown weary of being disrespected and underestimated by Democratic Party leaders in California. MAPA grew to have three dozen local chapters, becoming an important force, particularly in California politics.

In addition to forming political groups, individuals continued to seek electoral office in the Southwest. Four Mexican American political leaders from three different states serve as exemplars: US senator Dennis Chavez, New Mexico; Mayor Raymond Telles, El Paso, Texas; US Representative Henry B. González, San Antonio, Texas; and US Representative Edward Roybal, Los Angeles, California. These politicians created political space

24   *Latino Political Power*

for themselves in the local and state conditions within which they operated in the 1940s, 1950s, and 1960s. The first of this foundational group to be elected was Dennis Chavez, who became a US senator from New Mexico. Chavez grew up poor and did not finish high school, instead going to work to help his family. He was mentored by and later became an aide to New Mexico senator Andrieus A. Jones; he went to law school while working in Washington, DC, and became an attorney. He returned to New Mexico and was elected as a state representative. In New Mexico, Hispanos could be elected to the state legislature and at the local level, unlike in most other states. In 1930, Chavez was elected to the US House of Representatives. He held this position until the death of the incumbent US senator, Bronson Cutting (R). Chavez, who had run for this seat and lost to Cutting in 1934, was appointed to the Senate in 1935 and became one of the first Hispanic US senators.[16] In the 1930s, the Democratic Party grew in strength in New Mexico. Previously Hispanos were primarily registered as Republicans and were able to run and win some state and local elections, as Anglos were divided in their party loyalty. In this period, Democrats held power at the presidential level and in Congress, so through patronage power they controlled jobs and resources. The Democratic control of state jobs influenced Hispanos to join the Democratic Party, and Chavez became very influential in New Mexico politics.[17]

In the post–World War II era, New Mexico saw growth in the Anglo population and a corresponding decline in the Hispano population share. This wrought dramatic changes in the culture, economics, and politics of the state. In 1848, immediately following the Mexican-American War, over 80 percent of the Spanish-speaking people in the Southwest had resided in New Mexico. Up to World War II, the state's Spanish-surnamed population remained the majority in the Rio Grande Valley and was influential in both parties.[18] While northern New Mexico continued to reflect the influence of more than 350 years of continuous Spanish, Mexican, and Pueblo Indian culture and political institutions, in southeastern New Mexico the political conditions were more similar to those of neighboring Texas. Most of the Mexican Americans in this region were recent immigrants from Mexico, entering an Anglo-dominated economic and political system that kept them in a subordinate position.[19]

With more Anglos coming to New Mexico, US Senator Dennis Chavez (D) found it more difficult to hold on to his seat as the state grew increasingly conservative and Republican. He championed liberal causes throughout his service, including the 1944 introduction of the Fair Employment Practice Bill, designed to prohibit discrimination in employment on the basis of race, creed, or national origin. Twenty years later his pioneering efforts led to the passage of the 1964 Civil Rights Act.[20] Chavez was reelected five times, in hotly competitive races. He fought to open the political process to more Mexican Americans.

New Voices, New Contours of Political Power   25

In El Paso, Texas, during the 1940s and 1950s, the Mexican population swelled with new arrivals from Mexico. Most Mexicans lived in abject poverty in El Segundo District, located near the border with Juárez, Mexico. El Paso, like San Antonio, was located near military installations. An important political victory for Mexican Americans took place in 1957. A veteran of the Korean War, Raymond Telles, ran for mayor of El Paso in 1957. Telles was a conservative who ran primarily as an American and against strong opposition from the business community, whose members did not believe a Mexican was qualified to hold the mayoralty. Telles won with the support of 90 percent of eligible Mexican voters, demonstrating that the Mexican community would participate in politics if given a reason to do so.[21]

In San Antonio, the Mexican community became more politically active in the postwar period as its numbers grew. Mexican American voter turnout increased from 55 percent in 1948, to 69 percent in 1956, to 87 percent in 1964.[22] The leading politico of this era in the San Antonio area was Henry B. González. González was active for many years in community affairs. After an unsuccessful run for state representative in 1950, he won a seat on the city council in 1953. In 1956 he won a seat on the state senate, and in 1961 he won a special election for the US House of Representatives, where he served until 1998. González was an independent voice during his tenure on the San Antonio City Council and fought to desegregate public facilities. As a state senator, he carried out a filibuster against segregationist bills in the legislature in 1957.[23]

Edward Roybal, born in Albuquerque, New Mexico, moved to Boyle Heights in East Los Angeles when he was young. He served in the army during World War II. Following the war, he immediately got involved in local politics. In 1947, business and community leaders recruited Roybal, a thirty-seven-year-old social worker, to run for a Los Angeles City Council seat.[24] Following this unsuccessful electoral effort, with the help of Saul Alinsky and Fred Ross of the Industrial Areas Foundation (IAF)—a network of community organizations started by Alinsky in Chicago in the 1940s and dedicated to organizing poor people to fight for basic services in their communities[25]—he founded the Community Service Organization (CSO), with a mandate to carry out community action, conduct voter registration, and improve voter participation. Roybal again ran for the same city council seat he had sought previously. His message—that all residents deserved a fair share of city services and benefits—transcended ethnicity and appealed to a majority of residents in the 9th Council District.

Roybal backed up his campaign platform with his own record of community service, civil rights, and social justice, including opposition to discrimination in all forms.[26] After a grassroots voter registration drive and get-out-the vote effort by the CSO, Roybal won a seat on the Los Angeles City Council in 1949, which he held until 1962, when he won a seat in the US Congress. Roybal's 1949 city council victory was a grassroots effort

26   Latino Political Power

that included strong support from labor as well as other minority and ethnic groups, including Jews, African Americans, and Asian Americans. While Latinos comprised around 34 percent of his district, he continued to receive support from other ethnic communities that resided there as well as from business associations.

The CSO played an influential role for many years in the Mexican American community and provided a place to train community activists. By the early 1960s, there were thirty-four chapters in California and 10,000 dues-paying members. Most of the CSO chapters were in farmworker communities in California. The CSO registered a half million Mexican American voters, offered citizenship classes, and helped thousands of people to become naturalized US citizens. More importantly, it provided the Mexican American community in California with a sense of power and a voice to exert pressure on city hall, the school board, and county government.[27]

Many CSO leaders came out of the labor movement, while others, once trained as CSO organizers, went into the labor movement. The CSO worked closely with IAF community organizer Fred Ross. Ross later came into contact with a farmworker in a poor San Jose, California, barrio known as Sal Si Puedes. Ross convinced this man to become a CSO organizer in the 1950s. The new CSO organizer went on to build a movement for farmworkers, eventually known as the United Farm Workers. The name of this humble community activist was Cesar Chavez.

Chavez's message as a CSO organizer to farmworkers in the 1950s was that they would only solve their basic problems—poverty wages, labor contractor abuses, and the lack of unemployment insurance—if they got organized. Gilbert Padilla, a UFW vice president, said of Chavez's vision, "He was talking about how someday the people should have some sort of representation in the political structure. And we were thinking that if we could get someone elected, then we could get some laws that would help farm workers."[28] The CSO's efforts to organize the barrios in the 1950s paid off with large numbers of new voters. The UFW was an important vehicle for farmworkers and for Chicano political empowerment in the Southwest.

The Viva Kennedy Movement

In 1960, the establishment of Viva Kennedy clubs across the country marked the first attempt by Latinos to influence the outcome of a US presidential election and the beginning of a more militant push for equal rights. The Viva Kennedy movement arose out of efforts by middle-class Mexican American leaders and organizations to gain more visible and effective participation in Democratic Party politics and that year's presidential campaign. While there had been other efforts after World War II to woo Latinos to support both Democratic and Republican presidential candidates, there had been no systematic nationally coordinated efforts. Viva Kennedy clubs spread throughout the Southwest and other parts of the country. Many local GI Forum groups temporarily shifted their agenda to transform into Viva Kennedy clubs.[29] The Viva Kennedy clubs brought Latinos together as Puerto Ricans, Cubans, and others from South and Central America joined.

In different states and regions, the form of the Viva Kennedy clubs reflected the political organization of Latinos at that time. In California the organizing was led by MAPA and CSO members; Congressman Roybal played a key role. These organizations functioned separately from the presidential campaign. In Arizona, La Alianza Hispano-Americana and Mexican American–dominated local unions and branches of the International Union of Mine, Mill, and Smelter Workers were the key political forces. In New Mexico, Senator Dennis Chavez led the campaign. In the Midwest, there were active Viva Kennedy organizations in Indiana, Illinois, and other states. In Texas, numerous local groups and individuals worked on the campaign, which connected national politics with local communities and "crystallized a new Mexican American politics."[30]

Following John F. Kennedy's victory in 1960, there were great expectations that finally Mexican Americans would be appointed to high posts in his administration, something that had not occurred under previous administrations. Leaders of the Viva Kennedy campaign also attempted to transform the campaign efforts into a political coalition, composed of leaders of the established organizations—the GI Forum, MAPA, the League of United Latin American Citizens (LULAC), and eighteen others—which banded together as the Political Association of Spanish-Speaking Organizations (PASSO). From PASSO's inception, its members held different points of view on how aggressively to pursue a political agenda. PASSO never got off the ground as a nationwide organization; instead, each of the groups went back to working on its own efforts. The Texas-based group would keep the name for a few years, but its activities remained focused in Texas.

The Campaign for "Los Cinco" in Crystal City, Texas

In 1962 and 1963, PASSO became involved in Crystal City, Texas, to help elect a slate of Mexican Americans to the city council. Crystal City, unlike many communities in South Texas, was not a product of Spanish settlement. It had incorporated as a city in 1910 and was principally an agricultural town with a high percentage of Mexican workers. While Mexicans made up more than 70 percent of the population by the late 1950s, Crystal City's city council and school board and the county court of commissioners were "all Gringos. Segregation continued in public and private facilities."[31]

While these conditions were common throughout the Southwest at the time, in Crystal City a series of discriminatory actions by the Anglo minority

28   *Latino Political Power*

sparked an electoral revolt by the Mexican American community. These actions included a land scandal that involved blatant discrimination against Chicano war veterans, denial of entrance into a predominantly Anglo private school to a prominent Mexican minister's son, and mobilization of the Anglo population to defeat a Mexican American candidate for school board in 1960.

In late 1962, Juan Cornejo, a Teamsters leader, formed an alliance with the newly created chapter of PASSO to hold a poll tax fund-raising drive. Throughout Texas at the time, all citizens who wanted to vote were required to pay a poll tax of $1.75. This severely hampered the political organizing efforts of poor Mexican and African Americans. After successfully completing the poll tax drive, raising funds for those who did not have the money to pay the tax, the coalition needed to run a slate of candidates. They found five Mexican Americans to run for city council; one was Cornejo himself. Through a grassroots campaign that relied heavily on the working-class base of Teamster cannery workers and agricultural workers, "Los Cinco" won the election.

The decision to actively participate in the Crystal City elections was controversial in PASSO, as some conservative members felt that the organization was becoming too involved in ethnic politics. For the more militant members of PASSO, Crystal City represented an important breakthrough in Mexican American politics. The election of Los Cinco showed that "hard work, good planning and coalition politics, could bring positive results at the ballot box and make it possible for Mexican Americans to control their own destiny."[32]

In the aftermath of the electoral victory, however, the new Mexican American officeholders and the community found it extremely difficult to maintain the unity they had exhibited during the campaign. The coalition between the Teamsters and PASSO broke up, and a slate put forward by PASSO was defeated in the next election cycle, in 1965, by an Anglo–Mexican American coalition. Nevertheless, Los Cinco made some changes that helped improve the quality of life for Mexican Americans in Crystal City. This included securing funds for street paving and other infrastructure improvements in the barrio.[33] Their election signaled the beginning of the end of the system of segregated politics in Texas. On a practical and symbolic level, the Crystal City electoral challenge was an important statement of the potential of Latino political power and was a harbinger of other political uprisings of Chicanos in the Southwest and Latinos in other parts of the United States.

The Rise of the Chicano Movement in the 1960s

The 1960s were a dramatic period for the nation's oldest and largest Latino ethnic group: Mexican Americans. The effort to elect Mexican Americans to the city council in Crystal City, Texas, was soon followed by other organizing efforts in the Southwest, including electoral campaigns, labor organizing, student organizing, community struggles for access to services, and attempts to end discrimination in jobs and housing. There were efforts that directly challenged the two-party political system and capitalism. There were numerous nontraditional organizing projects in various parts of the Southwest that changed the image of Mexican Americans in society and raised Chicanos' expectations about their right and ability to achieve sweeping political changes. The political leaders who launched these organizing projects responded to local conditions of poverty, neglect, and discrimination by the larger society. As a short overview cannot discuss all of the organizing efforts, we will focus on several projects that significantly contributed to Latinos' efforts to achieve political power.

Building a Movement of Farmworkers
In California, while Chicano community activists were active in numerous organizing efforts in the early 1960s, the most impressive campaigns erupted not in urban centers but in the agricultural fields. The Bracero Program, which imported seasonal workers from Mexico and other Latin American nations beginning in 1942, undercut farmworkers' wages and weakened working conditions. Farmworkers were excluded from the protections afforded other private-sector workers by the National Labor Relations Act of 1935.[34] The Bracero Program ended in 1964.[35]

In 1965, two separate organizing efforts joined forces to take on the agribusinesses that had for decades kept wages low and working conditions oppressive. The catalyst was a strike by mostly Filipino grape pickers in Delano, California, led by the Agricultural Workers Organizing Committee, formed by Larry Itliong, Philip Vera Cruz, and Pete Velasco. Cesar Chavez's National Farm Workers Association soon joined this strike, and together these two organizations expanded the strike of farmworkers, which eventually developed into a national boycott of grapes. In 1966, these two unions merged into one organization, the United Farm Workers Organizing Committee. In 1972, it would change its name to the United Farm Workers of America.[36] The strike ushered in a new era of militant labor struggles by workers of color and mobilized strong support from the Chicano community and the civil rights movement. The UFW, led by Chavez and Dolores Huerta, would build an international presence and generate support for many labor and civil rights, as well as for pro-labor candidates for office. The UFW maintained close ties with the liberal wing of the Democratic Party and viewed itself as a labor organization; however, it was also known for supporting numerous Chicano causes and advocating for peace and justice.[37]

In Texas, another state with a large farmworker presence, organizing agricultural workers was problematic. Texas is a "right-to-work" state, which means workplaces are open shops where unions have only limited

30   *Latino Political Power*

rights. Workers can choose not to be part of a union; this weakens unions' effectiveness. Organizing workers into unions in this antilabor environment was extremely difficult. The long border with Mexico made the importation of low-wage labor easy for employers. Decisions handed down by hostile local courts and the actions of the antilabor Texas Rangers also greatly hampered organizing efforts.[38]

In 1966, however, a strike by farmworkers against eight growers in Starr County in South Texas for a higher minimum wage became a catalyst for the emerging Chicano movement.[39] Chicanos from all over the state joined in a farmworker-led march from Rio Grande City to the state capitol in Austin. Well-known civil rights groups, including LULAC, the GI Forum, and PASSO, supported the marchers.[40] The march concluded with a huge rally of 10,000 people in Austin, attended by Cesar Chavez and other political leaders. The march and the support it received spurred other forms of community organizing among Mexican Americans in Texas.

Community and Land Struggles in the Southwest

Another significant struggle involved efforts to reclaim or to retain land and water rights in northern New Mexico, an area with a strong historical Hispano presence. One organization, Alianza Federal de Pueblos Libres, was organized in 1962 by Reies López Tijerina. The Alianza powerfully symbolized the issue of historical sovereignty for Mexican and Indian people. As one author states, "The Alianza was formed to reclaim for descendants of land grantees, both Mexican and Indian, hundreds of thousands of acres of Spanish and Mexican government land grants dating from before the takeover by the United States" following the end of the Mexican-American War in 1848.[41] It grew from a moderate pressure group into a militant organization that held demonstrations and used more aggressive tactics, including taking over the Tierra Amarillo courthouse in 1967.[42] While the Alianza's actions did not result in the return of lands to the original descendants, the issues of land, rural poverty, and governmental control were introduced and provided many in the Chicano and other movements with an awareness that Mexicans had a rightful claim to land and political power that predated modern political realities. The Alianza helped spur the development of the Chicano movement in New Mexico and throughout the Southwest.

A third node of political organizing during this period was the Crusade for Justice organization, formed in Denver, Colorado, under the leadership of Rodolfo "Corky" Gonzales, a former Democratic Party activist. In 1966, the Crusade was born as a civil rights organization. It focused on building alternative institutions, fighting Denver's poor educational system, and opposing the war in Vietnam. It successfully hosted two national youth liberation conferences, which helped galvanize an upsurge in Chicano youth organizing in colleges and secondary schools throughout the Southwest.[43]

The Texas Chicano Student Movement and
La Raza Unida Party

Political activities among Latinos in South Texas increased as the energy and enthusiasm that grew out of Crystal City spread to other communities in the region. In 1967, a group of Chicano student activists at St. Mary's University in San Antonio formed the Mexican American Youth Organization (MAYO). MAYO, like the United Mexican American Students in California and other student groups in the late 1960s, was born out of a combination of ethnic pride and a desire to be activists for Chicano power.[44] One of MAYO's first actions was a 1969 campaign to elect Chicanos to the city council in San Antonio. The students helped form the Committee for Barrio Betterment, challenged the status quo, and offered alternative candidates. Soon they also launched the Winter Garden Project in other communities in South Texas.

In one of many actions in this era, in 1969, Chicano high school students walked out of their classes to protest racist practices, including a discriminatory process for selecting high school cheerleaders in Crystal City. Working with MAYO organizers, they called a boycott of elementary, junior high, and high schools that lasted for more than one month. The students won most of their demands. This was one of thirty-nine boycotts organized by MAYO between 1967 and 1970.[45]

The success of this well-planned boycott and other organizing efforts culminated in the formation in 1970 of a new organization, La Raza Unida Party (LRUP). The party's launch was a bold call to action by Chicano activists to build a political party that would challenge the hegemony of the two-party system. LRUP viewed itself as an alternative to the dominant parties, an organization that could give voice to Chicanos' desire for self-determination of their political destiny. Initially focusing on South Texas, LRUP ran candidates for city councils and county and school boards in Crystal City and other towns. It was successful in winning city council and school board majorities and mayoral positions in several small towns, defeating the Democratic Party, the dominant political power in the region.[46]

By the summer of 1972, the concept of an independent political party for *la raza* caught on in other communities. LRUP expanded its organizing base to various counties where Mexicans were the majority population; it held a Texas State convention that was attended by delegates from twenty-five counties. A young attorney, Ramsey Muñiz, ran for Texas governor and garnered 219,000 votes, or 6.4 percent. Other LRUP candidates for statewide office fared poorly; at this juncture the strength of LRUP was evident mainly in local communities in South Texas.[47]

The idea for a third party was not unique to Texas; Chicano activists in California, Colorado, New Mexico, and Arizona also formed LRUP organizing committees. In 1972, a national LRUP conference brought together representatives from eighteen states. The conference resolved not

32   Latino Political Power

to endorse either of the two major-party candidates for US president; however, differences regarding organizing strategies and ideology went largely unresolved. In some areas LRUP was a pressure group, while in others it sought to function as a political party and post candidates for electoral office. LRUP activists continued to organize throughout the region and in the Midwest during the 1970s. The party failed to grow substantially, though, as it competed with the Democratic Party for voters and fought internal battles over strategies and tactics for building the movement.

Outside South Texas, the LRUP model of achieving political dominance at the local level faced numerous obstacles. Local LRUP chapters in Northern and Southern California were active in organizing around community issues and also began to participate in local politics. In East Los Angeles, LRUP activist Raul Ruiz ran against Richard Alatorre, a Mexican American Democrat, in the Forty-Eighth Assembly District in 1971. Ruiz's candidacy generated enough support to split the Mexican American vote and contributed to a White Republican winning office in a Mexican-majority district.[48] LRUP had proved that it could compete in electoral contests outside Texas; yet here the result was to deny a Mexican American candidate the opportunity to win a valuable state representative seat at a time when Latinos had no representation in state government.

Significantly, LRUP and other Chicano activists provided leadership to a campaign to incorporate the East Los Angeles area into a city. This area housed the largest concentration of Mexicans in the state, but without incorporation, residents had virtually no political representation. The members of the County Board of Supervisors of Los Angeles were all Anglos who paid little attention to the needs of the Mexican American community. In 1974, a community campaign to win incorporation and gain community control was defeated by conservative community elements, who argued that incorporation would mean higher taxes for residents and would result in inferior services, including law enforcement. The forces opposed to incorporation also raised the specter of militants taking over and turning East Los Angeles into a radical Chicano city of poor, undocumented workers with rampant crime and no tax base.[49] The incorporation defeat marked a turning point for LRUP in California, and it slowly declined in influence and attraction for Chicano activists, who joined other political groups.

According to one knowledgeable participant, a number of external factors led to LRUP's demise by the late 1970s and early 1980s, including the end of the protest era of the 1960s and 1970s, Democratic Party co-optation, the system of two-party financing that makes it extremely difficult to raise sufficient funds to run credible campaigns, and restrictive electoral structures, such as winner-takes-all systems. Also, there was the "incessant political, judicial, ideological, social, and physical pounding" by those who sought to maintain the status quo.[50]

Certain internal factors also weakened LRUP, including disagreements over ideology, lack of a unified political organizing strategy, and limited funds.[51] Yet, while not successful in achieving electoral victories, except in South Texas and to a small degree in New Mexico, LRUP provided an important vehicle for dissatisfied Chicanos of this period to engage in political action: "The Raza Unida Party inspired a whole generation of Mexican Americans to participate in the electoral process on a scale never before attempted."[52]

Seeking New Means to Build the Movement

In California, despite the problems with building the LRUP, the UFW continued to organize among farmworkers in the 1970s, including the three-year lettuce strike and boycott in the Salinas Valley. Other important organizing efforts during the period played a role in shaping the politics and orientation of the Chicano movement. In Los Angeles, Chicano high school and middle school students protested the lack of quality education in their schools by conducting mass walkouts. These "blowouts" by more than 10,000 Chicano students highlighted the unequal, poor-quality, and racist education in East Los Angeles in 1968.[53] This was followed by the largest Chicano anti–Vietnam War march, on August 29, 1970. This event, called the Chicano Moratorium Against the Vietnam War, drew over 20,000 people to East Los Angeles.[54] The police savagely attacked the peaceful event and killed three people, including famed *Los Angeles Times* news reporter Ruben Salazar.[55]

Community groups focused on Mexican workers made important contributions to the Mexican American community's understanding of economics and class-based analysis during this period. A progressive organization that functioned in the Mexican community was Centro de Acción Social Autónoma—Hermandad General de Trabajadores (CASA). Established in 1968 by veteran Mexican American community activists and labor organizers Bert Corona and Soledad Alatorre in Los Angeles, CASA was a mutual-aid organization to provide services to undocumented Mexican workers. By 1970 CASA had expanded to include autonomous local affiliates in other California cities and in Texas, Colorado, Washington, and Illinois, providing immigration counseling and notary and legal assistance to undocumented workers.[56] In 1973, CASA helped to establish the National Coalition for Fair Immigration Laws and Practices, which sought to promote a positive view of immigration from Mexico. Later, in the 1970s, CASA disbanded as a national group, having made important contributions to the debate about a more humane immigration policy, the need to view the US-Mexico border as an artificial barrier, and the critical role of Mexican workers in the US economy.[57]

Another organization influential in the Southwest during the 1970s was the August 29th Movement. Formed from several local collectives, including several in California, the August 29th Movement was predominantly Chicano

34   *Latino Political Power*

but also included non-Chicanos. The political orientation was Marxist, and the stated principal task was to build a revolutionary party to overthrow the capitalist system. It actively participated in labor, land, community, and student campaigns, advocating self-determination for Chicanos in the Southwest.[58] The significance of groups such as the August 29th Movement was their focus on an economic analysis of US capitalism and the central role of US workers, combined with the call for political power for Chicanos.

The formation and development of such social movement organizations in the 1960s came about in part due to a vacuum of political leadership within the Mexican American community. Chicanos were effectively excluded from the political process in most places. In 1970, virtually no Latinos were elected to office. In Los Angeles, there were no Chicanos on the city council or the county board of supervisors. After Edward Roybal left the council in 1962 to join the US Congress, no other Latino was elected. The situation was not much better in other southwestern states. At the state legislature level, Chicanos were significantly underrepresented compared to the size of their population (see Table 2.1).

A Campaign to Win a Chicano Majority in Parlier, California

While there were few Latino elected officials in 1970, there was a strong potential for local political control by Chicanos in many communities, such as in Crystal City, with sustained organizing efforts and as some voting restrictions were eased or challenged in court. The process of Chicano empowerment was tested in Parlier, California, a rural town of fewer than 2,000 people in the San Joaquin Valley. In 1970 85 percent of Parlier's residents, primarily farmworkers, had Spanish surnames. It was a traditional farm town, with the major industry and employers tied to agriculture. The town's political and economic elites were mostly Anglo and to a lesser

Table 2.1   Chicano Electoral Representation, 1970

State	Total Number of Legislators	Number of Chicano Legislators	Percentage of Chicano Legislators	Chicano Percentage of Total Population
Arizona	90	11	11.1	18.8
California	118	5	4.2	15.5
Colorado	100	4	4	13
New Mexico	112	32	34	40.1
Texas	181	10	5.5	18.4

Source: Garcia and de la Garza 1977, 107.

degree Japanese American farmers. From 1921 to 1972, there was only one Spanish-surnamed elected official. In 1971, the city council passed over a Mexican American who was an eighteen-year veteran of the police force in favor of a less experienced Anglo officer for the position of Parlier police chief. When challenged by the Chicano community to rescind its decision, the council refused. Following a year of protests and boycotts of local businesses by the Mexican community, and after two recall petitions were thrown out due to technicalities, a voter registration drive was launched and a slate of Chicano candidates put forward. After sixteen months of continuous struggle, the Chicano majority won all electoral positions; they "were now in control of local government and could now pursue policies which would bring about important changes to the community of Parlier."[59]

The previously unorganized Chicano community was brought together by a grassroots organization, the Parlier Fact Finding Committee, which sought to involve the entire community. After the new council took power, its views were reflected in the Parlier General Plan for 1973: "What's really unique about Parlier is that the City Council represents our majority population: Mexican-American. This is the only place in California where this has ever happened in American history: majority Mexican-Americans voted minority Anglo Americans out of elected authority."[60] Before the 1970s, four rural communities and one urban community in California had elected Chicano-majority city councils. After the Parlier decision, five other towns established Chicano-majority city councils.[61] The Parlier struggle was echoed in other California communities in the following decades, as Chicanos used various paths to achieve electoral power. The Parlier campaign was similar to the Crystal City struggle: in both places Mexican Americans organized themselves and launched political empowerment efforts to unseat intransigent Anglo officials. They sought political incorporation into the local political system to have an equal voice in their government. These were the opening salvos in a broader movement for political inclusion by Mexican Americans.

Puerto Rican Politics in the United States in the 1940s and 1950s

Following World War II, Operation Bootstrap, an economic development plan by the US government to industrialize Puerto Rico, was launched. It resulted in the displacement of tens of thousands of farmworkers, who then migrated to the United States to seek postwar jobs. Puerto Rican migrants fanned out to many states to work in low-wage jobs in agriculture, manufacturing, and service industries.[62]

The Puerto Rican government sought to oversee the employment and adjustment experience of migrants with the creation of the Migration

36 *Latino Political Power*

Division—or the Office of the Commonwealth, as it came to be known.[63] It not only served as a clearinghouse for migrants but also represented the interests of Puerto Ricans on the mainland. During the 1950s and 1960s, however, the existence of the office hindered the development of Puerto Rican politics in the United States, for many assumed that "political leaders, patrons, were unnecessary so long as Puerto Ricans were represented by the Commonwealth Office."[64]

The relative calm of the Puerto Rican migration was shattered in 1954, when five Puerto Rican nationalists, led by Lolita Lebron, opened fire in the gallery of the US House of Representatives, shouting, "Long live a free Puerto Rico." Five Congressmen were wounded in the assault. This violent action placed the question of Puerto Rico's colonial status on the world agenda. It followed a United Nations vote on a US motion declaring that the issue of Puerto Rico "was an internal matter for the United States."[65] The attack on Congress was the Puerto Rican *independistas'* response, a stark reminder that the question of independence for Puerto Rico was never far from the surface during this period. The five were imprisoned for twenty-five years and pardoned by President Jimmy Carter after a long campaign by the Puerto Rican community for their release.[66]

Meanwhile, Puerto Ricans continued to find themselves welcomed by neither of the political parties, even though they were eligible to vote. The 1950s were marked by limited economic and political progress for Puerto Ricans. In New York City, the Democratic Party and the Tammany Hall machine had been on the decline since the 1930s, when the government, not the party, began to provide social services for the needy. By the 1950s, the Democratic machine had little to offer the newcomers for their votes. In the chill of Cold War tensions and anticommunism, the establishment viewed Puerto Ricans as troublesome. The city's Democratic Party comprised primarily Whites who had no use for poor, nonwhite workers.[67]

Puerto Rican Politics in the 1960s

Before the 1960s, many in the Puerto Rican community viewed US politics only in the context of issues pertinent to Puerto Rico. As noted earlier, many had been enticed to come to the mainland to provide low-wage labor in the wake of Operation Bootstrap. The priority for Puerto Rican workers was not achieving political power but rather obtaining jobs and economic rewards. Many sought to earn enough to return to the island; however, as their numbers grew, Puerto Ricans became a substantial population in several cities. More than one million Puerto Ricans came to the United States between 1946 and 1964, but most found only low-paying manufacturing and service jobs.[68] The new migrants were forced to live in urban ghettos in overcrowded

New Voices, New Contours of Political Power   37

and dilapidated housing. These socioeconomic conditions were to spawn militant actions by Puerto Ricans in the late 1960s and 1970s.

In the early 1960s, groups such as the Puerto Rican Day Parade Committee, the Congress of Puerto Rican Hometowns, and an educational group known as ASPIRA developed in New York to build cultural and social networks and develop leadership. These social service organizations "offered a springboard from which several Puerto Rican activists would later enter into the political arena."[69] ASPIRA, founded by Antonia Pantoja, continues to provide services to the Puerto Rican community today in the field of youth leadership development.

A spontaneous action signaled the frustration many Puerto Ricans felt in the face of years of poverty, police harassment, and racism in major urban centers. In 1966, in the Division Street neighborhood of Chicago, a White policeman shot a Puerto Rican man; for the next few nights, the Puerto Rican community protested against police brutality. They also looted neighborhood businesses, leaving some fifty buildings destroyed and causing millions of dollars in damages.[70] Underlying the actions of the rioters were severe socioeconomic problems that existed in many Puerto Rican *colonias* in the United States. The difficulties faced by most new migrants may have impacted migration to the United States from Puerto Rico, which slowed dramatically during this period as work opportunities became more limited.[71]

Accommodation and Confrontation in the Puerto Rican Movement

Despite slowing migration, political activities increased in the 1960s. Two political trends emerged in the Puerto Rican community in this decade: the first was to work within the system and seek positions in electoral politics, and the second involved militant confrontational politics that challenged the political system. The first trend was represented by Herman Badillo, who emerged in the 1960s as a reformer in the Democratic Party. He was elected as borough president of the Bronx in 1965 and became the first Puerto Rican elected to Congress in 1970. He also ran for New York City mayor unsuccessfully several times. He even joined the administration of New York mayor Ed Koch in 1977. Another notable active during this period was Gilberto Gerena Valentin, a longtime labor and community activist who moved to the United States in the 1930s, worked as a union organizer, and headed a division of New York City's Human Rights Commission under Mayor John Lindsay in 1966.[72] He also served on the New York City Council in the 1970s. A third figure who emerged was Ramon Velez, who rose from the antipoverty programs of the 1960s to lead various ethnic groups, antipoverty funds, and organizations in the South Bronx.[73] These

38 *Latino Political Power*

three leaders were prominent in New York City's electoral and political institutions for their influence throughout the 1970s and 1980s in the Puerto Rican community and in the city.

In 1970, no city council members and only a handful of state representatives were Puerto Rican. By 1978, three New York City Council members, seven state representatives and senators, and one member of the US Congress were Puerto Rican. Yet Puerto Ricans were still woefully underrepresented. In fact, until redistricting in the 1990s, Puerto Ricans focused on achieving representation. During the 1990s, Puerto Rican representation finally reached parity with the community's share of the electorate. By 2000, twenty-one of the twenty-three serving Latino elected officials in New York City were of Puerto Rican origin, and the other two were Dominican.[74]

Formation of Militant Puerto Rican Organizations

While these leaders operated within the political system, the Black Power and antiwar movements and the struggle for Puerto Rican independence from the United States contributed to the development of a more radical and confrontational style of Puerto Rican politics. Three main groups emerged within this trend: the Movimiento Pro Independencia, which later changed its name to the Puerto Rican Socialist Party; the Young Lords Party, which later became the Puerto Rican Revolutionary Workers Organization; and El Comité—Movimiento de Izquierda Nacional Puertorriqueño.

While the population center of the Puerto Rican community was in New York City, the Young Lords formed out of a Puerto Rican youth group in Chicago. The Young Lords actually arose out of the Chicago Lords, a street gang that had formed in the 1950s. A leader of the Chicago Lords, José "Cha Cha" Jimenez, became politicized while incarcerated, and when he got out of jail, he organized the Young Lords Organization to protest urban renewal in the Puerto Rican community.[75] In 1969, Puerto Rican community activists in New York City formed a second chapter of the Young Lords. In 1970, the elements in New York split from the Chicago organization and formed the Young Lords Party. Its politics combined emphasis on social justice stateside and support for independence for Puerto Rico.[76] Its members included youth who had grown up in Puerto Rico and others who had grown up in the United States. In 1969 the Lords led protests in East Harlem over infrequent garbage pickups, and they occupied a church, where they set up a free breakfast program, day care center, and health clinic. In 1970, the Young Lords occupied Lincoln Hospital in the South Bronx to expose the inadequate health care it provided to community residents.[77]

The Puerto Rican Socialist Party likewise attempted to organize for both Puerto Rican independence and the social and political struggles of

Puerto Ricans in the United States. It had its roots in Puerto Rico, where the group known as Movimiento Pro Independencia formed. A chapter was established in 1964 in East Harlem, composed essentially of first-generation Puerto Ricans. Later it would expand to include second-generation activists and serve as a bridge organization between Puerto Ricans residing in the United States and those living in Puerto Rico.[78] In addition to leading the campaign for independence for Puerto Rico, this organization participated in organizing migrant workers and other campaigns for democratic rights in the United States.

El Comité began in early 1970 when a group of residents on the West Side of Manhattan took over a storefront to oppose the city's plans to displace local residents and businesses in order to make room for new high-rise developments. El Comité comprised mostly Puerto Ricans but also included other Latinos; its leader, Federico Lora, was a Dominican. El Comité initially supported bilingual education and community control. Later it evolved into a consciously leftist organization and sought to build support for socialism in the United States.

By the late 1970s each of these organizations experienced internal difficulties, and they all eventually dissolved. However, in the late 1960s and early 1970s, they represented an important new trend in the Puerto Rican community of seeking to resist capitalist exploitation and US imperialism. The Puerto Rican radical community created new forms of collective identity and built strong ties to the labor movement and the New Left movement that arose during this period. Together with other leftist forces in the Chicano movement, the radical Puerto Rican forces represented an important alternative to mainstream machine politics during the 1960s.

Conclusion

At the beginning of the 1960s, Latino politics were poised to take off. While organized political activity was still extremely limited in most areas with substantial Latino population, the pioneers of Latino politics were already positioned within the political system to represent at least the Mexican American segment of the community on a national level. The formation of Viva Kennedy clubs marked a new effort to unite Latinos. However, due to a lack of organizational resources and political will on the part of all participants, these efforts were not sustained through the 1960s. Puerto Ricans' political influence, with very few elected officials, was limited to the New York City area. The impoverished conditions of Mexican and Puerto Rican *colonias* led to explosions of protest and demand in the 1960s. Other Latinos had not made their political presence felt in this country.

This period represents a significant advancement from the 1940s, when political incorporation efforts were still only nascent. The next chapter

40 *Latino Political Power*

explores the efforts by both Latinos who had resided in the United States for decades (and much longer in the Southwest) and new immigrants from Cuba, Dominican Republic, Central America, and South America in the late 1960s to the 1990s to build their political efforts through government institutions, the legal system, and continued electoral and grassroots movements for political power.

Notes

1. Gonzalez 2000.
2. Westad 2005.
3. Dominquez 1999.
4. Ong, Bonacich, and Cheng 1994, 8–9.
5. Bluestone and Harrison 1982.
6. Hunner 2001, 29–40.
7. Geron 2005, 19–33.
8. "Bracero History Project" 2021.
9. R. Taylor 1975, 88–89.
10. Ramos 1998.
11. Ibid.
12. Gonzales 1999, 177.
13. Griswold del Castillo and De León 1996, 106.
14. M. T. Garcia 1994, 195–196.
15. Ibid., 197–203.
16. Coy 2017, 25–30.
17. Acuña 1988, 241–242.
18. F. C. Garcia 1974, 179.
19. Ibid.
20. Vigil 1996, 28.
21. M. T. Garcia 1989, 113–144.
22. Acuña 1988, 283.
23. Rosales 2000, 71–72.
24. Pla and Ayon 2018, 47–52.
25. Industrial Areas Foundation, n.d.
26. Underwood 1997b, 4.
27. R. Taylor 1975, 84–86.
28. Ibid., 90.
29. I. M. Garcia 2000, 53.
30. Ibid., 88–103.
31. A. Navarro 1998, 20.
32. I. M. Garcia 2000, 150.
33. A. Navarro 1998, 47.
34. Gould 1993, 34–35.
35. Calavita 2010.
36. United Farm Workers of America, n.d.
37. Gomez Quiñones 1990, 105–107.
38. Gomez Quiñones 1994, 254.
39. Montejano 1987, 284.
40. Acuña 1988, 328.

41. Gomez Quiñones 1990, 115.
42. A. Navarro 2000, 178.
43. Ibid., 80–94.
44. A. Navarro 1995, 53.
45. Ibid., 117.
46. A. Navarro 2000, 31–33.
47. Ibid., 50.
48. Ibid.,140–144.
49. Ibid., 165.
50. I. M. Garcia 1989, 226.
51. A. Navarro 2000, 272–282.
52. I. M. Garcia 1989, 231.
53. Acuña 1988, 336.
54. Munoz 1989, 86.
55. Ibid., 173–174.
56. Gutiérrez 1995, 190–191.
57. M. T. Garcia 1994.
58. Muñoz 1989, 94; Gomez Quiñones 1990, 152.
59. Sosa Riddell and Aguallo 1979, 11.
60. Ibid., 19.
61. Takash and Avila 1989.
62. Gonzalez 2000, 82–95.
63. Sánchez Korrol 1994, 225.
64. Jennings 1977, 77.
65. Libertad 1994.
66. Ocasio Rivera 2012.
67. Baver 1984, 45.
68. Perez y Gonzalez 2000, 64.
69. Baver 1984, 46.
70. Padilla 1987, 145–146.
71. Bean and Tienda 1985, 105.
72. Baver 1984, 47.
73. Ibid., 48.
74. Falcon 2003.
75. I. Morales 1998, 212.
76. Abramson 1971.
77. Baver 1984, 49.
78. Velázquez 1998, 49–51.

3

The Struggle
for Inclusion

Over the past century and a half, diverse Latino communities have mobilized to demand political inclusion. Latino politics is founded on generations of prior struggles for inclusion. These struggles have been organized around a consistent set of demands that began in the 1960s to challenge the inequalities in electoral structures that disadvantaged Latinos. As these structural barriers racialized voting and gerrymandered districts came down (only for new ones to be erected), political incorporation efforts blossomed, as did grassroots efforts to elect Latinos to office. This chapter explores the growth of Latino legal organizations and their role in changing the rules to level the playing field in the electoral arena to give Latino voters a fair chance to elect someone of their own choosing and Latino candidates an equal opportunity to seek political office. We also explore efforts to build national and local "rainbow" political coalitions and other grassroots organizing efforts, the emergence of strong Latina leaders and community organizations, and finally the development of new Latino political voices in the 1990s.

Political, Legal, and Organizational Challenges to Exclusion

In 1968, a new civil rights organization, the Mexican American Legal Defense and Education Fund (MALDEF), was founded. This organization, the idea of Texas attorney Pete Tijerina, was modeled on the National Association for the Advancement of Colored People's Legal Defense Fund and was initially funded by the Ford Foundation, the nonprofit arm of Ford Motor Corporation.[1] While initially viewed with suspicion because of its financial support from corporate America, MALDEF would soon prove critical in the struggle to advance the voting rights of Latinos.

44   *Latino Political Power*

By the mid-1970s, many of the groups that had emerged in the late 1960s were in decline due to internal conflicts, inexperience, massive police interference in their activities, and the changing external context. Meanwhile, several other developments would dramatically change the options and potential for Latino political incorporation. By 1975, many of the inhibitors to voting, as well as districting practices that had proved detrimental to the election of Latinos, were beginning to be addressed.[2] For example, in 1970, in a landmark decision in *Garza v. Smith*, MALDEF won its challenge to Texas election laws that had enabled voting officials to assist physically handicapped voters but not those who were not proficient in English. The argument in *Garza* foreshadowed the broadening of the Voting Rights Act to Texas. In 1975, the Voting Rights Act was extended to states and counties that had historically failed to provide multilingual election materials.[3]

The elimination of barriers to registration and voting often did not result in the election of minority candidates, however, even in locations with large numbers of minorities. Several structural roadblocks remained: multimember districts (including at-large elections), racial gerrymandering, and malapportionment.[4] These barriers diluted minority voting strength, as racial voting among Anglos combined with certain election rules to prevent a cohesive bloc of minority voters from electing candidates of their choice. After the extension of the Voting Rights Act in 1975, numerous vote-dilution legal cases produced some form of single-member district elections in most major Texas cities, including Houston, San Antonio, and Dallas. (A single-member district is an electoral district where one officeholder is elected to the position.) The fact that between 1975 and 1990 the Justice Department brought 131 objections to voting procedures in the state of Texas alone illustrates the high level of litigation.[5] As electoral rules and structures were changed, the number of elected minority officials seeking office grew, and their election to office increased.

As a result of Texas voting litigation, in 1982 Congress amended the Voting Rights Act, clarifying that a discriminatory result produced by an at-large election was sufficient proof of minority vote dilution. This change in the law meant that discriminatory intent need not be shown; the result of an at-large electoral system alone could substantiate a claim. Legal challenges were also used in other states where Latinos had historically been unable to elect their own candidates. Legal challenges remain an important weapon in determining electoral opportunities for Latinos.

Puerto Ricans and Voting Rights

While Mexican Americans were beginning to build successful legal and mobilization strategies to achieve electoral office, Puerto Ricans built civil rights and advocacy groups. Among the new organizations that formed was the National Puerto Rican Coalition (1977), an umbrella advocacy organization that continues to provide a public forum to express the views of the Puerto Rican community. In 1981, the National Congress for Puerto Rican Rights was founded by former Young Lords Party members and others involved in progressive Puerto Rican politics. The Institute for Puerto Rican Policy, a research and policy think tank, was founded by Angelo Falcon during this period.[6] These organizations advocated for the rights of Puerto Ricans and also worked with the Puerto Rican Legal Defense and Education Fund (PRLDEF), a civil rights advocacy group similar to MALDEF founded in the 1970s.

The PRLDEF filed several voting rights suits. In New York City, it stopped the 1981 municipal elections and forced the federal courts to eliminate the proposed district boundaries.[7] The redrawn council districts opened up electoral opportunities for Puerto Ricans and produced several more independent Puerto Rican officials in addition to the candidates backed by local machine politics.

In Chicago, MALDEF and PRLDEF, a group of Black voters, and the Republican Party joined together to challenge the state of Illinois's legislative assembly district lines. The suit was settled out of court, and the resultant redistricting map enabled the 1982 election of Jose Berrios, the first Puerto Rican to serve in the state assembly of Illinois.[8] The redistricting map of the Chicago City Council districts was challenged in 1982. Voting rights law was used by civil rights attorneys to apply pressure to change the jurisdiction of long-standing machine aldermen.[9] Following both the 1990 and 2000 censuses, Puerto Ricans continued to propose district lines that would allow fair representation of Puerto Ricans. The PRLDEF developed a strategy in 2000 to open up the redistricting process to the Latino community. Working in eight states on the East Coast, they created the Latino Voting Rights Project to educate Latino communities about the legal and political aspects of redistricting at the local, state, and national congressional levels.[10]

Increasing the Voting Potential of Mexican Americans

In addition to attempts to reform political structures through legal pressure, in 1974, William Velásquez, a former Mexican American Youth Organization student activist, founded the Southwest Voter Registration Education Project (SVREP) in Texas. The SVREP focused on securing resources and support to build voter education and registration campaigns in the Southwest. An affiliated organization, the Midwest Voter Registration Education Project, expanded these efforts into the Midwest. Through the work of the SVREP in Texas, the number of Mexican American registered voters in that

46   Latino Political Power

state rose from 488,000 in 1976 to approximately 1 million by 1986.[11] Even with low turnout rates, this increase in the number of Mexican American voters, combined with changes in the political structure, enabled more Mexican Americans to seek office with a reasonable chance of being elected.

The SVREP continues to play a critical role in the Southwest and Midwest. It holds training and organizing sessions throughout the country to teach Latino community activists how to organize effective voter registration and get-out-the-vote campaigns. Its research arm, the William C. Velásquez Institute, gathers and analyzes information to improve political participation in Latino and other underrepresented communities. From its inception, the SVREP has organized more than 2,200 voter registration campaigns in fourteen states and has trained over 100,000 volunteers.[12] As a result of these efforts and the work of other organizations, Latino voters have increased dramatically, from 2 million in 1974, when the SVREP began, to 7.7 million in 2001. The SVREP continued to build on its previous efforts; in 2004 it set a goal of 10 million Latino registered voters and 7.5 million votes cast in the presidential election.[13]

Pan-ethnic Latino Political Leaders Organizations

The increase in Latino elected officials prompted the formation of other organizations that would represent their interests. In 1975, Congressman Edward Roybal formed the National Association of Latino Elected and Appointed Officials (NALEO). This organization, composed of elected and appointed officials from both parties, has provided issue analysis, training, and advocacy at the local and national levels. NALEO grew from a small organization of Latino activists and elected officials into a prominent political institution well known for its research and analysis of issues related to the election of Latinos, as well as naturalization and citizenship issues.

In addition to this national organization of Latino elected officials, organizations have formed to serve the needs of Latinos at specific levels of government. In 1976, the National League of Cities established the Hispanic Elected Local Officials constituency group to encourage communication among local elected officials. It also makes recommendations to the League of Cities on major public policy issues affecting Latino communities. Later, the National Association of Hispanic County Officials, a constituency caucus of the National Association of County Officials, was formed to represent the interests of Hispanic elected officials at the county level.

At the federal level, the Congressional Hispanic Caucus was established in 1976. Five original Latino members of Congress—Herman Badillo (New York), Baltasar Corrada (Puerto Rico), E. "Kika" de la Garza

(Texas), Henry B. González (Texas), and Edward Roybal (Californina)—were involved in forming the caucus. Its purpose was to monitor legislative and other government activity that affects Hispanics.

Breakthroughs by Latinos in the 1980s

In the wake of these legal efforts and the development of Latino leadership organizations, Latino politics in the 1980s expanded as candidates were elected to a number of important public offices. At the statewide executive level, Toney Anaya was elected as New Mexico governor with the backing of an estimated 85 percent of the Mexican vote in 1982.[14] He was the second Hispanic elected as governor in that state, following Jerry Apodaca, who was elected in 1974. Anaya was only the third Latino elected to a state governor's office in the contemporary period. He served only one term.[15]

At the municipal level, Federico Peña became the first Mexican American mayor of Denver, Colorado, in 1983. Peña was a MALDEF attorney in the 1970s. In 1978 he won a seat in the Colorado legislature, rising to become the minority speaker of the Colorado House of Representatives.[16] In 1983, Peña ran for mayor of Denver, a city where Mexicans were not a majority population and had little access to the corridors of power.[17] Even though Mexican Americans comprised 18 percent of the population and only 12 percent of voters, they played an important role in his election. The SVREP had recently registered 6,000 new Latino voters, and they contributed to Peña's margin of victory. Peña was known not as a strong Hispanic-identified candidate but as a politician who happened to be Hispanic.[18] He built an electoral coalition that included downtown developers, unions, liberals, Blacks, and the Mexican American community to win office. His politics could be characterized as moderately pro-growth and pro-development.

In 1982, Henry Cisneros became mayor of San Antonio, Texas, the largest US city with a Mexican-majority population. Cisneros, descended of an elite family that had migrated to the United States during the Mexican Revolution, was closely identified with the large Mexican American community. Cisneros's ability to run as an at-large candidate served him well when he decided to run for mayor of the city in 1981. He won the election by forging a citywide electoral coalition of downtown business interests and the Chicano majority population. Cisneros was able to mobilize the diverse currents within the Chicano community while keeping the support of the city's Anglo elites. His skillful use of personal politics that transcended the barrio made him electable to citywide office. Peña and Cisneros both were able to achieve prominent local elected political office by winning the backing of multiple class and racial forces at the same time.

Emergence of Cuban American Politics in South Florida

While Mexican Americans and Puerto Ricans were using legal challenges to force open previously gerrymandered districts, Cuban Americans in South Florida used a combination of legal challenges and naturalization and registration drives among first-generation refugees to gain a limited number of electoral offices by the early 1970s. The first Cuban elected to office, Manolo Reboso, was elected to the Miami City Commission in 1973 after being first appointed to the position. The difficulties of penetrating the Democratic Party's nomination process, combined with the generally held view that the John F. Kennedy administration had let the Cuban community down during the Bay of Pigs invasion and Cuban Missile Crisis of the early 1960s, led the majority of Cuban Americans away from the Democratic Party and spurred the exiles to register as Republicans.[19]

However, others did not meet the growth of Cuban political influence with support. Instead of a cooperative atmosphere, a growing divide emerged: "The growth of Cuban voting power, together with a sudden new wave of a large number of refugees brought by the Mariel exodus, soon touched off a backlash among Whites in Dade County."[20] A 1980 referendum attempted to nullify Dade County's support for bilingualism. The referendum passed easily. The vote polarized along ethnic lines, with 71 percent of non-Hispanic Whites voting for it and 85 percent of Latinos voting against it. This tension between Hispanics and non-Hispanics would sharpen as the electoral strength of Cubans grew in the 1980s.

As the geographic concentration of Cubans grew into sprawling ethnic enclaves, Whites left the City of Miami and Miami-Dade County too, which increased the opportunities to elect Cubans to multiple offices. This further enhanced the power of the Cuban exile community. One manifestation of their growing influence was the establishment of the Cuban American National Foundation (CANF) in 1981. While other Latinos were focusing their efforts on garnering political power to address domestic issues and win political office, Cubans were strongly concerned with US foreign policy. CANF raised and spent large amounts of money lobbying members of Congress to support legislation that kept up the pressure on Cuba.[21]

The growing political clout of the Cuban American community was evident after the redrawing of electoral districts and the creation of new single-member districts. In the early 1980s, following redistricting, Cuban Americans were elected to the Florida legislature, and a Cuban American caucus soon formed. At a national level, the Republican Party reached out to the Cuban community to build a base "to establish itself in the usually Democratic-controlled state."[22] The electoral strategy was to run Cuban candidates against Democrats and to promote Cubans into government posts. One result of these efforts was clearly evident in 1984; 80 percent of Cubans voted for Ronald

Reagan for president, a far higher percentage than among Puerto Ricans (18 percent) or Mexicans (30 percent).[23]

Outside the South Florida area, Cuban Americans are usually not the dominant Latino group in urban centers; in Chicago, Boston, and other cities, they are less tied to the Republican Party and more interested in forging multiracial electoral coalitions.[24] For example, former New Jersey congressman Robert Melendez, the son of Cuban immigrants, was born in New York City. He eventually moved to New Jersey, and in 1974 he was elected to his first position on the Board of Education of Union City, New Jersey. From 1986 to 1992 he served as the mayor of Union City; he served in the New Jersey State Assembly from 1987 to 1991 and the New Jersey Senate from 1991 and 1993. After this long career in local and state politics, in 1992 he was elected to the US House of Representatives and became the first Hispanic from New Jersey to serve in Congress (he was later elected as US senator from New Jersey).[25]

Multiracial Coalition Politics, 1983–1993

As Latinos made important electoral gains in the early 1980s through legal challenges, changes to the Voting Rights Act, reapportionment, and voter registration growth, both parties began to court Latinas and Latinos as candidates for office. Multiracial coalition politics with a goal of achieving minority group political incorporation were put to the test in the 1980s in some of the major metropolitan areas.

In Chicago, Latinos had a small presence in city politics prior to 1983. No Latinos had been elected to the city council, and only 2 percent of the city's employees were Latino, even though Latinos comprised 19 percent of the city's population.[26] In 1983, African American congressman Harold Washington defeated two White candidates in the Democratic primary, including incumbent mayor Jane Byrne and Richard M. Daley, son of the legendary machine mayor. Washington fashioned a liberal-progressive coalition that included almost all segments of the African American community plus liberal and progressive Whites, Asians, and Latinos. While the established Latino community leaders initially supported the two White candidates, a group of Latino activists decided to back Washington because of his opposition to the Simpson-Mazzoli immigration bill and his fight against attempts to dilute the Voting Rights Act.[27] When Washington won the Democratic primary,[28] most Latino voters switched their support. Latinos voted 75 percent for Washington in the general election and helped provide the margin of victory against the White Republican Party candidate.[29] Latinos then served in the Washington administration and helped build a progressive multiracial administration both as insiders and as advocates for the Latino

50   *Latino Political Power*

community through the newly formed Mayor's Advisory Commission on Latino Affairs.

In 1986, as a result of a legal challenge to the drawing of the city council districts, the courts ruled that the 1981 district map was discriminatory and required the city to develop an alternative plan. Four majority-Latino wards were drawn in the revised plan, in addition to several new majority–African American wards. The Latino wards were split evenly between the two major concentrations of Latinos in the city: two on the North Side, where most Puerto Ricans resided, and two on the near South Side, where the majority of Mexicans lived. In a special election held that same year, four Latinos were elected to the Chicago City Council, increasing Latino representation from the previous one member.

The Latinos on the council represented different political allegiances, with two of the four closely aligned with Harold Washington: Jesus "Chuy" Garcia (who later became a state senator and now is a US congressman) and Luis Gutierrez (who later became the first Puerto Rican US congressman from the Chicago area). These two viewed themselves as part of a progressive and reform agenda to transform Chicago politics. Both had risen from grassroots community organizing to become local elected officials.[30] The other two were more closely identified with the Democratic machine. Also, in 1986, Miguel del Valle was elected state senator from District 5 in Chicago, which contained a slim Latino population majority but not a Latino registered-voter majority; del Valle demonstrated the ability of Latino candidates to get elected in districts where the majority of registered voters were not Latinos.[31]

Unfortunately, in 1987, a year after the election of the four Latinos to the council, Washington collapsed and died after successfully winning a second term in office. In the ensuing election, African Americans were divided between two Black candidates. Richard M. Daley ran again and emerged victorious in 1989. This time, the majority of Latinos voted for Daley.[32] Daley's electoral victory in 1989 broke up the progressive "Black and Brown" coalition at the city level, as he built his own electoral coalition, which included a large turnout of White voters who were not divided between White Democratic Party candidates, combined with a small percentage of Black voters (the others being divided between multiple Black candidates) and strong majorities from the Latino population. The Latino voters shifted from 70 percent support for Washington in the 1987 Democratic primary to 50 percent for the African American candidate in the special election. By the 1995 mayoral elections, more than 80 percent of Latinos voted for Mayor Daley.[33] Among those who supported the Daley electoral coalition in the late 1980s was Luis Gutierrez, who had come out of the Puerto Rican independence movement and sat on the city council. Gutierrez would later win support from Daley for a new congressional seat created by apportionment in 1992.[34]

The Struggle for Inclusion   51

In Philadelphia, Wilson Goode was elected mayor in 1983, having won a close Democratic primary against former mayor Frank Rizzo. Goode also built an African American–Latino–liberal alliance. The Latino demographic made up only 4 percent of the city's population in 1980, with nearly three-quarters of these Puerto Rican. Given the predicted closeness of the election, Latino voters were courted. Puerto Ricans voted for Goode more than two to one in the primary and by 77 percent in the general election.[35] In 1987, when Goode ran for reelection, his percentage of the Latino vote was 70 percent in the primary. The rate was lower because state representative Ralph Acosta endorsed Goode's opponent, Ed Rendell, who would become Philadelphia's mayor in the 1990s.[36]

In Boston, a progressive African American candidate, Mel King, ran for mayor in 1979 and 1983. Both times he lost; however, he successfully built a multiracial coalition, including strong support from Latinos.[37] During the 1983 race, the combination of a Latino candidate for office and the Mel King campaign brought out large numbers of Latino voters, with a "Latinos for Mel King" committee drawing wider attention to their presence in the campaign.[38] In all three cities, multiracial coalitions headed by African American candidates were the focus of the campaigns.

Jackson Campaign and the Rainbow Coalition's Impact on Coalitional Politics

The success of the Mel King and Harold Washington multiracial electoral coalitions, combined with African Americans being taken for granted by the Democratic Party, prompted the Reverend Jesse Jackson to seek the party's nomination for president in 1984. Jackson called for the formation of a "rainbow coalition" of all groups historically disenfranchised by the political system—minorities, women, youth, and poor people. In many northern cities, African American and other voters participated in electoral politics for the first time. This included many Latinos who had previously viewed electoral politics as ineffective at best. The Jackson campaign was part electoral campaign and part social movement; the energy and enthusiasm it generated attracted many who were either alienated from society or part of its historically disenfranchised elements: Blacks, Latinos, Native Americans, Asian Americans, and the poor.

In 1984, Jackson, who had been largely unknown in the Latino community, except in Chicago, captured 33 percent of the Puerto Rican vote and 17 percent of the Mexican American vote in the Democratic primaries. Jackson's support for the Farm Labor Organizing Committee (FLOC) in its fight for better wages and working conditions won its endorsement. FLOC organizers campaigned for Jackson in Texas and helped him win delegates to the state convention in Hidalgo County, South Texas.[39] In New York City,

52 Latino Political Power

where Jackson won every Latino-majority district, the organizing was carried out by grassroots activists with little help from elected Hispanic leaders, none of whom endorsed Jackson.[40] In New York and other parts of the country, grassroots "Latinos for Jackson" committees were formed, with varying degrees of success.

In 1988, when Jackson ran for president for the second time, he garnered seven million votes nationwide in the Democratic primaries. A highlight of Jackson's second run was his winning of the popular vote in New York City with the strong support of Puerto Ricans. Jackson won 53 percent compared to 40 percent for Michael Dukakis, his primary opponent. This time, all of the major Puerto Rican elected officials in New York supported Jackson. Jackson also garnered considerable support from the city's labor unions, notably Local 1199 of the Health and Hospital Workers, which had a large Latino membership.[41]

In contrast, while Jackson increased his vote total from 1984, he won only 21 percent of the Mexican American vote in the Texas primary.[42] While Jackson made significant inroads in the Latino community, his opponent, Dukakis, did better outside the Northeast. In Texas, Dukakis carried 55 percent of the Mexican American vote, which was pivotal for him to win this state's primary. By the time California held its primary in June, Dukakis already had secured the nomination and won the Mexican American vote by a two-to-one margin. In Los Angeles the "Latinos for Jackson" committee included many community activists. Some of them would go on to enter electoral politics themselves; for example, Gil Cedillo and Gloria Romero, who were leaders in the "Latinos for Jackson" committee, became state senators from the Los Angeles area. Throughout the 1988 presidential campaign, Latinos played an important role in boosting Jackson's vote totals but also in securing the nomination for Dukakis. Latinos demonstrated that even without fielding their own candidate for president, they could be influential in determining who received the Democratic nomination.[43]

After the Jesse Jackson campaigns for president in 1984 and 1988, other biracial and multiracial campaigns followed. In 1985, Black and Latino political leaders in New York City could not agree on a candidate to challenge incumbent mayor Ed Koch. Herman Badillo announced that he would run and sought the endorsement of African Americans. However, the Black community leaders felt Badillo's attempt to run for mayor in 1977 had divided their efforts to elect a Black candidate. Rather than support Badillo, several Black leaders endorsed an African American state assemblyman instead; Black and Latino voters divided their votes, and Koch easily won the race.[44]

Despite these problems, efforts at building rainbow coalitions in New York City continued four years later in the mayoral race of 1989. An African American, David Dinkins, the Manhattan borough president, was elected with the majority votes of African Americans and Latinos and a substantial minority (35 percent) of White voters. The Dinkins campaign again demonstrated the power of multiracial coalition building. Dinkins successfully united Black leadership and won the support of many Latinos and White liberals. As in Chicago, the chance to elect the city's first African American mayor mobilized large turnouts in the Black community. In the Democratic primary, Dinkins had bested incumbent mayor Koch, and in the general election he defeated Republican candidate Rudolph Giuliani. Dinkins also won the support of almost half the White liberals, a majority of Latinos, and a quarter of the White ethnic Democrats.[45]

Four years later, in 1993, Dinkins lost his rematch with Giuliani, a federal prosecutor, as White ethnics turned out in higher numbers to support him, while African American, Latino, and White liberals turned out in lower numbers for Dinkins. Latinos supported Dinkins but at a reduced percentage and with a lesser voter turnout.[46] With African Americans not as numerous a voting group as they were in Chicago, and faced with strong interethnic tensions, Dinkins was unable to keep the multiracial coalition together. Some Latinos were disappointed that Mayor Dinkins had not done more to address some of their long-standing problems.[47]

Rainbow politics also spread to other communities. In Hartford, Connecticut, Puerto Ricans built a progressive coalition with White liberals and African Americans and won control of the city government in 1991. Having begun to participate in this city's electoral politics in the early 1970s, Puerto Ricans had emerged from having only one representative on the city council in the late 1970s to win three of the nine council seats in the 1991 election. These candidates captured the majority of votes in a city where Latinos made up less than 28 percent of the population and were only the third-largest racial group after Whites and Blacks. Puerto Ricans used identity politics to build in-group coherence but also used multiracial politics to have a citywide impact.[48]

The Hartford multiracial coalition, however, was unable to maintain political control, and a more conservative slate replaced it in 1993. The coalition had found it more difficult to work together to achieve legislation and policy agreement in office than to mobilize as candidates for office. As noted in an account of this period, "Only a few understood that although black and Puerto Rican interests were different, a mutually beneficial coalition was possible."[49]

At the end of the rainbow politics period, multiracial electoral coalitions were generally hard-pressed to demonstrate their ability to maintain dominant local governing coalitions capable of holding on to power and advancing the interests of Latinos and the other underrepresented racial minority groups. However, efforts to build cooperative Black-Brown political coalitions continue, because in most large urban centers these two groups, along with Arab Americans, Asian Americans, and Native Americans, find themselves living and working side by side.

Latino Empowerment Efforts in Majority Latino Population Communities

In addition to Latinos' efforts in large cities to build multiracial coalitions and their own political base of support, their actions in communities where Latinos were the majority or near-majority population brought important breakthroughs in this period. In many towns and cities, Latinos had recently become the majority population or had been the majority population with limited or no representation. A series of political organizing efforts in California in the mid-1980s to early 1990s illustrate the stirring of a growing Latino electorate.

Gomez v. City of Watsonville, a 1985 lawsuit challenging the unfairness of the at-large electoral system, was emblematic of numerous voting rights litigations filed during this period. After the defeat of city council candidate Maria Bautista, community activists met with representatives from the Mexican American Legal Defense and Education Fund. They discussed the possibility of a lawsuit against the city of Watsonville for a discriminatory at-large electoral system that prevented the election of Latinos to office due to the racialized voting patterns of Whites in the city. Soon after, MALDEF attorney Joaquin Avila filed suit on behalf of three Chicano residents of Watsonville: Waldo Rodriguez, Patricia Leal, and Cruz Gomez. The suit charged that Watsonville's at-large system violated the Voting Rights Act of 1965 by systematically denying Latino representation.

In 1987, a US district judge ruled against the plaintiffs. In July 1988, the US Ninth Circuit Court of Appeals overturned the decision, finding historical and contemporary racial discrimination against Latinos in California. The appellate court ruled Watsonville's at-large method of electing city officials violated the Voting Rights Act, as it diluted Latinos' voting strength. The court said creating two majority-Latino districts, as proposed under the MALDEF plan, would create a politically cohesive voting group.[50]

As the city was deciding whether to appeal the decision, the Chicano community was organizing to demand the court's decision be accepted. On January 10, 1989, Chicano community residents packed the city council meeting; representatives of the League of United Latin American Citizens, the United Farm Workers of America, and social service organizations were present, along with cannery workers, other union activists, and the plaintiffs in the case. They told the city council the Chicano Mexicano community was tired of the history of discriminatory treatment by city government, including discrimination in city employment and an inferior level of services in the Chicano neighborhoods. Despite united and vocal opposition, the city decided to appeal the decision to the US Supreme Court in 1989.[51]

On March 20, 1989, the Supreme Court refused to hear the city's appeal. This caused city leaders to cancel the at-large elections set for May and to instead schedule district elections. The electoral campaign for the first district elections was intense. For the first time, Chicanos and Latinos realized they had a realistic opportunity to win an election. In the seven district races, five Latinos and one Native American ran for various council seats. However, only one Latino, Oscar Rios, won a seat on the council, for the city's District 2, a predominantly Latino neighborhood.

Following the election, some questioned whether the change to district elections had benefited the Latino community, since only one Latino was elected. However, this analysis neglects an important point. Latino voters had turned out in record numbers for the first time in Watsonville, doubling the 1987 turnout in the same precincts. The district campaign unleashed pent-up frustration with the local political system. To elect Rios, a grassroots campaign of volunteers was organized, including cannery workers, Chicano students from surrounding colleges and Watsonville High School, and community residents. The community-wide effort went door-to-door, several times to every household, to solicit support.[52]

A similar, albeit different, process took place in nearby Salinas, California, in Monterey County, an agricultural regional center, where Latino empowerment efforts resulted in a change in the electoral structure of district elections and eventually led to the city's elected leadership becoming majority Latino.[53]

Another important community campaign for political incorporation occurred almost at the same time as the Watsonville voting rights campaign. The city of Pomona, California, located in eastern Los Angeles County, began undergoing a major demographic shift in the late 1970s and went from majority White to majority Black and Latino by the 1990s. Between 1965 and 1984, out of sixteen candidates from racial and ethnic minorities who sought election to the city council, only two Latino candidates were successful. In 1985, five Pomona residents filed a lawsuit claiming that the city's at-large system violated the Voting Rights Act. In 1986, the US District Court dismissed the lawsuit, but in 1990, Pomona voters adopted a district election structure. By 1993, the city council had become majority Latino with four Latino members and with one Black member.[54] Pomona was an important example of how racial and ethnic groups have joined together to achieve political incorporation in a local community.

In southeastern Los Angeles County, a number of suburban cities had transformed from predominantly White working-class communities into predominantly Mexican working-class communities by the 1980s. As growing numbers of Latino working families moved into affordable housing in Bell, Bell Gardens, Commerce, Cudahy, Huntington Park, Pico Rivera, Maywood, and South Gate, Whites moved to outer suburbs farther south and east. Yet, in these communities, despite the demographic changes, there was not a corresponding demographic change in the elected and appointed officials. Latino electoral representation was almost nonexistent.

56   *Latino Political Power*

In Bell Gardens, Latinos grew frustrated with the lack of representation and took decisive action. Bells Gardens' population of 43,000 was nearly 90 percent Latino. It was home to predominantly poor working-class renters. In 1990, the all-White city council passed a zoning ordinance that attempted to control population density by rezoning properties; this would have led to the demolition of hundreds of homes and apartment buildings and eliminated the use of "granny apartments," garages that had been turned into living quarters.[55]

The predominantly Mexican American residents got angry and decided to do something about this injustice. They went out, registered voters, and organized a recall election that threw the mayor and three other White city council members out of office in December 1991. The political establishment was stunned, as city leaders had cultivated the support of prominent Chicano politicians, including Congressman Marty Martinez. The residents had been successful by organizing a grassroots campaign that went door-to-door to build support to overturn the new zoning ordinance and recall the incumbents. At the next election, a majority of Latinos were elected to the city council. The Bell Gardens story was viewed initially as a "revolt that would bring majority rule to all the Southland cities where local governments defy demographics."[56] Other efforts to elect Latino representation followed in other nearby cities. By 1994, most of the city councils in southeastern Los Angeles County were becoming majority Latino.

However, in many of the poor and working-class communities, such as Bell Gardens, Maywood, and Cudahy, the achievement of Latino political leadership in local government came at a time of scarce economic resources. This severely limited the ability of the new crop of Latino elected officials to address problems of poverty, crime, and unemployment. Nevertheless, the Bell Gardens campaign initiated a new era of Latino politics in the county, as grassroots leaders emerged who were more representative of the population in numerous Latino-majority communities. Now Latinos also had multiple locations to gain experience in local politics, so these city councils provided an important training ground for future leaders.

With the growth of Latino elected leadership, the issue of representation takes on a different character: Latino candidates for office must distinguish themselves from other Latino candidates based on their record of community service, community ties, interest group support, and get-out-the-vote operations. As Latinos have been elected to office, questions have arisen: How representative is the local government responsible for carrying out public policy? Should the local administration reflect the demographic characteristics of the population?

Political incorporation theorists Rufus Browning, Dale Marshall, and David Tabb view the composition of the workforce hired or appointed to city jobs as an important measure of minority groups' political incorporation.[57]

As Latino elected officials have assumed power, they have also changed the composition of civil service and key appointed city offices to reflect the demographics of the community and to improve communication with a largely Spanish-speaking population. In many of these Latino-majority cities, Latinos hold key management positions such as city manager, city attorney, and police chief. In other Southern Californian cities, where Latinos were not the majority population, there were still few Latinos in key management positions by the start of the twenty-first century. When surveyed at that time, local Latino elected officials were concerned less with the ethnicity of the applicants for these key administrative positions and more with their qualifications.[58] Nevertheless, having a representative bureaucracy remains an important measure of whether Latinos are politically incorporated. When Latinos are in charge of political decisionmaking, they will have the power to hire a diverse government administration, including more Latinos.

The majoritarian representation principle that is a hallmark of US democracy is now evident in these majority-Latino communities. However, the economic resources to solve many of the systemic problems are often not available. Doing away with poverty is not the same as achieving political representation for Latinos. Ongoing stark racial and class stratification and discriminatory behavior also compel the development of community activism.

Politics by Other Means:
Nontraditional Methods of Political Struggle

In addition to participation in electoral politics in many barrios and *colonias*, grassroots organizing efforts to challenge the status quo and fight for specific demands have served as means to achieve political influence. The history of such organizing dates back to when Mexicans were first denied access to the political process as Anglos became the dominant population in the Southwest.

Later, as new immigrants arrived from Latin America in the twentieth century, they moved into ethnic enclaves and barrios, often without legal documentation. Many Latinos organize around their values and their beliefs about their rights, based on their sense of cultural belonging rather than on their formal status as citizens.[59] For many Latinos, their physical communities are locations of opposition to controlling structures and of the construction of a collective identity as a people. Day-to-day relationships among neighbors, families, and coworkers provide the basis for group mobilization efforts. While this book's focus on electoral political activities precludes a longer discussion of this important topic, it is important to note the role that

58 Latino Political Power

Latinas from distinct ethnic communities have played in politics in various forms, as often these local campaigns transform individuals into community activists and candidates for office.

Often the key organizers in issues and struggles that affect Latinos are women, who enter politics having been excluded from the male-dominated political arena in their own communities and from the larger society: "Their activity tends to be collective. The issues raised [are] intimately connected to the community."[60] Women's organizing can take the form of developing a community program to promote literacy, supporting coworkers in a workplace, or reclaiming cultural identity.[61] In Boston, Latinas built grassroots efforts that emphasized "the connection between everyday survival and political action [and focused] on the connectedness between people at the local level as they struggle for social change."[62] While Latinas organizing in their communities is not a new phenomenon, in the 1980s and 1990s these efforts blossomed throughout the nation and transnationally. For example, in Denver, Chicanas and other Latinas formed Hermanas en la Lucha to build alliances with indigenous women outside the United States. They targeted the struggle and women in Chiapas "in part because they saw their struggles for resistance as having important parallels with their own battles in the United States."[63]

In Los Angeles, one organization among many that formed during this period was the Mothers of East Los Angeles, established in 1984. A group of several hundred women came together to oppose the construction of a state prison in Boyle Heights. The group emerged from a Catholic parish on the east side of the city. The women marched, protested, and lobbied, leading to the defeat of the proposed construction site in 1992.[64] Later the group organized to oppose a municipal waste incinerator and an oil pipeline that were to be located in their community. These women provided an independent voice and organizing strength that resembled efforts in other communities.

For many Latinas, the struggle for social change is simultaneously a struggle to create community. Often it takes the form of defense of their dignity on the job. In San Antonio, 1,100 workers who had labored for many years in a Levi-Strauss plant were laid off in 1990 when the company moved its US plant to Latin America to stay competitive with other clothing manufacturers, even though the plant was profitable. The laid-off workers, predominantly Latinas, formed an organization known as La Fuerza Unida. These women then traveled throughout the country speaking against corporate greed. They launched a national boycott of Levi's labels. Their effort to improve the settlement package for laid-off workers has been an example to others victimized by corporate greed and globalization.[65]

In El Paso, displaced women workers formed La Mujer Obrera in 1981 after a long textile workers' strike against the Farah clothing company. La Mujer Obrera has survived for more than forty years as a grassroots community-based organization. Led by women of Mexican descent, the organization supports low-income women workers and their families.[66] In 1990, La Mujer members organized a hunger strike and chained themselves to their sewing machines to dramatize the poor working conditions and the flight of companies to Mexico and other low-wage locations. Later they pressured federal, state, and local government agencies to provide assistance to workers displaced by the North American Free Trade Agreement.[67]

Latinas have also acted as community watchdogs once Latino officials achieve elected office. Latina community networks and organizations are often the first to challenge the effectiveness of an elected official who fails to stay in touch with or represent the interests of a community. Grassroots community organizations, as well as labor unions, in Latino communities supply an important link to constituencies historically unrepresented by those in power.

The Arrival of Dominicans and Their Emergence in US Politics

In addition to the arrival of Puerto Rican migrants and Cuban political refugees, a large exodus to the United States of people from the Dominican Republic began in the mid-1960s. For thirty-one years, the Dominican Republic was ruled by Rafael L. Trujillo, who had installed himself as president and been a ruthless dictator. In 1961, he was assassinated, and in 1963 a progressive leader, Juan Bosch, was elected. Several months later, Bosch was removed from office by a coup d'état organized by an alliance of military officers and big-business interests.[68] In response, a military faction allied with the popular forces attempted to reinstate Bosch. The US government sent in 40,000 troops to prevent what it feared was another communist revolution (as had occurred earlier in Cuba). The US military occupation marked the beginning of a thirty-year period of political instability in the Dominican Republic. To defuse the postelection crisis, US officials hastily facilitated a mass exodus of pro-Bosch supporters. Many Dominicans came to New York as political exiles.[69] However, unlike Cuban refugees, the Dominicans were not classified as political refugees and received no federal assistance upon arrival. Many of the Dominicans who arrived in the United States in the 1960s had skills similar to those of the Cubans. They were generally highly educated and politically conscious; some had economic resources and started up small businesses in New York City. Subsequently, however, large numbers of working-class immigrants, faced with limited avenues for advancement, arrived, many of them undocumented. By the late 1990s, Dominicans were one of the poorest Latino groups on average in the United States. They had an average per capita household income

60 *Latino Political Power*

of $11,065 in 1999, with higher rates of unemployment than the national average.[70] Dominicans had a poverty rate of 27.5 percent, the highest among all Latino groups.[71]

Their main destination was the Washington Heights area of Upper Manhattan. More than 400,000 Dominicans legally migrated to the United States between 1961 and the mid-1980s. There were 332,713 Dominicans living in New York City in 1990, according to the census. If one takes into account the large number of undocumented Dominicans, the population was above half a million people. The intensity of politics in the Dominican Republic, the political skills of many of those who left their homeland, and the high concentration of Dominicans in one area of the city with limited political visibility led to the development of numerous grassroots political organizations.

The first political efforts centered on issues of concern in the homeland. In the 1960s, a number of autonomous, voluntary ethnic associations were established that did not run candidates but helped local Democratic candidates through leafleting and voter mobilization.[72] As the new political exiles arrived, the ethnic associations began to take on a new character that reflected their needs and interests. In the 1970s, the various associations combined businessmen who could obtain funding from city agencies and younger US-educated Dominicans who became active in New York politics. Dominicans were rallied to support and vote for Democratic candidates.[73]

By the 1980s, Dominicans were actively participating in party politics and educational reform in Washington Heights. The Dominican Day Parade grew in size, indicating the growth of the community's presence, with over 100,000 in attendance by 1983. That same year Dominicans organized to gain representation in the city's antipoverty bureaucracy, including the Community Development Agency and its locally elected advisory group, known as the Area Policy Boards. Until then, no Dominicans had served on a policy board. These organizing efforts resulted in significant increases in funding for Dominican groups in Washington Heights.

In addition, the lack of decent public education in New York City led Dominican community activists to form parents' and teachers' groups and enter into mainstream politics to address their concerns, running for local school boards and other positions.[74] The 1980s also witnessed a significant increase in Dominican participation in New York City school board politics. The school boards are decentralized and democratically elected and allow noncitizens to vote. Several Dominican community organizations focused on gaining control of their local educational institutions. The movement of parents and community activists to address school overcrowding and substandard education led to the election in 1983 of teacher and community activist Guillermo Linares to the Washington Heights area Community School Board (at the time it was one of thirty-two decentralized school boards in New York City). Linares relied heavily on parents and community residents, both citizen and noncitizen alike, to win the election.[75]

The Struggle for Inclusion   61

In 1991, after pressure from the Dominican and Puerto Rican communities and Puerto Rican elected officials, a redrawing of New York City's electoral maps created a Dominican-majority city council district in Upper Manhattan.[76] After a highly competitive race, Guillermo Linares emerged as the first Dominican to be elected to the city council. In 1992, the redistricting of the New York State Assembly created a strong majority-Latino district in northern Manhattan, with a 78 percent Latino population. Longtime incumbent Brian Murtaugh ran and won election that year, however, defeating a Dominican and a Puerto Rican candidate.[77]

In 1996, Adriano Espaillat defeated Murtaugh in the Democratic primary and won the general election. The campaign focused on representation and national origins, and Espaillat stressed his ability, given his Dominican origin, to better represent the district's residents.[78]

The 1980s and 1990s saw the Dominican community grow numerically and politically. They competed with other ethnic and racial groups for political influence and gained a limited level of political incorporation in New York City. By 2000, the US Dominican population was estimated at 579,000, an increase of 240,000 since 1990. Dominicans were nearly 27 percent of the Latino population, up from 19 percent in 1990, while Puerto Ricans declined from 48 to 38 percent (830,000) of all Latinos.

The Dominican population grew rapidly. According to the 2000 census, the Dominican American population had spread to numerous cities and communities beyond New York City. An important issue for Dominicans and other Latinos was the 2000 census undercount of Latinos in the United States. The wording of the census questionnaire required all Latinos other than Mexicans, Cubans, and Puerto Ricans to write in another Hispanic category, but no examples of other categories were offered to orient respondents, as had been given in 1990. For this reason, an unprecedented number of Dominicans and other Latino groups gave no specific information on their ethnic origin, so that 6.2 million, or 17.6 percent, were counted as "other Hispanics"—a far larger number than previously recorded. Most of them were new immigrant Latinos, with the result that many distinct Latino groups were undercounted. The Lewis Mumford Center, using 1998 and 2000 Current Population Survey data, estimates that the Dominican population was on average significantly higher than what was counted in the 2000 census.[79]

Dominican migration and incorporation into the United States has been limited by both economic and racialized discrimination. Dominicans have faced the intense stereotyping, prejudice, and discrimination "to which all people of African origin are subjected."[80] According to one author, Dominicans' migration to the United States at some point in the 1980s "gained enough economic and political weight in the life of the island to speak about a transnational community."[81] The Dominican migration includes participation in both the Dominican Republic and US politics. The Dominican American community is a large contributor to various political parties and

62   *Latino Political Power*

candidates in national Dominican elections.[82] New York State politicians regularly visit the island nation to maintain political relationships.

Overcoming the extreme poverty in the Dominican Republic that fuels emigration requires continued financial and other assistance from the overseas Dominican community. The electoral fortunes of Dominicans in the United States will continue to be closely connected politically and financially to their home country for many years to come.

Central Americans Emerge

Another important addition to Latino politics in the 1990s was a growing activism of new Latino immigrants and refugees in politics. Central Americans, including Salvadorans, Hondurans, Nicaraguans, and Guatemalans, began to come to the United States in the 1960s, continuing into the 1970s and 1980s, as their countries' economic and political conditions deteriorated. During the 1980s and early 1990s, many who fled civil conflicts began to support activities in the United States for the struggles being waged in their homelands for greater democracy and an end to military repression.

As civil conflicts came to an end in the 1990s, many Central Americans turned their efforts to obtaining legal status in the United States and fighting for the rights of political refugees. While Cubans were readily able to obtain political refugee status, many Central Americans who fled political conflict have been unable to do so. Many remain in this country on temporary visas or are undocumented. A whole generation of Latinos from Central American countries cannot naturalize and therefore cannot participate in the full range of political activities available to most Americans, such as voting. They are unable to qualify for most government services or for government jobs and continue to face an uncertain future.

Central Americans, despite numerous challenges, began to participate in community and US electoral politics. In Los Angeles, significant Central American refugee services, such as the Central American Refugee Center, were developed to serve the hundreds of thousands of refugees; the Coalition for Humane Immigrant Rights of Los Angeles was formed in 1986 to "advance the human and civil rights of immigrants and refugees in Los Angeles."[83] In the electoral arena, California state senator Liz Figueroa, the first Latina elected to the state legislature from Northern California, represented the 10th District—the vicinity of the city of Fremont in the San Francisco Bay Area. The daughter of Salvadoran parents, she was a small business owner before joining the state legislature in 1994. In the state of Maryland, Ana Sol Gutierrez, a Salvadoran American, was elected to the state's House of Delegates in 2003. She previously was elected to the Montgomery County School Board in 1990, after first organizing people to register to vote in her community. Gutierrez's election represents the growing presence of Salvadorans in the area. In Washington, DC, there were already 135,000 Salvadorans in the early 2000s, and they constitute the nation's second-largest Salvadoran community after Los Angeles. In the coming decades, other Central and South Americans would also participate in the political process and be elected to offices in different parts of the country.

Getting a Toehold in Politics for Nonmajority Latino Groups in Local Contexts

Establishing a toehold in politics in the United States for Central and South Americans is made more difficult by the fact that, in most locations where they live, they are usually minority members of the Latino population. For example, in Los Angeles County, in 2020, there were 4.8 million Latinos, of which 76 percent were of Mexican descent (3.6 million); the remaining 24 percent were Central Americans and Latinos from Puerto Rico and South America (1.1 million). In South Florida, the Nicaraguan population is heavily concentrated in cities such as Sweetwater; however, Cubans, who arrived earlier and have well-established political machines, dominate the political leadership in this city.

In some instances, nonmajority Latinos have achieved electoral office. In Miami, Maurice Ferré, a Puerto Rican, was elected mayor from 1973 to 1985 after building an alliance of Black and White liberals.[84] However, once Cubans became the dominant electoral group in the 1980s, this seat went to a succession of Cubans, including Manuel Diaz, who was elected in November 2001. In Connecticut a Peruvian American, Democrat Felipe Reinoso, was elected as the state representative from the city of Bridgeport, where there are large numbers of Puerto Ricans. Representative Reinoso was elected president of the Association of Peruvian Organizations of the United States and Canada, which works for the full participation of the 1 million citizens of Peruvian descent living in the United States, of whom 65,000 lived in Connecticut in 2000. Reinoso said, "Peruvian-Americans currently constitute the most rapidly growing segment of the Latino population. In Connecticut we contribute to the overall economy of the state as we pursue active roles in business, education and various other professions, as well as increasing involvement in civic and community endeavors."[85]

Other Latinos elected in an area where they are not a member of the dominant Latino ethnic community include Republican Juan C. Zapata, Florida's first Colombian American state representative. He was elected in Miami-Dade County, where Cuban Americans are the largest Latino group and Colombians are a much smaller segment of the population. His Republican Party credentials, his ties to Cuban American elected officials, and his

64 *Latino Political Power*

Latino heritage enabled him to win election. In Chicago's Near North Side, Mexican American Cynthia Soto was elected to the state assembly from a predominantly Puerto Rican area. She had to overcome opposition not only from the Daley machine but also from some who thought the seat should be reserved for a Puerto Rican. However, her pro–working family agenda and her political ties to Congressman Luis Gutierrez and other prominent Puerto Rican elected leaders enabled her to win victory in 2001.

Backlash, Voting Strength, and Growing Diversity in the 1990s

In the midst of growing Latino influence in society and politics, particularly in areas where there are large numbers of Latinos, an anti-Latino, anti-immigrant backlash emerged. Much of this anti-immigrant sentiment can be traced to nativism and a xenophobia that has existed throughout US history in different forms and is directed by those wielding power at different groups based on extant economic, social, and political conditions at the time.[86]

To understand the anti-immigrant, anti-Latino backlash in the 1990s, it is important to review government actions around immigration policy action in the twentieth century. In the 1930s and 1950s, hundreds of thousands of Mexicans were targeted and subjected to racialized mass deportations by the US government during challenging economic times and in the midst of political turmoil.[87] Hundreds of thousands were removed indiscriminately, including US citizens of Mexican descent. In the next decade, after much debate, the US Congress passed the Hart-Cellar Act, which President Lyndon Johnson signed into law in 1965. This immigration act abolished the national-origins formula that effectively excluded migration from many nations; it thereby enabled the large influx of many peoples historically excluded from the US immigration process.

The passage of this act followed the ending of the government sponsored Bracero Program in 1964. The Bracero Program brought seasonal Mexican and other workers to the United States to work in agriculture and other low-wage jobs. These combined actions set in motion both increased restrictions on the migration of Mexican workers and greater demand by employers for low-wage workers.[88]

By the 1970s, immigrants from Mexico continued to cross the US-Mexico border, lured by promises of work and an escape from poverty. At the same time, anti-immigration voices grew louder and more persistent in the United States. They were opposed to the 1965 Immigration Act and sought stronger measures to stop legal migration and unauthorized immigration. Immigration reform advocates continued to advocate for passage of a more comprehensive immigration reform package in the 1970s and 1980s that would address those living and working in the United States without legal status.

After years of lobbying and advocacy on both sides of the immigration issue, a compromise bill passed Congress and was signed by President Ronald Reagan in 1986. The Immigration Reform and Control Act (IRCA) created an amnesty program for millions of immigrants who had entered the United States prior to January 1, 1982; the law also included employer sanction provisions, which immigrant advocates feared would be used to increase discrimination against all immigrants.[89] Some labor unions, fearful of low-wage competition from undocumented workers, pushed for sanctions for employers who knowingly hired undocumented immigrants.[90] Funds were also allocated to the Border Patrol to bolster enforcement efforts at the US-Mexico border.

The passage of IRCA in 1986 did not stop the efforts to restrict new migration. In the early 1990s, calls to restrict unauthorized immigration again used anti-immigrant rhetoric. These efforts resulted in a series of federal laws adopted in the 1990s. One effort was implemented in 1993 by the former head of the El Paso Border Patrol, Silvestre Reyes; called Operation Hold the Line, it was designed to create a visible deterrent for people attempting to cross the border in the El Paso, Texas, area. This effort was followed soon afterward by Operation Gatekeeper, which expanded a fence along the Tijuana, Mexico, and San Diego, California, border. These efforts also included enhanced surveillance of the border and an immigration court to hold hearings for and deport those caught entering without authorization. A similar program, Operation Safeguard, was launched in the border area near Tucson, Arizona. These regional targeted efforts to slow unauthorized migration were designed to highlight federal government efforts to restrict southern border crossings and address anti-immigrant sentiments held by a segment of the US population.[91]

Anti-immigrant Backlash: Proposition 187 in California

In addition to these targeted efforts to restrict border crossings, in 1994 a combination of economic, political, and demographic factors dramatically changed the political landscape for Latinos in the United States, with broad implications for the future of US politics. In California, a small group of anti-immigration activists in Orange County, fed up with the proliferation of Latino and other immigrants in the Southern California region, put an initiative on the California ballot to cut off all services for anyone without legal status. The initiative was designed to deny government services, including public education and health care, to undocumented immigrants. The proposition also required teachers and health care professionals to

66 *Latino Political Power*

report individuals suspected of being undocumented to the Immigration and Naturalization Service (INS).[92]

At the time, Governor Pete Wilson was in the midst of a reelection campaign and needed an issue to promote his candidacy and propel himself into a run for president in 1996. The ballot proposition passed overwhelmingly with 60 percent support, though it was opposed by 70 percent of Latino voters. The organized opposition by the Latino community signaled a new day for Latino politics and contemporary American politics.

At the state level, Proposition 187 had the effect of politically mobilizing widespread segments of the Latino community, including mutual-aid associations, social service organizations, elected officials, and owners of Spanish-language media. One month before the November election, more than 100,000 Latinos demonstrated against the bill in downtown Los Angeles.[93] The demonstration culminated a series of rallies organized by Latinos, labor unions, teachers, students, and medical practitioners in both rural communities and large urban centers. There were also school walkouts by middle and high school students, who proudly waved Mexican and other Central American flags in heavily Latino school districts. The Catholic Church and the Spanish media in the state opposed the measure as well.

Although civil rights and community organizations mobilized communities of color to oppose the measure, recessionary fears, anti-Latino and anti-immigrant sentiments, and the heavy promotion of Proposition 187 by Governor Wilson combined to pass the initiative. Afterward, civil rights organizations immediately challenged the proposition, arguing it violated the Supreme Court ruling in *Plyler v. Doe* (1982) and that immigration is a federal rather than a state issue. Eventually, the law was not implemented as the courts ruled it was unconstitutional and violated the equal protection clause of the Fourteenth Amendment to the US Constitution, which protects individuals regardless of citizenship status.

If political opposition to immigration and the mobilization of the California Latino community were ignited in 1994, they caught fire in 1996. Anti-immigrant efforts went national in 1996 with the passage of the Personal Responsibility and Work Opportunity Act (Welfare Act) and the Illegal Immigration Reform and Immigrant Responsibility Act (IIRIRA). The Welfare Act removed many federal services for noncitizens, and the IIRIRA reduced many of the due-process procedures that had been required to deport those apprehended without US immigration documents.

The Latino response to these and other anti-immigrant efforts is still being felt on a nationwide basis. Before Proposition 187 passed in 1994, naturalization rates for Mexican and Central Americans were extremely low, as most Mexicans and Central Americans expected to return home when conditions improved or civil wars ceased. Following the passage of Proposition 187, many Latino immigrants sought the protection of US citizenship through naturalization. Many formerly undocumented Latinos who had obtained amnesty under IRCA were now highly motivated to become naturalized citizens.[94] Between 1994 and 1997, citizenship applications to the INS grew from 540,000 to 1.4 million, and most were made by Latinos. Between 1990 and 1996, 876,000 Latinos naturalized, and their voting behavior has changed the nature of the Latino electorate. Analyses of voting from the 1996 national elections indicated naturalized Latino citizens were more likely to register and vote than native-born Latinos.[95]

Also, among newly naturalized Latinos in the post–Proposition 187 period, voter turnout was higher than that of other Latinos in California; the turnout rate was also higher in Texas and Florida, where there was no major anti-immigrant legislation at that time.[96] Another indication of the impact of new and energized Latino voters was California's 1996 elections for president, Congress, and the state legislature. Latinos voted as a unified bloc and voted Democratic by a majority of 70 percent statewide, much higher than their previous rate of 60 percent.[97] In 2002 NALEO observed that 68 percent of Latinos in Los Angeles and 59 percent of Latinos in Houston had registered to vote since 1995.[98]

The emergence of new Latino voters and voices in Latino politics in the 1990s is an indication of the growing diversity within the Latino community. As Latinas, new immigrants, emerging ethnic constituencies, third-party officeholders, gays and lesbians, and others infuse new perspectives into Latino politics, and as the strength of Latino voters grows, together they will extend Latino political influence in the United States into areas not exclusively populated by Latinos.

Conclusion

Starting in the 1970s, Latinos moved from being political outsiders to filling a growing number of elected and appointed offices. During the "rainbow politics" period, 1983 to 1993, the number of Latino elected officials in the nation increased by 48 percent, which compared favorably with the 53 percent growth in the Latino population during the same period. More impressively, the number of Latinas in public office increased by 194 percent during that period and has continued to grow subsequently.[99]

Many of the new crop of Latino elected officials were part of biracial or multiracial coalitions in large urban areas. In the 1990s, Latinos also made gains in heavily Latino-majority towns, cities, and county districts as restrictive at-large electoral systems, gerrymandering of districts, and low Latino voter participation began to change. In 1994, an anti-immigrant measure on the California ballot helped inspire large numbers of Latinos to become active in politics to defend the rights of Latino citizens and noncitizens.

68   *Latino Political Power*

Also, new energy from Latino immigrant political voices created a distinct independent presence.

In short, Latino political incorporation from the 1970s to the 1990s increased dramatically, particularly in locations with high concentrations of Latinos. In most large metropolitan areas with a concentration of Latinos, usually in at least one neighborhood or more that has become an electoral district, Latinos have been elected to local, state, and some federal offices. This reflects a change from nonvisible representation to symbolic representation and, in some places, to substantive representation. Latinos by the end of the 1990s were becoming influential in many of the dominant political coalitions that run urban governments. They have matured politically and can compete and win office in many cities. The next chapter explores the dynamics of the growth of Latino politics in the first two decades of the twenty-first century.

Notes

1. Mexican American Legal Defense and Education Fund, https://www.maldef.org/our-history/.
2. Gomez Quiñones 1990, 159.
3. Brischetto et al. 1994, 242.
4. Ibid., 243.
5. Ibid., 246.
6. Gonzalez 2000, 179.
7. Baver 1984, 54.
8. Lucas 1984, 111.
9. Córdova 1999, 42.
10. PRLDEF 2002, 1.
11. Brischetto 1988b.
12. Southwest Voter Registration Education Project, n.d.
13. Ibid.
14. Acuña 1988, 419.
15. Gomez Quiñones 1990, 170.
16. Griswold del Castillo and De León 1996, 157.
17. Munoz and Henry 1990, 183.
18. Acuña 1988, 420.
19. Gonzalez-Pando 1998, 61.
20. Gonzalez 2000, 180.
21. de Los Angeles Torres 1999, 117.
22. Ibid., 122.
23. Southwest Voter Registration Education Project 1984.
24. de Los Angeles Torres 1999, 124.
25. US Library of Congress, n.d.a.
26. de Los Angeles Torres 1991, 166–167.
27. Ibid., 171.
28. Betancur and Gills 2000, 67–69.
29. Córdova 1999, 40.

30. Ibid., 47.
31. Fraga 1992, 118.
32. Starks and Preston 1990, 88.
33. Pinderhughes 1997, 131.
34. Gonzalez 2000, 184.
35. Ibid., 180.
36. Keiser 1990, 66.
37. Travis 1990, 119.
38. Hardy-Fanta 1993, 107–108.
39. Collins 1986, 190.
40. Ibid., 186–187.
41. Falcon 1992, 154.
42. R. Smith 1990a, 225–226.
43. de la Garza 1992, 172–173.
44. Bonilla and Stafford 2000, 49.
45. Mollenkopf 1997, 109.
46. Gonzalez 2000, 185.
47. Ibid., 110.
48. Cruz 1998, 211.
49. Ibid., 178–187.
50. W. V. Flores 1992.
51. Takash 1990, 342–344.
52. Geron 1998.
53. Geron 2005, 161–188.
54. Gottleib 1993, B4.
55. Davis 1992.
56. Ibid.
57. Browning, Marshall, and Tabb 1984.
58. Moret 1998, 105.
59. W. V. Flores with Benmayor 1997, 1–6.
60. Rosales 2000, 189.
61. W. V. Flores with Benmayor 1997, 1–6.
62. Hardy-Fanta 1993, 103.
63. Sampaio 2002.
64. Pardo 1998.
65. Louie 2001, 207–208.
66. La Mujer Obrera. www.mujerobrera.org, accessed January 9, 2004.
67. Louie 2001, 202–204.
68. Gonzalez 2000.
69. Jordan 1997, 38.
70. Hernández and Rivera-Batiz 2003.
71. US Census Bureau 2004.
72. Georges 1984a and b.
73. Jordan 1997, 38.
74. Interview with New York City Council member G. Linares, July 16, 2001.
75. Ibid.
76. Jordan 1997, 40.
77. Graham 1998, 55.
78. Ibid.
79. Lewis Mumford Center 2001.
80. Duany 1998, 148–149.

70 Latino Political Power

81. Izigsohn et al. 1999.
82. Jones-Correa 2001.
83. "Our Mission," Coalition for Humane Immigrant Rights (CHIRLA), www
.chirla.org/who-we-are/about-us/mission-history (accessed December 12, 2021).
84. Gonzalez 2000.
85. Reinoso 2001.
86. Ngai 2014.
87. Goodman 2020.
88. Zepeda-Millan 2017, 26.
89. Ibid., 33.
90. Flores-González and Gutierrez 2010, 7.
91. Nevins 2002.
92. Chavez and Partida 2020.
93. Acuña 1996, 158.
94. Pachon, Sanchez, and Falcon 1999, 170–172.
95. Vargas 1999–2000, 7.
96. Pantoja, Ramirez, and Segura 2001.
97. Segura, Falcon, and Pachon 1997.
98. NALEO 2002.
99. NALEO 1994.

4

Latino Politics in the Twenty-First Century

Entering the twenty-first century, Latino politics were on the rise. Yet underlying challenges emerged while electoral successes continued. The anti-immigrant legislation passed in the 1980s and 1990s escalated after the September 11, 2001, terrorist attacks on the United States. In addition to the rise of numerous federal laws, the adoption of state- and local-level anti-immigrant laws also impacted the Latino community. While there were a few modest efforts to enable noncitizen immigrants to vote in local jurisdictions, many efforts to restrict voting rights directly impacted immigrants and the Latino community.

The US presidential election in 2000 launched a decade of continued political contestation that directly involved Latinos. The presidential race pitted two southerners, Al Gore from Tennessee and George W. Bush from Texas. Of the two candidates, George W. Bush's appeal to Latinos was connected to his direct experiences as governor of Texas. In 1998, when Governor of Texas, Bush had a "targeted effort to seek Hispanic support through public policies such as bilingual education reform and funding and opposition to anti-immigrant and English-only initiatives."[1]

Bush's appeal to Latino voters helped propel him to narrow victory in 2000. Razor-thin victories in Florida and other states helped Bush to win election in 2000 and 2004. While the majority of Latinos voted for Bush's Democratic Party opponents, Latinos helped Bush in some strategic states by, according to some estimates, upward of more than 30 percent in 2000, and 40 percent of Latinos voted for Bush in 2004,[2] but still the fortunes of Latinos in the United States did not measurably improve in the Bush era. Bush did appoint a few Latinos to his cabinet and other high-level posts. Yet many Latinos continued to struggle economically, and issues such as immigration, voting rights, and other social and economic concerns continued to

72   *Latino Political Power*

impact the Latino community and received the attention of Latino politicians at the local, state, and federal levels.

Growth of Latino Elected Officials in the 2000s

At the beginning of the twenty-first century, there was a noticeable increase in the number of Latinos holding elected and judicial offices from 3,743 in 1996 to 6,084 in 2014 and 6,833 in 2019—nearly a 55 percent growth in less than twenty-five years. Between 1996 and 2007, the percentage of Latina elected officials grew by 74 percent compared to 25 percent growth for Latino elected officials (LEOs). Latina elected officials made up 24 percent of all LEOs in 1996 and grew to 34.5 percent in 2014 and 38.5 percent in 2019. Between 1996 and 2014, there was a 142 percent increase in Latinos being elected outside traditional areas of Latino population concentrations, with Latinos serving in forty-three states in 2007, up from thirty-four states in 1996. While the state locations did not increase for LEOs in 2019, their numbers continued to grow.

Latino Congressional Representation
at the Dawn of the Twenty-First Century

At the start of the twenty-first century, Latinos had limited representation in the US Congress. While their overall numbers had risen from four in 1961 to seven in 1971, nine in 1981, and fifteen in 1991, the number of elected representatives was not reflective of the numbers of Latinos in the population. In 2001, twenty-one Latinos were elected to the US House of Representatives, including a delegate from Puerto Rico. There were two Republicans and eighteen Democrats. There were no senators of Latino descent. By 2003 to 2005, there were twenty-three Hispanics in the House of Representatives. Republican Hispanics formed a separate caucus that includes five members. Together, Latinos comprised 5.3 percent of all members of the House. Between 1975 and 2005, there were no Latino senators elected to office. With the election of Republican Mel Martinez of Florida and Democrat Kenneth Salazar of Colorado to the US Senate in 2004, Latinos made up just 2 percent of that chamber. Even with these electoral victories in the Senate, Latino representation in Congress remained extremely limited.

From 2001 to 2021, the Latino presence in both houses of Congress more than doubled from nineteen to forty-six, representing 8.6 percent of all seats; this is the highest percentage of Latinos in Congress but still significantly below the Latino percentage of the US population, which was 18 percent as of 2019. Both political parties have seen a growth in their num-

Latino Politics in the Twenty-First Century 73

bers, with Democrats more than doubling their numbers from seventeen to thirty-six and Republicans increasing from three to ten since 2001. The spread of LEOs into more states and locations reflects not just the expansion of the Latino population but also the growing electability of Latinos in distinct political contexts and conditions beyond the traditional locations where Latinos are the majority population.

While this chapter focuses on the first two decades of the twenty-first century, some of the Latinas and Latinos in office started in the late 1980s or early 1990s and continued to serve into the twenty-first century. These Latinos were the pioneers or part of a second wave of Latinos elected to Congress. It is important to discuss Latinos elected to the US Congress before 2000 and their trajectory into the twenty-first century.

Ileana Ros-Lehtinen was elected in 1988 to Congress and served for thirty years. Ros-Lehtinen was born in Cuba and became a political refugee, arriving in the United States at a young age with her family after Fidel Castro came to power in 1959. She attended Miami-area schools, earned a PhD in higher education, assisted immigrant parents needing assistance, and helped start a school in the Miami area.[3] In 1982 Ros-Lehtinen won a seat in the Florida House of Representatives; she was the first Latina to serve in the state legislature. In 1986, she won a seat in the Florida Senate and three years later ran in a special election to fill a vacancy due to the death of US Representative Claude Pepper. Ros-Lehtinen won the special election and became the first Latina and the first Cuban American elected to the US Congress. During her tenure in the US Congress, Ros-Lehtinen served on the Foreign Affairs Committee, where she championed human rights, support for the embargo against Cuba, and issues related to her South Florida district. She also opposed numerous anti-immigrant pieces of legislation; often times she and fellow Cuban Americans Lincoln Díaz-Balart and Mario Díaz-Balart were the only Republicans to oppose legislation that included anti-immigrant policies in Congress.

José E. Serrano retired from the US Congress in 2020 after serving as a representative since 1990 from the Bronx, where he won a special election to fill the vacancy caused by the resignation of US Representative Robert Garcia, also a long-standing Latino member of the US Congress. Serrano was born in Puerto Rico and served in the US Army in the 1960s and later in the New York State Assembly from 1975 to 1990. Serrano was an outspoken leader in his thirty years in Congress and a member of the Progressive Caucus. He did not seek reelection in 2020 and was succeeded by Ritchie Torres.

Nydia M. Velázquez was born in Puerto Rico in a small town, and after obtaining her degree in political science at the University of Puerto Rico, she came to New York, where she earned a master's degree from New York University. In 1983, Velázquez worked for Democratic congressman Edolphus

74 Latino Political Power

Towns of Brooklyn. One year later, she became the first Latina appointed to serve on the New York City Council. In 1986, Velázquez became director of the Department of Puerto Rican Community Affairs in the United States.

In 1992, Velázquez ran a grassroots campaign and was elected to Congress, defeating a nine-term incumbent and other Latino candidates. She became the first Puerto Rican woman elected to the US House of Representatives. In 1998, she was named ranking Democratic Party member of the House of Representatives' Small Business Committee, the first Latina to serve as ranking member of a full House committee. In 2006, Velázquez was named chairwoman of the House Small Business Committee and was the first Latina to chair a full congressional committee. She is also one of the longest-serving Latina/os in Congress and continues to serve her constituents in New York's 7th Congressional District.

Congressman Luis V. Gutiérrez, after a long political career in Chicago politics, which included a seat on the city council, was elected in 1992 to the US House of Representatives, where he served until stepping down in 2018. Gutierrez was a leader on many issues in Congress related to the immigrant community. Congressman Gutierrez was instrumental in elevating national opposition to SB 1070, a bill adopted in 2010 in Arizona that, among other provisions, required a person stopped by law enforcement to produce their immigration papers, if requested, and allowed law enforcement to investigate immigration status if they suspected they were undocumented. He was also a strong advocate for the rights of the undocumented, including a pathway to citizenship for the estimated eleven million residents without legal status in the United States.[4] He introduced and supported numerous pieces of legislation to address the immigration crisis and the rights of the undocumented; while these efforts did not always result in legislative success, he is highly regarded for standing up for those with limited options who live in the shadows in this country without legal status. Gutierrez was succeeded by Jesus "Chuy" Garcia, a longtime progressive Mexican immigrant in Chicago's Latino community.

Lucille Roybal-Allard was first elected to US Congress in 1992, after serving in the California State Assembly. She was the first Mexican American woman to be elected to the US Congress. She was born in Boyle Heights, a neighborhood in East Los Angeles. The daughter of Edward R. Roybal, who served in Congress from 1963 to 1993, she was elected to his congressional seat when he decided not to run for reelection. Roybal Allard coauthored the 2001 Development, Relief, and Education for Alien Minors (DREAM) Act to provide a pathway to citizenship for undocumented young people. She continued to advocate for the rights of immigrants and the undocumented and decided to retire at the end of her term in 2022.

Another pioneer, Democrat Hilda Solis, is a daughter of working-class immigrant parents from Mexico and Nicaragua, both of whom were labor union members. After serving in the state assembly and senate, in 2000 Solis was elected from the San Gabriel Valley area, east of Los Angeles in Southern California, to the US Congress, having defeated nine-term incumbent Marty Martinez in the Democratic primary. This race was significant as Solis, a former Jimmy Carter appointee in the White House Office of Hispanic Affairs, had strong support from organized labor in the Los Angeles area; the county's labor federation had grown dissatisfied with Congressman Martinez and his moderate, pro-business positions and instead backed Solis, whom the federation viewed as a labor warrior.[5]

After Solis had served in Congress for eight years, in 2009, President Barack Obama appointed her US Secretary of Labor, making her the first Latina member of a US president's cabinet. She stepped down in 2013, and in 2014 she was elected to a seat on the Los Angeles County Board of Supervisors, succeeding her mentor, Gloria Molina, who had helped pave the way for many other Latinas. In this role, Supervisor Solis represents District 1, which is majority Latino and includes twenty-four cities, unincorporated East Los Angeles, and numerous parts of the City of Los Angeles. Solis has promoted environmental justice, housing for the unhoused, and the building of affordable housing.

Since 2000 the numbers of Latino Congress members have grown, as has their political and geographic diversity; Latinos have been elected in numerous states, which in 2021 included Arizona, California, Colorado, Florida, Idaho, Illinois, Massachusetts, Nevada, New Jersey, New Mexico, New York, Ohio, Texas, Washington, and West Virginia. Previously, for several decades, Latinos had been elected only from California, New Mexico, New York, and Texas. One of the most recognized and popular new members of the US Congress is Alexandria Ocasio-Cortez, who defeated a ten-term incumbent to win a seat in New York City's majority-Latino 14th District in 2018. Ocasio-Cortez, a thirty-something progressive activist and politician, is part of the new generation of Latina/o leaders. As the Latino population and its voting strength grow in the South, Midwest, and other regions, there will be more Latinos elected to the US Congress in the future.

Contemporary Latino Governors

In addition to growing their numbers in both houses of Congress, Latinos have also made gains at the governor level in several states in the past two decades. The governorship is the most powerful elected office in each state, so the stakes are high and the campaigns are expensive. In 2002, there were two high-profile governorships in the Southwest, in New Mexico and Texas. In Texas, two Latinos, Dan Morales and Tony Sanchez, squared off in the Democratic Party primary for governor in 2002. Tony Sanchez was victorious

76 *Latino Political Power*

and went on to lose in the general election to Rick Perry, a Republican. The Democratic Party primary was hotly contested between Morales, the widely known former state attorney general, and Sanchez, a wealthy businessman, who used a considerable amount of his own money to run ads introducing himself to Texas voters. He won overwhelmingly against Morales.[6]

Many characterized the general election as having racial overtones as the Perry campaign used television ads that appeared to link his opponent to Mexican drug dealers. Perry won White voters two to one in a state where they are the majority and thus won relatively easily despite Sanchez's considerable wealth. While many Texas Latinos had hoped for a change after many years of Republican leadership by former governors Bush and Perry, the expected expansion of Latino voters did not materialize.[7]

In New Mexico, well-known state politician Bill Richardson faced a Republican Hispanic candidate and won in a race for governor in 2002, in a state where Hispanics made up 42 percent of the population at the time. Richardson had already had a long political career at the time of his election. He previously served as a congressman for sixteen years (1982–1996), as US ambassador to the United Nations (1997–1998), and as secretary of energy under President Bill Clinton (1998–2000). Richardson was elected governor of New Mexico in November 2002, defeating Republican candidate John Sanchez. He took office in January 2003 as the only Hispanic governor in the United States and handily won reelection in 2006.

In 2011, Richardson was succeeded by Susana Martinez, the first woman Republican Hispanic governor of New Mexico. She served for two terms from 2011 to 2019 and was followed as governor by Michelle Lujan Grisham. It is notable that for three successive administrations, Hispanic governors were elected, two of them women, from both parties; this reflects the state's politics, which have leaned Democratic, although Republican leaders have been elected as well.

Also, in 2010, Republican Brian Sandoval was elected as governor of Nevada. He held this seat until 2018. Having served previously as the state's attorney general, he was a sitting federal judge when he successfully ran against a Republican incumbent governor in the 2010 GOP primary. He then went on to defeat Rory Reid, the son of Nevada US senator Harry Reid, in the general election. He left office in 2018.

Local Elections and Latinos

In addition to federal and gubernatorial positions, Latinos are actively pursuing and winning numerous other statewide, county and municipal positions, which reflects the growing diversity of the locations where they are being elected. The mayoralty is a high-profile office in a city. Since 2001, Latinos have sought to become mayors in some of the largest US cities.

Latino Politics in the Twenty-First Century   77

Fernando Ferrer was the first Latino to run a credible campaign for mayor of New York City in 2005, when he was defeated by incumbent Michael Bloomberg. In Los Angeles, the nation's second-largest city, Antonio Villaraigosa lost to James Hahn in a competitive race for mayor in 2001.[8] In 2005, Villaraigosa ran again and this time succeeded, becoming the first Latino mayor since 1872 in a city with nearly a majority-Latino population. In Houston, Texas, the nation's fourth-largest city, Orlando Sanchez lost to Lee Brown for mayor in 2001. While the mayor's race is nonpartisan, Sanchez was a Republican and had the backing of prominent Republicans, including the Bush family at a time when George W. Bush was the US president and former president George H. W. Bush lived in Houston. Sanchez, a Cuban American, ran in a city where the vast majority of Latinos are Mexican American and registered as Democrats. Nevertheless, Sanchez, as a Houston City Council member, was known in the Latino community and ran a credible campaign; still, Lee Brown was able to defeat him with a large turnout from the African American community.

In 2001, Latino candidates for mayor in three of the four largest cities lost their races; however, in San Antonio, Texas, Ed Garza won. Garza, a San Antonio City Council member, had targeted the most likely voters in the city, which included a high percentage of White as well as Latino voters.[9]

In San Jose, California, Democrat Ron Gonzales was elected in 1998 as the first Latino mayor of the city since the state was founded in 1850 and one of the first Latino mayors of a large city. The city of San Jose, located in the high-tech center of Silicon Valley in Northern California, is the state's third-largest city. Gonzales easily won reelection in 2002 and completed his term of office in 2006. Gonzales held numerous positions in and out of local government before becoming mayor.[10]

In 2019, there were 316 Latino mayors, plus an additional 173 mayors pro tem. Latino mayors in Texas numbered 121 out of a total of 1,200 in incorporated cities, which is 10 percent in a state where Latinos make up nearly 40 percent of the population. There were 83 mayors in California in a total of 482 cities, which is 17 percent of the total number in a state with a Latino population of 38 percent. These two states are the two largest cohorts among the seventeen states with Latino mayors. The other states include Arizona, Colorado, Florida, Georgia, Idaho, Illinois, Kansas, Maryland, Massachusetts, Minnesota, New Jersey, New Mexico, Ohio, Rhode Island, and Washington. In terms of partisanship, while most mayoral elections are nonpartisan, the party identification of candidates, alongside their policy priorities, is a cue for many voters. At the start of 2021, 64 of the country's 100 largest cities were affiliated with the Democratic Party.

In addition to winning high-profile mayoral elections in large cities, Latinos were also elected mayor in recent years in different regions of the United States, reflecting the growing diversity of Latino mayors. Wilda Diaz, of Puerto Rican descent, served from 2008 to 2020 as mayor of Perth

78 *Latino Political Power*

Amboy, a city of 50,000 in New Jersey. A diverse community, it is 65 percent Latino, primarily Puerto Rican and Dominican. Diaz was the only Latina mayor in New Jersey when she held office. Always an independent voice, she supported Bernie Sanders for president and challenged the local Democratic Party. She lost in a runoff to city council member Helmin Caba in 2020. Caba, born in the Dominican Republic and raised in Perth Amboy, headed the City's Democratic Party organization and was backed by labor unions.[11]

Democrat Michelle de la Isla served as mayor of Topeka, Kansas, from 2018 to 2022. In 2013, she was elected to the city council and served as deputy mayor in 2016. De la Isla was born in New York and grew up in Puerto Rico before moving to Kansas to attend school. As her city's Latina mayor, she carried out her duties while raising three children as a single mom.[12] Topeka is nearly 16 percent Latino and an overwhelmingly White community.

In McAllen, Texas, Republican Javier Villalobos, a former chairman of the local Republican Party, won a nonpartisan race for mayor by 200 votes over Democratic city council member Veronica Vela Whitacre. This city next to the US-Mexico border in Hidalgo County has a population of more than 143,000 and is nearly 85 percent Latino.

In Allentown, Pennsylvania, Democrat Matt Tuerk, a third-generation Cuban American, was elected mayor and defeated fellow Latino Tim Ramos, a Republican, in a majority-Latino city. Latinos are also a growing population in Pennsylvania; they are 69 percent of Reading, 29 percent of Bethlehem, and 15 percent in Philadelphia, where they grew by more than 48 percent in the recent census.[13] Local Latinos view the election of Tuerk and other Latinos to local office as long overdue; having people who look like them become their elected representatives will help address issues of exclusion and feeling left out of the political system. This diverse group of mayors is an indication that the regional influence of Latino politics can be expected to grow as the Latino population expands to new areas, plants roots, and begins to engage in politics.

Latino Local Politics in the Northeast

The high level of political interest in the Latino community is illustrated in the Northeast, including in New York City, where races have been hotly contested among Latinos and other candidates of color for election as local and state representatives in parts of the city with Latino density. When Dominican American New York City Council member Guillermo Linares was termed out of office in 2001, there were eight candidates for this position, reflecting the diversity of political viewpoints and allegiances within the community. The winner of this seat, Miguel Martinez, was president of a political club associated with assembly member Adriano Espaillat (who is

Latino Politics in the Twenty-First Century **79**

now the US congressman from this area). Other candidates had ties to Linares and other political alliances in the Dominican community. Also elected in 2001 in Brooklyn was another Dominican, Diana Reyna, a former aide to longtime assemblyman Vito Lopez. Both incumbents won reelection in 2003, running against many of the same rivals. Diana Reyna was the first Dominican American woman elected to public office in New York. Born and raised in Brooklyn, she was twenty-eight when she was elected in 2002 and served until 2013, when she was termed out. She most recently worked as a deputy borough president for Brooklyn borough president Eric Adams, who won election as New York City's second African American mayor in 2021.

Competitive races involving Dominican and Puerto Rican candidates in heavily Latino population centers in New York City are an indication of healthy debate in the numerous Latino communities over who can best represent the various ethnic Latinos in this city and their political allegiance to various political leaders. More recently, in 2016, Dominican American Carmen de la Rosa was elected for the state assembly in the heavily Dominican area of Washington Heights and Inwood. There was intense competition between the major Dominican American politicians who represented overlapping political turf in the area.[14] In 2021, de la Rosa was elected to the state assembly from this district, reflecting the rise of Latina elected officials.

Dominican Americans have also been elected to state and local offices in several other states. In Lawrence, Massachusetts, a former mill town that still receives new immigrants, as it did in the nineteenth century, two Dominicans and two Puerto Ricans were on the city council in 2005. A Puerto Rican and a Dominican ran for mayor of Lawrence in 2001, and the Puerto Rican candidate, Isabel Melendez, nearly won. Lawrence's Latino political leadership has continued to reflect its Latino-majority population with a current majority of Latinos on the nine-person city council as well as a Latino mayor, Kendrys Vasquez. With a 60 percent Latino population and 38 percent Latino voters in 2000—according to the 2010 census, the population had grown to 77 percent Latino (47 percent Dominican, 22 percent Puerto Rican, and 3 percent Guatemalan and others)—this city reflects how Latinos are becoming politically incorporated in towns not historically known as centers of Latino culture and politics.

In Rhode Island, Dominicans have also been elected to office from the Providence area: most recently, Sabina Matos was elected as Rhode Island's lieutenant governor, after serving on the Providence City Council. Democrat Grace Diaz is a Rhode Island state representative. She has represented Providence's District 11 since 2005. She was the first Dominican American woman elected to state office in US history. She was appointed vice chair of the Rhode Island Democratic Party and became the first Latina woman in Rhode Island to serve in such a high-ranking position.

80   *Latino Political Power*

In 2010, Dominican American attorney Angel Tavares was elected as the first Latino mayor of Providence.[15] In his tenure as mayor, he highlighted issues such as improving educational opportunities for the city's historically underrepresented students of color. On his election, the city faced fiscal stress and a significant structural deficit. In order to address the city's financial challenges, Tavares decided to close public schools, cut city department budgets, renegotiate city worker union contracts, and reduce pensions for city workers.[16] These fiscal challenges restricted his ability to create jobs for the Latino community; instead, he reduced the workforce by 10 percent, which limited opportunities for Black and Brown members of the community. Even though he had positive approval ratings, when he ran for governor of Rhode Island, he lost in the Democratic Party primary to state treasurer Gina Raimondo, who became Rhode Island's governor in 2014.[17] Raimondo was selected as secretary of commerce in the Joe Biden administration in 2021.

In addition to Dominican Americans, other Latinos have been elected or selected as mayor in the Northeast. Angel Tavares was succeeded as mayor of Providence by Jorge O. Elorza, who was elected in 2014 and took office in 2015. Elorza is of Guatemalan descent and was born and raised in Providence, the largest city in Rhode Island, with a 44 percent Latino population. In his second term, he had an expansive agenda, including reparations for Black residents of the community and major police-community reforms.[18] However, the ongoing fiscal challenges of the city—with a wealthy East Side versus other parts of the city facing economic hardship—were still evident in 2021 with the passage of the city's budget.[19]

In Connecticut, in the capital city of Hartford, Eddie Perez, a community organizer born in Puerto Rico, formed a multiracial, multiclass coalition and won election as mayor in 2001. He did not run for mayor as a Latino-empowerment candidate but sought to conduct a deracialized campaign, as have other Latinos running for citywide office, such as Federico Peña in Denver, Colorado.[20] Perez was the first Latino to become mayor of a major northeastern city. He served until 2010, when he was convicted on a corruption charge. Pedro Segarra became mayor in 2010 when Perez had to step down. Segarra was also born in Puerto Rico and became an attorney before holding the mayor's seat. He served in a number of appointed positions before being elected as a city council member. He also built a multiracial electoral coalition among the city's White liberals, African Americans, and Latinos. Segarra understandably focused on stabilizing the city's financial situation as he came to office following the 2008–2010 economic collapse. He was unable to expand his electoral coalition and lost his 2015 reelection bid to a White candidate.[21] These two Latino mayors, along with Tavares and Elorza in Providence, were some of the Latino electoral pioneers in the Northeast responsible for heading their states' capital cities, and they reflect the growth of Latino politics beyond the traditional centers.

Latino efforts to achieve electoral office are one part of shaping the political context in local communities where economic factors have played a major role in the political success of Latino mayors and others elected at the local level. Many of the Latinos elected since the recession and economic crisis that grew out of the 2008–2010 housing collapse found their cities and communities were hard hit with high unemployment, local economic crises, underfunded city services, high rates of homelessness, and numerous social challenges.[22]

In a 2019 study of Latino political leadership in Massachusetts, researchers observed that while Latinos make up a growing share of eligible voters in the state, Latino political leadership at the various levels of government is less than the Latino percentage of the state population. In only two cities, Chelsea and Lawrence, are Latinos elected to city council and school committees at a relatively comparable rate to their share of the local population. There are more Latinas than Latinos serving on school committees. They held only one seat in the state senate, where five seats would be proportionate to the statewide Latino population. They held none of the state's congressional seats.[23]

Latino Politics and Immigration Policy

While electoral victories have continued to grow as more Latinos are being elected to office in diverse locations and positions, other major issues have continued to impact Latinos and their political efforts, and Latino politicians play an important role in supporting pro-immigrant policies and opposing anti-immigrant laws. Immigration issues impact the form and shape of Latino politics as they often draw media and national attention, and Latino politicians are often front and center speaking out on immigration issues and other related concerns. In the past twenty years voices on both sides of the issue of immigration and reforming the broken immigration system have at times dominated the headlines. Some want to restrict both legal and undocumented immigrants and asylum seekers; others call for a pathway to citizenship for the estimated eleven million undocumented who are already in the country and seek a humane solution for those attempting to enter the United States without legal documents or as refugees escaping violence in their homelands. Latino politicians have been some of the most visible elected officials speaking out on the need to address the immigration crisis as the immigration issue continues to play a major role in the political activism of various segments of the Latino community.

In the first decade of the 2000s, the issue of immigration exploded into the largest mass protests the nation had seen. During 2006, hundreds of rallies and marches in America's largest cities, as well as in small towns, suburbs,

82 *Latino Political Power*

and rural communities, were held to oppose the passage of HR 4437, the Border Protection Anti-Terrorism and Illegal Immigration Control Act of 2005, proposed by Republican congressman James Sensenbrenner. The bill would have severely criminalized undocumented immigration by elevating it from a civil violation to a felony and punishing anyone who assisted or associated with those without legal status. Politicians like former Republican congressman Tom Tancredo from Colorado for many years called for the end of birthright citizenship for children born in the United States if their parents were not in the country legally.

In the 2000s, the anti-immigrant ballot initiatives of the 1990s in California weighed heavily on the Latino community, as many viewed them as efforts to weaken the growing Latino power in many states. There are differences in how Latinos view immigration, with the native-born more likely to favor restricting immigration and more recent immigrants believing that more immigrants should be allowed to enter the United States.[24] After the Immigration Reform and Control Act's passage in the 1980s, there was a spike in people applying for permanent residency by the 1990s. Service centers such as Catholic Charities were inundated with requests for assistance to apply for a green card and permanent residency, which is a major step toward becoming a US citizen after a minimum wait of five years. By the 1990s, many of these permanent residents began to naturalize as US citizens for both protection from future anti-immigrant legislation targeting noncitizens and for the ability to express their political views at the ballot box. One of the many responses to the anti-immigrant policies was a marked increase in naturalizations and voter registrations by the Latino community in the 1990s and 2000s.[25]

Another important factor in increasing immigrant rights efforts and resources was the reversal by the American Federation of Labor–Congress of Industrial Organizations (AFL-CIO) of its position on immigration. For many decades, the AFL-CIO had opposed immigration, viewing immigrants as competitors for good-paying union jobs. After several years of intense organizing by immigrant workers in Southern California and lobbying efforts by labor and community activists involved with the labor movement, the AFL-CIO, in February 2000, officially supported the legalization of undocumented immigrants and committed to organizing all immigrants, both documented and undocumented.[26]

With growing labor support for immigrant rights and continued efforts by grassroots and established civil rights organizations, there was a renewed energy to push forward for a more comprehensive immigration reform. Newly elected US president George W. Bush was open to some form of immigration reform, having previously served as governor of Texas, a border state with a large number of immigrants. The terrorist acts of September 11, 2001, in the United States dramatically changed the focus of the country's leaders to renewed anti-immigrant actions that focused initially on Muslim and Arab immigrants and grew to include others. Significant majorities of those polled in 2002 in the United States and European nations supported restricting immigration to combat international terrorism.[27]

Soon after, the passage of several new laws tied to terrorism had a negative impact on immigrants. The 2001 Patriot Act and 2002's Enhanced Border Security and Visa Entry Reform Act and Homeland Security Act combined with the 1990s anti-immigrant laws to create additional barriers to entry, swift deportations for those entering the country without legal status, tightening of entry rules, and increased surveillance. Frustration mounted among immigrants that their demands for just immigration policies were being drowned out by the anti-immigrant voices and the anti-terrorism regulations that made every immigrant a suspect.

In addition to anti-immigrant laws often couched in anti-terrorism rhetoric, the growing militarization of the US border over the past twenty years is another policy issue that impacts Latino politics. During the George W. Bush presidency, there was an escalation of legislation focused on immigration. Of the 2,000 bills introduced, 144 were signed into law, including increased scrutiny of immigrants, increased detention and deportation, heightened militarization of the border region with additional border patrol agents and new technology, restrictions on federal services and benefits to immigrants, and empowerment of local law enforcement to act as immigration agents.[28]

In addition, the Secure Communities Program of the Department of Homeland Security (DHS), started in 2008 under President Bush, enables Immigration and Customs Enforcement (ICE) to allow local police to send the fingerprints of persons arrested to DHS to match with immigrant records to expedite deportations, resulting in the removal of hundreds of thousands of individuals. The program was curtailed under President Barack Obama, revived by President Donald Trump in 2017 via executive order, and ended by President Biden in 2021 by executive order. The 287(g) Program, named after the 1996 immigration law, allows ICE to train and deputize law enforcement officers to assist with federal immigration policing to detect and deport persons with immigration status violations. This is controversial as some cities and counties have refused to sign memorandums of understanding with ICE.

In Arizona, two controversial laws were passed. Proposition 200, passed in 2004, required new forms of identification to vote, restricting Latinos' right to vote in particular; it was among the first voting rights restrictions adopted in the twenty-first century but has led to numerous other voter suppression laws adopted in many states. In 2006, a state referendum, Proposition 300, passed, stating that people without legal immigration status were not eligible for in-state tuition. Also, in 2005, the Minutemen organization began patrolling the Arizona border with Mexico to look for people

84 *Latino Political Power*

who were trying to cross. They said they were there just to assist the under-staffed Customs and Border Patrol.[29] Many in the Latino community viewed them as racist vigilantes, adding to the heightened racialized tension regarding US immigration policy.

While anti-immigrant legislation and initiatives grew, accompanied by anti-immigrant actions by federal, state, and local law enforcement agencies, many of them framed as anti-terrorist, there were also important efforts to address the growing immigration crisis and increase the rights of immigrants. In 2001, Senator Dick Durban of Illinois was a main sponsor of the Development, Relief, and Education for Alien Minors (DREAM) Act, which called for a pathway to citizenship for a segment of the undocumented youth population. It was not a comprehensive immigration reform package. Over the next twenty years, various legislators introduced at least eleven versions of the DREAM Act in Congress. While the many versions contained some key differences, all would have provided a pathway to legal status for undocumented people who came to this country as children. Despite bipartisan support for each version of the bill, none have become law. The 2010 version came closest to passage when it passed the House but fell just 5 votes short of the 60 needed to overcome the filibuster rule for passage in the Senate.[30]

An important galvanizing event took place in 2003, the Immigrant Workers Freedom Rides, launched in multiple cities by immigrant activists and supported by the labor movement. Over 1,000 people traveled by bus and car caravans, stopping in more than 100 communities and culminating with pro-immigration rallies in Washington, DC.[31] Religious organizations and leaders, many of which provided services for immigrant church members, also advocated for immigrant rights and in some cases provided sanctuary for refugees who faced deportation back to their former countries, where they faced political repression and violence.

Between 2003 and 2006, there were numerous attempts to introduce legislation both broad in scope and targeted toward a specific segment such as Dreamers. The 2005 SOLVE Act, a compromise immigration bill also known as the McCain-Kennedy Bill, sought a path to permanent residency for undocumented workers but also had many restrictions. These efforts did not materialize into passage of a bill.[32] At the same time, in late 2005 Congressman James Sensenbrenner and other Republican legislators passed an anti-immigrant law, HR 4337, in the US House of Representatives. Known as the Border Protection, Anti-Terrorism and Illegal Immigration Control Act of 2005, it would have criminalized undocumented immigrants and those who assisted them. The passage of this bill would soon to lead to a massive effort to defeat it.

HR 4337 was a key galvanizing issue for Latinos and others concerned with immigrant rights. People nationwide organized for months to create hundreds of actions in all regions of the nation. "Latinx workers organized through social institutions that had helped sustain their communities, including *comites civicos* from their home countries, workers' centers, labor unions, Catholic Church social justice committees, sports clubs, and civil rights organizations."[33]

There were marches and rallies in March 2006 and national immigrant rights events on April 10; on May 1, widespread actions called for immigrants to boycott work and school to oppose the Sensenbrenner bill in the US Congress and demand immigrant rights. While there have previously been important marches and rallies for immigrant rights in the United States, the scope, breadth, and scale of these actions was unprecedented, particularly because they included large numbers of immigrants, including the undocumented. Between February and May 2006, there were between 3.7 million and 5 million participants in 160 cities.[34] There were massive rallies in Chicago, Los Angeles, Dallas, Washington, DC, New York City, Phoenix, and San Jose, with crowds of at least 100,000. An estimated minimum of 650,000 people, and likely many more, took part in the Los Angeles May Day events.[35] Tens of thousands who rallied in cities such as Atlanta, Georgia; Detroit, Michigan; Fort Myers, Florida, and many others. There were also smaller rallies in numerous southern states, Idaho, North Dakota, and elsewhere. The impact of these actions was to be felt for years to come.

In the aftermath of the 2006 rallies, there were continued organizing efforts with the slogan "Hoy marchamos, mañana votamas" ("Today we march, tomorrow we vote"). Recognizing the importance of defeating anti-immigrant legislation and developing pro-immigrant legislation in the future, the We Are America Alliance, the Ya Es Hora! Campaign, and other group efforts launched both naturalization and voter registration drives in 2006 after the mass marches and rallies. These efforts resulted in significant growth in Latino turnout for the 2008 elections.[36] Latinos raised their turnout to an estimated eleven million voters, a 38 percent increase over the 2004 presidential election, representing 9 percent of the total voter turnout and signaling growing Latino engagement in electoral politics.[37]

In 2007, the Ya Es Hora! Campaign launched with more than 400 organizations participating. It targeted states with large Latino populations and presidential swing states with direct messaging on the importance of naturalizing and registering to vote. The campaign employed Spanish-language media and direct appeals to reach both those eligible to become permanent residents who had not been approached to do so previously and nonregistered US citizens who had not previously voted.[38]

Others involved in the 2006 immigration rights marches and rallies decided to participate in the presidential elections as another way to change immigration policy because efforts to develop immigration reform on a bipartisan basis continued to stall. Many joined the presidential nomination and elections campaigns in 2008 to support Barack Obama. While immigration

86   *Latino Political Power*

activists had high hopes for the passage of more comprehensive immigration reform with the Democrats gaining majority political control of both houses of Congress and the administration in 2008, the severe economic recession, foreign policy challenges, and the push to address health care reform took priority; immigration reform measures were stalled once again.

State-Level Immigration Policies

Although political gridlock around federal immigration action including HR 4437 did not become federal law, this did not stop state governments from passing anti-immigrant laws. In Pennsylvania in 2006, the state government passed the Illegal Immigration Relief Act, which fined landlords who rented housing to undocumented immigrants and business owners who hired them. The state of Arizona in April 2010 enacted SB 1070, the Support Our Law Enforcement and Safe Neighborhoods Act. The Obama administration challenged the law's anti-immigrant provisions legally. Immigrant rights groups also opposed the act for racial profiling. SB 1070 symbolized the growth of anti-immigrant sentiments and legislation and galvanized both those who supported and those who opposed the law not just in Arizona.[39] SB 1070, along with similar state-level legislation, was deemed unconstitutional by the courts because the US Constitution assigns control over immigration to the federal government, not individual states. These rulings are similar to one rendered regarding California's Proposition 187 in 1994, which the courts also struck down.

The states more likely to introduce legislation similar to SB 1070, seeking to restrict undocumented immigrants, were those in which the Republican Party held legislative control and where there was high unemployment.[40] While numerous anti-immigrant state and local laws were passed, others were passed that benefited immigrants, and undocumented persons in particular. In California, a pro-immigrant bill, AB 540 was signed into law on October 12, 2001; it authorizes any student, including undocumented students who meet specific criteria, to pay in-state tuition at California's public colleges and universities.[41] The bill's author, Marco Antonio Firebaugh, was born in Tijuana, Mexico, and came to the United States at a young age. He became a state assembly member from Los Angeles and was known as a champion of immigrant rights. The passage of in-state tuition for undocumented students in California led to its passage in other states.

According to the National Conference of State Legislatures (NCSL), twenty-one states provide in-state tuition for undocumented students: Arkansas, California, Colorado, Connecticut, Florida, Hawaii, Illinois, Kansas, Maryland, Michigan, Minnesota, Nebraska, New Jersey, New

Mexico, New York, Oklahoma, Oregon, Rhode Island, Texas, Utah, and Washington. In Virginia, in-state tuition covers those eligible for DACA. Seven states provide state financial aid to undocumented students. The California Dream Act (Assembly Bills 130 and 131) was signed into law in 2011, enabling students eligible for AB 540 to apply for state financial aid, including state-funded grants, institutional grants, and community college fee waivers.[42] However, the states are not united on providing in-state tuition to undocumented students. Three states—Arizona, Georgia, and Indiana—prohibit in-state tuition for undocumented students. Alabama and South Carolina go farther and prohibit undocumented students from enrolling at a public postsecondary institution.[43]

Another important issue in the immigrant community not addressed for decades was providing a driver's license for all residents of the state regardless of legal status. This legislation in California was prompted by intense lobbying by the Latino community and advocacy by assembly member Gil Cedillo, who sought for many years to have California, home to the largest number of undocumented, adopt a law to allow those in the country without authorization to obtain a driver's license if they met certain criteria. The bill, AB 60, was signed into law in 2013 by Governor Jerry Brown, nine months after Cedillo was termed out of office.[44]

According to the NCSL, sixteen states and the District of Columbia have passed laws to allow those who are undocumented and meet other criteria to obtain driver's licenses: California, Colorado, Connecticut, Delaware, Hawaii, Illinois, Maryland, Nevada, New Jersey, New Mexico, New York, Oregon, Utah, Vermont, Virginia, and Washington. These states can issue a license if an applicant provides documentation, such as a foreign birth certificate, foreign passport, or consular card, and evidence of current residency in the state.[45] In 2020, Virginia became the most recent state to enact legislation extending driver's licenses and identification cards to those without proof of lawful presence (HB 1211).

The question of how much we, as a nation, should provide rights to immigrants, both legal and undocumented, or deny them to those without legal status remains an ongoing debate that impacts Latino politics on several levels. When anti-immigrant voices translate into passage of laws that become government policy, whether at the federal, state, or local level, the full participation of Latino and other immigrant communities is limited. At the same time, efforts to pass anti-immigrant legislation have also sparked Latino political participation and grassroots organizing efforts to elect pro-immigrant representatives and pass pro-immigrant legislation. In addition to immigration, the issue of voting rights is also a major concern of Latino politics. The past twenty years have seen significant efforts to increase and restrict voting access at the local, state, and federal levels.

88 *Latino Political Power*

Voting Rights Protections and Challenging Existing

The passage of the 1965 Voting Rights Act (VRA) was the culmination of many years of effort by the civil rights movements, led by African Americans but including Latinos and other marginalized groups, to gain access to the vote without the historical discriminatory restrictions that limited their ability to elect their preferred candidates to office. While initially focused on Black people's disempowerment in southern states, amendments to the VRA later focused on Latino and other non-English-speaking racial minorities. In 1975 amendments (Section 203) extended coverage to linguistic minorities and broadened coverage to fourteen states. The VRA and its amendments entailed significant gains for Latinos in the electoral process, resulting in a significantly increased number of Latino voters and consequently leading to the election of more Latino officials. This in turn enabled the distribution of more resources and political and economic opportunities to the many Latino ethnic communities. The growth of the Latino population and its rising electoral clout have also produced a backlash in the area of voting rights.

With the 2008 election of Barack Obama, several states across the nation passed numerous measures to make it more difficult for voters, particularly Black people and Latinos, as well as the elderly, students, and people with disabilities, to exercise their basic right to cast a ballot. Many states have sought to limit the voting rights of Latinos and others through various methods. According to the Brennan Center for Justice, between 2010 and 2013 thirty-three state legislatures introduced ninety-two laws restricting voting rights.[46] Meanwhile, during this same time period, ten states passed thirteen bills in 2013 to expand voting opportunities, and eight states passed nine restrictive laws. Efforts to restrict voting have continued. After the 2020 elections, in 2021, there were three times as many bills designed to restrict voting as there had been in 2020 at the same time. In twenty-eight states, 108 bills were introduced that would restrict voting rights.[47]

Throughout the first two decades of the twenty-first century, the restrictions included efforts to require voters to show proof of citizenship in addition to a voter registration card. Also, there were efforts to require higher levels of identification to register and cast one's ballot, known as voter identification laws. Other changes included limiting early voting before Election Day, reducing the number and location of voting places, ending drop-off mail ballot locations, ending twenty-four-hour voting locations, and many other harsh restrictions, which would limit access to voting for many, including Latinos.[48] The most recent effort to restrict voting rights followed the 2020 national elections, when Joe Biden won several states that Hillary Clinton lost in 2016. By the end of 2021, in numerous states, including Texas, lawmakers had passed laws that restrict voting in various ways.[49]

Also, in 2021, a US Supreme Court case decided two issues from Arizona that have the effect of limiting voting access by upholding Arizona's voting rules that ban the practice of "ballot harvesting," which enables a person to give his or her ballot to another individual or group to turn in. The Court also upheld the legality of discarding a ballot submitted in the wrong precinct by a voter. Both of these provisions will make it more difficult to challenge election regulations under the VRA.[50]

Latinos and the Obama Administration, 2008–2016

Latinos, while not a monolithic group of voters, did support Barack Obama two to one over his opponent, John McCain, in 2008. Obama received an estimated 66 percent of Latino votes compared to John McCain's 32 percent.[51] Following the excitement of electing the nation's first Black president, and with Obama winning in states where Latino votes helped make the difference, Latinos had high hopes that long-standing issues impacting the Latino community would be addressed. Obama, in one of his first actions with long-term consequences, nominated Sonia Sotomayor to the US Supreme Court. Sotomayor's confirmation in 2009 as the first Latina to sit on the Supreme Court was historic and meaningful for women and the Latino community.

Many in the Latino community demanded that Obama address the immigration crisis. However, the Obama administration, like other presidential administrations since that of Ronald Reagan, found it difficult to advance a comprehensive immigration reform package. With other legislative priorities such as providing health care to more Americans and reigniting the economy after the economic recession brought on by the housing crisis, immigration went from the front to the back burner. Although the Obama administration stopped the workplace raids launched by the previous Bush administration, the steady drumbeat of mass deportations continued, with more than 5.2 million people removed during the Obama administration between 2009 and 2016, including border apprehensions, removals, and voluntary returns. This was a far lower amount than during both President Bill Clinton's administration, with more than 12.2 million deportations from 1993 to 2000, and George W. Bush's, with more than 10.3 million from 2001 to 2008. The Obama administration had higher rates of removals and lower rates of voluntary returns to home countries.[52] Most of the people removed from the United States were sent back to Mexico, with a growing number from Central America as economic and political conditions deteriorated. Asylum seeking continued during the Trump administration as economic conditions and violence grew in some Central American nations, prompting desperate efforts to come to the United States to escape.

90   *Latino Political Power*

With the Obama administration distracted by other priorities, the task of passing a comprehensive immigration solution fell to those in Congress who sought to pass legislation that included a pathway to citizenship for at least some of the eleven million undocumented persons. The DREAM Act, first introduced in 2001, failed to pass despite numerous introductions. In 2010, a revised version of the DREAM Act was introduced in the House of Representatives (HR 6497) and passed, then died in the Senate. Senator Dick Durbin sponsored the DREAM Act in 2011 (S. 952), but the legislation had lost important support from congressional Republicans and was not passed. After these legislative defeats, President Obama, following years of growing pressure by a movement of mostly undocumented Latino youth,[53] decided to act and initiated the immigration policy known as Deferred Action for Childhood Arrivals (DACA) in June 2012. This presidential action in the midst of Obama's reelection campaign was politically risky, but after nearly four years of no movement on immigration reform, Obama acted independently of Congress. In the years since, DACA's legality has continued to be contested in the courts.

DACA gives a two-year reprieve from deportation and provides eligibility for a work permit and a driver's license, among other temporary benefits. This presidential action, which only applies to a small percentage of those in the country without legal status, was praised as enabling some undocumented young people to gain a modicum of relief from deportation, but criticized for not addressing the need for relief of DACA recipients' parents and guardians, who did not receive the same benefit, or of the millions of undocumented farmworkers and other workers in the United States.

In the 2012 presidential election, among all Latinos, an estimated 71 percent of Latino voters supported Obama for reelection, with Latinas supporting him by 11 percent more than Latino males. While Obama did well in several states where the race was close, in Florida, a key battleground state, the growing non-Cuban population, including Puerto Ricans in central Florida, contributed to President Obama's advantage among Latino voters with 60 percent supporting Obama while 39 percent voted for his opponent, Mitt Romney.[54] Obama also did well among Latinos in other states, garnering 61 percent in Colorado, 70 percent in Nevada, 65 percent in Wisconsin, and 68 percent in North Carolina. The major issue for Latino voters in 2012, as in 2008, was the economy.

In 2016, even though the Latino potential vote share increased to 12.7 million voters, as compared to 11.2 million in 2012, the percentage was similar to 2012 as overall vote totals had increased. An estimated 47.6 percent of those eligible voted, which means a majority of eligible Latinos did not vote.[55] Given the group threat openly espoused by Trump, his anti-immigrant and anti-Mexican rhetoric had been expected stimulate higher Latino voter turnout. While the Latino vote did increase by 1.5 million, which is a large surge, the majority of Latinos did not turn out. Researchers found, however, that Latinos angered by Trump's rhetoric and policy proposals were more likely to engage in political activities, including voting.[56] Yet the challenge of mobilizing greater numbers of Latinos remains.

Obama's administration, at the end of his term, noted its accomplishments expanding opportunities for Latinos. For instance, Latino unemployment dropped from a peak of 13 percent in August 2009 to 5.6 percent in March 2016. The administration had called for raising the minimum wage at the federal, state, and local levels, which would raise wages for millions of Latinos workers. (Only a minority of states have taken action on raising the minimum wage, mainly in states led politically by Democrats, and the federal minimum wage has not been raised since 2009, when it moved to $7.25 per hour.)

Under the Affordable Care Act (ACA), also known as Obamacare, the uninsured rate among Latino adults dropped by 27 percent, which corresponds to more than four million Latinos gaining health care coverage. The ACA also invested heavily in community health centers, which increased access to affordable health care by almost 35 percent for Latino patients who use these local centers. The Obama administration directed resources to assist Latino young people such as investing $4 billion in Head Start programs for low-income children; 38 percent of Head Start participants are Latino. The Obama administration also "invested more than $12 billion in research grants for Hispanic-serving colleges, scholarships, training programs, and other resources that will help Hispanic students enroll and succeed in college."[57]

The Federal Housing Administration reduced the annual premiums for new borrowers by half a percentage point, which made homeownership more affordable for Latino families. The Obama administration also worked on behalf of Latino families for equal access to housing opportunities and secured funds that benefited people who faced housing discrimination. The Department of Housing and Urban Development, led by Julián Castro, launched an internet-access program that benefiting hundreds of thousands of low-income households, including Latinos.

In addition to taking action on these important issues, Obama, beyond nominating Sonia Sotomayor to the Supreme Court in 2009, also placed several Latinos in his cabinet, including Hilda Solis and Thomas Perez, both as secretary of labor, Julián Castro as secretary of housing and urban development (HUD), and Ken Salazar as interior secretary. He also nominated Latinas and Latinos to other high-ranking positions in his administration.

While these are laudable accomplishments and appointments, many actions taken or not taken by the Obama administration directly impacted Latinos, such as the failure to pass a comprehensive immigration reform package when the Democrats had control of both houses of Congress and

92   Latino Political Power

the presidency from 2008 to 2010. The massive deportation of millions caused some Latinos to be less supportive of the Obama presidency than one would have predicted given the strong support he received coming into office. In a survey taken in 2016, 48 percent of Latinos had a positive view of the Obama administration's accomplishments, with 36 percent saying its failures outweighed its accomplishments. Among the total US population, 49 percent believed the administration's accomplishments outweighed its failures, as compared with 44 percent who believed its failures outweighed it successes. By comparison, when Latinos evaluated President George W. Bush's administration in 2008, only 19 percent said that administration's accomplishments would outweigh its failures; a year later 64 percent said its failures would outweigh its successes.[58]

Given the high visibility of immigration issues, it is important to note that among Latinos, the undocumented (37 percent) viewed the Obama administration's achievements as outweighing its failures, which is similar to those undocumented Latinos who viewed the failures as outweighing the accomplishments (37 percent). Obama did propose to expand relief to other undocumented immigrants beyond DACA in late 2014 by also including unauthorized immigrant parents of US-citizen or legal-permanent-resident children. There were an estimated 3.9 million in this category in 2012, but this second executive order was blocked by the courts and not implemented.[59] At the end of the Obama presidency in 2016, while the Latino community made some notable advances, the Latino perception of the Obama administration's accomplishments was mixed, and not just among conservative Latinos.

Latinos and the Trump Administration

The election of Donald Trump in 2016 was unexpected by many political observers. He was competing against Hillary Clinton, the first woman to head a major political party's ticket. Clinton was well known and well funded, had served as an elected US senator from the state of New York, and had the backing of the majority of Latinos, including most Latino civil rights organizations. Donald Trump was a billionaire real estate owner with name recognition due to his reality shows but had not previously held elected office. Trump's campaign for president began with strong anti-immigrant rhetoric, and his anti-Mexican, anti-Latino, and anti-immigrant message was a constant tag line in his campaign speeches and political advertising. In many respects, it is what propelled him to not only secure the Republican nomination but also win the general election. The painting of Latinos as a threat to the dominant White population did not begin with Trump; the racism toward specific Latino groups and Latinos as a whole goes back many generations.[60] Trump just amplified this view like no other presidential candidate in the twenty-first century.

While Trump ran his presidential campaign on a consistent message disparaging Mexican immigrants and other Latinos, whom he regularly characterized as gang members, murderers, and rapists, once he was elected, he began to translate his campaign messages into policies that institutionalized many of these campaign issues. He immediately issued an executive order that called for an increase in the US Customs and Border Patrol and the building of additional detention facilities along the border with Mexico. He also restricted access for asylum seekers who arrived at the US border. In addition, Trump also beefed up enforcement of immigration laws in the interior of the United States, including an increase in the number of ICE agents, and revived Secure Communities and Section 287(g) agreements between local police agencies and the Department of Homeland Security and the FBI.[61] By 2018, children arriving at the border were separated from their parents, and in January 2019 the DHS developed additional policies that kept asylum seekers in Mexico while awaiting an asylum hearing rather than allowing them to apply for asylum at the border, as has been the policy for decades. Other families and children who made it to the US border were kept in prison-like detention facilities, with thousands of children separated from the families who had brought them. He also reduced the total number of people the United States would take in as asylees from all countries to 11,814 in 2020, an 86 percent reduction from 2016.

These and other anti-immigrant and anti-religious actions, such as the ban on travel from mostly Muslim majority countries, imposed by the Trump administration reflect the strong belief of President Trump and his supporters that America was heading in the wrong direction and that allowing people from other parts of the world, outside White Northern Europeans, into the country would lead to further decline of the United States as a dominant world power. These anti-immigrant sentiments can be explained as a reaction to the Obama presidency and its more liberal policies, which fueled the backlash of many White voters who feel threatened by immigrants bringing new cultures and values to the United States and view them as a challenge to traditional Eurocentric US society. These fears about who is immigrating to the United States fundamentally influence White Americans' core political identities, policy preferences, and electoral choices, which Trump drew upon in his campaign and presidency.[62] The actions of the Trump administration were also designed to make the slogans "Make American Great Again" and "America First" prominent in all policy decisions while denigrating Latino and other immigrants, as well other groups.

Another prominent issue that impacts Latinos is the DACA program that former President Obama started in 2012 to provide temporary status to young people who were brought to this country without legal documentation.

94 Latino Political Power

President Trump opposed the DACA program as he stated that immigration policy should be determined by the US Congress, not the executive branch. He also viewed the DACA program as part of a larger failure of the United States to enforce existing restrictive immigration policies. Trump wanted to change future US immigration policy to focus on a merit-based system rather than on family reunification, which has been the cornerstone of US immigration policy since the 1965 Immigration Act. The Trump administration tried several times to end the DACA program by preventing first time applicants from being able to apply to participate in the program. However, a federal judge ruled in December 2020 that first-time DACA applicants should be able to apply for consideration of deferred action under the DACA program, and the judge also extended the renewal period for DACA renewals to two years from the one year that Trump had mandated. President Biden reestablished the DACA program in 2021, and soon afterward a federal judge in Houston, Texas, ruled the DACA program illegal and said no new applicants could be admitted until there was a proper public rule-making process.

In addition, Trump issued an executive order to exclude undocumented immigrants from the census count. He also diverted funds from the Defense Department budget to construct an expanded border wall between the United States and Mexico. While Trump used anti-immigrant rhetoric throughout his campaign, he also courted Latinos around issues of economic growth, support for small businesses, and law and order, and he targeted evangelical and pro-life Latinos. Like previous Republican presidents and candidates, Trump used these issues to maintain consistent support among a segment of Latino voters.

Conclusion

In the 2000–2020 period, the growth of Latino elected officials continued at the local, state, and federal levels. While Latino elected officials are still underrepresented in most jurisdictions, there has been significant growth in certain states with high percentages of Latinos, and where they are a visible presence in state and local politics. The presence of a Latino candidate is also a cue for Latino co-ethnics who identity with and are likely to be more engaged in politics and mobilizing turnout even with candidates from a different political party.[63] The presence of Latino legislators at the state level can have a negative impact on the passage of anti-immigrant legislation.[64] Latino electoral gains since 2000 can be linked to changing demographics and the growing number of Latinos in America, growing political awareness by Latinos of their role and place in electoral politics, greater attention sporadically to mobilization by both political parties, and more effective mobilization by

Latino organizations on the ground to reach and turn out Latinos. Our next chapter explores the contemporary state of Latinos in the United States.

Notes

1. J. Garcia 2017, 34.
2. Suro, Fry, and Passel 2005.
3. "Ros-Lehtinen, Ileana," n.d.
4. Magana and Silva 2021, 60–62.
5. Frank and Wong 2004.
6. Yardley 2002a.
7. Yardley 2002b.
8. Purdom 2001.
9. S. Navarro 2015.
10. Jimenez, Garcia, and Garcia 2007, 61–78.
11. Pizarro 2020.
12. Hrenchir 2018.
13. Cann 2021.
14. Bredderman 2016.
15. M. R. Smith 2011.
16. Orr, Morel, and Farris 2018, 225–245.
17. Ibid.
18. Booker 2021.
19. GoLocalProv News Team 2021.
20. Chambers and Farris 2018, 176–178.
21. Ibid., 184–185.
22. Orr and Morel 2018.
23. Ortiz-Wythe, Kelleher, and Torres-Ardila 2019.
24. Binder, Polinard, and Wrinkle 1997, 324–337.
25. Zepeda-Millan 2017; Pallares and Flores-Gonzalez 2010; V. Rodriguez 2005.
26. Milkman and Wong 2000.
27. Hoschschild and Mollenkopf 2011, 9.
28. Sampaio 2015, 57–66.
29. Garcia and Sanchez 2008, 299.
30. American Immigration Council, www.americanimmigrationcouncil.org, June 13, 2021.
31. Flores-Gonzalez and Gutierrez 2010, 17; Sziarto and Leitner 2010.
32. Flores-Gonzalez and Gutierrez 2010, 21.
33. Ortiz 2018, 174.
34. Voss, Bloemraad, and Lee 2011, 15.
35. Bloemraad, Voss, and Lee 2011, 19.
36. Milkman 2011, 175.
37. Ibid.
38. Zepeda-Millan 2017, 187–189.
39. Shaw 2011, 92.
40. S. J. Wallace 2014, 261–291.
41. Abrego 2008.
42. National Conference of State Legislatures, www.ncsl.org, accessed August 29, 2021.

96 *Latino Political Power*

43. Ibid.
44. Marrero, n.d.
45. National Conference of State Legislatures, www.ncsl.org.
46. Brennan Center for Justice 2013.
47. Brennan Center for Justice 2021.
48. García 2017, 136.
49. Brennan Center for Justice 2021.
50. Howe 2021.
51. Rosentiel 2008.
52. Chishti, Pierce, and Bolter 2017.
53. García Bedolla and Hosam 2021, 238–239.
54. Suh 2012.
55. File 2017.
56. Gutierrez et al. 2019, 960–975.
57. Office of the Press Secretary 2016.
58. Pew Research Center Staff 2017.
59. Krogstad and Passel 2014.
60. L. Chavez 2013.
61. Canizales and Vallejo 2021.
62. Abrajano and Hajnal 2015.
63. Baretto 2010.
64. Filindra and Pearson-Merkowitz 2013, 814–832.

5

Participation and the Contours of Power

In the past few decades, the tremendous growth of the Latino population has transformed the political landscape of the United States. The increased demographic presence has gradually resulted in growing Latino political influence and representation. This chapter explores the changing political landscape for Latinos and simultaneously the contours of racial politics in the United States. Latino political behavior has been forged in an environment historically dictated by others. An examination of Latino politics at the national, state, and local levels must consider several factors. The structural and legal dynamics that shape Latino electoral fortunes are themselves affected by a multiplicity of factors. This chapter addresses the roles of demographic change, party affiliation, voting behavior, types of electoral districts, and candidate characteristics. We will also discuss strategies used by Latinos to achieve political incorporation. To begin with, let's consider the contours of the US political system within which Latino politics operates.

The US Political System and Latino Politics

All politics takes place on a variety of levels; we participate as individual members of society and as members of communities of interest. The basic foundation of successful political participation combines group cohesion and individual motivation. While a group may long to have formal representation in government, ultimately this requires an individual to seek and win elective office. Likewise, while an individual may wish to hold an elective position, winning one takes more than personal will. It involves the efforts of one or more groups of people who cooperate to elect a candidate. Our winner-takes-all system, based on political entrepreneurship and interest

98 *Latino Political Power*

group politics, dictates that an individual who seeks office needs group support to achieve it. If we assume Latinos seek to further the interests of the Latino population, as do other demographic groups in a pluralistic society, then we can expect Latinos to participate in the political system as voters, volunteers, activists, and candidates. In these efforts candidates and elected officials will seek to further their individual goals and possibly to benefit their group's position in society (although not all Latino candidates run as ethnic candidates or identify with or seek to assist the Latino community directly).

The ability of any group, whether identified by race, gender, sexuality, ethnicity, age, or issue, to gain political influence is based on a number of factors, including political and economic resources, level of organization, and knowledge of how the system operates to maximize a group's gains. For Latinos and other minority groups, the political system has historically been more a barrier than a resource in the quest to gain full participation. The system of racial exclusion and domination has long worked to keep African, Latino, Native, and Asian Americans out of elective, appointive, and civil service positions. The civil rights movement of the 1950s and 1960s dramatically moved these issues to the front of America's social policy agenda. The goal of inclusion in government was twofold: to end discrimination in hiring, promotions, and election to office and to share in the benefits of government. This included increasing minority employment, hiring minority administrators, awarding minority contracts for business with government, promoting economic development in minority communities, providing housing, and offering decent public services in predominantly minority communities.[1]

Each underrepresented group has a particular history and justification for representation. Latinos have a unique claim in American politics: they are both the forerunners of the American political system and some of its newest participants. Some of the early Spanish and Mexican settlers established forms of governance in the Southwest that preceded the establishment of the US government. Since 1965, new immigrants from throughout Latin America have dramatically changed the ethnic composition of numerous cities and states, bringing different political experiences and an alternative perspective to US politics. Yet the majority of Latinos are born and raised in the context of the US system, where representation in government is an important measure of a group's political progress.

Growth of the Latino Population

According to the 2020 US Census, Latinos as a group are not growing as quickly as they once did. From 2010 to 2019, the US population increased by 18.9 million, and Hispanics accounted for more than half (52 percent) of this growth. In 2019, Hispanics reached a record 60.6 million and comprised 18.5 percent of the US population.[2] This is up from 50.7 million in 2010, when Hispanics were 16 percent of the population.[3] The number of Hispanics is growing more slowly than it previously did because of a decline in the annual number of births to Latina women and a drop in immigration, particularly from Mexico.[4] From 2015 to 2019, the Latino population grew by an average of 1.9 percent per year; this is similar to the 2.1 percent annual growth between 2010 and 2015 but down from the annual growth of more than 3 percent in earlier years.[5] There was serious concern by both political parties that the Latino population was undercounted. For example, states varied in either embracing census efforts or treating them as a low priority. States like Florida, Arizona, and Texas— Republican run states with large Latino populations—invested late or chose not to play a role in aiding the 2020 count, whereas states like Minnesota, California, and New York started between one and five years beforehand to get their people counted.[6]

Latinos are among the youngest racial and ethnic groups in the United States but saw one of the largest increases in median age over the past decade. Latinos had a median age of 29.8 in 2019, up from 27.3 in 2010. According to the 2020 US Census, 18.6 percent of the US population is under the age of eighteen, compared to 25.7 percent of Latinos.[7] Despite the slowdown, population growth among Latinos continues to outpace that of some other groups. The White population slightly declined, with an average growth rate that fell slightly below zero between 2015 and 2019, while the Black population grew less than 1 percent per year over the same period.[8] Only Asian Americans have seen faster population growth than Latinos, increasing by 2.4 percent per year between 2015 and 2019.[9]

According to the 2020 US Census, Hispanic or Latino ethnicity is defined as being "of Cuban, Mexican, Puerto Rican, South or Central American, or other Spanish culture or origin regardless of race."[10] Hispanics are the largest minority in the United States. By 2060, the Hispanic population is projected to reach the 111.22 million mark, a significant factor in US population growth.[11]

However, the 2020 US Census changed in that it relies entirely on self-reporting and lets each person identify as Hispanic or not. Essentially, the first question is based on how a person self identifies. The standard requires the US government to collect and report data for a minimum of two ethnicities: "Hispanic or Latino" and "Not Hispanic or Latino."[12] Considering the expanded opportunities that the 2020 question formats offered for respondents to indicate membership in multiple national origin and tribal subgroups under racial categories, the bureau is likely to collect very complex information about individuals' backgrounds. Accurately representing racial and ethnic identity may be more difficult when many individuals provide more granular detail about their heritage than before. The Census Bureau

100 *Latino Political Power*

must decide how much detailed information it can feasibly make available in various products and publications.[13] Scholars urge the US Census to provide as much precise data as possible.

With regard to the origin countries, more than 37.1 million (61.5 percent) of the Hispanic population was of Mexican descent in 2019. The second-largest Hispanic ethnic population is Puerto Rican (9.7 percent), and the next largest groups are Cuban Americans (3.9 percent), Salvadorans (3.9 percent), and Dominicans (3.4 percent). Overall, Central Americans make up 9.8 percent and South Americans 6.4 percent.[14] As of 2020, the three states with the most Hispanics also had the biggest increases: California at 39.4 percent, Texas at 39.3 percent, and New Mexico with 47.7 percent. These states accounted for about 42 percent of US Hispanic population growth during this time. The smallest increases came in West Virginia (1.9 percent), Maine (2 percent), and Vermont (2.4 percent).[15]

In addition to the variance in growth of Latino ethnic groups, the geographic dispersion of the Latino population is also important. About 29 percent of all Latinos live in ten states with the largest Latino populations: Arizona, California, Colorado, Florida, Illinois, Nevada, New Jersey, New Mexico, New York, and Texas. Latinos in New Mexico, at 48.79 percent of the state's population, had the highest Hispano percentage in any state. In Texas, the Latino population accounted for 11.1 million, or 39.34 percent of the total state population. In California, Latinos amounted to a little over 15.3 million, or 39.28 percent of the total state population.[16]

Another way to view the distribution of the Latino population and its political impact is to examine the numbers of Latinos in the ten largest US cities (see Table 5.1). In eight of the ten largest cities, Latinos comprise at least 27 percent of the population. In Los Angeles, they are close to majority status. New York City has the most Hispanic residents, though not a Hispanic majority. The more than 14 million Latinos in the ten largest cities represent more 23 percent of the total Latino population in the United States. This means much of the Latino population is concentrated in a few large cities. Of course, we must factor in the 22 percent of the Latino population who have not obtained US citizenship.[17]

In addition to their high concentrations in urban areas, Latinos are "the most significant and fastest-growing sector of the working class in the United States. Within a few years, Latinos will make up more than a quarter of the nation's total workforce, a proportion that is . . . larger than this group's proportion of the total population." As importantly from an economic point of view, Latino workers are located in the light manufacturing and service sectors of the economy, which hold strategic importance for US capitalism. In Los Angeles County, a center of postindustrial America, an estimated 12 percent of manufacturing workers are Latinos, both legal and undocumented, from Latin America.[18] The high percentage of working-

Table 5.1 Latino Population in the Ten Largest Cities in 2020

Cities	Latino Population	Total Population	Population Percentage
New York	2,562,019	8,804,190	29.1
Los Angeles	1,890,892	3,898,747	48.5
Chicago	790,959	2,746,388	28.8
Houston	1,037,061	2,304,580	45.0
Phoenix	685,067	1,608,139	42.6
Philadelphia	235,758	1,603,797	14.7
San Antonio	921,029	1,434,625	64.2
San Diego	420,240	1,386,932	30.3
Dallas	545,230	1,304,379	41.8
San Jose	320,183	1,013,240	31.6

Source: Author's calculations based on 2020 census.

class Latinos, the industries they work in, and their impact on the economy have made them an inviting and, under some circumstances, successful target for labor movement organization.[19]

Latino Demographics and Political Behavior

The Latino population continues to grow, with heavy concentrations in large urban areas and with Latino workers located in sectors of the economy that are strategically important. Yet demographic growth does not equate to the attainment of political power. A critical ingredient in building Latino political power is increased Latino political participation. Political participation involves acts by individuals and groups to influence the political system. Traditionally this takes the form of attempting to influence the policymaking process or participating in the electoral process. When one studies Latino political behavior, it is essential to understand different dimensions of the Latino population: (1) the total population of Latinos, (2) the Latino voting-age population (those over eighteen), (3) the citizen voting-age population, (4) the registered voting-age population, (5) the turnout of Latino voters, and (6) the native-born and non-native-born voting-age populations.

These distinctions are critical in an analysis of Latino political participation for a few reasons. First, disenfranchisement of Mexican Americans in the Southwest dating from the 1840s and of other Latinos who have

102 *Latino Political Power*

come to the United States has limited their full political participation historically. Second, the immigration of Latinos from throughout the Americas means large numbers are in the process of transitioning into US society. Among Latinos who migrate to the United States, only Puerto Ricans are US citizens, by virtue of Puerto Rico's status as a US territory. All other Latinos, including legal and undocumented immigrants and political refugees, such as Cubans, have had varying degrees of both opportunities and obstacles in becoming naturalized citizens, registering to vote, and voting. For example, 59 percent of Cuban Americans are citizens,[20] while only 34 percent of Mexican immigrants are citizens.[21] Large numbers of Latinos with roots in Central and South America are recent immigrants, and about one-third are naturalized US citizens.[22]

A high percentage of Latinos, unlike Whites and Blacks and like Asian Pacific Islanders, are not citizens. The high incidence of noncitizenship is the single most important factor limiting the political power of Latinos. In the 2020, 161 million voted in the presidential election.[23] According to the 2020 census, 16.8 percent of Latinos were over the age of eighteen compared to 14.2 percent in 2010.[24] In the November 2020 election, 61.1 percent of Hispanics were reported as registered to vote, 19.2 percent reported not being registered, and 38.8 percent of the total voting-age Hispanic population cast a ballot in the November 2020 election.[25]

In 2010's census and November midterm elections, 96 million people voted. Registered Hispanic voters were 33.8 percent, while 20.5 percent actually reported voting and 29.4 percent reported not being registered.[26] In the same election 47.8 percent of non-Hispanic Whites reported voting, compared to 67 percent who reported being registered and 16.4 percent who reported not being registered.[27] While the Latino population has grown rapidly in recent decades, as of 2020, many are not eligible voters. More than other racial or ethnic groups, many Latinos are young (18.6 million are under eighteen) or are noncitizen adults (11.3 million), more than half of whom are unauthorized immigrants.[28]

The impact of the foreign-born Latino population is important to note. Latinos have played a significant role in driving US population growth over the past decade, though the group is not growing as quickly as it once did. From 2010 to 2019, the US population increased by 18.9 million, and Latinos accounted for more than half (52 percent) of this growth.[29] The number of Latinos is growing more slowly than it previously did, due to a decline in the annual number of births to Latina women and a drop in immigration particularly from Mexico.[30] From 2015 to 2019, the Latino population grew by an average of 1.9 percent per year, down significantly from a peak of 4.8 percent from 1995 to 2000.

The number of Mexican unauthorized immigrants in the United States declined so sharply over the past decade that, according to new Pew

Research Center estimates based on government data, they no longer make up the majority of those living in the country without legal status. In 2017, there were 10.5 million unauthorized immigrants in the United States, including 4.9 million Mexicans.[31] The decrease in the Mexican born was the major factor driving down the overall population of unauthorized immigrants in the United States, which in 2017 was 1.7 million below its peak of 12.2 million in 2007. The number of Mexican unauthorized immigrants declined because more left the United States than arrived. Mexicans remain a much larger percentage of all unauthorized immigrants than those from any other birth country,[32] but their 47 percent share of US unauthorized immigrants in 2017 amounted to less than a majority for the first time since the beginning of a long era of growth in undocumented immigration. That era began after passage of a major overhaul of immigration in 1965, which imposed the first limits on immigration from Western Hemisphere countries, including Mexico, and coincided with the end of the Bracero Program that had allowed temporary farmworkers from Mexico to work legally in the United States.[33]

Not all lawful permanent residents choose to pursue US citizenship. Generally, most immigrants eligible for naturalization apply to become citizens. However, Mexican lawful immigrants have the lowest naturalization rate overall. Language and personal barriers, lack of interest, and financial barriers are among the top reasons for choosing not to naturalize cited by Mexican-born green card holders, according to a 2015 Pew Research Center survey.[34]

Approximately every thirty seconds, a Latino in the United States turns eighteen and becomes eligible to vote. These young people have the potential to swing every election—if they vote.[35] Latinos under the age of eighteen are projected to make up 27.5 percent of the American population by 2060.[36] According to NBC News exit polling data of early and Election Day votes, 13 percent who voted for president in 2020 cast ballots for the first time, compared to under 10 percent in 2016. One in ten of the new voters in 2020 was between the ages of eighteen and twenty-four. Youth voter turnout was significantly higher in 2020 than in 2016.[37]

Why don't Latinos vote in higher numbers? While all communities have some members who do not vote, Latinos generally have the highest rate of nonvoting. This is a particularly vexing problem for a community that is historically underrepresented and underserved. Using survey data of Latinos in 2020, scholars found registered nonvoters and nonregistered US citizens had similar characteristics: they had lower levels of education and income and were younger. Furthermore, not all Latino groups have the same voting characteristics: "Mexican Americans, the largest of the Latino national-origin groups, are significantly less likely to vote than Cuban Americans and Puerto Ricans."[38] However, as discussed in Chapters 3 and 4, the growth of anti-immigrant efforts in the mid-1990s helped spur Mexican

104   *Latino Political Power*

Americans and others in the Latino community to naturalize and begin voting in greater numbers.

Another potential obstacle to increasing Latino voting rates is poor access to registration. Voting requirements vary by state. Historically there were numerous obstacles to Latino voter registration, including poll taxes, White primaries, literacy tests, and language barriers. The 1975 amendment to the Voting Rights Act (VRA) of 1965 extended its basic protections to specific language minorities. Previously, in places like Uvalde County, Texas, registered Mexican American voters were not allowed to place their names on voting lists, election judges deliberately invalidated ballots they cast, and Mexican Americans were not allowed to serve as deputy registrars.[39] Today, states have different requirements for voter registration; some states' rules are more stringent than others, such as the requirement that voters register at least thirty days in advance of an election.

Campaigns do not target the high percentage of Latinos who are non-registered citizens because they are not on lists of likely voters. They receive little, if any, attention or encouragement to vote. If they do consider registering, the process is not simple and efficient; rather, potential voters must find a registration form, fill it out correctly, and submit it in enough time to make the deadline. While all potential voters face the same obstacles, they are particularly difficult for new citizens who are unfamiliar with the US political system. If you factor in the high percentages of non-English-speaking Latinos, then it becomes understandable why many Latino US citizens do not register to vote.

In addition to those who could potentially vote but do not, the enormous undocumented portion of the Latino population cannot vote. How large is this portion? According to various estimates, there are more than 10.35 million undocumented persons living in the United States, compared to 11.73 million in 2010. Thus, between 2010 and 2019, the undocumented population in the United States declined by 1.4 million, or 12 percent. This demographic trend is primarily driven by Mexican nationals voluntarily leaving the United States. Since 2010, the undocumented population from Mexico has fallen from 6.6 million to 4.8 million, or by 28 percent.[40] This large segment of the Latino community cannot participate in the voting process, except in limited circumstances in elections for school boards, such as in New York City, or in nongovernmental organizations. Nongovernmental organizations can serve as a conveyor belt to move new immigrants from inactivity and isolation to social and political activism, as they do not usually have citizenship requirements. For example, in labor unions, education, and civil rights and church-based groups, thousands of Latino immigrants get their first experience of participating in organizations and voting for candidates for positions within the group or for ratification of a union contract agreement. This is an important first step in civic engagement for a segment of the immigrant population. It enables them to learn the value of voting and participating in community affairs. It breaks through the stigma of being undocumented and the fear of taking part in American society. It acknowledges these immigrants' role and value as contributing members of barrios and community and labor organizations. For many Latino immigrants, these forms of civic participation were not always available in their homelands due to political repression.

Latino Voter Turnout

In addition to Latinos' general population size, citizenship status, and voter registration rates, the critical factor of Latino voter turnout must be explored if we are to gain a full understanding of Latino political participation efforts. Motivating Latinos to go to the polls has been problematic for a number of reasons. As with most groups, their voting rates (though not their numbers) have declined since the 1960s. Latinos have high noncitizenship rates and a large percentage of the population under eighteen; however, even among those registered to vote, Latinos participate at lower rates than other racial and ethnic groups.

To overcome this legacy of Latino nonpolitical participation, Latino civil rights organizations, legal defense organizations, and policy groups have been working to increase registration and voter turnout. These efforts have produced dramatic results. In 2020, 20.6 million Latinos voted, a 63 percent increase from the last presidential election. Looking at the past Latino voter turnout, the number of voters consistently goes up (see Table 5.2).

Despite these rapid gains, Latinos have lower voter turnout rates than Whites. Less than half of all eligible Latinos voted in the 2016 presidential election, compared with 65 percent of eligible White Americans. In 2014,

Table 5.2   Latino Voter Turnout

Election Year	Voter Turnout
2000	5.9 million
2004	7.6 million
2008	9.7 million
2012	11.2 million
2016	12.6 million
2020	20.6 million

Source: Gamboa 2021.

just 27 percent of eligible Latinos voted, the lowest rate ever recorded for Latinos in a midterm election.[41]

In the 2016 elections, the number of Latino voters increased from previous national elections; however, how to precisely measure the number of Latinos who voted in the 2016 presidential was the subject of much debate. The exit poll numbers of Latinos were wildly inconsistent, with dozens of pre-election polls demonstrating a larger than three-to-one advantage for Hillary Clinton. What happened? The exit poll reports for the Latino vote were profoundly and demonstrably incorrect.

The methodology used for this poll systematically misrepresented all voters of color, and this was demonstrated with actual precinct-level results. The precise detail of the 2016 exit polls were never made available to the public or press, which gave many pause when considering their accuracy. Moreover, since many high-profile media outlets actually paid for the polling (ABC, CBS, FOX, NBC, and the Associate Press), reporters and editors were instructed to use that data, not to critique it, and to disregard other data sources. The Current Population Survey (CPS) of the US Census Bureau is the most accurate national source that can be used to estimate the Latino share of the turnout. Even with many obstacles, the growth in Latino voting-age population is expected to translate into increased numbers of voters. The exit poll was never designed to capture subpopulations, like Latinos or any other minority. Instead, it was designed to offer one national estimate and to help news organizations predict outcomes.[42]

Social issues can become important motivators of Latino voter turnout. In Arizona, the state's remarkable transformation from red state to swing state in 2020 traces back to the Support Our Law Enforcement and Safe Neighborhoods Act (also known as Arizona SB 1070) and the Latino activists it energized. The November 2020 presidential election results indicated an estimated 700,000 Latinos voted in Arizona, with 71 percent turning out in favor of Joe Biden, flipping the state from red to blue. This was the first time in almost twenty-five years Arizona voted for a Democratic presidential candidate.

The seeds of this flip were planted in 2010. That year, the Arizona legislature passed SB 1070. It was the broadest and strictest anti-illegal immigration measure passed in the United States. The infamous "papers, please" law came during the notorious reign of then Maricopa County sheriff Joe Arpaio, who enforced and encouraged racial profiling to terrorize Latinos in the state.[43] The act made it a misdemeanor for an alien not to be carrying the required documentation while in Arizona and required state law enforcement officers to attempt to determine an individual's immigration status during a "lawful stop, detention or arrest" when there was reasonable suspicion the individual was undocumented. Latinos raised an alarm and vociferously stated their concerns but were ignored. The Supreme Court

Participation and the Contours of Power 107

decided the "show me your papers" provision was not preempted by federal law. However, Latino activists argued SB 1070 invited racial profiling of Latinos.[44] Hundreds of thousands of Latino Arizonians—many too young to vote at the time—viewed the bill as a seminal moment. Known as the SB 1070 generation, they were angered by this attack and became determined to act. SB 1070 reflected a state leadership that had given in to racism and division at the political and economic expense of all Arizonans. In 2020, Arizona Latinos not only helped flip the state from red to blue but elected two Latinas to statewide office as well as elevating a Latina to serve in the Arizona state senate's minority leadership. Table 5.3 shows the total Latino share of the vote compared to the total Arizona vote.

Changing Latino Voting Patterns in 2020?

New data from the 2020 presidential election shows a big swing in one voting group away from the Democratic Party. Latinos made a significant rightward turn.[45] In this presidential election, analysis of precinct after precinct revealed marked shifts. In South Texas, there were thirty-point swings in many counties. Donald Trump either won or came very close to winning counties that had voted for Democrats solidly in the 70 to 80 percent range since the 1890s.[46] And in South Florida and Florida generally, there was a 13 or 14 percent swing. Basically, wherever there were large concentrations of Latino voters, there were large swings in the 6 to 9 percent range. This national trend happened in many parts of the country. Among the biggest predictors of the switch from Democrat to Republican were attitudes toward crime and policing.

In Florida, Trump carried the Cuban vote with 56 percent, while Biden carried the Puerto Rican vote with 66 percent; they split the South American vote with 50 percent each. Overall, Biden won 54 percent of Latinos.

Table 5.3   Analysis of Arizona Latino Voters, 2020

Total population	7,172,000
Eligible voter population	5,042,000
Latino population	2,267,000
Latino eligible voter population	1,188,000
Total population: Latino share	31.6 percent
Eligible voters: Latino share	23.6 percent
Latino population: eligible voter share	52.4 percent

Source: US Census Bureau 2020b.

108   *Latino Political Power*

Trump made significant gains among Columbians, Venezuelans, and Nicaraguans compared to the last three presidential cycles. Miami-Dade, the state's biggest county, shifted from being reliably blue to what some experts are now calling purple, after Biden won by only seven points. Table 5.4 shows the Latino vote in proportion to the total population vote.

Outside Arizona and Florida, other Latinos have also reacted to issues of importance within their communities with strong turnout. When Trump was elected in 2016, he had labeled migrants from Mexico as rapists, criminals, and drug traffickers. He promised to build a border wall and force Mexico to pay for it and called for massive deportations. This rhetoric set the stage for Trump's first months in office, as he took measures to crack down on both legal and unauthorized immigration, much of it flowing from Mexico and Central America.[47] In the third year of the Trump presidency, many Latinos found themselves reflecting on their cultural identities, their place in US society, and the need to act—whether via social media, political engagement, or a shift in the trajectory of their personal and professional lives.

In the third year of Trump's presidency, the massacre in El Paso, Texas, galvanized those feelings for many. On August 3, 2019, in a mass shooting at a Walmart, Patrick Wood Crusius shot and killed twenty-three people and injured twenty-three others.[48] Three years later, Crusius, a twenty-one-year-old from Allen, Texas, faced ninety federal charges, including twenty-three counts of hate crimes resulting in death, twenty-three counts of use of a firearm to commit murder during and in relation to a crime of violence, twenty-two counts of hate crimes involving an attempt to kill, and twenty-two counts of use of a firearm during and in relation to a crime of violence.[49] The trial date had yet to be set as of this writing. The shooting was described as the deadliest attack on Latinos in modern American history. Police believed a manifesto with White nationalist and anti-immigrant themes, posted on an online message board shortly before the attack, was written by Crusius.[50] Many in the community blamed the Trump adminis-

Table 5.4   Analysis of Florida Latino Voters, 2020

Total population	21,299,000
Eligible voter population	14,342,000
Latino population	5,562,000
Latino eligible voter population	3,143,000
Total population: Latino share	26.1 percent
Eligible voters: Latino share	20.5 percent
Latino population: eligible voter share	56.5 percent

Source: US Census Bureau 2020b.

tration's anti-Latino, anti-immigrant rhetoric for creating or at least setting the context for racist attacks.

Impact of the Covid-19 Pandemic and the Economy

The Covid-19 pandemic and resulting recession wreaked havoc on the Latino community. Due to Latino workers being overrepresented in the industries hit hardest by the pandemic, Latinos faced large losses in employment, particularly Latinas in the service industry.[51] Latinos were 1.7 times more likely to contract Covid-19 than their non-Hispanic White counterparts, as well as 4.1 times more likely to be hospitalized for it and 2.8 times more likely to die from it.[52] Latinos, along with other communities of color, had been disproportionately harmed by the economic fallout: They accounted for 23 percent of the initial job loss due to the pandemic while making up only 16 percent of the civilian noninstitutional population—those sixteen years and older who are not incarcerated or serving in the armed forces. Latina women experienced disproportionate economic impacts. Women accounted for 100 percent of US job losses in December 2020, with Latina women alone accounting for 45 percent of that job loss.[53]

Party Affiliation of Latinos

Latinos are not a monolith or one unified force. The differences between communities are vast and deep. The United States is home to nearly 61 million Latinos, according to a Pew Research Center estimate, who vary in age, race, gender, religion, socioeconomic status, political ideology, and educational attainment. Historically, party affiliation has been a strong marker of the political behavior of social groups in the United States. Latinos in the United States come from all parts of Latin America, Central America, and Mexico. Some Latinos have lived in the United States for generations. There's a variety of Spanish dialects, languages, foods, and traditions. It should come as no surprise there are also differences in political ideology. Political campaigners need to engage with Latinos early and often, year-round, to understand the needs of individual communities. Puerto Ricans in New York City, for example, will have different priorities than Mexican Americans in the Rio Grande Valley. Latinos are a highly diverse population.

Because Latinos nationwide vote for Democrats in larger numbers than they do for Republicans, one misconception is that as the population of eligible Latino voters grows in the United States, so will votes for Democrats. Social scientists refer to this myth as "demography as destiny." Research shows that White voters made up as much as 85 percent of Trump supporters

110   *Latino Political Power*

in 2020.[54] But a number of Latino subpopulations are concentrated in swing states that play an outsize role in determining the outcome of national elections. While democratic strategists are deeply unsettled by Trump's gain nationwide among Latino and Hispanic voters—estimated at around eight to ten points, with the increase far wider in some key districts—most Democratic strategists appear to ignore a key reason for the shift. While pollsters parse messaging on the economy, immigration, and health care, few pay attention to the role of religious demagoguery.[55] Religious identity is one of the biggest divides among Latinos. A 2020 AP VoteCast exit poll showed that Latino Catholics voted 67 percent for Biden while Latino Protestants voted 58 percent for Trump.[56] Robert P. Jones, founder and CEO of the Public Research Religion Institute, observed, "Most Latino Protestants identify as evangelical, and in the American context, that shared religious identity with White evangelicals has brought along with it a Republican partisan identity and set of political attitudes and priorities."[57] This makes it more likely that Latinos will affiliate with Republicans.[58] In addition, party recruitment cannot be as simple as speaking Spanish during a political debate or opening a rally with mariachi music—symbolic cultural messaging to relate to Latino voters that lacks substance. As for all voters, life experience, not just ethnic or racial identity, informs the way Latino voters vote.[59]

In fact, according to the Pew Research Center, in 2018, 62 percent of Latino voters identified with or leaned toward the Democratic Party, while 27 percent leaned toward or identified with Republicans. But this is not widely recognized, and political pundits' surprise at Latino support for Trump on Election Day—the Cuban vote in Florida, for example—points to a lack of understanding of nuances among Latinos in the United States. Geraldo Cadava, author of *The Hispanic Republican* (2020), emphasized that in every presidential election since Richard Nixon won in 1972, between a quarter and a third of Latinos have voted for the Republican candidate— meaning there has been a half-century tradition of a significant minority of Latinos voting Republican.

The Cuban American population of Miami-Dade County, for example, has since the 1970s leaned toward the Republican Party. However, within the Cuban American community there exist nuances as well. Older Cubans who fled from the Castro regime are still more likely to vote for a Republican than younger generations. Donald Trump's 2020 campaign did make attempts to reach Cuban Americans by propagating an antisocialist message, one that might also resonate with other Latino groups who have their own antisocialist sentiments.[60]

So what do we know about Latino voters? For one, Republicans are gaining ground with them. According to Democratic pollster David Shor, White liberal elites are pushing the party to the left and alienating certain voter groups, including Latinos. From 2016 to 2020, both Trump and congressional

Republicans improved among Latino voters. Trump went from 28 to 32 percent of the Latino vote, while congressional Republicans improved from 32 to 36 percent. Some Senate Republicans did even better with Latinos in the November 2020 election; notably, John Cornyn of Texas won 42 percent of the Latino vote. Shor also contends that contrary to popular belief, the majority of Latinos are not Democrats.[61] In the 2020 election, party ID among Latinos was 48 percent Democrat, 20 percent Republican, and 32 percent Independent, presenting a real opportunity for Republicans going forward. The data also show ideology is one of the driving factors behind Latinos positioning in the middle. Forty-three percent of these voters self-identified as moderates, the largest group, followed by conservatives at 32 percent and liberals at 25 percent. By comparison, Democrats' self-identification broke down as 46 percent liberal, 43 percent moderate, and 10 percent conservative, meaning Democrats identify as liberal over conservative by thirty-six points.[62]

According to the Pew Research Center's 2018 National Survey of Latinos, party affiliation of Latino voters is tied closely to ethnic or nationality group. Among Puerto Ricans and Mexicans, more than half identify with the Democrats, while only 37 percent of Cubans identify as Democrats. Both Central and South Americans have a stronger affiliation with Democrats. When this information is examined by national origin, almost all Latino ethnic groups show strong support for Democrats (see Table 5.5).

Other than Cuban Americans, all major Latino ethnic groups were solidly in the camp of the Democrats. The Democrats' party affiliation advantage is strikingly high among Puerto Ricans (65 percent), Central Americans (59 percent), and South American (58 percent); these groups are located primarily in the US Northeast, with Puerto Ricans also having substantial numbers in the Midwest. Among Mexican Americans, the largest Latino population group, party affiliation with Democrats was 59 percent. While there is a high "Independent" segment of this voting population, previous research indicates Mexican Americans consistently vote for Democratic Party candidates.

Table 5.5   Party Affiliation of Latino Voters by Ethnicity or Nationality Group

Nationality	Democrat (%)	Independent (%)	Republican (%)
Puerto Rican	65.0	0.0	35.0
Mexican	59.0	n/a	41.0
Cuban	37.0	n/a	57.0
Central American	59.0	n/a	29.0
South American	58.0	n/a	40.0

Source: Latino Decisions 2020.

The voting rate for Latinos in the presidential election was 47.6 percent in 2016 and 48 percent in 2012. In 2008, the voting rate for Latinos was 49.9 percent.[63] Hillary Clinton won 66 percent of Latino voters on Election Day, a level of Democratic support similar to 2008, when 67 percent of Hispanics backed Barack Obama. However, Clinton's share of the Latino vote was lower than in 2012, when 71 percent of Latinos voted to reelect Obama. While Clinton underperformed among Latinos compared with 2012, Republican Donald Trump won 28 percent of the Latino vote, a similar share to Mitt Romney's 27 percent in 2012 and John McCain's 31 percent in 2008.[64] Latino voting surges were seen in Arizona, where their voting rate rose from 47.4 percent in 2016 to 60.8 percent in 2020, and in Texas, where it rose from 40.5 percent of eligible Latino voters to 53.1 percent.[65]

The number of Latino voters nearly doubled from 2014 to 2018 to nearly presidential-election-year levels. Overall, Latino voter turnout reached 11.7 million in 2018, up from 6.8 million in 2014, the single largest increase on record from one midterm election to another. In fact, turnout among Latinos was the second largest of any election year, presidential or midterm, trailing only the 2016 presidential elections. About twenty-nine million Latinos were eligible to vote in 2018, up from approximately twenty-five million in 2014.[66]

While party affiliation is a traditional marker to predict voter preferences, issues appear to play a strong role among Latino voters. Polling data in recent years have consistently demonstrated Latinos have very strong views on key issues that eclipse party affiliation. This is evident among Latino voters and in the views of Latino elected officials. Because the Covid-19 pandemic began in 2020, about eight in ten Latino registered voters indicated the economy (80 percent), then health care (76 percent), then Covid-19 (72 percent) were the top three issues. These views came as Latinos had disproportionate economic and health effects from the coronavirus outbreak.[67] Such issues of concern in the Latino community may not be taken up by either of the two major parties. For example, the topic of negative attitudes toward immigrants, a strong concern among Latinos, is not being discussed explicitly by either political party. Similarly, Latinos from both parties are willing to support a larger government to provide better educational opportunities even if it means higher taxes. The national parties, however, have not made education a top priority in their campaigns.

Latinos and the Contemporary Structure of US Politics

In addition to Latino demographics, voter turnout, and party affiliation, the political structure plays a role in shaping Latino electoral fortunes. Chapters 2 to 4 explored in depth the obstacles that have historically hindered Latino empowerment. However, if we are to understand the current level of Latinos' political progress, we must briefly review their group experiences. Since the United States was founded, Latinos have faced various discriminatory barriers put up by the government. There were very few Latinos outside the Southwest before 1848, when the United States annexed the territories of California, Arizona, Texas, New Mexico, and parts of Utah and Colorado following the end of the Mexican-American War of 1846 to 1848. Mexicans residing in these territories were incorporated as US citizens. Though they were nominally granted citizenship, their voting rights were extremely limited, except in areas where they were the numerical majority. In these locations they retained more citizenship rights, including the right to elect their own representatives. As more Anglos arrived in the former Mexican lands, however, Mexicans became the minority, and strict rules were laid down to limit the power of Mexican American voters, such as the poll tax, White primaries, and English-only ballots.

The Progressive era of American politics, which lasted from the late 1800s to the early 1900s, radically changed local electoral systems, as most jurisdictions changed to at-large elections during the first half of the twentieth century. This was particularly true of cities in the South and the West, which urbanized in the twentieth rather than the nineteenth century. By the mid-1970s, 74 percent of southern cities and 79 percent of western cities elected councils at large, compared to only 52 percent of eastern and 50 percent of midwestern cities.[68] In 1991, among US cities with populations larger than 250,000, 28 percent used at-large elections, 10 percent used district-only elections, and 61 percent combined district and citywide election systems; that is, 71 percent of cities elected councils through a district or mixed system.[69]

Such Progressive era reforms, while designed to root out corruption, had a negative impact on Latinos. Since, in most cities, Latinos tend to be segregated into barrios, the elimination of district elections, while other barriers to voting were retained, made it extremely difficult to elect Latinos to office. The change to at-large elections in the Southwest would exacerbate the lack of Mexican Americans holding elected office, except in New Mexico (where Hispanos were the dominant group), from the 1880s to the 1950s. While other Latino ethnic groups were present in the country during this period, this change had the greatest impact in the Southwest, where large numbers of Mexican Americans were concentrated. In many cities, Latinos found it extremely difficult to win in at-large elections. By the 1970s, Latinos were challenging the at-large electoral structure and the use of gerrymandered district boundaries to inhibit the election of Latinos.

The passage of the Voting Rights Act of 1965, with strong support from the Lyndon B. Johnson administration, was a result of the civil rights movement to end discriminatory practices that prevented Black people from voting

114 *Latino Political Power*

and being elected to office, particularly in southern states, where segregation of the races and discrimination against Blacks remained strong. Section 2 of the VRA prohibits minority vote dilution, which is the use of voting laws and practices that discriminate on the basis of race, color, or membership in a minority language group. All voting procedures are covered under the law, including voter registration, candidate qualifications, voting practices, and types of electoral systems. Section 2 also prevents local governments from using any electoral procedure that would deny racial and linguistic minorities a fair chance to elect candidates of their choice.[70] In 1975 the VRA was amended to extend voting rights protection to linguistic minorities. These amendments mandated bilingual ballots and oral assistance to those who spoke Spanish, Chinese, Japanese, Korean, and Native American and Eskimo languages. In 1982 the VRA was also amended to clarify that proof of discriminatory purpose or intent was not required under a Section 2 claim of voter discrimination.[71]

In 2010, Shelby County, Alabama, filed suit asking a federal court in Washington, DC, to declare Section 5 of the Voting Rights Act unconstitutional. Section 5 is a key part of the VRA, requiring certain jurisdictions with a history of discrimination to submit any proposed changes in voting procedures to the US Department of Justice or a federal district court in DC to ensure the change will not harm minority voters. In September 2011, the US District Court for the District of Columbia upheld the constitutionality of Section 5, and in May 2012, the US Court of Appeals for the District of Columbia Circuit agreed with the district court. Shelby County appealed the ruling to the Supreme Court, which agreed to take the case in November 2012. On June 25, 2013, the Supreme Court ruled the coverage formula in Section 4(b) of the Voting Rights Act, which determines which jurisdictions are covered by Section 5, is unconstitutional because it is based on an old formula. As a practical matter this means Section 5 is inoperable until Congress enacts a new coverage formula.[72]

One of the most critical structural elements governing the electoral process is the design of electoral districts. The design of electoral districts, whether based on nonpartisan or partisan positions, is a political act. Political parties and a wide variety of interest groups, including women, chambers of commerce, and racial and ethnic groups, seek to draw political boundaries to increase their opportunity to elect someone who will represent their interests.

As noted, a major obstacle to the election of minorities to office is the use of at-large, winner-takes-all seats, where candidates must run and win election in an entire school district, city, or county. In an at-large election system, there are no districts. A candidate can reside anywhere within the political jurisdiction, and all registered voters living within the political boundaries can vote for the candidate. Again, the at-large electoral system is part of the Progressive era reforms of the late nineteenth and early twentieth centuries, designed to eliminate the ethnic urban political machines that controlled politics at the local level.

In the 1970s, Latino and African American groups successfully challenged many at-large elections in locations where they had a history of being unable to elect someone of their ethnic or racial group to local office due to racially polarized voting. The goal was to create "district elections which would provide increased representation for minorities and facilitate their inclusion into urban governing coalitions, and lead to policy equity for underserved areas of the city."[73]

Today, however, a problem is evident with district elections: if a minority group is heavily concentrated in one district, and if there is voting along racial lines in that city, then the voting strength of the minority community may increase in the district where it is concentrated but weaken throughout the rest of the city, where it is less concentrated. District structures do tend to lead to deference to the wishes of council members on issues that concern their districts. Decentralization of power appears to increase council members' ability to deliver to their constituents and claim credit for doing so.[74]

Modern redistricting of political boundaries occurs after a census, which entails the counting of all Americans every ten years. Because the US Constitution requires that representation in the House of Representatives be based on state population, congressional districts must be redrawn by state legislatures to reflect population shifts. Through redistricting, the political party with the greatest number of members in a statehouse tries to ensure the maximum number of its party members can be elected to Congress. State legislatures are also responsible for redrawing any other district boundaries for state offices. Subunits of government within each state are responsible for redrawing their own political boundaries, such as at the county, city, and school district levels. The redistricting process often involves gerrymandering, the drawing of district boundaries to maximize the number of representatives from the political party in power in that state.

The process of redistricting also involves three types of claims of bias. State and federal courts have generally ruled out the claim of bias by either of the two main political parties based on redistricting schemes by state legislatures. In other words, there is no valid claim of bias if a district is "too Democratic" or "too Republican" in registration. This is understood to be the prerogative of the dominant political party in each state. Instead, the first basis for a claim is the "one person, one vote" principle from the Equal Protection Clause of the Fourteenth Amendment to the Constitution. This principle basically states each vote should count the same as every other vote; that is why all legislative districts must be drawn with roughly equal populations. According to the 2010 US Census, the target number was 711,000 people per congressional district. In 2020, each congressional district

116   *Latino Political Power*

increased to about 761,000 people. Too wide a variance from this target invites a lawsuit.[75]

A second group of claims are those brought under the Voting Rights Act by racial minorities who claim the political lines unfairly divide them among different electoral districts, thereby diluting their voting strength. For example, the Texas legislature cemented Republican Party dominance of the statehouse. Based on the 2020 census data, of the nearly 4 million people added to the population count, 95 percent were people of color. Nearly 2 million were Latino. Yet, the new US congressional district map drawn by the state of Texas gave White voters control of the two new districts, one in Houston and one in Austin. Specifically, 50 percent of new Texas residents in the past ten years were Latinos. In addition, there are 150 districts in the Texas House map. According to a report from the *Texas Tribune*, the majority of the districts are Republican leaning.[76] The new map drew criticism for potentially decreasing the influence of Latinos and Black voters. Compared to the previous map, Latinos make up the majority of eligible voters in thirty districts instead of thirty-three. Districts with majority Black voters went down from seven to six. However, districts with a majority of White voters increased from eighty-three to eighty-nine.[77]

As of this writing, in the Texas Senate there are twenty-one districts with a majority of White eligible voters, seven with Latino majorities, one with a Black majority, and two where no racial group makes up more than half the total.[78]

The map's lead author, Senator Joan Huffman, a Republican from Houston, said she drew the map "race-blind" but ran it by state lawyers to ensure it complied with legal requirements for the redistricting process. Under certain circumstances, lawmakers are required to consider racial demographics in the state to ensure they are complying with the VRA. But Huffman declined Democrats' requests to specify what measure she used to ensure maps complied with the law.[79] Many states have learned from Texas's conservative nature; Republicans effectively dominate the redistricting process in twenty states.[80]

The legal landscape for the Texas map and maps redrawn by Republican legislatures to favor their party was weakened by two major Supreme Court rulings. In the first, the court in 2013 gutted core protections for the Voting Rights Act in *Shelby v. Holder*. The court determined that Section 4(b), which laid out the formula used to determine which states were subject to preclearance, was unconstitutional. Without a formula in place to identify jurisdictions subject to preclearance, neither Texas nor any other previously covered jurisdiction needed to get federal approval for its district maps.[81]

In the second case, the courts in 2019 closed the door to federal court challenges to partisan gerrymandering in *Rucho v. Common Cause*.[82] According to the Brennan Center for Justice, the Supreme Court ruled 5–4

Participation and the Contours of Power 117

that partisan gerrymandering claims present political questions that fall beyond the jurisdiction of the federal judiciary. In addition, the Supreme Court remanded the case to a lower court with instructions to dismiss for lack of jurisdiction. In *Rucho*, the Supreme Court ruled that gerrymandering is a political issue and that no "limited and precise standard" exists to determine when partisan gerrymandering is too partisan.[83]

Running and Winning in Different Electoral Districts

Historically, the form of district that provides the best opportunity for racial minorities to elect candidates of their choice is known as the majority-minority district. Here boundaries are drawn such that racial minority populations are concentrated into districts where they are the majority population. If racialized voting can be demonstrated, with White and racial minority voters each voting for their own candidates and effectively limiting the voting choices of racial minorities, then the formation of a majority-minority district can be justified. It enables the voters in this district to elect a candidate of their own choice (whether minority or not).

Despite the use of majority-minority districts and other means to elect racial minorities, state legislatures around the country have made little progress in diversifying their ranks during the last decade, with many states losing ground in boosting their representation of people of color and White women. Even as the share of nonwhite Americans has grown, analysis of data from the National Conference of State Legislatures finds most state legislatures are lacking in diversity, with nearly every state failing to achieve racial and gender parity with its own population data. Despite efforts to diversify politics, progress in statehouses remains slow and halting. That's in contrast to the US House of Representatives and Senate, where a quarter of voting members (23 percent) are racial or ethnic minorities, making the 117th Congress the most racially and ethnically diverse in history.[84] Despite this gain, the data show every single state in the country has a legislature that is disproportionately White. Arizona stands out as the state legislature with the largest gain in racial diversity between 2015 and 2020: a ten point increase from 28 to 38 percent. Hawaii far and away leads the country in its share of nonwhite state legislators (71 percent). But like twenty other states in the nation, it saw a decrease in nonwhite representation. Five states saw no movement at all, and twenty-one saw slight movement of two percentage points or less. West Virginia and New Hampshire have the Whitest legislatures. A majority of statehouses, however, became Whiter or saw no increase in nonwhite representation over the past five years. Of the statehouses that did get increasingly diverse, many saw only a moderate improvement in nonwhite representation.[85]

118   *Latino Political Power*

In addition to district characteristics, candidates' ability to obtain endorsements and financial resources is crucial to their credibility. Such resources are usually acquired through working as a staff aide, party activist, or community or labor activist. Credibility is crucial: those who fund campaigns are most likely to donate to those with a reasonable chance of victory. Endorsements establish candidates' legitimacy and also draw in other resources. Entering into this political environment requires excellent connections and strong community-based ties. Name recognition is also a valuable commodity, whether due to familial ties or to demonstrated leadership in an area of expertise.

As electoral barriers to Latinos were removed, both males and females began to run for office in diverse locations and at different levels of government. The next section explores the fortunes of Latinos at different levels of government.

Latino Population Growth and Congress

The legislative branch of the federal government includes 100 senators and 435 members of the House of Representatives. Obtaining one of these offices is not easy; such seats are costly, extremely partisan, and very prestigious. Latinos historically have not been well represented in the legislative branch of the federal government. In the 1970s, only three congressmen (two from Texas and one from California) and one US senator (from New Mexico) were Latinos. In the subsequent decades, there were dramatic changes in the number and gender diversity of Latinos elected to the House of Representatives. Latinos will continue to make even greater gains in the US House and Senate in the next few years.

By 2020, the growing Latino population had dispersed beyond the traditional centers of concentration into suburbs, rural areas, and all regions of the country. Twenty-six districts, or 5.98 percent of the nation's 435 congressional districts, are now Latino majority. As of the 2020 election, there were forty-six Latino/a legislators (forty in the House and six in the Senate). Of the top fifteen congressional districts with the greatest share of Latinos, six had a more than 75 percent Latino population: five districts in Texas and one district in California (see Table 5.6). Another thirteen congressional districts were between 65 and 75 percent Latino, and two districts were more than 62 percent Latino. In twenty-six of the forty districts, the Latino population was greater than 50 percent. Fourteen districts had slightly less than 50 percent Latino populations, with both Republicans and Democrats winning elected office.

Following the National Association of Latino Elected and Appointed Officials' 2021 report, there were forty-six Latina and Latino congressional

Table 5.6　Latino Members of Congress

Name	State (Party)	Latino Percentage of the District Population	Percentage of Vote Received in 2020
Representatives (40)			
Ruben Gallego	AZ (D)	63.4	75.7
Raul Grijalva	AZ (D)	61.4	NE
Pete Aguilar	CA (D)	54.1	62.1
Salud Carbajal	CA (D)	35.2	58.7
Tony Cardenas	CA (D)	68.2	NE
J. Luis Correa	CA (D)	66.0	NE
Gil Cisneros	CA (D)	33.3	NE
Nanette Diaz Barragan	CA (D)	69.5	67.8
Grace Flores Napolitano	CA (D)	67.0	NE
Mike Garcia	CA (R)	37.4	54.9
Jimmy Gomez	CA (D)	63.8	53
Mike Levin	CA (D)	25.7	56.4
David Nunes	CA (R)	46.0	54.2
Lucille Roybal-Allard	CA (D)	86.6	72.7
Raul Ruiz	CA (D)	48.3	60.3
Linda Sanchez	CA (D)	61.2	74.3
Norma Torres	CA (D)	68.08	69.3
Juan Vargas	CA (D)	69.4	71.4
Mario Díaz-Balart	FL (R)	74.6	NE
Carlos A. Gimenez	FL (R)	67.3	51.7
Maria Elvira Salazar	FL (R)	68.9	51.4
Darren Soto	FL (D)	37.5	56
Jesus "Chuy" G. Garcia	IL (D)	69.8	Uncontested
Sires Albio	NJ (D)	55.5	74
Teresa Leger Fernandez	NM (D)	39.81	58.7
Antonio Delgado	NY (D)	8.27	54.8
Adriano Espaillat	NY (D)	54.38	90.79
Alexandria Ocasio-Cortez	NY (D)	48.80	74.6
Ritchie John Torres	NY (D)	66.0	88.9
Nydia M. Velázquez	NY (D)	39.30	84.9

continues

120 *Latino Political Power*

Table 5.6 Continued

Name	State (Party)	Latino Percentage of the District Population	Percentage of Vote Received in 2020
Representatives (40)			
Anthony Gonzalez	OH (R)	2.35	63.2
Joaquin Castro	TX (D)	69.64	64.7
Henry Cuellar	TX (D)	78.5	51.8
Veronica Escobar	TX (D)	81.03	64.7
Sylvia R. Garcia	TX (D)	77.09	71.1
Vicente Gonzalez	TX (D)	81.87	50.05
Filemon Vela	TX (D)	83.88	75.1
Tony Gonzales	TX (R)	68.34	50.6
Jaime Herrera Beutler	WA (R)	4.6	56.4
Alex X. Mooney	WV (R)	2.0	58
Senators (6)			
Alex Padilla	CA (D)		
Catherine Cortez Masto	NV (D)		
Ted Cruz	TX (R)		
Marco Rubio	FL (R)		
Ben Lujan	NM (D)		
Robert Menendez	NJ (D)		

Source: NALEO 2021.
Note: NE = nonelection year.

members, thirty-five of them Democrats and eleven Republicans. Four caucuses now represent Hispanic interests.[86] The Congressional Hispanic Caucus was formed in 1976 and has historically had a liberal social agenda. It now includes thirty House members, all of whom are Democrats. In 2003, House Republicans formed the Congressional Hispanic Conference, which at the time of this writing was composed of four members of Hispanic descent and two of Portuguese descent. This caucus was formed with the stated goal of promoting policy outcomes of importance to Americans of Hispanic or Latino and Portuguese descent. The impetus behind the conference's creation was the debate surrounding the nomination of Miguel Estrada to the DC Circuit Court of Appeals.[87]

While Latinos have steadily increased their numbers in the House of Representatives, they are still only 9.2 percent of the total number of members, less than a ten percent of the Latino total population. After the 2020 census, there were twenty-four congressional districts with Latino populations greater than 50 percent. In order for a larger number of Latinos to enter the House of Representatives, they will need to win in electoral districts where Latinos are not the majority population but perhaps a significant minority.

Though Latino fortunes have improved in the House of Representatives, the situation is not as optimistic for Latinos when it comes to winning US Senate seats, which requires winning at a statewide level. Before the election of Latinos to the Senate in 2020, there had been only nine Latino US senators in the history of the country.[88] The difficulty of putting together the economic resources, the political network, and a sophisticated campaign operation have until recently held Latinos back from winning any but a handful of statewide electoral victories.

It is no coincidence the only US senators of color elected consistently over the past forty years have come from the state of Hawaii. Asian Americans are the majority population in Hawaii, and they have consistently elected Asian Americans to both houses of Congress since Hawaii's statehood in 1959. As of 2022, there were four Native Americans serving in the House of Representatives and none in the Senate. There were three sitting African American senators: Tim Scott (R-SC), Corey Booker (D-NJ), and Raphael Warnock (D-GA). There were six Hispanic/Latino/a senators: Alex Padilla (D-CA), Catherine Cortez Masto (D-NV), Ted Cruz (R-TX), Marco Rubio (R-FL), Ben Lujan (D-NM), and Robert Menendez (D-NJ).[89] Although recent Congresses have continued to set new highs for racial and ethnic diversity, they still have been disproportionately White when compared with the overall US population.

State and Local Representation of Latinos

Other than the offices of president and vice president and seats in Congress, all elections in the United States involve contests for state or local offices. While Latinos have held elective office in this country since the early nineteenth century, before the 1960s they did so only in a few areas of the Southwest. Beginning in the 1960s, Chicanos in the Southwest began to win a wide variety of local and state representative elections. In the 1970s, Cubans and Puerto Ricans began to win elected office in the Northeast and Southeast. In the 1980s, other Latinos also began to win election to local offices in different regions of the country. In the 1990s, Latinos of different ethnicities ran for office in all regions. By 2020, Latinos held office in forty-three states. The breadth of officeholding by Latinos is an indication of their growth and potential strength nationally.

122   *Latino Political Power*

At the state representative level, there are different social conditions and ethnic demographics among the states. In 2020, there were 236 Latino state representatives and 88 state senators for a total of 326. Nationally in 2010, there were 179 Latino state representatives and 66 state senators for a total of 245. Not surprisingly, the southwestern states had the largest numbers and percentages of Hispanic state legislators. In terms of party affiliation, in 2020, 188 Hispanic state legislators identified with the Democratic Party, while 40 identified as Republicans and none identified as Independent. By 2021, 282 state senators identified as Democrats and 51 state representatives identified as Republicans.[90] In general, Latinos have historically found it difficult to win election for state representative except in majority-Latino districts.

This is clearly evident in Texas, where the House of Representatives is composed of 150 members: in 2021 thirty-seven were Latino (including twelve Chicanas), that is, 24.67 percent of the entire legislature. Twenty-two of the thirty-seven were elected from majority-Latino population districts. In New Mexico, Hispanic legislators numbered forty-four in total, or 62.86 percent of the legislature.

In California, the situation has begun to change: Latino state representatives are being elected in non-Latino-majority districts. In 2011, out of the eighty assembly districts in California, Latinos were 23 percent of the voting-eligible population.[91] As of 2020, Latinos were 30 percent of the voting-eligible population statewide but a majority in just 19 percent of districts. All of these districts were located in Los Angeles County, home to the greatest concentration of Latinos in the country.

In 2020, there were ninety-one Latino state senators from twenty-four states, which included eighty Democrats and eleven Republicans. New Mexico, with fifteen Latino state senators, had the largest contingent; California had ten, and Texas, Arizona, and New York were tied with seven. There were also 242 Latino state house representatives in thirty different states, including 202 Democrats and 40 Republicans. The largest contingents of assembly members include thirty-seven from Texas, thirty from Texas, twenty-nine from New Mexico, nineteen from California, and sixteen from Arizona and New York. However, in 2010 the total number of Latino state house representatives was only 3.97 percent of the total number of 5,739 seats nationally.[92] In only one state, New Mexico, does the percentage of Latino elected representatives exceed the state's percentage of Latino voting-age population; in all other states, it is lower. This is one way to measure whether Latinos have achieved equality throughout the country, and clearly, they have not done so.

At the local level, Latino officeholders hold positions in numerous states, as is evident in Table 1.1. While Latinos hold many high-profile seats as mayors and county supervisors and on city councils and school boards in urban areas, a critical look at these numbers indicates in many respects the process of electing Latinos to office is still in its infancy in many local areas.

Looking at the ten largest cities in the United States (see Table 5.7), Latino elected city council members are generally at a lower level of descriptive representation than their population.

In only one city, San Jose, California, is the percentage of Latinos on the city council greater than their population percentage. San Antonio, Texas, has rough parity, and Chicago, Illinois, is at near parity with its Latino population in the city.

In the area of public education, an issue Hispanics ranked as their highest priority in determining their choice for president in 2020,[93] there were a total of 2,592 Latinas and Latinos elected to school boards as of 2021. Of this total, 1,154, or nearly 45 percent, came from over a dozen different school district across Texas. There were 1,436 males and 1,156 (or 44.5 percent) females elected to school boards nationwide.

If we look at the numbers of Latino school board members in 2010, there were 1,804 scattered throughout the country, nearly 91.3 percent of them in three states: California (569), New Mexico (156), and Texas (916). There were 640 Latinas, or about 35.5 percent, among these school board members (see Table 5.8). School board members have surpassed city council members as the largest cohort of Latino elected officials. Yet consider that there are more

Table 5.7   Latino Descriptive Representation

City	Number of Latino Elected Officials (LEOs)/ Total Seats	Percentage of LEOs on Council	Latino Population Percentage in City
New York	11/51	21.5	29.1
Los Angeles	4/15	26.6	48.5
Chicago	12/50	24.0	28.8
Houston	2/16	12.5	45.0
Phoenix	3/9	33.3	42.6
Philadelphia	1/17	5.8	14.7
San Antonio	6/10	60.0	64.2
San Diego	2/9	22.2	30.3
Dallas	3/14	21.4	41.8
San Jose	5/10	50.0	31.6

Source: NALEO 2020.

124 *Latino Political Power*

Table 5.8   Latino Elected Officials, Education/School Boards

Year	Male	Female	Total
2010	1,164	640	1,804
2020	1,493	1,156	2,649

Source: NALEO 2010, 2020.

than 13,800 school districts in the country and that Latinos represent about 3 percent of the total number of elected leaders for public schools.[94] The small number of Latino school board members reflects a larger crisis in education for Latinos. In 2019, about 5.3 percent of Hispanic students in the United States dropped out of high school in grades ten to twelve. This is down from a high of 11.6 percent in 1995.[95] Latino and Black students nationally have lower test scores on average than other groups, and they also have low rates of admittance at many higher education institutions.[96] The lack of Latino representation on school boards and in administrative positions becomes an important issue to address. If Latinos are not included in local policymaking decisions, they will be relegated to outsider status with limited influence on policy outcomes.

Conclusion

The continuing growth of a diverse group of Latino elected officials will likely produce more Latino candidates who will work to build pan-ethnic Latino coalitions to seek elected office. In other situations, there will be intense competition among Latino candidates of different national origins to win seats in majority-minority districts. The ability of minorities to construct broad coalitions, both intra- and interethnic, will be critical to electoral success. Candidate-centered politics, as opposed to a common group effort by Latinos to occupy an electoral seat held previously by an Anglo, became the predominant means to achieve office in the 1990s. Today, ambitious Latino candidates are seeking to run for office in districts where Latinos are not the majority population; rather, they seek to run where Latinos are a sizable minority and can provide a base of support on which the candidate can build. Instead of focusing solely on turning out votes in the Latino area of an electoral district, they seek to expand their influence to non-Latino areas.

This chapter sets in motion a series of strategic questions for Latinos in the coming years. How can the number of seats where Latinos have a credible opportunity to win office be increased? How long will Latinos wait before challenging entrenched incumbents who now represent districts with majority or near-majority Latino populations? Should the creation and retention of majority-minority seats remain the primary objective of voting rights litigation? Or is it more important to create new districts where Latinos are the largest ethnic group but not necessarily a majority population, if Latinos are to extend their opportunities to win election? How can Latinos win elected office when states, like Texas, gerrymander districts using a "colorblind method" that essentially dilutes and marginalizes their growing population?

This chapter has provided a broad overview of Latino politics and the involvement of Latinos in the electoral process. There is not space to fully explore other avenues of political participation in which Latinos are engaged; however, as electoral participation is an established means of political involvement, it provides a marker of the progress of Latino politics. The next two chapters explore the process of Latino political empowerment in three cities and the political trajectory of Latinas in electoral politics as they move from political disenfranchisement to political incorporation.

Notes

1. Browning, Marshall, and Tabb 1997, 10.
2. Migration Policy Institute, n.d.
3. US Census Bureau 2001b.
4. Noe-Bustamante, Lopez, and Krogstad 2020.
5. Ibid.
6. Epstein and Medina 2021.
7. Noe-Bustamante, Lopez, and Krogstad 2020.
8. Ibid.
9. Ibid.
10. US Census Bureau 2021a.
11. Statista Research Department 2021.
12. Lopez, Krogstad, and Passel 2021.
13. Ibid.
14. Krogstad and Noe-Bustamante 2021.
15. World Population Review 2020.
16. Ibid.
17. Passel, Lopez, and Cohn 2022.
18. Los Angeles County Economic Development Corporation 2017.
19. Ibid.
20. Blizzard and Batalova 2020.
21. Israel and Batalova 2020.
22. Babich and Batalova 2021.
23. Goldsmith 2020.
24. Jones et al. 2021.
25. US Census Bureau 2021b.
26. US Census Bureau 2010, https://www.census.gov/.

126 *Latino Political Power*

27. Ibid.
28. Noe-Bustamante, Budiman, and Lopez 2020.
29. US Census Bureau 2020b.
30. Passel and Cohn 2014.
31. Budiman 2020.
32. Ibid.
33. Lopez, Passel, and Rohal 2015.
34. Gonzalez-Barrera 2017.
35. World Staff 2020.
36. Dominquez-Villegas et al. 2021.
37. Acevedo 2020.
38. Krogstad 2020; Gramlich 2020.
39. de la Garza and DeSipio 1997, 75.
40. Center for Migration Studies of New York 2021.
41. Krogstad et al. 2016.
42. Latino Decisions 2016.
43. D. E. Henry 2020.
44. Nowicki 2010.
45. Garcia-Navarro 2021.
46. Barron-Lopez, Rodriguez, and Rayasam 2020.
47. Reny, Wilcox-Archuleta, and Cruz Nichols 2019.
48. Attanasio 2019.
49. Perez 2021.
50. Dearman 2020.
51. Gould, Perez, and Wilson 2020.
52. US Centers for Disease Control and Prevention 2021.
53. US Bureau of Labor Statistics 2021.
54. Equis Research 2021.
55. Ibid.
56. Schor and Crary 2020.
57. As quoted in Stewart 2022.
58. NALEO 2022.
59. Abrajano 2010.
60. Willis and Seiz 2020.
61. Levitz 2021.
62. Ibid.
63. US Census Bureau 2016.
64. Krogstad and Lopez 2016.
65. Gamboa 2021.
66. Flores and Lopez 2018.
67. Krogstad and Lopez 2020.
68. Sanders 1979.
69. Bridges and Underwood 2000, 51–52, based on Renner and de Santis 1993.
70. Center for Voting and Democracy, n.d.b.
71. US Department of Justice, n.d.
72. Lockhart 2019.
73. Bridges and Underwood 2000; Grofman and Davidson 1992.
74. Bridges and Underwood 2000; Polinard et al. 1994.
75. In 1983, the Supreme Court ruled in *Brown v. Thomson* that state legislative and local districts could vary by as much as a 10 percent range.
76. Barragan and Ura 2021.

77. Ashbrook 2021a.
78. Limon 2021.
79. Ibid.
80. Desilver 2021.
81. "Shelby County v. Holder" 2018.
82. Morales-Doyle 2021.
83. Ibid.
84. Schaeffer 2021.
85. Bettridge and Kania 2020.
86. Venezuela Democracy Caucus, Congressional Hispanic Caucus, Congressional Hispanic Conference, and Congressional Central America Caucus.
87. Bonilla et al. 2003.
88. "Hispanic American Senators," n.d.
89. Manning 2022.
90. NALEO 2020.
91. McGhee, Paluch, and Hsieh 2021.
92. NALEO 2010, 2020.
93. NALEO 2020.
94. National School Boards Association 2018, 3.
95. Duffin 2021.
96. Hussar et al. 2020.

6

Political Power
in the Sunbelt

The face of American politics is changing, and so is the nation's local politics. Latinos were once almost totally excluded from city politics. In the 1980s, researchers Rufus Browning, Dale Marshall, and David Tabb documented, "Latinos rose from exclusion to positions of authority as mayors, council members, and top managers and administrators" in local government. To study the progress of Latino politics at the local level, this chapter focuses on minority group mobilization, governing coalitions, incorporation into the institutions of power, and policy responsiveness to racial minority interests. While each local arena undergoes a unique political development, there are also patterns of electoral (dis)empowerment. In addition to demographic and individual-level characteristics, factors such as the extent of coalition building, financial resources, political support, and many others have an impact on electoral results. The three case studies in this chapter were selected to highlight Latino group experiences in different regions and in different local contexts in order to compare Latinos' pathways to political incorporation.

The first case study is Miami, Florida, a large metropolitan area. In only a few decades, Cuban American immigrants have transformed this city and become the dominant politic force in the region. The second study is San Antonio, Texas, where Mexicans, who led local politics until the 1840s, over time lost control to Anglo newcomers. For the next 140 years Mexican Americans were marginalized politically, even though they were the majority population. In 1981, a Mexican American mayor, Henry Cisneros, was elected; Mexican Americans Ed Garza and Julián Castro were elected to the office in 2001 and 2009, respectively. We will consider why it took so long to win political leadership in a city originally dominated by Mexicans, why Mexican Americans were unable to retain the mayoral seat after the early

130   *Latino Political Power*

1980s, and how they were able to win the office again in 2001 and again in 2009. Since 2001, both non-Latinos and Latinos have held the mayor's seat, with Castro being elected in 2009 after losing in his first effort in 2005. When Castro left to take a position with the Barack Obama administration in 2014, he was succeeded by the first African American mayor, Ivy Taylor, who won the election in 2015 and was defeated by current mayor Ron Nirenberg in 2017.

The third case study is Los Angeles, California, the city with the second-largest number of Latinos in the country, yet a city that did not elect a Latino mayor in the twentieth century. Latinos make up the largest ethnic or racial group in Los Angeles but were not able to build a successful coalition to win the mayor's seat until 2005. This case study explores the pathways to office for Latinos in Los Angeles and analyzes some of the reasons why Latino political incorporation has been slow in the nation's second-largest city, even though the population is nearly majority Latino. The 2005 mayoral election of Mexican American Antonio Villaraigosa, then, after he was termed out in 2013, of Eric Garcetti, who is of mixed racial identities, including Mexican heritage, reflect the latest chapter.

Cuban American Politics in South Florida

In some cities in the 1980s, Latinos and African Americans worked together on issues of reapportionment and single-member districts and built multiracial electoral coalitions. In other places, however, strong working relationships were not forged. One location of sharp racial divisions is the South Florida area. The 1965 Voting Rights Act and subsequent amendments provided legal justification for fair representation of racial minorities in areas of concentration. While African Americans and Latinos nominally worked together in South Florida, reapportionment after the 1980 and 1990 censuses did not result in greater coalition efforts. Instead, White liberals and African Americans alike viewed the rapid growth of the largely conservative Cuban American community as a threat to their power and authority. The "natural allies" of Latinos in other cities were not their allies in Miami-Dade County. Why did this conflict occur? What pathways to political empowerment did Cuban Americans adopt to achieve electoral success?

As Cubans began to arrive in Miami in the early 1960s, African Americans were embroiled in a long battle for civil rights. After many years of struggle, in the 1970s and 1980s African Americans gained a limited number of elected and appointed positions in Miami-Dade County through the implementation of single-member districts in large cities and concentrations of voters in small communities. They won the majority of city council seats in Opa Locka and Florida City, as well as seats on the Miami City Commission and the Miami-Dade County Commission. While African American electoral success grew, systemic economic problems remained unresolved and boiled over in the 1980s into four riots, all precipitated by incidents with the police, that "crystallized a widespread anger among Black Miamians over both the failure to keep pace economically and the lack of a political voice."[1]

In the 1980s, Black Miamians struggled to advance economically in an environment where they were geographically divided into separate neighborhoods that were not connected to one another and politically isolated from potential allies. Historically, due to the race-conscious placement of some Black settlements in unincorporated areas, Black people had played an almost insignificant role in the politics of municipalities, with most residing in unincorporated parts of Miami-Dade County where they lacked political clout.[2]

As African American fortunes stalled, Cuban American political fortunes grew dramatically in the 1980s. Much of the political change occurred because of changing demographics in Miami-Dade. A look at the demographics of the county reveals the rapid change from an Anglo to a Latino majority in six decades (see Table 6.1).

The Cuban American population grew in numbers and economic strength; political incorporation came later. At first, prominent exile leaders such as Manolo Reboso and Alfredo Duran, who participated in the Bay of Pigs invasion in Cuba in 1961, escorted Anglo politicians to Little Havana, Hialeah, and Westchester to build ties with them and gain whatever small number of Cuban American votes were available at the time. This symbolic politics approach is typical of first-generation immigrant politics in the

Table 6.1 Miami-Dade County Population, 1960–2020

Year	Non-Hispanic White (N)	Non-Hispanic White (%)	Black or African American (N)	Black or African American (%)	Hispanic (N)	Hispanic (%)	Total (N)
1960	748,000	79.8	140,000	14.9	50,000	5.3	938,000
1970	788,000	61.6	190,000	14.9	299,000	23.5	1,275,000
1980	776,000	47.3	282,000	17.2	581,000	35.5	1,639,000
1990	614,000	31.2	398,000	20.3	953,000	48.5	1,965,000
2000	466,000	20.7	457,000	20.3	1,291,000	57.3	2,253,000
2010	381,573	15.2	431,649	17.2	1,633,415	65.2	2,505,379
2020	361,517	13.3	400,002	14.8	1,856,938	68.7	2,701,767

Sources: Boswell 1994; US Census Bureau 2000b, 2010, 2020a.
Note: N = number.

132   *Latino Political Power*

United States, where prominent members of the immigrant community serve as a link to the larger society. In the early stages of their resettlement, Cubans refugees had not yet gone through the process of becoming citizens and registering. Anglo politicians would identify community leaders and "reward them with political patronage, access, and influence."[3] Later, leaders from the Cuban American community developed their own political machines capable of delivering votes.

For their efforts in supporting Governor Reubin Askew and other Anglo politicians, both Reboso and Duran were appointed to local political office in Miami beginning in 1972. They were Democrats and heroes within the Cuban exile community because of their participation in the Bay of Pigs. In 1972, Reboso was appointed to an open seat on the Miami City Commission, the first Cuban exile to hold this position, and later won reelection in 1974, carrying seventy-one out of eighty-two precincts. In 1973, Duran was appointed to fill a vacancy on the Dade County school board and became the first Hispanic on this board. Even though he was a Democrat, and this was still a traditionally Southern Democratic stronghold, he was ousted from office by the voters in the 1974 countywide election due to local Democrats' hostility toward Cuban American candidates.[4] Another Hispanic would not be appointed to the Dade County school board until 1980.

During the 1970s, the number of Cubans who became American citizens more than doubled: in 1970, 25 percent of the Cuban exiles had become citizens; by 1980 the proportion had risen to 55 percent.[5] Thus Cubans were now poised to expand their electoral influence. In 1978, Jorge Valdés was elected mayor of the city of Sweetwater, and Raul Martinez was elected mayor of Hialeah; both cities bordered Miami and had rapidly grown into Hispanic enclaves with strong Cuban American political influence. Around this time Cubans also began to be elected to office in the Little Havana section of Miami, where they had settled upon arrival in the early 1960s. The highest concentration of Cubans has remained in Little Havana, where they still make up 70 to 90 percent of the population. While Blacks in Miami-Dade County are dispersed, a majority of Hispanics reside in various geographically connected municipalities. These settlement patterns and the large numbers of Cubans in cohesive, contiguous neighborhoods provided a natural base from which to build political power.

As demographic change was occurring, a trend developed of employing district elections at local levels and for state offices. Given the high concentrations of Cubans in densely populated areas of the county, the adoption of district elections facilitated the election of more Hispanic city and county officials, and several of them went on to win other local, state, and federal offices. During the 1980s, the Cuban exile community began to discard its earlier reservations about participation in American politics. With the political enfranchisement of thousands of newly registered Cuban

Political Power in the Sunbelt 133

American voters and the reapportionment of new electoral districts with high concentrations of Hispanics, Cuban candidates had opportunities to quickly move into important elected positions. Based on the redrawing of district boundaries in 1982, Cubans from South Florida, where Cubans were heavily concentrated, captured three seats in the Florida State Senate and eight seats in the Florida House. Having had virtually no representation up to this point, they gained immediate visibility and political clout. This was a dramatic leap for an ethnic minority group that had had virtually no presence in the area before 1960. In 1988, the burgeoning numbers of Cuban American legislators prompted the formation of the Cuban American Caucus in the Florida state legislature. It was formed consciously as a Cuban American, not Hispanic, caucus.[6]

Another important milestone for Cuban American politics occurred when Cuban exile Xavier Suarez was elected mayor of the city of Miami in 1985. He defeated former mayor Maurice Ferré, a Puerto Rican American Democrat, and Raul Masvidal, a Republican and Cuban American National Foundation board member. By 1986, Latinos totaled 53 percent of Miami's registered voters, had majority control of the city commission, and held almost all of the city's major administrative positions.[7] Since 1985, except for three years in the mid-1990s, the mayor's seat has been held by Cuban Americans. Suarez held the post from 1985 to 1993, lost it, and then won it back in 1997, only to have the election results overturned by the courts because of absentee ballot fraud. Joe Carollo became the city's mayor from 1996 to 1997 and then also regained the seat from 1998 until 2001. Mayor Carollo reduced the city's debt and created a surplus but was defeated in his reelection effort after numerous conflicts with members of the city's management team and personal problems.[8]

The 2001 mayoral race included four major candidates, three of them Cuban American and one of Puerto Rican descent. Carollo and Suarez split the largest share of Cuban votes in the initial round and did not make the runoff. The runoff pitted Maurice Ferré, the only non-Cuban in the race and a proven vote-getter among liberal White and Black voters, against Cuban American Manny Diaz, a local attorney with strong business ties who had represented Elian Gonzalez's Miami-based family in the suit for him to remain in the United States.[9] Diaz's victory, like the earlier wins of Carollo and Suarez, was largely attributable to the Cuban American vote. He defeated former mayor Ferré by 55 to 45 percent. As Ferré's campaign manager, Manny Alfonso, put it, "If you're not Cuban in Miami, you don't have a chance."[10] Diaz won 71 percent of the Hispanic vote but only 12 percent of the Black vote and 32 percent of the White vote. In the heavily Cuban neighborhoods of Little Havana and West Miami, Diaz averaged 70 percent of the vote.[11] However, Diaz was not strictly a high-identity Cuban mayor: "Diaz seems likely to be a mayor who is Cuban. He didn't make

134   *Latino Political Power*

ethnicity an issue during the campaign . . . and has a good rapport with Blacks and White non-Hispanics, unlike Carollo."[12]

Manny Diaz served as mayor from 2001 to 2009, when he was termed out. Diaz was credited with moving the city from financial hardship to a more stable economic foundation, as well as with promoting sustainability, infrastructure investment, poverty issues, and the arts. While the position of mayor is nonpartisan, Diaz became an Independent and later was elected president of the US Conference of Mayors in 2008; he also endorsed Barack Obama for president in 2008. In a book Diaz wrote after finishing his term, he expressed his view of politics: "My premise is that we need to restore pragmatism in politics through a renewed investment in our cities. Unless we do so, we will head down a very perilous road."[13]

Diaz was succeeded as Miami's mayor by Tomas Regalado. Born in Cuba, he came to the United States at the age of fourteen as one of many unaccompanied children in Operation Peter Pan in the 1960s. Regalado grew up in the Miami area and became a journalist, even becoming the first Cuban American to join the White House press core. He later returned to Miami and served as a city commissioner from 1996 to 2009 before being elected as Miami's mayor in 2009 and reelected in 2013, winning those races with more than 71 and 78 percent of the vote, respectively. He is recognized for balancing Miami's budget, expanding the city's role in emerging technology, and promoting research about sea-level rise.

Regalado was termed out in 2017, and Francis Suarez was overwhelmingly elected mayor with 85 percent of the vote. Suarez was born in Miami and is a registered Republican. He previously served as District 4 city commissioner from 2009 to 2017. He is the son of former Miami mayor and Miami-Dade County commissioner Xavier Suarez. Mayor Suarez and former mayor Regalado have both highlighted the threat of rising sea levels to the city's infrastructure. Suarez was reelected in 2021 with nearly 79 percent of the vote.

In addition to engaging in city- and state-level politics, Cuban Americans were busy seeking regional and federal offices in South Florida. From the late 1980s to 2004, four prominent Cuban politicians were elected, solidifying the growing influence of Cuban Americans in the region. In 1989, in a special election to replace longtime congressman Claude Pepper, State Senator Ileana Ros-Lehtinen won by mobilizing more than 94 percent of the Cuban American vote. Ros-Lehtinen was the first Cuban American candidate for Congress who had a real chance to win. She enjoyed near unanimous support in the Cuban American community. Her opponent carried all the other blocs of voters—Jews, Anglos, and Blacks—but they represented only 47 percent of the electorate.[14] In this election, the important factors in the victory were strong political mobilization and solid ethnic-group voting by Cubans. The significance of Ros-Lehtinen's victory went far beyond South Florida, because she became the first Latina and the first Cuban American ever to serve in Congress.

In 1992, following reapportionment, a second Cuban American, State Senator Lincoln Díaz-Balart, was elected to Congress in Miami-Dade County. Here a seat that had always been held by a Democrat was conceded to Cuban American Republicans.[15] Unlike in the polarized election of Ros-Lehtinen, Díaz-Balart had only weak opposition in the Republican primary and no Democratic opponent in the general election. Díaz-Balart comes from a powerful Cuban family that was involved in government politics in the island nation before the Cuban Revolution.

Following the 2002 reapportionment, Mario Díaz-Balart, younger brother of Lincoln Díaz-Balart, became the third Cuban American member of Congress from the South Florida region. Mario Díaz-Balart was born in the United States and began his political career as an aide to Miami mayor Xavier Suarez in 1985. He later served in both houses of the Florida legislature. In 2000, Assemblyman Díaz-Balart headed the committee that drew the new congressional district lines within the state. He then won the seat in November 2002. Within twelve years, Cuban Americans had won three congressional seats and established themselves as a solid conservative voting bloc in South Florida.

Another political milestone for Cubans and Hispanics began in 1990. Hialeah council member Alex Penelas won a seat on the Miami-Dade County Commission after defeating Jorge "George" Valdés, who in the early 1980s had become the first Cuban American to ever sit on this commission. Penelas, a Cuban American Democrat, was a young attorney fresh out of law school and only recently elected to the Hialeah City Council. At the time, all eight of the county commissioner seats were at-large; candidates could reside in separate geographic districts but had to compete across the county. Penelas won on the strength of Democratic Party support among liberal Black and White voters (he received 85 percent of Anglo votes); he did not win a majority of the Cuban vote. Penelas managed to attract only 38 percent of the Latino vote, whereas Valdés won 62 percent.[16]

The Miami-Dade County government underwent a dramatic structural change in 1992, when it was required to change from at-large to single-member district elections. An alliance of Black and Latino leaders had mounted a successful federal court challenge that compelled this change. The courts also abolished the position of county mayor, which left a vacuum, as no commissioner represented the entire county.

County Commissioner Alex Penelas proposed to modify the commission's structure by establishing the position of executive mayor. The person holding this position would be directly accountable to the voters, as opposed to a county manager appointed by the commissioners. The executive mayor would be elected countywide and would provide checks and

136   *Latino Political Power*

balances to the newly elected district commissioners. County voters approved the initiative in 1992, with the election to take place in 1996.[17] This structural change laid the basis for Penelas's run for this office. In the 1996 race, Penelas was pitted against African American Republican and fellow county commissioner Arthur Teele. Teele sought to win the Hispanic vote by appealing to his party identification. Penelas sought to win Democratic Party votes among Black and White voters and have the Hispanic vote swing toward him along ethnic lines.

Penelas won the election. The significance of his electoral victory lay in the power of ethnic voting. Penelas is a Democrat; yet he received virtually the entire Cuban American vote, which normally votes heavily Republican, and almost none of the African American vote. He won over 60 percent of the total vote, including 60 percent of the Hispanic vote, but only 3 percent of the Black vote. Teele won 84 percent of the Black vote but could only garner 2 percent of the Hispanic vote.[18] In the heightened racialized atmosphere of South Florida, party identification meant less for local electoral office than ethnic identification.[19]

This type of bullet voting is not unique to Cubans in South Florida; many ethnic and racial groups in other locales exhibit similar behavior when given the opportunity to vote for "one of their own." The party-crossover voting pattern of Cubans resembles the voting behavior of African Americans in Chicago in the 1980s, when Harold Washington ran for mayor and received more than 97 percent of the votes of fellow African Americans, with an astounding 85 percent voter turnout.[20] Asian Americans crossed traditional party lines and voted for Republican Matt Fong for US senator in California in 1998. During the 2001 Los Angeles mayoral race runoff, Latino candidate Antonio Villaraigosa won between 80 and 90 percent in heavily Latino precincts.[21]

While the vast majority of Cuban Americans have been in the United States only for two generations, most of the first generation of Cuban community leaders trace their fate back to the homeland politics in which their families participated before the Cuban Revolution. This is a powerful common denominator among the first generation of political refugees and many of the American-born second generation of Cuban Americans.

The impact of ethnic voting was never more evident than in the Elian Gonzalez case. As an elected official of a diverse county government, Penelas had managed to govern from the center on most issues. However, during the critical months of the Elian Gonzalez saga in 2000, Penelas returned to his ethnic roots and stood shoulder to shoulder with other Cuban American community leaders and elected officials to oppose US government intervention in the case. This made him a hero in the Cuban American community of South Florida, but many Democrats were angry and accused him of being a closet Republican, particularly after he did not intervene in the

Political Power in the Sunbelt 137

recount of the 2000 presidential race in Miami-Dade County. Even though Al Gore won Miami-Dade County by 30,000 votes, Democratic critics felt Penelas should have supported the continuation of the county recount. The difficulty of being both a Democrat and a Cuban American in South Florida is evident in a comment by Penelas: "Let me tell you, it is not easy being a Cuban-American Democrat. It has been very, very difficult for me to remain a Democrat because of the incredible pressure I've gotten from the Cuban-American community that's predominantly Republican."[22]

In the aftermath of the highly charged Elian Gonzalez case, Penelas faced a difficult political future. His effort to win the US Senate seat in Florida in 2004 resulted in a poor showing in the Democratic Party primary. After terming out as mayor, Penelas stepped back from politics. In 2004, he was succeeded in office by Carlos Alvarez, a Republican and the public safety director for Miami-Dade County. Alvarez defeated several better-known elected officials, running on an anticorruption and political-reform platform that appealed to middle-class suburban voters.[23]

Alvarez sought to strengthen the power of the county mayor and wrest for that office control of the procurement process from the county commission. The county commission resisted this effort, so in 2007, Alvarez won voter approval for a strong-mayor system with the county mayor becoming the chief executive officer for the county and taking most of the executive power away from the county manager. The county mayor was given the power to hire and fire county managers and most department heads. Soon afterward voters eliminated the county manager position and moved its executive powers to the county mayor in 2012.[24]

While Carlos Alvarez won reelection handily in 2008 with two-thirds of the vote and enjoyed voter support in 2010 for strengthening the powers of the county mayor, his support for public financing of a baseball stadium soured him with the voters being asked to fund the project to the tune of $2.4 billion over many years. Other ill-advised economic decisions included proposing a 12 percent increase in property tax rates in 2011.[25] Led by a wealthy Republican donor who opposed big government and with growing opposition to Alvarez, an initiative launched in 2011 successfully recalled Alvarez and another county commissioner. More than 88 percent of the voters voted to recall Alvarez, at the time the largest municipal recall vote in US history.

A recall election entails not just the question of whether to remove someone from office but who should replace that officeholder. The campaign to succeed Alvarez drew many into the race, including Carlos Gimenez, who was the sole county commissioner to oppose the baseball stadium deal and the 12 percent property tax increase. Also entering the race was Hialeah mayor Julio Robaina, who held similar positions to Gimenez but supported the building of the baseball stadium and had the backing of real estate interests. In a close runoff, Gimenez bested Robaina

138 *Latino Political Power*

51 to 49 percent, a difference of 4,000 votes, by securing White voters and Hispanic-majority cities such as Coral Gables and Miami Beach, whereas Robaina received the votes of Blacks and working-class Hispanics.[26]

Before Gimenez was elected Miami-Dade County mayor, he had previously served as a firefighter and fire chief and as Miami city manager. Gimenez was reelected in 2012 and 2016 as Miami-Dade County mayor. During his tenure in this office, he sought to roll back the 2010 property tax increase, which led to a challenge to his 2012 reelection by Joe Martinez, a county commissioner who opposed the rollback of the property tax increase. Martinez supported the county labor unions who believed the tax rollback would force them to make significant concessions, which the unions opposed. Gimenez easily won reelection in 2012 and defeated Martinez. Gimenez was term-limited in 2020, when he sought and won a hotly contested seat for the US House of Representatives. He was victorious over the Democratic incumbent, Representative Debbie Mucarsel-Powell, the nation's first Ecuadorian congressperson.[27]

In the neighboring congressional district, Cuban American Maria Elvira Salazar defeated the Democratic incumbent, Representative Donna Shalala, who was President Bill Clinton's Health and Human Services director and a former president of the University of Miami. These two victories and Joe Biden's close margin of victory over President Donald Trump in Miami-Dade County reflect a continuing influence of Cuban American and other conservative voters in this Florida county. Salazar, the daughter of Cuban immigrants and a former Spanish-language television reporter, was well known in the Latino community and lost to Shalala in 2018. This time Salazar won by almost three percentage points, even though Joe Biden beat Donald Trump by more than three percentage points in the same congressional district, which includes most of the city of Miami, Miami Beach, and coastal Miami-Dade County. Salazar raised $3.7 million, far more than average for House races, and was just short of incumbent Shalala's $3.8 million total.[28]

It is noteworthy that Miami-Dade County is 87 percent Black (17.7 percent) and Hispanic or Latino (69.4 percent). The continuing political influence of Cuban American elected officials reflects the resilience of the Cuban American community's political efforts. In a county that has 27.8 percent Republican registration, 39.5 percent Democratic Party registration, and 31.2 percent no affiliation, Cuban Americans have been able to sustain and grow their numbers of elected leaders in multiple communities and at all levels of government.[29] This indicates the continued ability of Cuban Americans to elect members of their community to congressional as well as local and regional offices.

Although Cuban Americans account for fewer than a third of Florida's Hispanics, all three of the congressional seats, all three of the state senate seats, and nearly all of the eleven state house seats in majority Hispanic districts were held by Cuban Americans in the early 2000s. Both partisan and national-origin factors lie behind this. Cuban Americans bloc-vote in high percentages, and 90 percent vote Republican. The Republican Party controls the state legislature, where district lines are drawn, and a study by Allan Lichtman found that 83 percent of Cubans in Miami-Dade and Broward counties were put into majority-Hispanic House districts, compared with only 55 percent of non-Cuban Hispanics. This concentrated the votes of Cuban Hispanics, whereas the votes of non-Cuban Hispanics were more diluted.[30]

While Cuban political influence on Miami-Dade politics will continue into the foreseeable future, in neighboring Broward and Palm Beach counties, respectively, a more diverse contingent of South Americans and Puerto Ricans, as well as Cuban Americans, is being elected to office. Broward County from the 1990s–2000 was 17 percent Hispanic, compared to neighboring Miami-Dade County, where 60 percent of the population is Hispanic. Six Hispanics, from judges to city commissioners, held political office during the decade between 1990 and 2000. Many Broward residents are recent arrivals from South America. Thousands of Venezuelans, Peruvians, Argentines, and Colombians live in Broward, and many of them are more likely to tune into their home country via the internet than into local politics. Some are dual citizens and still participate in their home country politics. Others, such as Cubans and Nicaraguans, are barred from participating in home country politics. Many Central and South Americans purchase homes in South Florida as a hedge against political unrest in their home countries.[31]

By 2021, there were fifteen Hispanic elected officials in both counties combined out of 433 elected positions. This is a small percentage, far below the Hispanic population in each county, and reflects the new immigrant migration pattern, with Hispanics dispersed in multiple communities with limited density as compared to Miami and Miami-Dade County.[32]

With the numbers of Latinos moving into different areas of Florida, such as Orlando, where Puerto Ricans and other Hispanics are 38 percent of the population, and Tampa, where Hispanics are 28 percent of the population, the continued growth of Latino political power will extend beyond the Miami-Dade South Florida region to other parts of the state.

Mexican American Politics in San Antonio

The contemporary struggle for political empowerment for Mexican Americans is largely a post–World War II phenomenon. However, to understand current politics, it is necessary to look back briefly at San Antonio's history and race relations. One hundred years before the establishment of the Republic of Texas in 1836 and the state of Texas in 1845, Tejanos exercised

140 Latino Political Power

self-government through the *ayuntamiento*, a local form of government. The colonization of Spanish Texas began in 1716, and the province's first *ayuntamiento*, called San Fernando de Bexar, formed in 1731. This form of government continued into the Mexican rule of Texas, from 1821 to 1836, and its influence persisted afterward.[33] White settlers and a few Tejanos declared their independence from Mexico in 1836. Subsequently, a war of independence and eventually a war of conquest was waged by the United States against the Mexican government to gain control of the land and resources in the Southwest.

In 1837, the Republic of Texas gave San Antonio a municipal charter, under which the city formed an eight-person board of aldermen. The first councilmen all had Spanish surnames, and the mayor was Anglo. In the years following 1836, city councils were composed of a majority of Mexicans. Up to 1844 the Mexican electorate outnumbered the Anglo vote in San Antonio. In 1840 and 1842, Juan Seguin was elected as mayor; however, he was to be the last Mexican American mayor until Henry Cisneros in 1981. By 1845, European Americans had squeezed Mexican Americans out of their dominant position on the city council.[34] The Mexican elite's influence declined as the newcomers monopolized banks and commercial enterprises.[35]

In 1850, Mexican Bexareños composed 47 percent of the population; by 1880 their share had declined to 30 percent, and by 1900, the Mexican population was only 25 percent of Bexar County, where the city of San Antonio is located. From the 1880s until the 1940s, White political machines were able to maintain power through the use of patronage. World War II brought military bases to San Antonio, however, and with them came federal civil service jobs that the local political machine could not control. Mexican Americans remained marginalized from local politics.[36] As alternatives, Mexicans built strong community organizations; many of these groups were based in or had active chapters in San Antonio, including the League of United Latin American Citizens (LULAC), formed in 1929. After World War II, middle-class Latinos in San Antonio, particularly businessmen, formed ethnic chambers of commerce. Other local Mexican veterans' organizations appeared, such as the Loyal American Democrats. Civic and political groups such as the West Side Voters League and the Alamo Democrats also formed in San Antonio.[37]

Meanwhile, the Good Government League (GGL) formed in 1954, the latest in a long series of Anglo local political machines. This group was based in the city's affluent North Side. One of the organization's strengths was nominating slates of candidates for city council. In the 1955–1971 period, the GGL won seventy-seven of eighty-one seats. The council candidates "consisted primarily of Anglos (78 percent), although there were a few token Mexican Americans (one in 1955, two from 1957–1971, and three in 1971)."[38] The GGL controlled not only who got elected but, more

Political Power in the Sunbelt 141

importantly, the policy agenda. The Anglo businessmen who led the GGL controlled the city's economic development and enhanced their economic interests. Through the control that GGL held over city council seats and the selection of the city manager, they were able to determine city priorities, which included urban growth and an economy tied to the military.[39]

In 1969, the GGL began to falter as the Chicano community began to organize to challenge the at-large electoral structure of city elections and to run independent candidates from the barrio. The Committee for Barrio Betterment was formed in 1969 by Mexican American Youth Organization (MAYO) activists and Barrios Unidos, a community organization. This group was not tied to the Democratic Party machine or to the GGL, which had battled each other for electoral control for many years.[40] While not successful due to the at-large electoral system, the Committee for Barrio Betterment swept the Chicano precincts against all the GGL candidates.

From 1971 to 1975, Mexican American voters expressed their opposition to the ruling Anglo political elite by supporting Mexican American candidates not supported by the GGL over Anglo and Mexican American GGL candidates. From 1971 to 1973 the GGL's Mexican American candidates received less than half as many votes in the predominantly Mexican American precincts as they did in predominantly Anglo precincts.[41] In 1971, high voter interest in the Chicano community was sparked by a campaign for mayor by Peter Torres, who challenged the GGL candidate, John Gatti. Voter turnout climbed from 33 percent in 1969 to 53 percent in 1971, "a level of participation which has not been repeated since."[42] The 1971 election marked the beginning of the end for the GGL, as its grip on the nomination of city council members began to weaken. In 1973, several prominent GGLers broke ranks and backed other non-GGLers, and GGL-backed candidates won only four seats. Conflict among San Antonio's elites enabled new organizations and political voices to emerge.

One important independent voice that formed during this period was Citizens Organized for Public Service (COPS), which came together in 1974 to demand greater equity in city services and improvements in the barrios of the South and West Sides. COPS was initiated by Eddie Cortes, who was trained by Saul Alinksy's Industrial Areas Foundation in Chicago. He believed that for an organization to last, it must be anchored by institutions with deep ties to the community: "They discarded the PTAs as too caught up in school board politics, and settled instead on the Catholic parish networks."[43] Although COPS did not formally endorse candidates for political office, the organization worked through the Catholic parishes to conduct voter registration drives and to improve the political influence of those who had been historically locked out. According to two scholars of Mexican American politics, "The concentration of Mexicans in the Westside, and the presence of a stable community encouraged the growth of COPS and made

142   *Latino Political Power*

possible an effective voter registration program."[44] COPS became an influential independent voice that remains active in San Antonio politics today.

A beneficiary of the transition in political leadership who brought his own personal political skills was Henry Cisneros. Part of the Cisneros family had arrived in New Mexico long before the American Revolution, whereas Henry's grandfather had come from Mexico in the aftermath of the Mexican Revolution. The Cisneros family was well known and active in both Mexican and American politics. Henry Cisneros was a professor of public administration who had received his education in Ivy League universities after growing up in West San Antonio. He returned to San Antonio in 1974 and began his political career as part of the GGL slate of city council candidates in 1975. His uncle, Ruben Munguia, an influential political operative in San Antonio politics, recommended him for the GGL slate, and the GGL, desperate to find new potential leaders, nominated him. Cisneros won his seat with much assistance from the influential GGL. He ran his own campaign and at age twenty-seven became the youngest councilman in the city's history; that year he was the only GGL candidate to win without a runoff. Cisneros won the election with 52 percent of the vote. He received more votes from Anglos than Mexican Americans. For example, in heavily Spanish-surnamed precincts Cisneros received only 44 percent of the vote.[45]

Meanwhile, a recent annexation into the city had prompted a review by the US Department of Justice based on the 1975 voting rights amendment. The annexation, which added more White voters, diluted the majority status of the Mexican American population. The Justice Department indicated that unless the city changed its method of electing council members to provide equitable representation of linguistic and racial minorities, the area would have to be de-annexed.[46] The city council proposed, and voters agreed, to change the city charter to replace at-large elections with a council of ten persons elected from single-member districts and a mayor elected at large.

Cisneros joined in the successful campaign for passage of the referendum. The transition to single-member districts created potential for institutionalized independent voices from the diverse communities in San Antonio. The 1977 elections produced the first city council with a majority of racial minority members. Mexican Americans won five of the ten seats, and an additional seat was won by an African American candidate. This was a major shift, not only in the descriptive representation of the city council but in the transfer of power to a more diverse set of political leaders less tied to the traditional power brokers of the GGL. While the new commission's public policy did not radically shift away from the pro-growth policies of previous commissions, it signaled the end of the "business as usual" type of politics in the city.

Political Power in the Sunbelt   143

The 1981 elections for mayor and city council were a watershed for Mexican American politics. For the first time in the United States, a Mexican American was elected as mayor of a major city. Cisneros won a convincing victory, capturing 64 percent of the vote, with large majorities in the predominantly Mexican American precincts and an average of 43 percent of the vote in predominantly Anglo Districts 8 and 10. Cisneros relied heavily on energizing the Latino, African American, and labor votes; the San Antonio Teachers Council, for example, ran his phone bank operation. Cisneros was an effective ethnic candidate who relied on his West Side base of support and won in eight of the ten city council districts. He was defeated only in Districts 8 and 10, which were majority White.

When Cisneros vacated his council seat to seek the office of mayor in 1981, a less well-known but equally important political effort unfolded. A group of local Chicana activists established an informal group to discuss running a Chicana for the city council seat, and they nominated Maria Berriozábal to run. The Chicana activists backed Berriozábal during a difficult campaign, and she went on to win election as the first Mexican American woman to serve on the city council. Her victory was viewed as a victory for all Chicanas. Berriozábal's election grew out of a collective process, and she brought a new style of politics that included empowerment for the neighborhoods she represented. She was known for bringing people she represented to the council chambers to speak for themselves, which was her definition of providing leadership.[47] Berriozábal's victory signaled the emergence of a Chicana movement capable of electing its own candidates, and it demonstrated the electoral potential of Latinas nationwide. Similar efforts took place to elect Gloria Molina to the California State Assembly from Los Angeles in the early 1980s.

During his time as mayor, Cisneros governed from the center with a pro-growth economic development philosophy, but he did not alienate his Chicano and Mexican constituency as he addressed issues of jobs, education, and improving neighborhoods. Mayor Cisneros supported major development projects, including the Alamodome sports arena, and annexation and tax breaks for the Sea World and Fiesta Texas theme parks. His administration lasted until 1989, when he decided not to run again.

The personal politics of Cisneros did not translate into another Mexican American winning the mayor's seat. Former mayor Lila Cockrell, who was not Latina, succeeded him. The Cockrell victory signaled maintenance of the business-development philosophy in the city. Cockrell left after two years, and Mexican American council member Berriozábal ran for mayor in 1991. Berriozábal lost in a runoff, and a Mexican American would not wage a serious contest to win the mayor's seat for another ten years. Not until 1995 did Mexican Americans regain five seats on the city council, capturing the

144   *Latino Political Power*

sixth seat in 1997. Then, for the first time, the descriptive representation on the council reflected the city's Mexican population.

Post-Cisneros Era

In 2000, San Antonio was America's eighth-largest city; 58 percent of the population was Latino, and roughly 34 percent of registered voters had Spanish surnames. Ed Garza, District 7 council member, announced his candidacy for mayor in late November 2000. As Bruce Davidson of the *Express News* saw his chances, "To become the city's second Hispanic mayor in modern times, Garza must energize the West Side while attracting a healthy percentage of the North Side's votes."[48] San Antonio's West Side is predominately Latino, and the North Side is predominately Anglo.

Garza had grown up in the city's Jefferson neighborhood, then a mixed Anglo and Mexican American middle-class area. He became active in the local neighborhood association as a teenager and then went on to graduate from Texas A&M University with an undergraduate degree in landscape architecture and a master's in urban planning.[49] He worked as an aide for one San Antonio council member and subsequently worked for state representative Pete Gallego. In 1997, at age thirty, he won a seat on the San Antonio City Council representing District 7.[50] After serving two terms, Garza had his sights on the mayor's office. In 2001, Garza faced Councilman Tim Bannwolf, representing District 9, for mayor of San Antonio. The race came to involve questions more of personality and style than of policy substance. Garza stressed neighborhood services and infrastructure, while Bannwolf stressed his commitment to job growth and education. Each was aided by the backing of one or another segment of the city's business leadership.[51] In late spring of 2001, Garza won the mayor's office with 59.2 percent of the vote, compared with Bannwolf's 29 percent.[52]

At the age of thirty-two, as San Antonio's second Mexican American mayor, Ed Garza parlayed his experience as an architect for a development firm to secure business community support. The pro-growth interests that heavily influence politics and economic decisionmaking in the city did not view him as a threat. According to one observer, "San Antonio's electorate is very divided in racial and ethnic terms. Anglo districts vote for Anglos; Hispanics vote for Hispanics."[53] Even though Mexican Americans are the majority population, an Anglo can more easily win a mayoral election because Anglos are usually more likely to vote than Mexican Americans. Mexican American candidates must cross over and appeal to Anglos to win an election.[54]

In contrast to Cisneros, who had campaigned heavily in the Latino community, Garza campaigned less in the Mexican neighborhoods and more in the heavily Anglo North Side communities, as he counted on winning the support of the Mexican American community. A study by the

Political Power in the Sunbelt 145

William C. Velásquez Institute found that nearly 97 percent of Latino registered voters cast their vote for Garza, while only 52 percent of Whites voted for him. Latinos represented 60 percent of Garza's total support and 36.6 percent of the total votes cast, though they make up nearly 59 percent of the city's population.

While Los Angeles voters chose to elect an Anglo Democrat for mayor in 2001, San Antonio voters, both Mexican American and White, supported a Mexican American candidate. It appears that even in a city with a long history of marginalizing Mexican Americans and deeply racialized voting patterns, a Mexican American candidate who can appeal to both Mexican and White voters can succeed in citywide elections. The electoral victories of Cisneros and Garza demonstrate the power of different types of crossover candidates.

Like other San Antonio mayors before him, Garza faced divisive issues well outside his agenda. His most challenging issues presented themselves early in his tenure. The Lumbermen's Investment Corporation announced plans to develop a 2,800-acre golf resort, the "PGA Village," on the North Side over the aquifer recharge zone, just beyond the city limits; it would use special state legislation to create a "conservation and improvement district" that would capture all the property, sales, and hotel taxes in the district to pay for public improvements.[55] The city council initially supported the special district, but over the fall, the proposed resort turned into a heated controversy over the loss of tax revenue, the potential threat to the city's water supply, and the appeal of gaining the national visibility of a Professional Golfers' Association (PGA) resort.[56] Garza sought to find a compromise that included greater environmental protections, together with a commitment to a living-wage agreement to satisfy COPS. But after the council approved the development agreement by a 9–2 vote, local environmentalists who organized as the Smart Growth Coalition joined COPS in a petition campaign to put the resort project agreement on the ballot.[57] By June 2002, the coalition had collected over 77,000 signatures, enough to force a November vote. The Lumbermen's Investment Corporation was unwilling to see a vote and withdrew the project from city review, effectively killing it.[58]

The PGA saga exemplified some realities of the post-Cisneros era. Although the mayor continued to play the role of chief jobs promoter, he was seriously hampered by the four-year maximum imposed by term limits. Major deals, particularly if they provoked the long-standing divide between the city's North and South Sides, could not be readily managed even in two mayoral or council terms. And as before, success in winning a mayoral election did not necessarily translate into a capacity to win public approval for a project or a proposal at the polls.

In early 2002, Garza faced a serious problem with his city council colleagues: corruption. In October of that year, the FBI had arrested two city council members, a lobbyist and a local lawyer, on bribery charges, and a third

146   *Latino Political Power*

member pleaded guilty to misusing campaign funds for personal purposes.[59] The arrests were a deep embarrassment to the mayor and the city. However, the mayor, who, as the *San Antonio Express News* editorialized, had "been in no way personally tainted by the scandal that hit City Hall like a bomb," managed an easy reelection victory in May 2003 with 68.3 percent of the vote, boosted in part by the February 2003 announcement that Toyota would build a major truck manufacturing plant to employ some 2,000 on the city's South Side.[60] The most telling commentary, however, was the turnout of just 5.5 percent.[61]

The public's assessment of city hall was further sullied three months later when overt conflict broke out between a majority of council members and the city manager, Terry Brechtel, ultimately ending in her firing.[62] The origins of this conflict were born out of the relationship between Garza and Brechtel, who came into office together. Brechtel was appointed two months prior to Garza's election. One of Garza's first acts as mayor was suffused with the kind of negative symbolism no public official should aspire to upon taking office.[63] He ordered a door built to shut off the mayor's office from the city manager's office in what, for years, had been an open suite, leading many to believe there was an internal conflict. This strained relationship came to a head when Garza summoned Brechtel to city hall one night at 10:30 p.m. and calmly asked her to resign, claiming that "he had enough votes to get rid of her. Calmly she said she wouldn't."[64] At that time, city hall observers, including former leaders, pointed out that this feud was another "black eye" for a city still reeling from the bribery convictions of two former councilmen.[65] One local columnist summed up Garza's mayoral tenure as follows: "Garza was not a bad mayor. What he was, was an extremely bad leader and communicator."[66] It was a modest legacy for an individual once touted as the "next Henry Cisneros."

The May 2001 election that brought Ed Garza to the mayor's office also saw the election of his replacement representing District 7. From a field of six, Julián Castro won the seat with 61 percent of the vote. Castro, at age twenty-six, was the youngest council member in the city's history. He and his twin brother, Joaquin, had been raised in an intensely political home environment. Their mother, Rosie, had worked for the Mexican American Unity Council, had run for city council as part of the Committee for Barrio Betterment in 1971, and had later chaired the Bexar County Raza Unida Party.[67] Growing up in the tumult of West Side politics, the twins were clearly primed for public service careers. At Stanford University, Julián wrote his senior honors thesis on the mayoralty of Henry Cisneros, before completing a law degree at Harvard and beginning a legal career in San Antonio.[68]

Over a year before Garza's second term ended, incumbent council members began to position themselves for the mayoral contest in May

2005. The early contenders were District 7's Julián Castro and Carroll Schubert from District 9. Schubert was aided by early support from development interests who viewed him as a pro-growth, low-tax conservative. Castro, in contrast, had won the opposition of many in the business community for his vote against the PGA project.[69] A small group of local businesspeople, including *Express News* publisher Larry Walker, sought an alternative candidate to Castro and Schubert, someone with both experience and no attachment to the city council.[70]

The 2005 election began as a three-man race between Castro, Schubert, and Phil Hardberger, a recently retired chief justice of the Fourth Court of Appeals with no city council experience. He was Walker's candidate. Hardberger's decision to run for mayor in early 2004 was somewhat of a surprise to the general public because no one without a city council background had been elected mayor of San Antonio in modern history. In the spring of 2004, Hardberger met with *San Antonio Express News* associate editorial page editor Bruce Davidson. Any candidate desiring to run for mayor met with San Antonio editorial staff. The essence of Hardberger's message in the meeting with Davidson was "I'm running for mayor. See you in October."[71] The following day, Hardberger set sail for the East Coast in his forty-two-foot trawler. Hardberger had essentially skipped out on fund-raising and campaigning until the fall of 2004. This left the other candidates wondering if his bid was serious. Upon his return, Hardberger took out a personal loan of $300,000, and just like that, he became a serious contender for the office of mayor.[72]

In the spring of 2005, Castro and Hardberger moved on to the runoff, winning 42 and 30 percent of the vote, respectively. Schubert, a four-year council veteran and active Republican, was eliminated from the race. Winning only 26 percent of the vote, he finished in third place. It is important to note, however, that a mere 17.7 percent of eligible voters cast ballots in the May race.[73] Shortly after the general election, Schubert endorsed Hardberger; his business supporters and their dollars followed. An overwhelming 90 percent of Schubert voters supported Hardberger; 77 percent of Schubert supporters were White. Turnout in this election was the highest in precincts where Latinos comprise less than one-third of the population and lowest in precincts where Latinos were a majority of registered voters.[74]

In the May race, among Whites, 79 percent cast their ballot for a co-ethnic: 35 percent voted for Schubert, and 44 percent voted for Hardberger. Castro won only 20 percent of the White vote. In the initial May race, Latinos voted 72 percent for Castro, 16 percent for Hardberger, and 9 percent for Schubert.[75] Typically, runoff elections have a lower turnout than general elections. The opposite was true here. Turnout increased by 15,760 votes, an overall total of 1 percent but a 14 percent increase over the previous race. The increased turnout was significant in several ways. Schubert voters, who

148 *Latino Political Power*

were overwhelmingly Republican and conservative, did indeed return to the polls to support a candidate with a well-established association with liberal causes and Democratic Party politics.[76] Not only did the Schubert supporters show up to vote, but so did more than 15,000 additional voters who had not participated in the election just one month before, bringing the total turnout to 18.8 percent. All of that said, turnout in the runoff was still quite low. In terms of ethnicity and turnout, over half of Latino supermajority precincts (66 percent or more) turned out to vote at a rate of 16 percent or less. In two-thirds of the precincts where Latinos comprised less than 25 percent of registered voters, turnout was at 17 percent and above.[77] The turnout increased in Latino-majority precincts but did not match the increase in White voter turnout.

In the two-man race, 73 percent of Latino voters supported Castro, and 79 percent of Whites supported Hardberger. Particularly striking were the overwhelming conservative and Republican levels of support for Hardberger, given his clear pattern of solidly Democrat and liberal identification.[78] Many liberal establishment voices endorsed and contributed to Hardberger; among them were high-profile Democrats, including former congressman Ciro Rodriguez, union advocates Jaime Martinez and Rosa Rosales, State Senator Leticia Van de Putte, and Congressman Charles Gonzalez.

In terms of partisan identification, ideology, and vote choices, Latinos were less cohesive than Whites. In this race they voted overwhelmingly in support of the same candidate with strong ties to the Democratic Party. Thirty five percent of the city's Hispanic voters, a significant break from past voting, was enough to elect the seventy-year-old Phil Hardberger mayor of a city where 59 percent of residents were Hispanic. "Hispanic voters find it easier now to look beyond skin color."[79] Both Cisneros and the city's outgoing mayor, Ed Garza, had won significantly larger shares of the Hispanic vote than Castro was able to command. Hardberger won with 51.1 percent of the vote and a margin of fewer than 4,000 votes out of nearly 130,000 cast.[80] In a race that close, many factors were seen as decisive. But one surely was that Hispanic voters departed from the past practice of giving near-unanimous support to the Hispanic candidate. Castro was unable to hold together the Hispanic vote because Hardberger had long-standing ties with the Mexican American community. Hardberger, as a former judge and lawyer, had represented Hispanic causes in Texas courts. Castro was a Stanford- and Harvard-educated lawyer elected to the city council at age twenty-six. Rodolfo Rosales, political scientist at the University of Texas, San Antonio, said, "The race was decided by political alignments, not racial or ethnic divisions. The Anglo vote did bloc vote. But this time there was enough Mexican American votes to make the difference."[81] Hardberger said he was able to grab as much as one-third of the Mexican American vote because those voters were willing to look past skin color.

Political Power in the Sunbelt 149

"I have a long history of working for Hispanic causes, and that's how I was able to get a third of their vote."[82]

When Hardberger was reelected in 2007, Castro positioned himself as the leading candidate for office in 2009. He told *San Antonio Express News* editor Bruce Davidson in June 2007, "We came close in 2005. I have spent the last two years building bridges with folks who did not support my campaign in 2005."[83] With Castro's mayoral bid nearly certain, the more relevant question was who would oppose him. In the fall of 2008, public relations executive Trish DeBerry emerged as a contender. However, she had no previous electoral experience and little name recognition citywide. In the end Castro won with 56.2 percent of the vote, while DeBerry garnered 29 percent. Turnout was just 11.6 percent of registered voters.[84]

The policy questions Castro faced in his first few weeks in office were somewhat different from his personal agenda. The city-owned utility CPS Energy proposed expanding the South Texas Nuclear Plant to serve growing energy needs. The cost for more nuclear energy was estimated to be $5 billion, likely forcing an increase in electricity rates.[85] Castro sought a middle ground, but CPS's management provided him with a unique opportunity. A leak from CPS revealed that the cost estimate was significantly higher than initially stated. Public confidence in the utility's management and the city's oversight was shaken. In the end, Castro forced out the CPS board chair and promised a new direction.[86] He used his limited authority but high public visibility to both shape a policy and appear to be a strong leader. He was emulating Henry Cisneros.

In fact, Castro's leadership style and public relations mirrored Henry Cisneros mayoral tenure. In 2010, Castro created SA2020, modeled after Cisneros's Target '90 effort. SA2020 included a broad section of the San Antonio community and was tied to specific goals—in arts and culture, downtown development, education, government accountability, and transportation—to be monitored and reported on. With SA2020, Castro was committed to rebuilding downtown San Antonio.[87] This broad coalitional support of various members in the community signaled the affirmative to both developers and central-area property owners, promoting both new construction and adaptive residential reuse in former industrialized zones and gentrification in some older neighborhoods.

In late 2010, Castro also unveiled plans for a "brainpower initiative," using a city sales tax increase to aid some facets of local education.[88] With SA2020 and the focus on local education, Castro positioned himself for reelection. In May 2011 he drew no substantive opposition and won with 81.4 percent of the vote.[89] The brain power initiative or task force focused solely on early childhood education with a program dubbed "Pre-K for SA." The prekindergarten program was designed to offer full-day pre-K classes for eligible four-year-olds.[90] It also targeted economically

150 *Latino Political Power*

disadvantaged students. In short, it was designed to appeal to a local electorate (particularly more affluent North Siders) that might be reluctant to embrace another sales tax increase.

The vote on the Pre-K tax in November 2012 proved a victory for Castro and his policy vision. Pre-K won with 53.6 percent of the vote. Even before the successful Pre-K vote, Castro had emerged on the national political scene.[91] At the 2012 Democratic National Convention, he served as the keynote speaker, which provided him the opportunity to tell his personal story and position himself as an up-and-coming Democratic politico.[92]

Castro easily won the May 2013 mayoral contest and his third term with 66.5 percent of the vote.[93] And as he became more visible in national Democratic politics during 2013, some local issues began to emerge as overtly conflictual.[94] Within a few months of his election, rumors surfaced that he was being considered for a cabinet position in President Obama's administration. News broke in mid-May 2014 that Mayor Castro would be nominated by President Obama as the next Housing and Urban Development secretary. Castro followed the path of Henry Cisneros in taking this cabinet position, which offered him greater executive experience and opportunity for national visibility. It also allowed him to sidestep growing controversial local issues. In 2019, he launched his campaign for the 2020 Democratic nomination for president of the United States. He dropped out of the presidential race in January 2020.

Julián's twin brother, Joaquin, also had political aspirations. He ran for Texas House of Representatives from the 125th District in San Antonio in 2002. In the Democratic primary, he defeated incumbent representative Arthur Reyna by 64 to 36 percent.[95] Political observers attributed Castro's victory to a combination of name identity and grassroots campaigning. Castro and his operatives engaged in extensive door-to-door campaigning efforts. In the general election, he defeated Republican nominee Nelson Balido by 60 to 40 percent. He was twenty-eight at the time of his election.[96] In 2004, he was reelected unopposed.[97] In 2006, he was reelected to a third term, defeating Balido by 58 to 39 percent. Two years later, in 2008, he was reelected to a fourth term unopposed. In 2010, he was reelected to a fifth term, defeating Libertarian Jeffrey Blunt by 78 to 22 percent.[98]

In June 2011, Castro announced his candidacy for Texas's newly drawn 35th Congressional District's seat in the US House of Representatives. Initially, he was set to challenge fellow Democrat and nine-term incumbent Lloyd Doggett, whose home in Austin had been drawn to include San Antonio, in the Democratic primary.[99] Doggett had received support from the Democratic Party over Castro. Within a few weeks of his announcement, Castro received a call from Congressman Charlie Gonzalez of the neighboring 20th District, which is nestled into San Antonio, that he was going to retire. On November 28, after Gonzalez publicly announced his retirement after seven terms, Castro announced that he would run instead for the 20th District seat. This was the second time in over fifty-seven years that the state's District 20 congressional seat had opened up.[100] The first was in 1997, when Henry B. Gonzalez became ill and announced that he planned to step down; the second was in 2011, when Gonzalez's son and successor, Charlie, decided not to seek an eighth term in office. Castro was unopposed in the Democratic primary, all but assuring him of winning the general election in this heavily Democratic, Hispanic-majority district. In November 2012, Castro defeated Republican nominee David Rosa by 64 to 34 percent, becoming only the fifth person to represent this district since its creation in 1935.[101] The Castro brothers were coming into their own as political players in San Antonio.

Garza and the Castro brothers were a leading force in Latino political incorporation. San Antonio voters illustrated that Latino political behavior cannot be generalized from the city politics of Los Angeles, Denver, or Miami. Unique political and demographic dynamics shape local politics and history.

Latino Political Incorporation in Los Angeles

In contrast to Cuban Americans' rapid rise to political incorporation in Miami-Dade County, the rise to power of Mexican Americans in Los Angeles has been a long, slow process. Unlike the new refugee population arriving with both economic and political resources, the Mexican population in Los Angeles has had a visible presence since the 1700s. Mexicans actually provided the political leadership for the city until the mid-1800s. Unlike the Cuban refugees, who were provided with various government assistance programs upon arrival, Mexicans in Los Angeles were ignored by the federal and local governments and forced to live in segregated neighborhoods in the eastern portion of the city and in unincorporated East Los Angeles. A manipulation of boundaries between city and county residents divided the population in half and weakened the political strength of the Mexican American community. This artificial political division was part of a much larger political disenfranchisement of Mexicans in the east side area and throughout the state. District boundaries for state assembly and senate seats divided barrios into safe seats for White incumbents, while the political establishment largely marginalized Mexican Americans.[102]

The contemporary political incorporation of Latinos in Los Angeles began after World War II, with East Side community activist Edward Roybal's election to the Los Angeles City Council in 1949. Roybal held that office until 1962, when he ran and won a seat in Congress from the East Los Angeles area. That same year the city council seats were reapportioned, and East Los Angeles was divided among seven council districts. One scholar noted, "As a result of this fragmentation, Latinos could not be a

152   *Latino Political Power*

majority in any one of the city's fifteen districts, although they heavily populated seven of the council's fifteen districts."[103] Although Roybal sought to have another Latino appointed to fill his unexpired term, he was the only racial minority on the city council, and African Americans successfully lobbied the council to appoint Gilbert Lindsey to this seat. Lindsey then became the city's first African American officeholder.[104]

From 1962 to 1985, no Mexicans or other Latinos were elected to city council or citywide offices in Los Angeles. This period was politically volatile, and the lack of elected local leadership weakened the influence of Latinos in city politics. Latino political influence in Los Angeles grew, however, at the federal and state levels. In addition to Congressman Roybal, two Mexican Americans elected to the state assembly, Richard Alatorre (1972) and Art Torres (1974), were the other Latino elected officials from the Los Angeles area in the pre-1980s period. These elected officials not only had to represent the interests of their constituents at the state and federal levels but also became the de facto political leaders of California's whole Mexican American community because they were the only Latinos elected to state and federal office at the time. By all accounts, the local political incorporation of Latinos during this period was low.

The gerrymandering of Los Angeles–area political districts to limit the political participation of Mexican Americans, combined with their historically low voting rates, made it extremely difficult to elect a Mexican American to the city council. In the vacuum of leadership, outsider groups such as the La Raza Unida Party (LRUP) challenged the dominance of the two-party system and sought to establish their own electoral base in the early 1970s in the Los Angeles area. The LRUP ran a candidate for a state assembly seat in East Los Angeles, and although unsuccessful, this bid demonstrated that at least a segment of the Mexican American community was willing to consider third-party candidates. In 1974, the City Terrace chapter of the LRUP unsuccessfully led a campaign to incorporate East Los Angeles as a city. Unincorporated East Los Angeles included over 100,000 residents, more than 90 percent of them Mexican. Real estate and business interests that opposed the incorporation effort defeated this effort, and the Mexican American community remained politically weak.[105]

Meanwhile, in the city of Los Angeles during the 1970s and 1980s, a biracial coalition was being forged between White liberals and African Americans. African American Tom Bradley was elected to city council in 1963, lost a racially charged mayoral race in 1969, and won the mayor's seat in 1973. He held this office for twenty years, retiring in 1993. While working-class Latinos were strong supporters of Bradley, the Latino community was at best a junior partner in this coalition and received only limited policy rewards and a few notable appointments to positions in the Bradley administration. Latinos were largely viewed as uninterested in politics. They had very low voter turnouts in city elections, and their voices and votes did not play a major role in Los Angeles politics until the 1980s.

Furthermore, as noted, a large percentage of the Latino population lived in unincorporated East Los Angeles, which bordered the eastern portion of the city. These residents of Los Angeles County were unable to vote in city elections. Between the 1960s and 1980s, Latinos were heavily concentrated in two council districts, the ninth and fourteenth. Gilbert Lindsey held the 9th District council seat until he died in office in 1990. He had held this seat for twenty-seven years, and when it became vacant, another African American, Rita Walters, was appointed to fill it.

Two Anglo politicians held the 14th District from 1943 to 1985. This district included the heavily Latino East Los Angeles and the largely White Eagle Rock neighborhood. While numerically it had a smaller number of residents, it turned out a higher number of voters, thus perpetuating Anglo rule on the East Side. Art Snyder held the seat from 1967 to 1985, when he resigned after defeating a strong challenge by community activist Steve Rodriguez in the 1983 council race, then surviving a recall effort in 1984. While East LA was in turmoil from the late 1960s into the 1970s, with the walkouts of tens of thousands of Latino high school and junior high school students in 1968, the Chicano Moratorium Against the Vietnam War in 1970, and numerous other struggles, Latinos were forced to operate in a political system in which each city council seat represented 200,000 people. Without strong financing, it was not possible to challenge incumbents who could afford to mount door-to-door campaigns and mail out campaign literature. Also, many residents were not yet citizens, and many of those who were citizens did not vote. So, Snyder retained the 14th District council seat for eighteen years, only adding to the frustration and powerlessness of Los Angeles Latinos.

Meanwhile, African Americans in the city were more successful than Latinos in winning political representation, city jobs, and appointed positions.[106] While African Americans were able to win three of the fifteen city council seats, Latinos had no representatives on the council from 1962 to 1985. In 1985, however, Mexican American state assemblyman Richard Alatorre gave up his seat to seek the city council position vacated by Snyder. He was elected in the overwhelmingly Latino 14th District twenty-three years after Roybal had left the council.[107]

Alatorre held this seat until 1999. After he decided not to seek reelection in 1999, then mayor Tom Bradley appointed him to the Los Angeles Regional Transportation Commission, the forerunner of the Los Angeles County Metropolitan Transportation Authority (MTA). Alatorre became the first MTA chairperson and led the successful approval of the Gold Line, which extended light rail into East Los Angeles.[108]

In 1986, as a result of a federal lawsuit contesting the 1982 reapportionment of district lines, an additional Latino district was created, resulting

154 *Latino Political Power*

in the election of Gloria Molina to the city council in 1987. The emergence of Molina and Alatorre in the 1980s reflected not the simple addition of Brown faces to the Black and White biracial coalition but the importance of the use of legal challenges and political recruitment networks by Latinos. Alatorre had emerged as a legislative aide to a non-Latino assembly member in the 1960s, and by 1972 he had won a seat in the assembly in an increasingly Latino district. In 1982, he was placed in charge of the assembly committee responsible for reapportionment. Most of the Latinos holding significant elected positions in the early 1980s gathered in a meeting and decided whom to support for various positions that would become available following reapportionment.

Two legislative aides sought support of the group for the state assembly seat vacated by Alatorre's move to the city council in 1982. Richard Polanco, an aide to Alatorre, and Gloria Molina, then an aide to assembly member Art Torres, competed against each other in the Democratic primary. Molina won the primary and then the general election. At this point Molina became the first of a number of Mexican American women to run and win office in Los Angeles. In 1986, Molina again challenged the Chicano political establishment by not supporting its candidate for the seat vacated by Alatorre, who had won election to the Los Angeles City Council. In 1987, Molina decided to run for another seat, the vacated District 1 council position. She bested the Alatorre-supported candidate handily and was now well positioned to achieve an even more significant electoral post.

Molina, the daughter of a farmworker, had worked in the Jimmy Carter administration in the 1970s; she built a grassroots base of young and working-class Chicanas into a strong electoral machine. As an outsider, Molina challenged the Anglo-Black political establishment and the old-boy network of Chicano officials.[109] In the 1980s and early 1990s, the Alatorre and Molina camps put up rival candidates for almost every local election in the Los Angeles area. The recruitment networks provided money, resources, expertise, and campaign workers. Only a rival network could effectively compete with this level of campaign organization.[110]

In addition to the lawsuit charging malapportionment of city council districts, another lawsuit filed by the Department of Justice and the Mexican American Legal Defense and Education Fund challenged Los Angeles County's 1981 reapportionment plan, which combined heavily Latino districts with White-dominant communities to dilute the Latino vote. The five members of the Los Angeles Board of Supervisors served a population of 8.5 million people and controlled a budget of over $13 billion in 1990. A Mexican had not been elected to this board for 115 years. In June 1990, a US district court ruled in *Garza v. County of Los Angeles* that the supervisors had violated the federal Voting Rights Act. New district lines were drawn to create a district that was 71 percent Latino. In a 1991 election,

Political Power in the Sunbelt 155

Los Angeles City Council member Molina was elected to the LA County Board of Supervisors after a hard-fought campaign against three other Latinos, including her former boss, Art Torres.[111]

When Molina left the city council to run for the Los Angeles County Board of Supervisors, a seat opened up on the Los Angeles City Council. Mike Hernandez won the endorsement of Supervisor Molina and was elected to office in 1991, defeating an Alatorre-backed opponent. The growing influence of Molina acted as a counterbalance to the more entrenched Alatorre forces. In addition to redistricting at the local government level, reapportionment for congressional districts occurred following the 1990 census. In the newly redrawn 30th Congressional District, the conflict between the Molina and Alatorre forces continued as longtime representative Edward Roybal resigned and both sides put up candidates. The Molina-backed candidate, assembly member, Xavier Becerra, went on to win the contest. In the nearby, newly created 25th Congressional District, Roybal's daughter, Lucille Roybal-Allard, won easily and became the first Mexican American congresswoman.

The 1990 reapportionment brought a dramatic increase in the number of Latinos elected to office in the Los Angeles area. The redistricting of the 7th District created the conditions to elect a third Latino to the city council. As Latino numbers continued to grow, other groups felt a corresponding decline in their political influence. In 1994, another Latino, Richard Alarcón, was elected to the city council from the northeast San Fernando Valley. Alarcón held this position for four years before he left to run for state senator in 1998. His razor-close election to this state senate seat showed the growing influence of Latinos in the San Fernando Valley section of the city and county of Los Angeles. For the first time, a Latino held a seat traditionally held by an Anglo. Perhaps more significantly, Alarcón won his election by defeating a prominent and well-funded former assembly member, Richard Katz. Alarcón's ability to turn out new Latino voters demonstrated how they could be mobilized. Spurred by his get-out-the-vote effort, Latino participation doubled, rising from 6 percent of the primary voters in the district in 1994 to 12 percent in 1998.[112] Alarcón's victory was in part prompted by the rapid growth in the Latino population in the San Fernando Valley, which had reached 27 percent of the total valley population; in some parts of the northeast valley, Latinos became the majority population.

After Alarcón vacated his city council seat, twenty-six-year-old Alex Padilla won a hard-fought campaign in 1999, defeating the candidate backed by the Los Angeles labor movement and Alarcón. Padilla, the son of Mexican immigrants, had returned from college on the East Coast and gotten involved in local politics. The Padilla race was preceded by the 1996 election of Tony Cardenas to the 20th Assembly District seat in the same part of the San Fernando Valley. Padilla worked for Cardenas and in turn

156 *Latino Political Power*

had his support for his own race. These two developed a stance of independence from the East Side political machines. They were tied neither to the Molina forces nor to any other East Side forces. This represents a growth in Latino political power in another section of the city and county of Los Angeles and enhanced the overall presence of Latinos in political power in the region.

Two other electoral campaigns provide further evidence of a diversity of views and a jockeying for electoral positions among Latinos, reflecting the growing sophistication, intergenerational conflicts, and political influence of Latinos in Los Angeles: the 2001 race for mayor and the 2003 race for the 14th District of the Los Angeles City Council. The 2001 race for LA mayor demonstrated that the Latino community is not monolithic, as it initially backed different Latino candidates, Antonio Villaraigosa and Xavier Becerra, who competed in the general primary. Villaraigosa obtained the largest vote total, but not 50 percent, in the nonpartisan primary and so was forced into a runoff with the next highest vote-getter, City Attorney James Hahn.

While most Latinos backed Villaraigosa's candidacy, then assembly member Tony Cardenas and council member Padilla did not support him in either the general contest or the runoff, instead backing Hahn, an Anglo. Hahn was also endorsed by Richard Polanco, the former state senator who had lost to Gloria Molina in the 1982 state assembly contest that launched her electoral career. Polanco and the two San Fernando Valley officeholders were the most prominent Latinos to support the opponent of Villaraigosa.

In the runoff, Villaraigosa did very well among Latinos, garnering 82 percent of the vote, but he was unsuccessful in securing the majority of White and Black votes and lost to Hahn. While Latinos comprised nearly

Table 6.2 Exit Poll Results for Los Angeles Mayor in 2001 (percentage)

	All Voters	Hahn	Villaraigosa
Total	100	54	46
White voters	52	59	41
Black voters	17	80	20
Latino voters	22	18	82
Asian voters	6	65	35
Liberals	49	41	59
Moderates	29	62	38
Conservatives	22	73	27

Source: Los Angeles Times 2001.

50 percent of the population in Los Angeles in 2000, they were only 22 percent of the voters (see Table 6.2).

The final vote total showed that moderate and conservative voters, African Americans, and San Fernando Valley voters were more inclined to support the liberal White Democrat, Hahn, who was viewed as tough on crime. Hahn won a decisive 80 percent of the Black vote for several reasons. First, he had longtime family ties to the African American community, something that Villaraigosa did not have. His father was the longtime county supervisor for the area and had helped mentor a number of senior African American leaders there. African American politicians decided en masse, except for one prominent leader, to back Hahn in exchange for Hahn's continued support of African American police chief Bernard Parks. In the aftermath of the 1992 LA riots, police-community relations had been poor; Parks rose to become police chief in 1997 and had strong backing in the African American community.[113] Another reason for Villaraigosa's defeat, according to some observers, was Hahn's use of negative campaign materials that trafficked in racial stereotypes, including a last-minute campaign ad that criticized Villaraigosa for supporting amnesty for a drug dealer and linked his image with the use of crack cocaine.

However, the raw numbers in Los Angeles politics overrode any other factor at play in the mayor's race. Latinos made up 46.5 percent of the population but were not an equivalent percentage of the voters. The Latino electoral participation has been rising rapidly, from 8 percent in the 1993 mayoral election to 22 percent in 2001, but it remains far below a level commensurate with the Latino population. Again, part of the reason is that Latinos are a young population, with a sizable number still too young to vote. The other factor is a high proportion of noncitizens, including undocumented persons who reside in the city.

Beyond victory or defeat in this particular election, a significant potential ally for some Latino politicians emerged. Villaraigosa was a former union organizer, and he won the backing of the Los Angeles labor movement, which was growing and energized. The Los Angeles County Federation of Labor, an effective, well-organized political machine with more than 800,000 members in 350 local unions at the time, was then under the leadership of Miguel Contreras, a former United Farm Workers organizer. The federation voted to back Villaraigosa and put hundreds of its members into the streets to help elect him, even after several union locals with large numbers of African Americans had decided to back Hahn. The federation is a very influential labor council and has helped elect local, state, and federal officials who support labor's agenda.

The building of a labor-Latino alliance in Los Angeles represents a convergence of shared agendas by two rapidly growing segments of the population. Organized labor, unlike the national decline in union strength in

158 *Latino Political Power*

many places, has been growing in Los Angeles County. More importantly, the LA County Labor Federation has brought together various unions from the public and private sectors, predominantly those representing immigrants, to work to elect labor-friendly candidates, many of them Latino. The Latino population is also heavily immigrant and working-class, as well as increasingly unionized. Many are becoming citizens and registering to vote.

In the city of Los Angeles in 2001, union leader Contreras estimated that 175,000 union members were registered to vote and that 31 percent of them were Latino.[114] While these numbers are not large enough to swing a citywide election by themselves, in combination with other allies they can have a decisive impact on a city council, state assembly or senate, or congressional race. The changing demographics, the increase in Latino voters, and the strategic alliance between Latinos and the burgeoning labor movement played a significant role in elections in the Los Angeles area, helping to shape positions on such critical issues as affordable housing, living wages, and economic development in the neighborhoods.

In addition to the mayor's race, four additional Latinos were elected to the city council, including Eric Garcetti (District 13) and Ed Reyes (District 1) in 2001 and Tony Cardenas (District 6) and Antonio Villaraigosa (District 14) in 2003. By 2003, then, with Padilla, five of the fifteen Los Angeles City Council members, or one-third, were Latinos. While Latinos had a growing influence on a council on which they had no members as recently as 1984, they were not necessarily united on all issues. These differences reflect the reality that these officeholders had risen to office in different parts of the city, with different constituencies and political influences. The diversity indicates that the dominant political machines of the 1980s and early 1990s no longer exist in the same fashion; nor do they control the political fates of Latino politicians. Others have important influence as well, including the San Fernando Valley politicians, East Los Angeles County politicians, Latino Congress members, and new political leaders, many of whom are women. With the establishment of term limits in California politics, the jockeying for positions, particularly in the heavily Latino Los Angeles County, is constant and relentless, and at times it overshadows the important problems that need to be addressed in the community.

The ongoing conflicts that erupted within the Latino community in 2001 were again evident in the 2003 race for the 14th City Council District seat. The race pitted Los Angeles City Council member Nick Pacheco against Antonio Villaraigosa. Pacheco had won his seat in 1999 in a crowded field seeking to replace Richard Alatorre, who had decided not to run for reelection after holding office for fourteen years. Pacheco did not win the support of Gloria Molina and State Senator Richard Polanco in his first run for office, so had built alliances instead with Los Angeles mayor Richard Riordan and Congressman Xavier Becerra. When Becerra ran for mayor in

2001, Pacheco backed him. When Pacheco came up for reelection in 2003, he had Becerra's and ex-mayor Riordan's support. However, in a two-person race, Villaraigosa, who also had strong ties to the district, more political endorsements, and an effective get-out-the-vote operation, won 56 percent of the vote and defeated Pacheco.

After being elected to the city council, Villaraigosa built alliances with fellow council members, including Martin Ludlow, an African American, who worked on Villaraigosa's staff in the California State Assembly and later became the LA County Labor Federation's political director. Ludlow won his city council race at the same time Villaraigosa won his city council seat. Villaraigosa also drew on the citywide connections that he built in his 2001 campaign for mayor to run again in 2005. He further expanded his base of support in the African American community by gaining the support of Karen Bass, a former community organizer from South Los Angeles who won a California State Assembly seat in 2004. Bass supported Villaraigosa in 2005 for mayor, as did several other prominent Black community leaders. Villaraigosa was able to build support from his base and network in the Latino community and expand his support with African American and White supporters as well as Asian Americans. Villaraigosa was also able to take advantage of a rift between some in the African community who were not happy that Mayor Hahn had brought in New York City police commissioner William Bratton to head the Los Angeles Police Department and replace Black police chief Bernard Parks. Several prominent African American leaders shifted their support to Villaraigosa, and Hahn lost support from African American voters. Hahn also was vocal in his opposition to a secession movement in the San Fernando Valley to leave the city, which turned off more conservative White voters.[115]

The labor movement, which was divided between Villaraigosa and Hahn in 2001, continued to be divided with the formal endorsement going to the incumbent Hahn and individual unions organized to support Villaraigosa's candidacy. Villaraigosa won the 2005 election by 58.6 to 41.4 percent and won an estimated 60 percent of the union vote.[116] Latinos made up 25 percent of the vote, although they were nearly half of the city's population, whereas White voters cast 50 percent of all ballots although they made up 28 percent of the city's population.[117]

After his election as LA mayor, Villaraigosa brought several progressives into the city administration to lead key departments. He tackled a wide range of issues from homelessness to public safety, public transit, and the environment while limiting racial conflicts that had plagued the city since the 1960s. However, other issues, such as gentrification of working-class communities like Boyle Heights, the community where Villaraigosa grew up in East Los Angeles, have continued to simmer, with longtime Mexican American residents fighting to preserve their ethnic community

160   Latino Political Power

while other outside business interests seek to expand into this community that is located near LA's downtown. Also, Villaraigosa, a former teacher's union representative, was determined to influence the direction of public education in the Los Angeles area as, by standard metrics, the vast majority of schools were low performing. He tried a variety of measures to reform public education, many of which were stymied, so he focused on backing candidates for the Los Angeles Unified School District school board who supported allowing charter schools to grow over the objections of the United Teachers of Los Angeles, the union that represents tens of thousands of educators. Villaraigosa supported the public school choice measure, passed by the Los Angeles school board in 2009, allowing groups outside the school district to bid for control of new and low-performing schools. The results were mixed, and without having direct control of the public schools, Villaraigosa was limited in how much he could influence the direction of public education.

Villaraigosa also tackled the issue of improving public transportation and reducing automobile travel. He supported the passage of Measure R in 2008, a Los Angeles County initiative that raised the sales tax by a half cent to fund county transportation projects, and he promoted what he called the 30/10 initiative that sought to fast-track thirty years of transportation projects in ten years.[118] This effort resulted in expansion of rail lines to South and West Los Angeles and continued with his successor, Eric Garcetti. Villaraigosa easily won reelection in 2009 and, limited to two terms, left office in 2013.

The 2013 mayoral election featured a competitive race between Eric Garcetti and Wendy Greuel, the city controller and a former city council member from the San Fernando Valley. The great-grandson of Italian immigrants who settled in Mexico, Garcetti identifies as part Latino and part Jewish and ran as a mixed-heritage candidate. With a historically low turnout, Garcetti won with 60 percent of the Latino vote and 59 percent of the White vote, but only 31 percent of the Black vote. Many well-known women leaders, such as County Supervisor Gloria Molina and labor leader Dolores Huerta supported Greuel, but in this relatively low-key election, the LA County Federation of Labor's endorsement was not sufficient to win the mayor's office.[119] Garcetti, like Villaraigosa, highlighted his Latino heritage but did not run as a Latino candidate; nor did he identify as a Latino mayor. Garcetti easily won reelection in 2017 with 81 percent of the vote but only 20 percent turnout. The LA mayoral election date was changed to align with statewide elections, with the next election taking place in 2022.

While the LA mayoral contest grabs the headlines, the size and scope of Latino politics in Los Angeles County and the surrounding counties are also of significance, as the Latino population and its political influence have expanded beyond the core areas where Latinos, predominantly Mexican descendants, have lived for many decades. The LA City Council is

Political Power in the Sunbelt 161

comprised of fifteen elected members, and in 2021 there were four Latinos serving, including the city council president, Nury Martinez, who represents District 6, which is located in the east San Fernando Valley area, in Pacoima. The first Latina to head the council, she is the daughter of Mexican immigrants. As presiding chair of the city council, she has influence over local legislation, economic development, and public policies. She also oversaw redistricting for the city of Los Angeles for the council in 2021.

At the state level, Latino elected officials for LA County are influential. Out of forty total state senators, nine are Latino, three of whom are based in Los Angeles County. The head of the California Latino Legislative Caucus is State Senator Maria Elena Durazo, a former union leader, who represents the downtown and East LA area. Of the twenty-one Latino assembly members, out of eighty seats statewide, five are based in different parts of LA County, including Anthony Rendon from southeast LA County, who has also been the Speaker of the California State Assembly since 2016. Rendon, a former university educator and nonprofit executive director, is the fifth Latino assembly Speaker since the late 1990s, which reflects Latinos' growing influence in state-level legislative politics.

The combined political influence of Latinos who hold 30 of the 120 legislative seats, or one-quarter, reflects the community's growing political power, and there is still room to grow by capturing additional seats in the state legislature and congressional seats to reflect the state's Latino population of 40 percent. It is noteworthy that with his appointment as California's US senator after the election of Kamala Harris as vice president of the United States, Alex Padilla became the first Latino US senator from California. Padilla, the son of working-class Mexican immigrants, previously served as a state senator and a LA City Council member from the San Fernando Valley. In addition, Ricardo Lara, also a former state assemblyman and state senator from southeast LA County, is the state's insurance commissioner and was elected statewide.

The growth of Latino political power in the Los Angeles region and beyond in the state has been significant since the early 1990s, when anti-immigrant legislation dominated California politics. Today, the state is a leader in pro-immigrant legislation at the local and statewide levels.[120]

However, in this context, there are still challenges. In a detailed study of Latino/a electoral efforts in LA County, Christian D. Phillips documented the multiple challenges Latinas face in joining the inner circle of Latino political leaders and being considered for open seats that come available. The relationships between labor, Latino Democratic Party leaders, and immigration activists have created a traditional pipeline for possible candidates that usually includes serving as a legislative staff member, working for a labor union, earning consideration for elected office by working on numerous electoral campaigns, and building a network of allies and supporters. Latinas

162   *Latino Political Power*

have had to challenge the male-dominated Latino Democratic political leadership and run as outsiders or disrupters.[121] These internal challenges tied to relationships and the relative power dynamics of the labor movement, the Democratic Party, and community advocates means that efforts to develop new Latina leaders with the full support of long-standing, relatively entrenched male Latino leaders is a work in progress.

With the power of other organized interests in the Los Angeles area, this means that while Latino political influence will continue to grow, there are no clear pathways to continued growth. The most recent example is the race to replace LA mayor Eric Garcetti, whom the Biden administration nominated to serve as ambassador to India. LA City Council member Kevin de Leon ran against several other announced non-Latino candidates, including the favorite, Karen Bass, an African American congresswoman, and a billionaire businessman, Rick Caruso. De Leon did not make it out of the primary race in June 2022. His inability to mobilize a significant portion of the Latino community and fashion a broad, diverse electoral coalition resulted in his coming in third with 8 percent of the vote. He was defeated by a popular African American candidate and an extremely wealthy White business candidate, both of whom made it into the general election in November. The results of this mayor's race mean the Latinos in the city of Los Angeles, with a near majority population, will once again have neither a Latino as mayor nor parity with their population in city council seats. This reflects the continuing challenges facing Latinos in building political power at the local level, while they are growing their political influence in the state legislature.

Conclusion

One of the most dramatic political changes in American urban politics in the past thirty-five years has been the rise of Latino politicians in local cities. These three case studies highlight the complexity of Latino political inclusion. In three large Sunbelt cities with different political contours, histories, local economies, and political cultures, Latinos have achieved varying levels of incorporation. Latinos in Miami have gained full incorporation in just a few decades of concerted political activity. In San Antonio, Mexican Americans had what would be called in labor relations "a break in service." Before 1848, they led the city out of the transition from Mexican province to independent republic to statehood; they were then unceremoniously excused and did not appear again as serious political actors until the 1960s, when, in less than a decade of concerted effort, they retook the mayor's seat. Twenty years later, they took the majority of the city council; however, not until 2001 would the Chicano majority obtain in the electoral arena what had been theirs in the 1840s: the majority leadership of the council and the mayor's seat. In

San Antonio, Chicanos have become more politically incorporated; yet they are not able to retain and hold on to the mayoral position.

In Los Angeles, Latinos also have yet to achieve full political incorporation. They have won five of the fifteen the council seats in a city where they are the dominant ethnic group, with nearly 50 percent of the population, but not yet a majority or near majority of the voting population. Structural barriers, low voter turnout, a high rate of noncitizenship, racially polarized voting, and internal conflicts have weakened their power base in a polyglot world city, slowing progress toward full political incorporation and inclusion. Latinos in Los Angeles have achieved more than weak incorporation but have not yet gained strong incorporation. This could take the form of the election of a Latino mayor and/or several more Latino city council members. However, given the demographics of the city and chronic low voter turnout rates, Latinos will need to build alliances with other racial and ethnic groups to advance toward full incorporation.

These three case studies provide a window into the difficulties of translating population numbers into electoral victories. In each location, Latinos have grappled with the problem of voter registration and turnout. In Miami, Cuban Americans were able to overcome this hurdle more quickly. In San Antonio, consistent voter registration efforts coupled with higher voter turnout rates of Mexican Americans enhanced Latino candidates' opportunities to win office. In Los Angeles, the city with the largest Latino population in the nation, despite continued voter registration drives and educational campaigns, Latinos' vote share is less than their voting-age population. As Latino voting rates increase, so will the opportunities for additional Latino representation and political influence.

Together these studies highlight the diversity of political situations confronting Latinos in politics in large urban centers. Other large cities with significant Latino populations, such as New York, Chicago, Houston, and San Jose, also demonstrate that the structural barriers, the political obstacles, and the pathways to elected office and political incorporation are complex and multifaceted. Taken as a whole, these case studies provide a glimpse of the diversity of methods being employed by Latinos to obtain political power in large urban communities. In the next chapter we explore the rising influence of Latinas in politics.

Notes

1. Grenier and Castro 1998, 37.
2. Warren and Moreno 2003, 287.
3. Gonzalez-Pando 1998, 60.
4. Ibid.
5. Ibid., 61.

6. Moreno and Warren 1992, 135.
7. Mohl 1989, 149.
8. Dahlburg 2001.
9. Warren and Moreno 2003.
10. Ross, Weaver, and Corral 2001.
11. Ibid.
12. T. Bridges 2001.
13. Diaz 2013.
14. Moreno 1996.
15. Moreno and Warren 1992, 179.
16. Grenier et al. 1994, 183.
17. Moreno, Hill, and Cue, 2001.
18. Grenier and Castro 2001.
19. Moreno, Hill, and Cue, 2001.
20. Hirsch 2001.
21. Tomas Rivera Policy Institute 2001.
22. A. C. Smith 2003.
23. Moreno and Ilcheva 2018, 210.
24. Ibid.
25. Ibid., 213.
26. Ibid.
27. Vignor 2020.
28. Haley and Bryner 2021.
29. Florida Division of Elections, https://dos.myflorida.com/elections.
30. Date 2002.
31. Kripalani 2003.
32. Man 2021.
33. "Tejano Politics," n.d.
34. Booth and Johnson 1983, 6.
35. Acuña 1988, 29.
36. Muñoz and Henry 1990.
37. "Tejano Politics," n.d.
38. Booth and Johnson 1983, 23.
39. Sanders 2018, 73.
40. Rosales 2000, 118–119.
41. Brischetto, Correll, and Stevens 1983.
42. Ibid.
43. Sekul 1983.
44. Navarro and Acuña 1990, 213.
45. Diehl and Jarboe 1985.
46. Brischetto, Correll, and Stevens 1983, 88.
47. Rosales 2000, 163–167.
48. B. Davidson 2000.
49. Casey 2001d.
50. Ibid.
51. Hood 2001.
52. *San Antonio Express News* 2001.
53. Saunders quoted in Zars 2001.
54. Ibid.
55. Needham 2001.
56. Pack 2001b.

Political Power in the Sunbelt 165

57. Pack 2001c.
58. Patoski 2002.
59. Castillo 2002.
60. *San Antonio Express News* 2020; Powell 2004.
61. Anderson 2003.
62. Castillo 2005; Rivard 2004.
63. Ibid.
64. Koidin 2004.
65. Ibid.
66. Stinson 2004.
67. Castro 2018.
68. Ibid.
69. K. Rodriguez 2004d.
70. Gurwitz 2005.
71. K. Rodriguez 2004b.
72. R. Rodriguez 2005a.
73. Bexar County Elections Office 2005.
74. R. Rodriguez 2005c.
75. Sanders 2018; Manzano and Vega 2013.
76. R. Rodriguez 2005b.
77. Welch 2005.
78. R. Rodriguez 2005c.
79. Welch 2005.
80. Bexar County Elections Office 2005.
81. Welch 2005.
82. Ibid.
83. B. Davidson 2007.
84. Russell 2009a.
85. Russell 2009b.
86. B. Davidson 2009.
87. Stroud 2011.
88. Baugh 2011.
89. Bexar County Elections Office 2011.
90. Jervis 2012.
91. Hendricks 2012.
92. Thomas 2012.
93. Bexar County Elections Office 2013.
94. Davila 2012.
95. M. Flores 2002.
96. "Our Campaigns—TX State House 125 Race" 2002.
97. Texas Secretary of State 2004.
98. "Information for Rep. Joaquin Castro" 2011.
99. Hicks 2011.
100. G. Garcia 2019.
101. "Our Campaigns—TX District 20 Race" 2012.
102. Acuña 1988, 318.
103. Regalado 1988.
104. Sonenshein 1993, 43–44.
105. Acuña 1988, 368.
106. Sonenshein 1997, 52–53.
107. Clayton 1985.

166 *Latino Political Power*

108. Alatorre 2016, 391–412.
109. Griswold del Castillo and De Leon 1996, 156.
110. Guerra 1991, 130–131.
111. Acuña 1996, 72–74.
112. Dallek 1998.
113. Skelton 2001.
114. Ibid.
115. Shiau 2018, 139–140.
116. Drier et al. 2006, 45–52.
117. Shiau 2018, 143.
118. Shiau 2018, 156.
119. Guerra and Gilbert 2013.
120. Williamson 2018; Gulasekaram and Ramakrishnan 2015; Collingwood and O'Brien 2019.
121. Phillips 2021.

7

Latinas: Political Activists and Leaders

Chicanas and Latinas have a long history as political actors, dating as far back as the Mexican Revolution.[1] Yet scholarly research has only begun to address their contributions to American politics. In this chapter, we delineate the increasing presence of Latinas and Chicanas in electoral politics in roles from activist, to candidate, to officeholder. We look specifically at the intersection of gender, sexuality, and ethnicity as central to Latinas' fight for political incorporation.[2]

What motivates Latinas to become involved in political activity, and what barriers do they confront in their efforts? Do they typically follow the conventional paths of men and women from other races and ethnic groups? As elected leaders, do they have unique political perspectives and/or skills gleaned from their cultural backgrounds or life experiences? What cost or risks are involved in running for office? Finally, how, if at all, do their identities influence their political perspective? To answer these central questions, we describe and analyze the political stories of Latina and Chicana women who have reached public office at the federal, state, and local levels. These detail-rich case studies, derived primarily from personal interviews, are intended to provide readers with a multidimensional understanding of Latinas' and Chicanas' political leadership. As Alessandro Portelli, a leading scholar utilizing oral history, explains, "Oral sources tell us not just what people did, but what they wanted to do, what they believed they were doing and what they now think they did."[3] As much as possible, we substantiate their subjective stories with primary data and other sources.

According to the Directory of the National Association of Latino Elected and Appointed Officials (NALEO), as of 2021, among a total of 6,882 Latino elected and appointed officials, there were about 2,692 Latinas

(39.1 percent).[4] This is up from NALEO's 2010 count of 1,858 Latinas (32 percent) out of 5,739. All 2,692 Latinas were randomly solicited over a period of seven months. Follow-up emails and calls were made, but the challenges of coordinating a date and time for an interview proved unworkable for the following reasons: a pressing national legislative agenda, participation in budgetary committees, states with year-round legislative sessions, campaigns for primary mid-term elections, campaigns for other state or local offices, and limited communication because of staff reductions. Every effort was initiated to interview (either via phone or Zoom) as many Latina elected officials as possible. In the end, seven Latinas were interviewed.

We fully recognize the limitations of our sample size. Our decision to use a case study approach allowed us to delve more deeply into the lives of each of our subjects. This provides for a rich, experiential analysis.[5] However, our conclusions are thus limited to these individual women. Although we are unable to generalize to all Latina public officials, we believe these shared experiences will encourage others to pursue other methods to further this research.

Despite their improved numbers and significance to the success of both political parties, Latinas continue to be politically underrepresented in the highest political offices and institutions of power. Senator Catherine Cortez Masto from Nevada stands out as the lone Latina *ever* elected to the US Senate, despite the fact that with over 60 million people, Latinas/os/xs constitute the largest racial/ethnic minority population in the United States. In 2022 there were thirteen Latina US representatives and nine Latinas serving in statewide office (Table 7.1).

Latina women also serve in various state legislative/assembly, city, and school board offices—too many to list here. President Joe Biden's administration was said to be one of most diverse cabinets in history, with the inclusion of Latino members like Xavier Becerra (Health and Human Services), Alejandro Mayorkas (Homeland Security), Dr. Miguel Cardona (Department of Education), and Isabel Guzman (Small Business Administration).[6]

Latinos are a powerful and growing political force in the United States. In the five largest Latino majority-minority states (Arizona, California, Florida, Nevada, and Texas), President Joe Biden led former president Donald Trump among Latino men by nineteen points (58–39) on average and among Latina women by thirty-three points (65–33) in the 2020 presidential election. Latino men and women were most united on the candidates in California and Florida and most divided in Nevada, where men split roughly even among the two candidates while women preferred Biden two to one.[7] In short, Latinas have consistently shown up and been present for political candidates, parties, and movements but without a reciprocal investment in their representation.

While research on intersectionality, descriptive representation, and political incorporation has been growing over the past decade, a distinct but

Latinas   169

Table 7.1   Latina US Representatives and Statewide Officeholders

Name	Ethnicity/Race	Party	Roles	State
Lisa Cano Burkhead	Latina	Democrat	Lieutenant governor (2021–2022)	Nevada
Stephanie Garcia Richard	Latina	Democrat	Land commissioner (2019–2022); state representative (2013–2018)	New Mexico
Nellie M. Gorbea	Latina	Democrat	Secretary of state (2015–2022)	Rhode Island
Michelle Lujan Grisham	Latina	Democrat	Governor (2019–2022); US representative (2013–2018)	New Mexico
Lea Marquez Peterson	Latina	Republican	Corporation commissioner (2019–2024)	Arizona
Sabina Matos	Black, Latina	Democrat	Lieutenant governor (2021–2022)	Rhode Island
Susana A. Mendoza	Latina	Democrat	Comptroller (2017–2022); state representative (2001–2011)	Illinois
Jeanette M. Nunez	Latina	Republican	Lieutenant governor (2019–2022); state representative (2011–2018)	Florida
Anna M. Tovar	Latina	Democrat	Corporation commissioner (2021–2024); state senator (2013–2014); state representative (2009–2012)	Arizona

Source: Center for American Women and Politics, n.d.

related question—the impact of ethnic diversity and, more specifically, geographically concentrated minority communities on the election of Latina women and those who identify as LGBTQ+—has received much less attention. This gap in the literature is rather surprising, given that this question has important policy implications. Moreover, it is not at all obvious what

170   *Latino Political Power*

impact, if any, the size of the ethnic minority population will have on female legislative representation and/or agendas.

The judicial branch has also witnessed a slow growth in Latina political incorporation. Since 1789, only 140 of the more than 3,400 federal judges have identified as Hispanic or Afro-Latino; of those, 34 have been women, according to the Federal Judicial Center.[8] Although Latinos compose 18.7 percent of the US population, forming the country's largest minority, they represent around 7 percent of all federal judges. For Latinas, that number hovers at around 2 percent. That percentage has been practically unchanged since 2009, when Sonia Sotomayor became the first Supreme Court justice of Latino descent.[9] Myrna Pérez, a voting rights expert, was confirmed in October 2021 as a Second District Court of Appeals judge.[10] The Biden administration in 2021 nominated Linda Lopez, Cristina D. Silva, Ruth Bermudez Montenegro, Katherine Menendez, and Evelyn Padin as district judges. They have all since been confirmed.[11] Thus, it is essential that we study Latinas and Chicanas and their role in politics.

The Emergence of Latina Politicians

In the 1930s, women helped build middle-class organizations such as the League of United Latin American Citizens and were leaders in a number of labor organizations among cannery and farmworkers.[12] For example, in 1938 in San Antonio, pecan shellers went on a spontaneous strike after their pay was cut by 20 percent. A young, dynamic labor radical, Emma Tenayucca, played a leading role in helping to organize the strike. After six weeks, living on tortillas and frijoles, the workers won the strike and established a union.[13] In the 1960s, Chicanas sought a leadership role in the emerging Chicano movement and to articulate a distinct identity out of the long history of exploitation they suffered as women and Mexicans.[14] Puerto Rican women played similar roles in building community organizations as activists and leaders in the 1960s and 1970s Puerto Rican movement. The experiences in these movements led many of them to form separate organizations focused on Chicana, Latina, or Hispanic women's issues.

Latinas also began to seek political office in the 1960s and 1970s. Virginia Musquiz was active in the Crystal City, Texas, struggle in the 1960s and ran for city council and for state representative. She also organized the high school walkouts in 1969 and the political campaign to take control of city government.

In the 1970s, however, only a handful of Latinas were elected to office. A pioneer of Latina legislators was Olga Mendez, a state senator from New York. Elected in 1978, she was the first Puerto Rican woman to serve in a state legislative body. She remained in this position until 2004, when, after changing her party affiliation from Democrat to Republican, she was defeated by New York City Council member Jose M. Serrano. Texas has had the largest delegation of Chicanas in elected office: Irma Rangel of Kingsville was elected in 1976 as state representative, and later Lina Guerrero of Austin was elected as state representative as well. Judy Zaffirini of Laredo was elected to the Texas State Senate in 1984 and held this position for decades. In 1987, according to NALEO, there were 592 Chicana/Latina elected officials nationwide, but none in federal office.

In 1989, this changed when Ileana Ros-Lehtinen (R-FL), a Cuban American, became the first Latina elected to Congress. Her election was followed in 1992 by the election of two additional Latinas, one from New York City and another from Los Angeles: Nydia Velázquez (D-NY) became the first Puerto Rican woman and Lucille Roybal-Allard (D-CA) the first Chicana elected to the US Congress. Subsequently, more Mexican American women legislators have been elected from Southern California: Grace Napolitano, Hilda Solis, Loretta Sanchez, and Linda Sanchez. The election of five Latinas from one region of one state is not a coincidence, as there is a growing presence of Latina political leaders throughout the Southern California area. Each of them has built strong electoral coalitions based on local political forces. The elections of these Latina congresswomen reflect their strong ties to their communities and their political sophistication. These women are important role models and community leaders on issues of concern to the Latino community.

The election of a growing number of Latina elected officials at all levels of government was due to a combination of factors, including new open seats created by redistricting after the 1990 US Census, term limits in many states that forced longtime politicians out of office, mentoring and development of candidates by Latina networks and existing Latina officeholders, and changing attitudes of Latino and other voters. Latina elected officials emerged from a wide variety of experiences as community leaders, progressive activists, professionals, business owners, and intellectuals.

In 1992, Puerto Rican Nydia Velázquez won the Democratic Party nomination over New York congressman Stephen J. Solarz, at the time a nine-term incumbent. She won the general election to New York's 12th District with over 75 percent of the vote, and in 1994 she was reelected with over 90 percent of the vote. Loretta Sanchez (D-CA), a Mexican American and daughter of immigrant parents, defeated eight-term incumbent Bob Dornan, a controversial maverick Republican, in 1996 in Orange County, California. Orange County, a traditionally conservative area, has seen large growth in its Latino population, and many of these Latinos became Democratic Party voters. Sanchez won by a razor-thin margin and then had to endure charges that noncitizens had voted illegally to bring her victory. These charges were eventually dropped.

172   *Latino Political Power*

In 2000, Hilda Solis (D-CA) challenged nine-term incumbent Marty Martinez in the Democratic Party primary in the San Gabriel Valley area of Los Angeles County. Most viewed defeating a fellow Mexican American incumbent legislator in the primary as an extremely difficult task. However, Solis easily outdistanced Martinez by 68 to 31 percent. This convincing victory was due to several factors, including the incumbent's positions against gun control and abortion, among other stands that alienated his base, and the strong support for Solis from labor, women, and the community.

In many states, women must overcome various institutional and gender barriers. In New Jersey, by the 2000s, three Latinas had been elected in the state assembly, where county political party chairpersons (predominantly male) had strong institutional power to control who gets party nominations. Women of color in particular have a difficult time breaking into and succeeding at politics in this environment dominated by party and personal loyalties.[15]

Majority-Minority Cities and States

Latinas' and Chicanas' potential to win races for highly competitive offices has been generally underestimated. In some communities where Latinos have a sizable population presence, Latinas hold some of the highest-ranking elected positions. El Paso, Texas, is located in the Chihuahuan Desert of extreme western Texas, along the Rio Grande River. It adjoins both the state of New Mexico and the country of Mexico (across from Ciudad Juárez) with the Franklin Mountains. By the 1970s, El Paso's population was approximately 340,000 with a predominately Hispanic population. Alicia Rosencrans Chacón's political orientation began with her involvement in the Democratic Party and as president of the Ysleta Elementary PTA. Her first elected office was as a member of the Ysleta Independent School Board, on which she was the first Hispanic person to hold a seat.[16] She decided to run for the school board in order to improve the poor conditions in Ysleta and Lower Valley schools.[17] Within a few years, in 1974, Chacón was the first woman elected to El Paso government when she became county clerk.[18] Between 1983 and 1987, she served two terms on the El Paso City Council, the first Hispanic woman to serve on that body.[19] In 1990 she became the first woman and first Hispanic person in 100 years to serve as the county judge for the El Paso area.[20] In 1996, she served as president of the El Paso County Employees Union and advocated for a salary increase for El Paso County employees.[21]

The second Hispanic female elected as El Paso County judge was Dolores Briones, a Democratic Party activist who worked in the health field before winning office as the chief administrative officer of the county government in 1994; she presided over the county's governing body, the Commissioners Court.[22] She won reelection in 1998 and in 2002, serving until 2006.[23] She has received high marks as a bridge builder between conservative and liberal perspectives on the county commission.

In 2005, Veronica Escobar, along with Robert Francis "Beto" O'Rourke and others, considered entering public service; they started to discuss grassroots strategies with the goals of improving urban planning, creating a more diversified economy with more highly skilled jobs, and ending systemic corruption among city leadership. At the time, Escobar was a nonprofit executive and a communications director for Mayor Raymond Caballero.[24] In 2006, Escobar decided to dip her toes into electoral politics by running unopposed and was elected as a county commissioner of El Paso County. In 2010, she was elected as the county judge with 62 percent of the vote.[25] She would be the third Hispanic female to serve as county judge in a majority-minority Hispanic city. She was swept in as county judge after the FBI raided the county courthouse in a corruption investigation. She led a massive overhaul of governance policies during her tenure. Escobar, along with O'Rourke and others who ran for office during the same period and won, became collectively known as "The Progressives."[26] Before completing her first term as county judge, Escobar resigned in 2017 to run full-time in the 2018 election to succeed Beto O'Rourke in the US House of Representatives for Texas's 16th Congressional District.[27] The heart of this solidly Democratic, majority-Hispanic district sits in El Paso. Whoever won the Democratic primary was heavily favored in November.[28] Escobar won the six-way Democratic primary with 61 percent of the vote.[29] She became the first woman and the second Hispanic ever to represent the 16th District.

Escobar acknowledges that women get their political experience at the most basic level. She said, "Local offices like school boards, city councils, and commissioner courts are important training ground for women considering running for higher office because they learn how to govern and campaign."[30] Escobar is also cognizant of the barriers and challenges to running a campaign and winning office.

> Part of the problem is that women shoulder more responsibilities and obligations than men do and don't always feel they can run for office because of their family.[31] The harder offices are state government and federal government because you're away from home. If you have children, even if you're in the most equitable partnership, frequently it is the woman that is the primary caregiver and that many times has stood in the way of women wanting to serve. They feel that their kids are their first obligation and it would be too difficult to sacrifice the time that child rearing takes.[32] Even in local government, it's harder for a woman to run for office than a man. It's a luxury for most women like me to have the time and money to run for office.[33]

174   *Latino Political Power*

At the same time Escobar was running, Texas state senator Sylvia Garcia of Houston was also running for the US House of Representatives for the 29th District. Unlike Escobar's introduction into politics, Garcia's political career started in the early 1980s when she was appointed as the chief judge of the Houston Municipal System by then mayor Kathryn Whitmire. Garcia was the first woman and youngest person ever to hold the post. She served for an unprecedented five terms under two mayors.[34] In 1998, she was elected city controller, the second-highest elected official in Houston city government and its chief financial officer.[35] She earned a reputation as the taxpayers' watchdog, fighting to protect the pocketbooks of working families and ensuring the city was transparent and accountable.

In 2002, she was elected to the Commissioner's Court of Harris County, home to NASA, the nation's largest petrochemical complex, the Houston Ship Channel, and the Port of Houston, the sixth-largest port in the world.[36] The first Latina elected to the seat, she lost it in 2010 to Republican Jack Morman.[37] In 2013, Garcia defeated State Representative Carol Alvarado in a special election runoff to replace the late state senator Mario Gallegos. Garcia took the oath of office of state senator on March 11, 2013.[38] She served on the Criminal Justice, Intergovernmental Relations, Natural Resources and Economic Development, and Transportation committees. Garcia ran unopposed in the 2016 general election.[39]

While still serving as a municipal judge, Garcia ran in the Democratic primary for the newly created 29th District congressional seat in 1992. She finished third in the five-way primary—the real contest in this heavily Democratic, Latino-majority district—behind City Councilman Ben Reyes and State Senator Gene Green. Green won the runoff and held the seat for twenty-six years. In November 2017, Green announced his retirement, and Garcia, a state senator, entered a crowded seven-way Democratic primary. The district was still a Democratic stronghold and 80 percent Latino.[40] It was taken for granted that whoever won the primary would be overwhelmingly favored in November. Garcia got a significant boost when Green endorsed her, saying, "She's a legislator, and that's what a member of Congress should be."[41] She won the primary with 63 percent of the vote.[42] She and Veronica Escobar became the first Latina congresswomen from Texas. Escobar and Garcia are two out of the thirty-six-member congressional delegation representing Texas.

The mid-term elections of 2018 in many ways presented a picture of a divided country as Republicans maintained their control of the Senate. This was good for the Democrats, who assumed control of the 435-member House of Representatives for the first time in eight years, picking up at least 35 Republican seats. Republican women had more luck with the Railroad Commission, State Board of Education, and Texas Court of Criminal Appeals, winning a total of sixteen races.[43] Not only were Latinas making

Latinas 175

inroads at the federal level, but their numbers have been steadily growing at the state level.

State Legislators

The Texas Legislature is a bicameral institution that consists of 150 House representatives and 31-member Senate. It meets in regular session on the second Tuesday in January of each odd-number year. The Texas Constitution limits the regular sessions to 140 calendar days. State legislators in Texas make $600 per month, or $7,200 per year, plus a per diem of $221 for every day the legislature is in session.

In Texas, cultural changes in the state over recent decades have increased the diversity of the Texas Legislature. The number of officeholders who are members of ethnic minority groups has grown, both in Texas and across the nation. However, women and people of color are still underrepresented in the Texas Legislature compared with their proportions of the state population. In the 86th Texas Legislature (2019), people of color made up 58 percent of Texas's population, yet accounted for only 36 percent of the legislative seats. Likewise, while women account for 50 percent of the state population, they hold only 22 percent of the seats in the Texas Legislature.[44] The number of women legislators in Texas increased from a single woman in each chamber in 1971 to a total of 48 out of 180 in 2022. As of 2022, 44 Latinos served in the Texas Legislature; of this total, 2 Latinas were serving in the state senate and 12 were serving in the state house.

Celia Israel is one of these Latina state representatives. Her district is nestled in North Austin, Pflugerville, and east Travis County. Austin is the third-most populous city in Texas and the second-most populous state capital city after Phoenix, Arizona.[45] As a result of the major party realignment that began in the 1970s, central Austin became a stronghold of the Democratic Party, while the suburbs tend to vote Republican. Overall, the city blends downtown liberalism and suburban conservatism but leans to the political left as a whole.[46]

Israel has represented House District 50 since 2014. When she was growing up, her parents were not politically active; nor was politics discussed in the home. Israel knew that her mother had voted for Richard Nixon but never talked about it, perhaps because "she was embarrassed because he was impeached."[47] Raised in El Paso, Texas, Israel moved to Austin to attend the University of Texas in 1982 and never left. Representative Israel's introduction into politics was when she heard Governor Ann Richard's speech in 1988 at the Democratic National Convention. "That was my inspiration," Israel states. She connected with Richard's message, and when Richard decided to run for governor of Texas, Israel contacted a

176   *Latino Political Power*

former University of Texas professor, Sarah Weddington, and asked for a recommendation to assist in the campaign.[48] Israel was unaware of how campaigns worked and thought she needed a special contact to help.[49] In 1991, Ann Richards won the governor's race, and Israel eventually went to work for her administration.

Israel defines politics as "campaigning, raising money, and gathering volunteers. Organizing the get-out-the-vote efforts." She has admitted that her view of politics has changed. As an elected official, she knows "there is a lot of gray areas and there's different ways of creating policy." Israel found her voice and political confidence when she first ran for Travis (Austin) County commissioner in 2004. She lost but gained the political confidence she needed launch her next race. "I earned a lot of respect from people because I ran a good campaign." Israel was planning her next run. She knew that if she wanted to pursue a higher office, she needed the right career, one that would supplement her salary as a state representative. Israel obtained her real estate license. She wanted to ensure that her family would not pay a financial price for her choice to run as a state representative.

Israel remained active in the community, until her state representative, Mark Strama, viewed as having a promising electoral career, abruptly resigned to head Google Fiber in Austin. In the meantime, Israel worked to combat mental illness and hunger, also serving on the police monitor board and Austin Independent School District school safety task force. She also advocated for small business by serving as chair of the Advocacy Committee. Strama's resignation triggered a special election set for November 2013. Israel recognized the political opportunity of an open seat and what it signaled to a minority female, and many others, thinking of running for it; she had a good chance winning. The candidate pool consisted of Israel, attorney and former assistant district attorney Rico Reyes, and business owner Jade Chang Sheppard, as well as Republican chiropractor Mike Van-DeWalle.[50] In November, no one took a majority of the vote in the special election, forcing a runoff between the top two vote-getters: VanDeWalle, who received 39 percent of the vote and Israel, who received 32 percent of the vote.[51] In January 2014, Israel bested VanDeWalle by 59.6 to 40.4 percent to become the new state representative for District 50.[52] Her current term ends in January 2023. In January 2022, State Representative Israel formally announced her candidacy for mayor of Austin.

Reflecting on her decision to run for office, Israel acknowledged barriers that she as a Latina encountered:

> First, do I have it in me? Do I have what it takes? Can I lead? Women are more introspective. Men just wake up and think, "What can I get done today? Who can I lead today. I am in charge today." Second, do I have the resources, that means financially? Do I have the networks that will con-

tribute to my campaign for that level of office? Because generally, Latina women do not have the personal financial wealth to run a campaign or to self-fund a campaign. Third, while serving on boards and commissions helped me define my issues, that wasn't necessarily helpful with community organizing, and I think that the traditional way of making connections with the community, through activism, would have helped.

Latinas as political candidates often face risks.[53] Israel contextualized her risk this way: "As a Latina, you have to have a good sense of self-worth because the negative campaigning against you will happen. There is a personal cost because you are sacrificing time with your family. Sacrificing time with your business. So, you have to ask, 'Is this the right thing for me to do right now?'" Israel is the first openly gay state representative serving the Austin area. Given Texas's conservative political climate, her sexuality was only a consideration in her own mind when she thought about running. She describes it this way: "It was my own fear. It turned out to not be a thing. My sexuality was not an issue at all. It was like having brown hair." Israel was overthinking her sexual identity as a possible barrier to her election, particularly in light of Austin being voted one of the friendliest cities in America for lesbian, gay, bisexual, and transgendered people.[54] In short, her sexual identity was not a factor, but her involvement on boards and commissions was. She had invested time in building her connection to the community.

State Representative Jessica González represents the 104th District in Texas. This district is nestled in central and eastern Grand Prairie and a portion of West Dallas. Out of a district population of 185,500, 70 percent is Hispanic, 14.9 percent White, 12.1 percent Black, and about 2.6 percent Asian.[55] In 2019 González ousted a twenty-six-year incumbent, Roberto Alonzo, in the Democratic primary by 62.5 to 37.5 percent. She went on to win the general election.

González's introduction into politics happened by chance when she first attended a rally with her older sister who was in college at the time. She reminiscences, "We participated in some rallies that were related to immigration issues that were going on then. That was my first taste of activism."[56] Once she completed law school and opened up her own law firm, she began thinking about running for office. She knew that her city council representative was being termed out, and "people were starting to talk to me about it; they were encouraging me to run for city council." However, she knew that serving on city council was a full-time job, and it did not make financial sense given the infancy of her law firm. When she turned a run for city council down, the conversation shifted to another elected office: state legislator. Texas politicians were focusing on cultural war grievances rather than the nuts and bolts of governance.[57] The state legislature was addressing cultural issues like barring the teaching of critical

178   *Latino Political Power*

race theory in K-12, book bans, restrictions on transgender participation in youth sports and transgender kids' receiving gender-affirming care,[58] restrictive election laws, and so on. Community members were encouraging her to run, she recalls, some saying, "Hey, what about you running for the legislature? With your skill set you will be able to do a lot more and it's more conducive with being a lawyer and having your law practice." Another supporter said, "You're a lawyer, you're from the neighborhood, you're a perfect fit." She gave it some serious thought and had several discussions with her law partner about a possible run. González knew there would be push back from the old guard in the political party. When she mentioned that she was thinking of running to party officials, she was told "'to wait your turn' which was met with 'If I wait my turn, it's never going to happen.' The reality was that there had never been a woman to represent this district." She ultimately decided to run for office, she said, because "I was frustrated with what I was witnessing. We saw a lot of attacks on women, the LGBTQ community with the bathroom bill and so on. For me, it was about the issues."

For González, politics is a "necessary evil. I mean, it is a set of actions or a group of people that come together to influence government or just influence policy decisions and that can be a good thing. I think when people use politics to hurt people, that's the evil."[59] Having been in office one term, González has realized that politics is about relationship building. With encouragement from various community members, González did not take running for office lightly. She came face-to-face with real challenges. The first was fund-raising. She acknowledged that many women find it difficult to ask for money or have to build the networks. "We don't like to ask for help. I also think it is culturally across the board. We [Latinas] don't like to ask for help. We are raised a different way. We tend to do things on our own. But I try to remind myself that it is not about me asking for money for me. This is about asking for money for the right to continue to do work for my district. . . . We tend to not want to make those phone calls or to make those asks." The second challenge was paying the bills. González knew that service in the Texas Legislature is a part-time job with a salary of $7,200. She would have to take time away from her practice, and her law partner would have to carry the full load of cases while she was in Austin. She and her law partner made a commitment to start Gandara & González, PLLC, in 2015, and her law partner had to be all-in for González to run. The third challenge was child care and maintaining a home. "Women are caretakers, and it would be a struggle for those that have children. I don't have children yet, but I can anticipate the struggle."

One of González's concerns and a possible risk was how the community would receive her. González identifies as LGBTQ+. She frames her thoughts this way:

I wasn't sure, I mean, I didn't try to focus on the fact that I was LGBTQ. When I ran for office, I was openly LGBTQ. But this district has changed a lot over the years. It is very progressive, more diverse not only in demographics but political views. It turns out that it wasn't an issue, but I was concerned that, you know, it would come up, and there would be some, maybe, potential attacks, and that's not what you want your family to see. But that did not happen.

González also believes that it can be difficult to find a balance between her private practice and being away from home. However, the work she has been able to do for her community makes the sacrifices worth it. She has received multiple awards for her legislative work. In 2021, she was awarded the Matt Garcia Public Service Award by the Mexican American Legal Defense and Education Fund for her work during the legislative session on voting rights.[60] *Texas Monthly* named her the "Bull of the Brazos," a title given after each session to a lawmaker who sets aside niceties on the issues that matter most to them, regardless of the political price.[61] It was the first time a woman received that recognition. *USA Today* named her Woman of the Year for 2022 for her work on behalf of voting rights and protecting the LBGTQ+ and other marginalized communities.[62] González acknowledges that she is in a very privileged position and expresses gratitude every day.

The Delaware General Assembly is a bicameral legislature composed of twenty-one senators (seven of whom are women, including two African Americans and one Argentinian) and forty-one representatives (twelve of whom are women; five of these are African American, one of whom is a practicing Muslim). It convenes on the second Tuesday of January in odd-number years, with a second session of the same assembly convening likewise in even-numbered years. These elected men and women earn a salary of $45,291 a year.[63]

State Senator Laura Viviana Sturgeon, the daughter of Argentine immigrants, was born in Florida but raised in Delaware in a bicultural and bilingual home. Her father had a PhD in engineering, and they often traveled abroad for his work. Her mother had an Argentine degree in writing contracts. Sturgeon grew up hearing her parents talk about Argentine and US politics and how very different the two countries were. She believes those conversations helped shape her understanding of politics.[64]

Sturgeon received her bachelor's and master's degrees from the University of Delaware. She taught in Delaware public schools for over twenty years and served as a leader in the Delaware State Education Association, the largest union in Delaware.[65] A combination of factors sparked her run for office. First, her involvement in education left "her feeling frustrated that teachers were not often at the table when big decisions were being made around education policy." Second, she started to notice that her local

180   *Latino Political Power*

representative had gone unopposed election cycle after election cycle. "If he had opponents, they were kind of last-minute candidates that were just put on the ballot just so that there was another choice and I said to myself, 'I grew up here,' and I just knew in my heart of hearts that this is not a super conservative area. That I could not possibly be the only Democrat."

Her district had been represented by a conservative for close to twenty years. Sturgeon really did not know how to run a campaign, but she knew that she had a student whose mother was an elected representative. Having had plenty of conversations with her in the past, she thought she could get some tips on how to get started with a campaign. Sturgeon also signed up for the Campaign School at Yale University.[66] With advice from her student's mom and the political education she received at the campaign camp, Sturgeon started knocking on doors two year prior to the 2018 election. She knew the incumbent had an incredible war chest, which she would never be able to match as a new challenger, and that the only way to beat him was to "outwork him." On Election Day, Sturgeon beat her opponent with 53 percent of the vote in a state senate district that was 78 percent White, 5 percent Black, 3 percent Hispanic, 11 percent Asian, and 2 percent other.[67] She is the first Hispanic (Argentinian descent) to serve in the Delaware General Assembly.

Since her election, Sturgeon's definition of politics has evolved with her tenure in office. She defines politics as "the intersection between advocacy for good policy and the relationships that you have to build across both aisles to move policy forward." Reflecting back on her race for state senate, she recognizes barriers to campaigning.

> First, raising money to run a campaign. The second issue is I think being taken seriously when you're a woman. I was told it's not your turn. There is this guy we want to run for that seat and he's got, like, more connections. He's got more ability to raise money. He is interested in running for the seat. So, maybe you should pass. Third, I had to be prepared for the negativity that comes with campaigning. I had to prepare my family. I had to tell them not to take it personally.

For Sturgeon, the risks of campaigning for an elected office involved two factors: caring for children and maintaining a job. She states,

> I can't imagine what it's like for women who have jobs and children while trying to campaign. If I had children while trying to campaign, I would have been pulled into too many directions. I would have been scattered. The other issue to consider is a job. If had no choice but to work, it would have been difficult. I couldn't afford to quit working. Thankfully, I am married, so I did not have to worry about being the sole income provider as many other women do who contemplate running for office.

Sturgeon, like Israel and González, realized that family responsibilities and financial security are still factors that Latina women have to consider when running for office. The costs and risks are no less serious. Both González and Sturgeon had to prepare their families for the negativity that comes along with campaigning. However, the potential for negativity did not deter them from running.

Although Sturgeon is the first Hispanic woman to serve in the Delaware General Assembly, she argues that her biculturalism provides her with a unique perspective on how she views policy issues. She states, "Being Latina has played a very small role in how I'm seen by others because I am White. I have blue eyes and dirty blond hair. I have no markers, audibly or visually that would cause people to think of me as Latino when they see me." For Sturgeon, her Hispanic identity did not play a role in her electability.

Sturgeon's interest in women's rights and desire to help mold public education policy inspired her to run. She hopes to continue serving in the state legislature. As she put it, "I feel like I'm right where I should be."

The California State Legislature is a bicameral body consisting of the lower house, the state assembly, with eighty members, and the upper house, the state senate, with forty members.[68] California's voters imposed term limits on their state senators and assembly members in 1990. Senators could not serve for more than two terms (a total of eight years) and assembly members could not serve for more than three terms (a total of six years). California voters modified these limits in 2012 to allow legislators to serve twelve years total, but they could spend all twelve in either chamber (a total of three senate terms or six assembly terms). The California legislature has been full-time since 1966.[69] Women consist of only 32 percent of the legislature compared to 50.8 percent of California. Hispanics make up 20 percent of the California State Assembly and 10 percent of the California State Senate.[70] There are a total of eleven Hispanic females in the assembly and eight serving in the senate.[71]

California State Assembly representatives serve two-year terms, while state senators serve four-year terms. California imposed term limits for the state legislature. As a result of Proposition 140 in 1990 and Proposition 28 in 2012, members elected to the legislature prior to 2012 are restricted to two four-year terms (eight years), while those elected in or after 2012 are allowed to serve twelve years in the legislature in any combination of four-year state senate or two-year state assembly terms.[72]

Susan Talamantes Eggman is the state senator from California's 5th District, one of forty senate districts in the state. The district is centered on the northern end of the San Joaquin Valley and forms the gateway between the Delta, the San Francisco Bay Area, the Sacramento metropolitan area, and Gold Country. Eggman's district population sits at around 1,051,930, which is approximately 38.2 percent White, 41.7 percent Latino, 6.7 percent Black, 15.1 percent Asian, 1.6 percent Native American, 0.8 percent

182 *Latino Political Power*

Hawaiian/Pacific Islander, and 0.26 percent other.[73] Prior to being elected to the state senate in 2020, she was a member of the California State Assembly representing the 13th Assembly District (from 2012 to 2020), as well as being a Stockton City Council member and associate professor of social work at California State University (CSU) at Sacramento. From the time she was first elected to the assembly in 2012 to her last election in 2018, Eggman won each general election with close to 65 percent approval.

Growing up, Eggman was surrounded by politics. Her grandparents became citizens so that they could vote for John F. Kennedy as the first Catholic president. "My parents and grandparents were staunch Democrats. They had a very strong belief in equality, choice, public education, everything that was important for society to thrive."[74] Politics was always talked about in the home. She recalls asking her mom, "What was the most important political time in your life?" Her mother answered, "Oh, it was the [Nixon] trials that were so fascinating."[75] Eggman really didn't become personally involved in politics until she was pursing her doctorate at Portland State University. She was involved in some organizing around providing access to mental health and health care in general to the Latino community in Portland, Oregon.

As Eggman stepped into her teaching role as a professor of social work at CSU, Sacramento, she saw how then president George W. Bush's social welfare was "detrimental to the most vulnerable. It was just one of those life-altering moments." She recalls attending a faculty meeting and "everyone was sitting around, saying, 'Oh my God, what should we do? What do we need to do?'" She then offered some direction in the meeting by saying, "Why aren't we teaching our students to organize and run for office to change the direction of policy?" Eggman remembers the brief silence in the room before she jumped in and said, "I'm running for the next office that comes available." In 2006, Eggman ran for an open seat on the Stockton City Council and won with 42.2 percent of the vote.[76] Eggman had never run for political office before but felt compelled to do so out of a sense of policy frustration. She served on the city council until 2012, when she ran for Assembly District 13 and won with 65.4 percent of the vote. She held that seat until she ran for Senate District 5 in 2020. She won with 54.9 percent of the vote.[77]

Eggman defines politics "as the necessary part of the people having a voice to further advance equity." With each passing year, Eggman acknowledges, her view of politics changes. "It evolves, dances through time." Serving in office at the state level allows Eggman to address policies she cares most about for all Californians. She was not able to do that at the local level. While serving in state office, she authored the End of Life Option Act enacted into law in 2015. This law allows mentally capable, terminally ill adults with six months or less to live the option to request prescription medication they can decide to take to peacefully end unbearable suffering.[78]

Running for any office involves consideration, and like Israel, González, and Sturgeon, Eggman thought about her family. Her wife had health issues, and Eggman wanted to make sure she was supportive. She also wondered how her running for office and being away from home would impact her daughter. Eggman is a lesbian, and when she first ran, people advised her not to disclose her orientation. "My response was 'Well, I have been with my spouse for twenty-five years. Who am I supposed to say she is, my cousin?' I couldn't lie to potential voters and ask them to vote of me. So, I ran as out, and it was somewhat of an issue, but nothing I didn't overcome. I have never lost an election." Like Israel, González, and Sturgeon, she ran as her authentic self and never looked back.

According to Eggman, the barriers or challenges to running for office can prove to be insurmountable. First, "men fall over themselves to run for every office and they may be marginally qualified. Latinas are unsure if they are qualified. They believe they have to be more prepared than they already are. The second obstacle is raising money. We struggle in this area. The last barrier is thinking about how nasty the political environment has become." Eggman's assessment of the perceived barriers are similar to those of the Latinas previously mentioned in this chapter.

Like González, Eggman believes that risks can frighten women from running because "whatever you might have done in the past will be brought out for display. You have to have thick skin. You have to have your North Star and understand that the service you provide to the community outweighs the personal."[79] Eggman reflects back on her career and highlights the fact that she authored legislation in 2015 establishing the National Guard's Discovery Challenge Academy. This program targets students who have dropped out of or did not do well in high school. The objective is to turn their lives around.[80] It was one of the proudest legislative pieces of her career.

Latinas Elected in Small Urban Cities and Rural America

Delano, California, is located thirty-one miles north-northwest of Bakersfield. The population is just under 52,000. The demographic profile of Delano is 5.3 percent White alone (not Hispanic or Latino), 77.4 percent Hispanic Latino, 4 percent Black or African American alone, 12 percent Asian alone, and less than 1 percent American Indian and Alaskan Native.[81] The mayor and council members are elected "at large"; that is, they do not represent separate districts. There are five city council members and a mayor. Currently, Veronica Vasquez serves as mayor pro tem. In 2020, she was first elected as a council member. Vasquez's first introduction to politics can be attributed to her deep roots in the United Farm Workers movement. Her grandparents led the fund-raising for the United Farm Workers union to

184 *Latino Political Power*

educate workers on the importance of labor, grassroots organizing, and politics in general. Vasquez said, "This experience prepared me for college and provided me the skills need to serve in the student senate. I then earned two internships, one with Senator Barbara Boxer in San Francisco and then with the Congressional Hispanic Caucus Institute in Washington, DC."[82] She ultimately graduated with a master's in social work from California State University at East Bay.

Her view of politics has been shaped by her upbringing and her involvement with labor unions and electoral politics. She defines politics as "ugly and cutthroat. I used to see politics as being a game changer for the community, helping the community. I think it's lost its meaning." She decided to run for city council because she believed that elected officials, at the time, were not utilizing money granted by the Coronavirus Aid, Relief, and Economic Security (CARES) Act as it was intended.[83] "I just felt like what needed to get done during a very important time was not getting done. When I decided to run and told my family and friends they replied, 'We've been waiting for you to run for office,' and I was like 'Oh.' To me it was like something new because I had not even thought of running of office."

Vasquez acknowledges the barriers to running a campaign by reflecting on her experience.

> First, there is a stereotype of women and that they should know their place. We are not judged by our merits. The second is the family and all of the responsibilities that come with a family. There is a question of whether having a family will affect their ability to focus on what is needed. Third, the lack of money and a support group. I didn't have the support to guide me but because of my experience in helping other candidates, that benefited me.

Irrespective of the level of elected office, the political experiences of Latina women seem to be the same.

Running for office also requires consideration of a number of factors. Vasquez had to ask herself, "Will this job pay be enough to pay my bills? How is the financial change going to affect my family? The other factor is negativity that comes with campaigning." Vasquez was running for office at a time in US history when the Covid-19 pandemic was unleashed. Shutdowns, quarantines, mask mandates, and social distancing were in place, so deciding to run for office brought challenges. The pandemic put a stop to door-to-door outreach, rallies, and town halls. "I had to make a lot of phone calls and that made campaigning a lot more difficult." Vasquez is aware of the differences in a campaign and formulating the support candidates need and how taxing it can be when one is the actual candidate. The perspectives and needs are different. The costs and risks for her involve the question of "Will I be held to a different standard compared to other people?

I am very vocal in my views." Vasquez's goal is to ensure that public policy is enacted appropriately to benefit constituents.

Vasquez's identity originates in the environmental and social historical importance of Delano as it existed within the Chicano movement. Historically, Delano was a major hub of farmworker organizational efforts and Chicano movement politics.[84] She has generational ties to the community. She self-identifies as a Latina/Chicano with roots in the community where the Delano Grape Strike and Boycott began in 1965 and lasted for five years.

In 2015, Latinos running and winning in small rural towns started to gain national attention. The rural town of Wilder, Idaho, in 2015 elected its first Hispanic city councilor and first Latina mayor, Alicia Almanzan.[85] According to the 2020 US Census, Wilder has a population of just under 2,000, with a majority-minority Latino population of 75.9 percent.[86]

In 2022, West Liberty, Iowa, with a population of about 4,000, elected its first Latino-majority city council.[87] According to the 2010 census, West Liberty was the first town in the state of Iowa to achieve a Hispanic-majority population (52.2 percent).[88] Research indicates that Latino candidates in small towns may have advantages over those in bigger cities. Urban areas tend to have gerrymandered election districts that favor the establishment power structure, and the media there play a larger role in shaping public opinion. In smaller places, people mobilize by word of mouth.[89] Others believe that running and winning in rural towns gives Latinos the platform to demonstrate their ability to lead diverse communities, thereby addressing one of the biggest issues facing potential Latino leaders in conservative towns.[90] The new reality is that Latinas are running and winning in small rural towns across America where Latinos are less than 3 percent of the population. Hiawassee, Georgia, is another of these small rural towns.

Liz Ordiales serves as mayor of the city of Hiawassee. Located near the Appalachian and Southern Highroads trails, Hiawassee has a population of just under 1,001.[91] Hispanics in Hiawassee make up less than 2.08 percent of the population.[92] She became the first openly LGBTQ+, Cuban-descent mayor of Hiawassee in November 2017 and ran unopposed for her second term in November 2021. Mayor Ordiales was initially elected to serve in Post 5 on the Hiawassee City Council in 2015 and was selected by fellow council members to serve as mayor pro tem in spring 2017.[93]

Ordiales's introduction to politics came from her parents' discussion of Fidel Castro's takeover of Cuba. She was just a toddler when her family fled Cuba after the 1959 revolution. They lived in Spain for a year, then put down roots in the United States. "We bolted out of Cuba and finally ended up in Miami where my grandmother moved out to first. We established ourselves and made a little money."[94] After growing up in Miami and graduating college, Ordiales got a job at BellSouth. She moved to Atlanta in 1981 to oversee the company's twenty-eight-state Hispanic products division.

186   *Latino Political Power*

Ordiales met her partner in 1989, and they would visit a friend who owned a home in Hiawassee. "I just fell in love with this place. We're surrounded by lakes and mountains. It's just an awesome place."[95] The couple eventually bought a house there in 1994 and became full-time residents a decade later.

Ordiales dove deep into community activities. She volunteered for the Towns City Fire Core and Meals on Wheels, just to name a few. The more involved she became in various community activities, the more she noticed the need for revitalization. "It was a very stagnant city. There were many derelict buildings. Empty store fronts. This encouraged me to do something."[96] She started attending city council meetings and learned more about the community needs. She eventually decided to run for city council, then mayor pro tem. She describes her moment this way: "There comes a time when you either put up or shut up." She eventually became mayor because she believed "she had a particular skill set that maybe up here they [the citizens of Hiawassee] don't have."

Ordiales defines politics as "being in a position to really serve your city and your citizens and move it forward depending on what kind of vision the city has for what it needs." She knew running for mayor would be challenging. "Hiawassee is a retirement community that is primarily elderly and White so that presents challenges."[97] She knew being a "transplant to Hiawassee," as opposed to some someone born and raised there, would be difficult. "They [voters] thought I would have gay pride parades and paint the sidewalks rainbow colors. There was a lot of 'We don't trust her so much.'"[98] The perception is "You are coming into my town and wanting to change?" So "the lack of diversity—being someone different in any environment is challenging."[99] Another challenge is "how physically demanding campaigning can be. You are constantly going door-to-door, explaining your position and your vision. It takes a toll on you physically." A further challenge is "the demands of the office. It is the scrutiny you are under for every policy you create and implement. It is a demanding office because you spend more than fifty hours a week serving as mayor—if you are a full-time mayor and you are in here all day every day. It is demanding because you have meetings on Thursday nights. You have the Chamber functions. You have veteran events and so on."

Ordiales's dedication paid off, and she sailed into a second term. During her first term she worked on fixing the city's infrastructure. This second term she is tackling downtown revitalization. It is the most important policy agenda for her.

> We've got a lot of good solid plans for our city. We've just purchased two buildings downtown in 2019, and we plan on restoring them. They have been empty for twenty-seven years. Nothing has been in them. We are transforming those two buildings that will be the catalyst to revitalizing downtown. One of the buildings is going to be an anchor restaurant with a

rooftop bar and outside dining. The other building will serve as a business incubator. If you come to us with a business idea, we will help you set up a solid business plan, access to attorneys, marketing, and so forth. We will house your business at a reduced rent rate for twenty-four months and eventually if you get yourself established, we move you out and put you into an open store front.

Reflecting on her tenure in office and the risks or costs that come with serving on city council and then as mayor, Ordiales cites the lack of diversity anyone may find in a small city or town. The challenges in running for office when your demographic is less than 2 percent of the population are very real. As for Israel, González, and Eggman, her sexual identity was a consideration for "others" but did not prevent her from winning office.

Richfield is a suburban city in Hennepin County, Minnesota, with a population just under 37,000.[100] The ethnic and racial makeup of the city is 67.50 percent White, 17.5 percent Hispanic or Latino, 11.8 percent African American, 6.9 percent Asian, 4.4 percent from two or more races, 0.50 percent Native American, and 0.04 percent Pacific Islander.[101] The current mayor of Richfield is Maria Regan Gonzalez, the first Latina mayor in Minnesota history. Regan Gonzalez was a councilwoman in Ward 3 before being elected to the mayor's office in 2018.

Regan Gonzalez grew up in two cultures with her native-Minnesotan father and Mexican mother, who immigrated from Ciudad Nezahualcoyotl, adjacent to Mexico City. "My dad is from Mora, Minnesota, and he grew up in an Irish-Swedish immigrant family that were dairy farmers, and my mom was born in Mexico. I actually think my identity, as someone who comes from these two drastically different worlds, is a really perfect fit to lead Richfield."[102] When Richfield was first settled in 1860, half of all immigrants were from Ireland.[103] Consequently, she identifies as a biracial, bicultural Chicana. "I identify as both being White and a person of color. I understand that when I pass as White, I have a lot of privilege."[104] Regan Gonzalez credits being raised in a bicultural, bilingual, and biracial family, with half of her family living in extreme poverty in Mexico, as her political awakening. She states,

> The social and racial inequities were very clear from a very young age to me. My parents really talked about it a lot. They had really instilled in my brother and me that the only difference between the two of us and my cousins in Mexico is that we happen to be born in the US and living in the US. It was our duty to use our privilege to improve conditions for our family and for our community. That was like the very impetus for my political consciousness.

Regan Gonzalez claims that as she got older, her political consciousness continued to evolve. She eventually graduated from the University of

188   *Latino Political Power*

Minnesota with a master's degree from the Executive Program in Public Health Practice. When she started working for the local public health department, Regan Gonzalez began to see just how much local government affected everyday life. She said the killings of Trayvon Martin (in Florida) and Philando Castile (in Minnesota) were "the last thing that really pushed me, and I just thought there's like an all-out war on people of color and it's subliminal and subversive and it's also very blatant. I just couldn't sit there and do nothing. Even though I was helping my community, I needed to do more, and I decided that I was going to run for city council." Looking back, Regan Gonzalez understood why people in her community had been asking her to run for office. "I just thought they were crazy, and I was like, I would never do that. Why are they asking me? I am not interested in that." Regan Gonzalez just wasn't really into elections and did not vote in every single one. She admits to being an average voter and only voting in national elections. Now, she would be *asking* for votes.

Regan Gonzalez defines politics as the "ability to make change, and so politics and public policy are vehicles for the communities and individuals to make change in their community. There's a process and structure that we have to make those larger-scale changes. I think that it should be led by those people most impacted." Regan Gonzalez admits that she did not know anything about the political process outside voting. She did not know how to run a campaign or how to advocate for herself as a candidate. Regan Gonzalez ran for the Richfield City Council in 2016 and won 56.2 percent of the vote. With only two years under her belt, she learned that the mayoral incumbent would not be seeking reelection.[105] Community members began encouraged her to run. She didn't feel ready. "I was encouraged to make an announcement that I would run. And I did that. Then I took about a month to talk to the current mayor and the city manager, and I began to reflect and ask myself, 'Am I really the most equipped person for this position? Is there somebody else? Does this align with my values?' At the end of the day, after all my reflection, I said, 'Yes, I am ready to do this.'" As a self-proclaimed "public health nerd," Regan Gonzalez knew that she could improve her community's overall quality of health. "As a public health professional, I know that 80 percent of what creates health has nothing to do with the health care system. It is your social determinants of health, where you live, the color of your skin, your income, access to healthy foods." As mayor, she had the opportunity to improve road infrastructure, provide housing amenities, and create accessible green spaces. In November 2018, Regan Gonzalez ran unopposed for the mayor's office and won with 96.3 percent of the vote.[106]

Regan Gonzalez faced similar barriers to the Latinas mentioned earlier in the chapter. The first barrier was raising money to finance a campaign and serving in elected office where the salary is not conducive to maintaining a family. Regan Gonzalez summarizes her experience this way: "If you are not independently wealthy or retired, the struggle is there. This applies to all people, but especially women of color who are disproportionately impacted by all kinds of burdens. You know, we get paid less, we have more of the responsibilities with family."[107] The second barrier is flexibility in balancing work, family responsibilities, and elected office. Regan Gonzalez characterizes the position of the eldest Latina daughter this way: "We hold the eldest daughters, which I am an eldest daughter, like the matriarch. There is the grandmother, mother and then the eldest daughter, who has a lot of family responsibilities for their immediate family, in addition to their extended family, that other people might not have."[108] The third barrier or challenge is that people are constantly questioning her leadership.

> People undermine my legal leadership ability because I don't look or sound or come from the same cloth that they think a mayor should be cut from. I have a lot of power and ability to make huge changes, and I have, but the work that I have had to go through to get to this place has been tremendous, and not only do you have barriers of other people's expectations from the dominant culture weighing on you. You have the expectations of people from the Latino community on your shoulders. . . . There is really not an understanding of all the burden that is placed, especially on Latinas, from both the dominant culture and from our own community.

As we have seen with the previous Latina candidates in this chapter, the risks of running for public office are high. Regan Gonzalez maintains, "The biggest risk in today's world is the toxicity that the political candidates now face as candidates, especially people of color and women of color. I've had people threaten me. I've had people say they were going to come to my home and keep me accountable, and then there are those kind of underhanded remarks about hurting me." She knows of other mayors who have had people with rifles and guns in their yards for days at a time. To her, these are a real cause of concern and not at all uncommon.

Regan Gonzalez understands that leadership, politics, and policy involve taking time to foster relationships, build trust, and broaden one's understanding of issues before trying to disrupt and make changes.[109] One of her greatest accomplishments is instituting policy, protections, and support to keep Richfield's community housing affordable and accessible to everyone in her community. She fought against apartment purchases that displaced low-income families. "Before I was on the council and in the mayor's office, we did not have an affordable housing public policy agenda. Before I joined, there was the largest mass displacement of low-income community members in the state of Minnesota in Richfield. This is hands down the area of public policy that I have had the most impact."

Conclusion

There is no clearly delineated path to electoral office for Latinas. Some enter through participation in grassroots community efforts and social networks in the community. Others use a more traditional path to seek elected office by simply jumping into a campaign with both feet. The Latinas mentioned in this chapter highlight similarities that proved challenging as they meandered from the margins to electoral office or political incorporation. These women struggled to raise money to run a campaign. They had to think about whether they could afford to assume office since the salary is often less than what they were earning. Familial responsibilities and cultural expectations continued to give them cause for concern. González, Sturgeon, Eggman, Vasquez, and Regan Gonzalez endured sexist comments like "wait your turn" or had their authority questioned and were not taken as seriously as a man in the same office. These Latina women understand the power of relationship building and the importance of coalitions in moving legislation from bill to law. These Latina women understand that their sacrifice is for the betterment of their communities. Without a doubt Latina elected officials are changing the way we think about political inclusion.

Notes

1. Acosta and Winegarten 2003.
2. Bird 2016; Fraga et al. 2008; Hughes 2013.
3. As quoted in Stille 2001.
4. NALEO's Directory is dependent on officeholders' self-reporting. There are Latinas currently in office who have not completed the NALEO survey and hence are not counted.
5. Morse 2000.
6. National Association of Latino Elected and Appointed Officials, "The Dream Latino Cabinet," https://naleo.org/latinocabinet/.
7. Sonneland 2020.
8. "Hispanic Judges on the Federal Courts," Federal Judicial Center, https://fjc.gov/history/judges/search/Hispanic.
9. Cruz and Molina 2009.
10. Brennan Center for Justice. 2021. "Brennan Center's Myrna Perez Confirmed to Federal Bench." https://www.brennancenter.org/our-work/research-reports/brennan-centers-myrna-perez-confirmed-federal-bench.
11. "Judicial Nominations," Committee on the Judiciary, https://Judiciary.senate.gov/nominations/judicial?c=117.
12. Ruiz 1987.
13. Texas Civil Liberties Union 1938.
14. Sosa Riddell 1974.
15. Fitzgerald 2003.
16. *El Paso Herald-Post* 1970.
17. Flynn 2003, 5B.

18. A. Chavez 2000.
19. Keck 1991, 5; Long 2005.
20. Keck 1990, 1; Chabrán and Chabrán 1996, 282.
21. "E.P. County Union Seeks Pay Increase," *El Paso Herald-Post*, August 29, 1966.
22. "Election Archives," El Paso County Elections Department, https://epcountyvotes.com/election_archives.
23. Ibid.
24. A. Flores 2018.
25. "Election Archives."
26. Benson 2018, 79.
27. Svitek 2017.
28. Bassett 2017.
29. "Election Archives."
30. As quoted in Evans 2018.
31. Ibid.
32. Ibid.
33. As quoted in M. Mendez 2018.
34. Schwartz 2002.
35. "Texas State Directory" 2018.
36. Kinghorn 2005.
37. Morris 2012.
38. Molony 2013, A1.
39. Harris County Elections Division 2016.
40. *Houston Chronicle* 2020.
41. J. Wallace 2017, A006.
42. Harris County Elections Division 2018.
43. Murphy 2018, 9A.
44. Ura and Astudillo 2021 .
45. US Census Bureau 2020b.
46. Webb 2017, A5.
47. Israel, personal interview, February 2, 2022.
48. Sarah Weddington was an attorney and a member of the Texas House of Representatives. She is best known for representing "Jane Roe" in the landmark *Roe v. Wade* case before the US Supreme Court.
49. Israel interview.
50. Ibid.
51. Eaton 2013.
52. Kerr 2014.
53. Navarro and Hernandez 2016.
54. Theis 2014.
55. District Profile Texas House District 104 2021.
56. Gonzalez, personal interview, February 21, 2022.
57. Serwer 2021.
58. Lamagdeleine 2021.
59. Ibid.
60. In 2021, the Texas governor signed into law Senate Bill 1, which tightened state election laws and constrains local control of elections by limiting counties' ability to expand voting options. See Ura 2021.
61. Since 1973, *Texas Monthly* has published the biennial list of the best and worst legislators in a session. See Hooks, Ratcliffe, and Zelinski 2021.
62. Moritz 2022.

63. Delaware General Assembly, https://legis.delaware.gov.

64. Sturgeon, personal interview, February 14, 2022.

65. "About Laura" *Campaign website,* January 2, 2019. https://sturgeon4state senate.com/about-laura/.

66. The Campaign School at Yale University is a nonpartisan, issue-neutral political-campaign training program. Its mission is to increase the number and influence of women holding elected and appointed office in the United States.

67. State of Delaware, Department of Elections 2018. https://elections.delaware .gov/archive/elect18/elect18_general/html/index.shtml.

68. "California Constitution Article IV," Justia US Law, https://law.justia.com /constitution/california/article-iv.

69. Alexander 2009.

70. California Research Bureau 2020, https://public.tableau.com/views/Legislative Demographics2019-20/UserView?:showVizHome=no.

71. Ibid.

72. Jacobs 1990; Howard 2012.

73. American Community Survey 2021 and US Census Bureau 2020c, https:// www.census.gov/programs-surveys/acs/data.html.

74. Talamantes Eggman, personal interview, February 25, 2022.

75. Ibid.

76. "Part 1: Vote Totals, Election Outcomes and Text for City Ballot Measures," California Secretary of State, 2006, https://elections.cdn.sos.ca.gov/county-city -school-district-election-results/city_report_2006.pdf.

77. For 2012 through 2020, see "Statewide Election Results," California Secretary of State, https://www.sos.ca.gov/elections/prior-elections/statewide-election-results.

78. Mason 2015.

79. Ibid.

80. KXTV Staff 2015.

81. "Delano Population," US Census Bureau 2020, American Community Survey Office 2022, www.census.gov/.

82. Vasquez, personal interview, February 16, 2022.

83. The CARES Act of 2020 was a $2.2 trillion economic stimulus bill passed by US Congress. The bill provided a onetime cash payment to individual people who submitted a tax return in America, increased unemployment benefits, and created the Paycheck Protection Program to provide forgivable loans to small businesses, money to corporations, and money allocated to state and local governments.

84. "City History," Delano California, https://www.cityofdelano.org/512/City -History.

85. Rott 2015.

86. US Census Bureau, "P2 Hispanic or Latino, and Not Hispanic or Latino by Race," 2020 Census State Redistricting Data (Public Law 94-171) Summary file. US Census Bureau, 2020 Census, www.census.gov/.

87. Arena 2022.

88. Schaper 2011.

89. Planas 2015.

90. Rott 2015.

91. Hiawassee, Georgia Population 2020, World Population Review 2022, https://worldpopulationreview.com/us-cities/hiawassee-ga-population.

92. Ibid.

93. Towns Co Content Specialist 2019.

94. As quoted in Saunders 2021.

95. Ibid.

96. Ordiales, personal interview, January 26, 2022.

97. The racial makeup of the town was 95 percent White, less than 1 percent Black, less than 2 percent Asian, and less than 3 percent Hispanic; Hiawassee, Georgia Population 2020. World Population Review 2022, https://worldpopulationreview .com/us-cities/hiawassee-ga-population.

98. As quoted in Saunders 2021.

99. Ordiales interview.

100. US Census Bureau 2020, *American Community Survey 5-year Estimates*, www.censusreporter.org/profiles/79500US2701410-hennepin-county-bloominton-rich field-cities-puma-mn.

101. Ibid.

102. As quoted in Bonelli 2018.

103. Smetanka 2008.

104. Gonzalez, personal interview, February 18, 2022.

105. Otarola 2018.

106. City of Richfield Elections Department 2016 and 2018 (author conversation via phone).

107. Ibid.

108. Ibid.

109. Millard 2019.

8

Latino Political Power Today . . . and Tomorrow

The aim of this book is twofold: to describe Latinos' transition from disenfranchised outsiders to political leaders and policymakers and to explain to what degree Latino elected officials (LEOs) are sensitive to ethnic community concerns and seek to deliver policy benefits to their communities. Stated another way, the story presented here has explored the historical struggle of Latinos to overcome discriminatory barriers to full participation and to achieve political incorporation and obtain policy benefits. This book contributes to the larger study of Latino politics. First, it shows through case studies the different ways Latino communities have mobilized to achieve and consolidate Latino political incorporation. Second, it explores the demographics of Latino political leaders, the pathways they used to win elective office, and their views on contemporary policy matters. Third, it has summarized the many years of struggle by Latinos to receive, in the words of the Voting Rights Act, "an equal opportunity to participate in elections and to elect a candidate of their choice." This struggle is far from over for Latinos. Stricter voter ID laws, reductions in early voting and voting hours, partisan election administrators, elimination of voting drop-off points or mail-in ballots, mass purges of voter rolls, high rates of noncitizenship, lower voter registration and turnout rates, and racially polarized voting patterns have limited Latinos' access to and full participation in the political process and their election to office. Relative to the majority population, Latinos still do not have equal opportunity to participate in the electoral process.

Some have argued that Latinos have entered a post–civil rights era in which they are no longer victims of the political system and no longer in need of legal protection of the Voting Rights Act and its amendments to obtain their fair share of elected positions in a society that remains bounded by racial politics. However, one fact not in dispute is that Latinos continue

195

196 *Latino Political Power*

to live in residentially segregated areas that are more densely populated or overcrowded, with underfunded schools and lower levels of education and income than the average American. There remain numerous social struggles to achieve full equality in our democracy by Latinos and other racial minorities. These battles must continue to be waged, while others in the Latino community push the boundaries of who can be elected and where.

The core of majority-Latino districts that have elected Latinos should be viewed as a base, not a ceiling, for Latino electoral aspirations. The dilemma faced by Latino political strategists is how to expand the number of districts in each state to provide the greatest number of locations where Latinos will have the opportunity to elect the representatives of their choice. Should a certain percentage of majority-minority districts be broken up and new district lines redrawn to create greater numbers of electoral districts where Latinos could compete in non-Latino-majority districts to choose their representatives? This assumes non-Latino voters will vote for Latinos. While there is some evidence for this proposition in certain areas of the country, the legacy of prejudice and discrimination toward Latinos still hangs heavy over the political process in many communities. These challenges are not new. In 2001, this was said about one state: "Unfortunately, racially polarized voting persists in California, thus demonstrating the continued need for and enforcement of the Voting Rights Act. [The Mexican American Legal Defense and Education Fund's] consultants have conducted preliminary racial polarization analysis of elections occurring during the decade and have found evidence of polarization, particularly in Southern California."[1]

While the preservation of existing Latino-majority districts is a necessary feature of Latino efforts for equal opportunity to participate in the political process in the foreseeable future, at the same time, this should not restrict Latinos in their efforts to win elections in areas and regions where historically they have had a limited presence. Determining how to hold onto existing seats and expand into new electoral districts has become a controversial issue.

As discussed previously, Latinos have used at least four distinct pathways to achieve electoral office: legal challenges, demand/protest, coalition politics (including multiethnic and issue-based coalitions), and nonconfrontational individual efforts. Some of these efforts have been part of movements for political empowerment; others were separate from these efforts or even ran counter to them. The result, as discussed in Chapter 5, has been different types of candidates, different levels of political incorporation, and different types of representation.

The election of Latinos to office creates the potential for different types of representation. Hanna Pitkin posits four dimensions of representation.[2] The first level is *formal* representation, where officials are empowered to act on behalf of others by a process that enables the representative to attain more authority than those being represented. This takes place through an institutional arrangement such as an election. At the second level, *descriptive* representation, the elected representative reflects the social characteristics of the people he or she represents. This level is also important, as it provides a marker of the extent to which LEOs have achieved visible elected positions in society.

At the third level, *symbolic* representation, a representative is accepted and supported by the community that elected him or her to office. This is important to study, because LEOs often become role models in their communities. If a candidate or officeholder is identified by the community not just as a symbol of individual achievement but as a representative of the community's values and aspirations, then symbolic representation has been achieved.

A fourth level is *substantive* representation. At this level, an elected representative is expected to act "in the interests of the represented in a manner responsive to them."[3] There is a perceived close connection between the representative and the represented. The elected leader who strives to redirect resources to the community that elected her or him to office is viewed as representing the needs of the community. Constituents come to expect the representative will fight on their behalf. Those who do not will likely have a difficult time retaining their seats.

Strategies for Winning Office in Diverse Districts

Latinos are elected from a diverse range of electoral districts, from predominantly Latino-populated districts to those where Latinos are only a small percentage of the population. While they are mostly elected from districts where Latinos are a significant proportion of the population, Latinos have found creative ways to cross over and win in non-Latino-majority districts. Here we explore the strategies employed by Latinos to achieve elected office.

The election of Latinos in non-Latino-majority districts is an indication of the potential for more crossover Latino candidates from both parties in urban, suburban, and rural areas. In more conservative suburban or rural districts, crossover politicians tend to use campaign themes and craft their campaign messages to build a mainstream, noncontroversial platform that does not emphasize national origin or ethnic identity. In urban districts, where Latinos may or may not be the majority population, crossover candidates tend to include a multiracial platform and focus on interracial coalition building.

The existence of a majority-Latino district may lead us to assume wrongly that Latino candidates win elections there solely by appealing to

198 *Latino Political Power*

Latino voters. In a study of Los Angeles politics, Latino city council candidates used deracialized campaign strategies in order to win office in districts that had a majority-Latino population but included other ethnicities. In order to build cross-racial support, which was crucial where the Latino electorate was less than 50 percent of the voters, Latino candidates used political styles, issues, and mobilization strategies that deemphasized race.[4]

Whether Latinos are using mobilization strategies that deemphasize race, given the political realities of racial and ethnic politics in the United States, will have to be based on empirical data. Research into electoral politics indicates that hyperpartisan environments pressure minority candidates to move their race/ethnicity to the margins to secure victory.[5] Deracialization is tied directly to the long debate over Anglo attitudes about race and how these attitudes shape voting behavior. Racialized politics is generally believed to work against racial minority candidates in Anglo-majority areas, particularly at the local level.[6] Nevertheless, where Latinos are the majority population and Latinos have previously been elected to office, there is an *intraethnic* competitive character to electoral contests. Latinos now regularly compete against each other in districts for elected positions where they are the majority or near-majority population, and the ability to form alliances with selected voters often makes the difference between winning and losing. Name recognition, previous electoral experience, and strong family roots in the district are also usually essential factors for winning elections.

In areas where Latinos are not the majority population, employing a variety of approaches is crucial to elect Latinos. For both conservative and moderate Latino Republicans, the use of campaign messages that appeal to non-Latinos has been effective in suburban California districts and other parts of the country where large numbers of middle- and upper-middle-class homeowners are concerned about preserving property values, improving schools, and keeping crime rates low. In urban locations, where Latinos are not the majority population, Latinos must reach across ethnic and racial fault lines and build coalitions. The coalitional forms include the use of biracial, multiracial, multiple-issue, and labor-Latino alliances.

Each political environment contains its own set of circumstances. Former Speaker of the House of Representatives Tip O'Neill said, "All politics is local." This is an accurate description of the dynamics under which Latinos seek elected office. Latino political candidates and officeholders are affected by the local political structure, including the strength of political parties, the influence of a dominant political machine, and the level of political organization in the Latino community. Structural rules, such as whether positions are partisan or nonpartisan, also influence the degree to which officeholders are tied to party politics.

In theory, nonpartisan races limit the power of machine politics, and during the Progressive era in the early twentieth century, many local communities, particularly in the West and Southwest, moved to a system of non-partisan offices. However, the dominance of one of the two main political parties in most geographic areas means that while candidates may not run as party candidates, they have traditionally been nominated by, or received the support of, a local party committee. Party identification, while not nearly as strong as during an earlier era, is still a powerful predictor of electoral success in many communities. Only in strong reform electoral districts, where party affiliation is nonexistent or secondary to strong independent candidates, is partisanship not a decisive factor in election to local office.

Historically, the use of machine politics in government, with strong control by a political apparatus, is usually tied to the dominant political party. In urban areas, the dominant political influence was usually the Democratic Party machine, formed in the nineteenth century in urban areas by Irish and other European immigrants. The large numbers of Latinos in the Democratic Party and the presence of Cuban Americans in the Republican Party make monolithic party identification not completely useful in a discussion of Latino politics. Instead, "Latino machine politics" involves established political leaders, usually but not exclusively Latino, who have worked their way up the ladder of elected and appointed positions; these politicians seek to bring along the next generation of political leaders they have mentored and groomed for elected office. They also assist them with financial backing from influential supporters.

Learning from the Incorporation Process

A few general conclusions can provide some insights into how the process of political incorporation unfolds and the construction of political governing coalitions operates at the local level. First, for their genesis, movements for political representation do not require a singular major event that sparks protest and demands for change. These case studies indicate that several events triggered a reaction leading to movements for political incorporation.

Second, the presence of community organizations that mobilize to achieve the inclusion of Latinos has an important impact on the character of the political incorporation process. The community-led efforts to win district elections in San Antonio and Miami-Dade County built a strong foundation to carry forward the demand for full political incorporation. In Los Angeles, while district elections already existed, when Latinos began to seek inclusion, the struggle took the form of drawing district boundaries that enabled Latinos to have a fair chance at winning elected office. The formation of this organization and the mobilization of the Chicano community, combined with the sophistication of Chicano community activists, were indispensable to the electoral campaign to win district elections.

200 *Latino Political Power*

Third, a biracial coalition to achieve political incorporation is a tactic, not a strategic necessity. In places where Latinos are a minority of the population, Latino politicians will continue to work in alliance with an array of potential allies. For candidates aligned with the Democratic Party, this can include labor unions, African Americans, Asian and Pacific Islanders, and Native Americans, as well as other potential issue-based allies, to build electoral coalitions. In places where Latinos are the dominant majority, such as Miami, the role of White liberals or other potential allies was not critical in the ascension to political leadership. In Miami, White liberals and the conservative Cuban American community were at odds over many issues and failed to work together. The necessity of a biracial coalition was not evident in the political incorporation efforts of the Cuban Americans.

Others have observed a similar finding in some Latino-majority cities in the Southwest. The point is that when Latinos are the majority of voters, they are less likely to seek or need the assistance of White liberals, although, because of common ideological views, they want to work closely with Whites and other racial groups based on common policy aims and goals. This certainly was the case in San Antonio, Texas, where in 2009 Julián Castro won election as mayor with the support of both White and Mexican American voters. However, in numerous other cities, the achievement of political incorporation for Latinos and other racial minorities was based on the forging of bi- and multiracial coalitions.[7]

Emerging Leaders

Although Latino elected officials are generally older than the populations they serve, some enter politics at an earlier age than their more experienced counterparts. They come into office in a variety of ways, such as by defeating the incumbent candidate endorsed by the political machine or by working for an incumbent and jumping into the race when the position opens up. This "Millennial" cohort of young, ambitious elected officials who are not held back by their age or experience is a growing phenomenon. In centers of Latino politics and beyond—in Delano, California; Richfield, Minnesota; and elsewhere—they are running and winning important political offices. This cohort of political actors includes Mayor Maria Regan Gonzalez in Richfield, Mayor Pro Tem Veronica Vasquez, and several officials in New York City. Some of them are challenging the Latino political establishment in their communities. They are highly educated, well informed on issues, and determined to make their mark on politics.

Richfield mayor Maria Regan Gonzalez was first elected at the age of thirty-three in 2018.[8] She was the first in her family to go to school and get a master's degree. Regan Gonzalez proved to be a strong leader dedicated to building a more prosperous community-oriented city. State Representative Jessica González represents the 104th District in Texas. A fierce advocate of voting rights and LGBT+ protections in Texas, she was elected to office at the age of thirty-seven. In 2020, Joshua Garcia, at the age of thirty-five, became the first Latino (Puerto Rican) mayor in Holyoke, Massachusetts. Garcia had served as the town administrator of Blandford, Massachusetts, and as a fire commissioner and school committee member in Holyoke. He was able to garner support from Puerto Ricans, Whites, Irish, Blacks, Columbians, and Dominicans. Garcia campaigned for a "Holyoke with an experience that is Puerto Rican."[9] These emerging leaders reflect a growing trend of young people becoming engaged in politics.

LEOs are on average better educated and more financially secure than the general Latino population. Many of them were successful professionals or businesspeople before they sought electoral office. It is probably accurate to say, however, that many LEOs are ideologically somewhat more liberal than their constituents; yet in most respects they are representative of the broad masses of Latinos. Some LEOs are able to build consensus and work with politicians of other beliefs and races. Some continue to raise calls for social justice, equality, and an end to discrimination. Yet they are part of a much larger political structure that limits their ability to make dramatic changes.

Political Incorporation and Class Interests

Another finding drawn from the efforts of Latinos to achieve political incorporation is that governing coalitions contain multiple class interests. The character of urban government is a complex mix of influences, including commercial development, labor, neighborhood, environmental, and Latino and racial minority community interests that seek to steer local policy. The dominant governing coalition in cities where Latinos have been successful in the electoral arena does contain Latinos, including members of the city council and city bureaucrats; however, a combination of factors has limited the level of policy benefits being delivered to the working poor in the Latino community. These factors include slow economic investment in the city, systemic poverty in the Latino community that is produced by a low-wage labor market, and differing land-use and environmental policy agendas by elected Latinos and other local elected officials. Issues such as crime reduction, public safety, and debate over no-growth/pro-growth development have received the most attention and budgetary consideration by the city; meanwhile, desperately needed services in the Latino community, such as more varied employment opportunities, training for better-paying jobs, overcrowding in schools, improved educational services, and more after-school programs, have received fewer resources.

Latino political incorporation has meant, for the first time, not just the representation of Latinos in general; more specifically, low-wage Latino workers and the urban poor are now included in the dialog in some communities. Latino worker interests are usually part of the electoral coalition that elects many Latinos to office. Previously, local governments rarely addressed labor issues. Today, these concerns are likely to be openly discussed and debated since they relate to water issues, housing, education, and other social policies. In many cities, policies have been created that have benefited the working poor in Latino communities. These policies appear to be much stronger than the previous governing coalitions, which were dominated exclusively by downtown business interests. For example, in 2016, California became the first state to officially adopt a statewide minimum wage of $15 an hour, implemented by incremental increase, after a grassroots campaign by a community coalition that included numerous Latino worker organizations. Beyond 2023, the state will adjust its minimum annually for inflation based on the national consumer price index for urban wage earners and clerical workers.[10]

Another observation from the case studies and history of political incorporation efforts is that Latinos have not always acted with a common vision among their community stakeholders and officeholders. The need for an ongoing community-based movement of Latinos that can articulate the community's demands for policy equity, hold city leaders, including Latino council members, accountable for their actions, and push for a greater share of policy benefits in the future was an important lesson learned by community activists in places like San Antonio and Los Angeles. However, Latinos are not the dominant economic players in most communities and thus are still economically dependent on the same economic interests that have controlled local and regional politics for decades. For this reason, in cities like San Antonio, where Latinos are the majority of the governing coalition, the Latino community must negotiate a relationship with the dominant economic forces that shape the policy agenda. In these locations, there is a dual role to the governing coalition with both corporate influences, and by the efforts to redistribute resources to the working poor in Latino and other communities.

In Miami, where Latino business interests are influential, Cuban American politicians are also brokers for the wealth and power exercised by their fellow community members in the business world. There appears to be a more equitable relationship between race and class forces; however, this is highly unusual. In most cities, Latino politicians' role is to negotiate to achieve policy benefits for the Latino community in the context of supporting a large economic development project. This usually takes the form of attempting to obtain agreements from private developers to build affordable housing, hire from the community, and fund urban education or parks and recreation areas in Latino communities as part of development efforts.

Economic interests will continue to remain active where there are investment opportunities. This requires that they deal with the political forces that occupy the seats of power. Economic interests must adapt and find ways to compromise to achieve their financial goals or use their economic strength to negotiate the deal most favorable to them. This is the logic of the market system; Latinos in power in local and higher levels of government should continue to leverage their political power to obtain the best possible economic deals for their communities and for others in need of community development and social services.

Levels of Political Incorporation and Policy Benefits

The results of these case studies indicate the level of political incorporation is not an accurate predictor of the strength of Latino political power. The more important question is how political power manifests itself in the strength of policy benefits returning to local Latino communities. The level of political incorporation alone does not answer this question. Particularly in cities that use district elections, where candidates are elected from different neighborhoods with widely divergent socioeconomic conditions and issue formation, there are different types of Latino officeholders.

This study concludes that, at least in cities with district elections, the strength of the number of Latinos on a city council does not fully explain differences in policy formation among cities. Even in cities with at-large electoral systems, the ability of Latinos to get elected stems from the support of different voter bases. This in turn impacts the character and type of governing coalition that is created.

Not only is who is elected significant; the type of administrators hired into key positions, such as city manager, police chief, and head of economic development, is also important to understand how governing coalitions are constructed. These positions, in conjunction with the election of Latinos, share an equally powerful role at the local level. They shape local policy decisions and can steer cities in a variety of directions. For example, these usually nonelected local government leaders can provide leadership around an issue and direct resources to solve long-standing problems.

The final conclusion of the case studies is that, in addition to the important roles of economic interests, Latino politicians, and city administrators, vigilance and an ongoing, organized community-led movement of Latinos are vital for policy benefits to be returned to the community. The key lesson from the many political incorporation efforts is the need for the Latino community to continue to mobilize to receive its fair share of resources and to highlight broader social issues outside the electoral arena *after* the election of Latinos to office. This can take the form of a well-organized interest

204 *Latino Political Power*

group such as Citizens Organized for Public Service in San Antonio. However, when this does not take place, there is no mechanism other than electing different political actors to keep local government accountable to the needs of the Latino community. Latino politicians who run for office on a program to implement a Latino agenda may soon resort to a business-as-usual mentality that is disconnected from the most pressing needs of the community. This situation existed for a period in Los Angeles, where elements of the Latino elected leadership had grown removed and insulated from the grassroots needs of their communities.[11] This is a dangerous trend and adds to cynicism in the Latino community and the belief that the electoral arena is an ineffective and counterproductive vehicle for democratic action.

In a representative democracy, overreliance on the electoral arena and on elected Latino officeholders and a sole focus on achieving the maximum numbers of Latinos in office will not solve the complex problems in Latino communities. In addition to an examination of political leaders, issue-based neighborhood organizing in Latino communities is vital to address the structural inequalities facing the Latino community. Understanding the interplay between political incorporation efforts and empowerment efforts at the grassroots level is important for the study of Latino politics.

The community efforts usually begin as small and insignificant but form the basis for large-scale changes at a later date, such as the dramatic changes in the cities we explored. These efforts are difficult to maintain as the leadership and resources to sustain them can ebb and flow; yet the existence and maintenance of organized interest groups, neighborhood-based organizations, community activists, and local residents can extend inclusion into a governing coalition or force policy changes in cities as small as Richfield[12] and as large as Los Angeles.[13] More often than not, these efforts provide the spark that ultimately leads to the reevaluation of public policy, institutional changes, and the election of new leaders.

Final Thoughts

Pan-ethnic labels describing the US population of people tracing their roots to Latin America and Spain have been introduced over decades, rising and falling in popularity. The two dominant labels in use are Hispanic and Latino, with origins in the 1970s and 1990s, respectively. More recently, a gender-neutral term, Latinx, has risen as an alternative to Hispanic and Latino. While some Hispanics say Latinx should be used as a pan-ethnic term, few say they prefer it over others.

The diversity of political experiences of Latinos makes broad generalizations difficult. For example, the rapid rise to local political power of

Cuban Americans in South Florida is due to the combination of favorable US government policy and local political and economic underdevelopment in Miami that enabled Cubans to overcome the discriminatory obstacles created by the city's Anglo establishment.[14] The Cuban political experience is a different process of political incorporation than that of Puerto Ricans, who are citizens by decree of the US government; Mexican Americans in the Southwest and Midwest, who have suffered a much longer history of entrenched structural discrimination and social ostracism for generations; and recent immigrants and refugees from Central and South America, who have only recently begun to achieve electoral office.

In another example, Latinas (and those who identify as LGBT+) who have risen to Congress, state legislative office, and the mayoralty of small urban and rural cities have faced similar considerations and barriers as they have fought for political inclusion, such as raising money to run a campaign, questioning if they could financially afford to assume political office, being told to "wait their turn," juggling family responsibilities, and protecting their own safety, to name a few. They all view politics in relation to the betterment of their communities. This is consistent with other studies that examine Latinas in electoral politics.[15] In addition, Latinas studied in this book understand the importance of relationship building as a precursor to moving public policy from bill to law. Interestingly enough, the sexual identity of some Latinas had little to no influence on their electability. Instead, the skill sets they offered and the ability to work in other sectors of their communities had compounding beneficial effects in areas such as education, voting rights, health care, and so on.

Latinos do not share an identical political experience in this country, and there are limits to the use of various methodologies to study such a diverse group of people. Although Latinos have a common history of conquest and colonialism, their diverse paths to political officeholding and political power reflect a multiplicity of factors based on the structure of the conditions they entered as ethnic immigrants, their social and political status upon entering this new environment, and their efforts to change their status using a variety of traditional avenues as well as protest/demands. As such, this book has not attempted to capture the totality of Latino political experience; rather, it is a more focused exploration of how racial politics have unfolded in the post–civil rights era, where the contestation of racial identities, economics, and political power have manifested in specific forms. While we did analyze some of the political conflicts with Whites in some cities and the process of the transition of power from those who have held it for many decades, the book has not fully explored the dynamics of Black and Latino political relationships, except in specific locations. This is an important topic that others have more fully examined.[16] Also, we did not explore the challenges and opportunities for the Asian and Pacific Islander communities and Latinos for coalition politics. In many communities these heavily immigrant communities live in the same neighborhoods, compete against each other, and at times join together to support candidates from each other's respective communities, and this topic needs to be further explored.

This book has also sought to capture the contemporary thinking of Latino elected officials. The results of the original survey of LEOs demonstrates that they exhibit significant concern for the needs of the Latino community in their political behavior. The subsequent interviews conducted with LEOs confirmed the initial finding of the mail survey that most Latino political leaders were committed to being substantive representatives for the Latino community. They consciously sought to set policy that benefited the Latino community.

Having achieved political office, and in some cases having achieved political domination of the local political power structure, does this mean that all Latino efforts meant little as the limitation of their collective economic fortunes and lack of economic control have reduced their officeholding to "window dressing" to give the appearance that they have gained equality with Whites? It is our belief that Latino politics, as it is conducted in the centers of Latino politics and in numerous other locations, has the potential to create partnerships for economic development for Latino communities. This will not be easy, as Latinos do not control most of the economic resources in their communities; yet the sheer number of Latino voters is causing global economic interests to address their needs. The US Hispanic market is enormous, and the Latino community has the potential to shape economics and politics in the hemisphere. With the economic investment of China in Latin America, the effect of a major world power in the hemisphere will also need to be explored, for undoubtedly there will be a significant impact on the people of Latin America and US-based Latinos. Within the constraints of an unequal economic system in the United States and the additional political and economic uncertainty in the world, such as the Russian invasion of Ukraine in 2022 and the long-term impact of the Covid-19 pandemic on world and domestic economics and health care, Latino political power can at opportune moments redirect economic resources to solve some long-standing social problems at the local and regional levels.

Distinct pathways to political empowerment are available to Latinos as their numbers continue to grow in urban, suburban, and rural communities. There will undoubtedly be a growing variety of Latino candidates from both major parties and as Independents. More importantly, the poverty and social inequalities that continue to grow in many communities will result in new and varied forms of social movements being constructed to respond to the new conditions. Likewise, as many American-born Latinos move away

Latino Political Power Today . . . and Tomorrow   207

from the barrios to suburbs, the growth of middle-class enclaves of Latinos and the integration into non-Latino areas by Latino families will also present new challenges and new voting patterns within the Latino community. Furthermore, the continuing growth of anti-immigrant forces that fan the racial cultural wars will also prompt new and varied responses within the Latino and other immigrant communities. As old alliances fray, new ones may emerge.

Undoubtedly, this book is one piece of a larger puzzle. The types of electoral districts and candidates seeking office can be explored more systematically and also compared in qualitative studies. This book contributes to the growing body of literature on racial politics in American cities and adds greater validity to the development of Latino politics at the local and national levels. The field of Latino politics is still a relatively new subfield of social science investigation, and as various social theories are tested in the context of the experiences of Latinos, in interaction with others, these theories will be enriched to a greater degree.

In a society as diverse as the United States, equality for all remains an elusive goal. In a nation where physical and cultural differences have been used by a dominant majority to discriminate against and marginalize groups of people, gaining symbolic and substantive representation is a necessary step in a much longer process of obtaining full equality for historically underrepresented groups. The political representation of people of color is not exclusively the responsibility of those of the same racial or ethnic group; however, the historical divisions among peoples of color in this country require continued exploration of how minority representatives act to represent their own historically underrepresented group members and others in a similar situation. As Melissa Williams notes, "Although representation for marginalized groups is not in itself a cure for injustice, there is good reason to believe it is at least a healing measure."[17]

Notes

1. MALDEF 2001, 1.
2. Pitkin 1967.
3. Ibid.
4. Juenke and Sampaio 2010.
5. Krebs and Holian 2007; Orey 2006.
6. Citrin, Green, and Sears 1990; Highton 2004; Oliver and Mendelberg 2000; Sears, Sidanius, and Bobo 2000.
7. Hero 1997, 257.
8. Birt 2018.
9. DeForge and Hohenberger 2021.
10. Golden 2022.

11. Regalado 1998.
12. Gonzalez, personal interview, February 18, 2022.
13. Rosales 2000; Regalado 1998; Anner 1996; Medoff and Sklar 1994.
14. Moreno 1997.
15. Hardy-Fanta 1993; S. Navarro 2018.
16. Vaca 2004; E. Morales 2004; Jennings 1994; C. P. Henry 1980; Miles 1992.
17. M. S. Williams 1998, 243.

References

Abalos, David T. 1986. *Latinos in the United States: The Sacred and the Political.* Notre Dame, IN: University of Notre Dame Press.

Abrajano, Marisa. 2010. *Campaigning to the New American Electorate: Television Advertising to Latinos.* Stanford, CA: Stanford University Press.

Abrajano, Marisa, and Zoltan L. Hajnal. 2015 *White Backlash: Immigration, Race, and American Politics.* Princeton, NJ: Princeton University Press.

Abramson, Michael. 1971. *Palante: Young Lords Party.* New York: McGraw-Hill.

Abrego, Leisy. 2008. "Legitimacy, Social Identity, and the Mobilization of Law: The Effects of Assembly Bill 540 on Undocumented Students in California." *Law & Social Inquiry* 33, no. 3: 709–734.

Acevedo, Nicole. 2020. "Young Latinos Mobilized, Voted and Were Pivotal in 2020. Organizers Want to Keep It Going." *NBC News.* November 27. https://www.nbcnews.com/news/latino/young-latinos-mobilized-voted-were-pivotal-2020-organizers-want-keep-n1246853.

Acosta, Teresa Palomo, and Ruthie Winegarten. 2003. *Los Tejanos: 300 Years of History.* Austin: University of Texas Press.

Acuña, Rodolfo F. 1981. *Occupied America: A History of Chicanos.* 2nd ed. New York: Harper & Row.

———. 1988. *Occupied America: A History of Chicanos.* 3rd ed. New York: HarperCollins.

———. 1996. *Anything but Mexican: Chicanos in Contemporary Los Angeles.* New York: Verso.

Alatorre, Richard. 2016. *Change from the Inside: My Life, the Chicano Movement, and the Story of an Era.* Berkeley, CA: Berkeley Public Policy Press.

"Alex Padilla." 2001. *Latino Leaders: The National Magazine of the Successful Hispanic American* 22, no. 3 (June–July): 21–24.

Alexander, Kurtis. 2009. "Laird Leads Fight Against Part-Time Legislature." *Santa Cruz Sentinel.* September 26.

210 References

American Community Survey. 2021. *California State Senate District 5.* https://www.census.gov/programs-surveys/acs/data.html.

Anderson, Christopher. 2003. "Mayor Re-elected Analyst Says Garza's Tally May Signal Trouble Ahead." *San Antonio Express News.* May 4.

Anner, John, ed. 1996. *Beyond Identity Politics: Emerging Social Justice Movements in Communities of Color.* Boston: South End.

Arena, K. 2022. "Iowa Town Translates Its Diverse Population into a Majority Latino City Council." NPR. January 14. https://www.npr.org/2022/01/14/1072987317/iowa-town-translates-its-diverse-population-into-a-majority-latino-city-council.

Ashbrook, Maeve. 2021a. "Before and After: How Do the New District Maps in Texas Compare?" KVUE ABC. October 20.

———. 2021b. "Coalition of Latino Organizations Files Lawsuit Challenging Texas Redistricting Maps." KVUE ABC. October 18.

Attanasio, Cedar. 2019. "El Paso Shooting Suspect Pleads Not Guilty in 22 Deaths." APNEWS. October 10.

Avila, Joaquin G. 1997. "The Political Integration of Racial and Ethnic Minorities." Twelfth Annual Ernesto Galarza Lecture, Stanford Center for Chicano Research, Palo Alto, CA.

Ayon, David R. 2000. "Fault Lines Below Latino Politicians." *Los Angeles Times.* February 6.

Babich, Erin, and Jeanne Batalova. 2021. "Central American Immigrants in the United States." Migration Policy Institute. August 11. www.migrationpolicy.org/article/central-american-immigrants-united-states.

Baker, Lou, Linda Camacho, and Robert Salinas. 1995. *Latino Political Representation: The 1993–94 California Latino Legislative Caucus.* Chicano/Latino Policy Profile 2, no. 1. Berkeley: University of California, Institute for the Study of Social Change.

Barone, Michael, and Grant Ujifusa. 1999. *The Almanac of American Politics 2000.* Washington, DC: National Journal.

Barragan, James, and Alexa Ura. 2021. "Lawmakers Send to Governor Greg Abbott New Political Maps That Would Further Solidify the GOP's Grip on the Texas Legislature." *Texas Tribune.* October 15.

Barreto, Matt A. 2010. *Ethnic Cues: The Role of Shared Ethnicity in Latino Political Participation.* Ann Arbor: University of Michigan Press.

Barron-Lopez, Laura, Sabrina Rodriguez, and Renuka Rayasam. 2020. "Trump's Gains in Texas and Florida Don't Tell the Full Latino Story." *Politico.* November 6.

Bassett, Laura. 2017. "Meet the Woman Who Could Be Texas' First Latina in Congress." *Huffington Post.* September 8.

Baugh, Josh. 2011. "Mayor Eyes Sales Tax Increase." *San Antonio Express News.* March 3.

Baver, Sherrie. 1984. "Puerto Rican Politics in New York City: The Post–World War II Period." In *Puerto Rican Politics in Urban America.* Edited by James Jennings and Monte Rivera. Westport, CT: Greenwood Press.

Bean, Frank D., and Marta Tienda. 1985. *The Hispanic Population of the United States.* New York: Russell Sage Foundation.

Benson, Eric. 2018. "What Makes Beto Run? Does Beto O'Rourke Stand a Chance Against Ted Cruz?" *Texas Monthly.* January 13.

Berman, David R. 1998. *Arizona Politics and Government: The Quest for Autonomy, Democracy, and Development.* Lincoln: University of Nebraska Press.

Betancur, John J., and Douglas C. Gills. 1993. "Race and Class in Local Economic Development." In *Theories of Local Economic Development: Perspectives from Across the Disciplines.* Edited by Richard D. Bingham and Robert Mier. Newbury Park, CA: Sage.

———. 2000. "The African and Latino Coalitional Experience in Chicago Under Mayor Harold Washington." In *The Collaborative City: Opportunities and Struggles for Blacks and Latinos in U.S. Cities.* Edited by John J. Betancur and Douglas C. Gills. New York: Garland.

Bettridge, Keelin, and Claudia Kania. 2020. "State Legislator Demographics." National Conference of State Legislatures. December 1. https://www.ncsl.org /research/about-state-legislatures/state-legislator-demographics.aspx.

Bexar County Elections Office. 2005. https://www.bexar.org/1568/Elections -Department.

———. 2011. https://www.bexar.org/1568/Elections-Department.

———. 2013. https://www.bexar.org/1568/Elections-Department.

Binder, Norman E., J. L. Polinard, and Rovert D. Wrinkle. 1997. "Mexican American and Anglo Attitudes Towards Immigration Reform: A View from the Border." *Social Science Quarterly* 78: 324–337.

"Biography." N.d. Congresswoman Veronica Escobar Texas' 16th Congressional District. https://escobar.house.gov/about.

Bird, Karen. 2016. "Intersection of Exclusion: The Institutional Dynamics of Combined Gender and Ethnic Quota Systems." *Politics, Groups, and Identities* 4, no. 2 (January): 284–306.

Birt, Lydia. 2018. "Richfield Elects Minnesota's First Latina Mayor." *Kare11.* November 8. https://www.kare11.com/article/news/richfield-elects-minnesotas -first-latina-mayor/89-612526003.

Blizzard, Brittany, and Jeanne Batalova. 2020. "Cuban Immigrants in the United States." Migration Policy Institute. June 11. www.migrationpolicy.org/article /cuban-immigrants-united-states-2018.

Bloemraad, Irene, Kim Voss, and Taeku Lee. 2011. "The Protests of 2006: What Were They, How Do We Understand Them, Where Do We Go?" In *Rallying for Immigrant Rights: The Fight for Inclusion in 21st Century America.* Edited by Kim Voss and Irene Bloemraad. Berkeley: University of California Press.

Bluestone, Barry, and Bennett Harrison. 1982. *The Deindustrialization of America.* New York: Basic Books.

Bonelli, Cam. 2018. "Richfield Elects First Latina Mayor in Minnesota History." *Sun Current.* July 21.

Bonilla, Frank, and Walter Stafford. 2000. "African Americans and Puerto Ricans in New York: Cycles and Circles of Discrimination." In *The Collaborative City:*

Opportunities and Struggles for Blacks and Latinos in U.S. Cities. Edited by John J. Betancur and Douglas C. Gills. New York: Garland.

Bonilla, Henry, Lincoln Diaz-Balart, Mario Diaz-Balart, Devin Nunes, and Illeana Ros-Lehtinen. 2003. "We the (Hispanic) People . . ." *Wall Street Journal.* March 17.

Booker, Brakkton. 2021. "The Mayor Trying to Fix Policing." *Politico.* May 7.

Booth, John A., and David R. Johnson. 1983. "Power and Progress in San Antonio Politics, 1836–1970." In *The Politics of San Antonio: Community, Progress, and Power.* Edited by David R. Johnson, John A. Booth, and Richard J. Harris. Lincoln: University of Nebraska.

Bositis, David A. 2003. "Black Elected Officials: A Statistical Summary." Joint Center for Political and Economic Studies.

Boswell, Thomas D. 1994. *The Cubanization and Hispanization of Metropolitan Miami.* Miami, FL: Cuban American National Council.

"Bracero History Project." 2021. Library of Congress. November 12.

Bredderman, Will. 2016. "Battle for Charles Rangel's Seat Spills Over into Assembly." *Observer.* April 7.

Brennan Center for Justice. 2021. "Brennan Center's Myrna Perez Confirmed to Federal Bench." https://www.brennancenter.org/our-work/research-reports /brennan-centers-myrna-perez-confirmed-federal-bench.

Bridges, Amy. 1997. *Morning Glories: Municipal Reform in the Southwest.* Princeton, NJ: Princeton University Press.

Bridges, Amy, and Katherine Underwood. 2000. "Life After Districts." In *Minority Politics at the Millennium.* Edited by Richard A. Keiser and Katherine Underwood. New York: Garland.

Bridges, Tyler. 2001. "Hard Work, Elián Issue Gave Diaz a Major Boost: From Background to Spotlight, Candidate Quickly Built Up Image." *Miami Herald.* November 14.

Brischetto, Robert R. 1988a. "Electoral Empowerment of Texas Mexicans: The Case for Tejanos." In *Latino Empowerment: Progress, Problems, and Prospects.* Edited by Roberto E. Villarreal, Norma G. Hernandez, and Howard D. Neighbor. Westport, CT: Greenwood Press.

———. 1988b. *The Political Empowerment of Texas Mexicans, 1974–1988.* San Antonio, TX: Southwest Voter Research Institute.

Brischetto, Robert R., Charles L. Correll, and R. Michael Stevens. 1983. "Conflict and Change in the Political Culture of San Antonio in the 1970s." In *The Politics of San Antonio: Community, Progress, and Power.* Edited by David R. Johnson, John A. Booth, and Richard J. Harris. Lincoln: University of Nebraska Press.

Brischetto, Robert R., David R. Richards, Chandler Davidson, and Bernard Grofman. 1994. "Texas." In *Quiet Revolution in the South: The Impact of the Voting Rights Act, 1965–1990.* Edited by Chandler Davidson and Bernard Grofman. Princeton, NJ: Princeton University Press.

Brown, Anna, and Sara Atske. 2021. "Black Americans Have Made Gains in U.S. Political Leadership, but Gaps Remain." Pew Research Center. https://www

.pewresearch.org/fact-tank/2021/01/22/black-americans-have-made-gains-in-u
-s-political-leadership-but-gaps-remain.

Browning, Rufus P., Dale R. Marshall, and David H. Tabb. 1984. *Protest Is Not Enough: The Struggle of Blacks and Hispanics for Equality in Urban Politics.* Berkeley: University of California Press.

———, eds. 1990. *Racial Politics in American Cities.* New York: Longman.

———. 1994. "Political Incorporation and Competing Perspectives on Urban Politics." Paper presented at the American Political Science Association Annual Meeting, New York City, September.

———. 1995. "Mobilization, Incorporation, and Policy." Paper presented at the American Political Science Association Annual Meeting, Chicago, Illinois (September).

———, eds. 1997. *Racial Politics in American Cities.* 2nd ed. New York: Longman.

———. 2003a. "Can People of Color Achieve Equality in City Government? The Setting and the Issues." In *Racial Politics in American Cities.* Edited by Rufus P. Browning, Dale Rogers Marshall, and David H. Tabb. New York: Longman Press.

———, eds. 2003b. *Racial Politics in American Cities.* 3rd ed. New York: Longman.

Budiman, Abby. 2020. "Key Findings About U.S. Immigrants." Pew Research Center. https://www.pewresearch.org/fact-tank/2020/08/20/key-findings-about-u-s -immigrants.

Burkett, Lynnell. 2001. "Term Limit Issue Reawakens." *San Antonio Express News.* July 15.

Cadava, Geraldo. 2020. *The Hispanic Republican.* New York: Ecco.

Calavita, Kitty. 2010. *Inside the State: The Bracero Program, Immigration, and I.N.S.* New Orleans, LA: Quid Pro Books.

"California Constitution Article IV," Justia US Law, https://law.justia.com/constitution /california/article-iv?

California Research Bureau. 2020. https://public.tableau.com/views/Legislative Demographics2019-20/UserView?:showVizHome=no.

Canham, Matt. 2021. "Salt Lake City Makes History with Its Most Diverse Council Ever, Electing Racial and LGBTQ Majorities." *Salt Lake City Tribune.* November 5.

Canizales, Stephanie L., and Jody A. Vallejo. 2021. "Latinos and Racism in the Trump Era." *Daedalus* 150, no. 2 (January): 150–164.

Cann, Harrison. 2021. "Pa.'s Latino Community Has Growing Political Clout—and They're Going to Use It." *Capital-Star.* November 23.

Carlesso, Jenna. 2010. "Pedro Segarra Poised to Become Hartford Mayor." *Hartford Courant.* June 25.

Casey, Rick. 2001a. "City's Voters Could Handle the PGA Village Hot Potato." *San Antonio Express News.* November 4.

———. 2001b. "Forget Term Limits, Council Pay—Let's Talk About a Revolution." *San Antonio Express News.* July 11.

———. 2001c. "Garza Makes History, Carries North Side Suburb." *San Antonio Express News.* May 6.

214 References

———. 2001d. "Who's Running as Henry Cisneros?" *San Antonio Express News.* January 24.

Castillo, Elizabeth, Ben Christopher, Jon Osborn D'Agostino, Orlando Mayorquin, and Matt Levin. 2021. "How Diverse Is The California Legislature?" *Cal Matters.* February 16.

Castillo, Jaime. 2002. "Crisis of Confidence in City Hall—Mayor Wants to Restore Public's Trust in the Wake of Scandal." *San Antonio Express News.* October 13.

———. 2005. "Garza Has Made Few Friends, but He Hasn't Been a Bad Mayor." *San Antonio Express News.* January 29.

Castro, Julian. 2018. *An Unlikely Journey: Waking Up from My American Dream.* Boston, MA: Little, Brown and Company.

Center for Migration Studies of New York (CMS). 2021. "What You Should Know About the US Undocumented and Eligible-to-Naturalize Populations." CMS. August 4. https://cmsny.org/undocumented-eligible-to-naturalize-population -democratizing-data-release-080421.

Center for Voting and Democracy. N.d.a. "Latinos in State Legislatures." FairVote. www.fairvote.org/vra/stateleg2003.htm.

———. N.d.b "Voting Rights Act." FairVote. www.fairvote.org/vra/vra.htm.

Center for American Women and Politics (CAWP). N.d. "Women Elected Officials by Race/Ethnicity." CAWP. https://cawpdata.rutgers.edu/women-elected-officials /race-ethnicity?race_ethnicity%5B%5D=Hispanic%2FLatina&current=1& yearend_filter=All&level%5B%5D=Statewide&items_per_page=50.

Chabrán, Richard, and Rafael Chabrán. 1996. *The Latino Encyclopedia.* Vol. 1. New York: Marshall Cavendish.

Chambers, Stepfanie, and Emily M. Farris. 2018. "Two Latino Mayors in Hartford: Eddie Perez and Pedro Segarra." In *Latino Mayors in the Post-industrial City.* Edited by Marion Orr and Domingo Morel. Philadelphia: Temple University Press.

Chandler, Charles Ray. 1968. *The Mexican-American Protest Movement in Texas.* Ann Arbor, MI: University of Michigan Microfilms.

Chang, Benji. 2013. "Filipino American Farmworkers and Larry Itliong." In *Asian Americans: An Encyclopedia of Social, Cultural and Political History.* Edited by E. Park and X. Zhao. Santa Barbara, CA. ABC-CLIO.

Chavez, Adriana. 2000. "Ex–County Judge to Be Honored." *El Paso Times.* June 15.

Chavez, Herman Luis, and María Guadalupe Partida. 2020. "1994: California's Proposition 187." In *A Latinx Resource Guide: Civil Rights Cases and Events in the United States.* Edited by Suzanne Schadl and María (Dani) Thurber. Library of Congress. Last updated December 30. https://guides.loc.gov/latinx -civil-rights/california-proposition-187.

Chavez, Leo. 2013. *The Latino Threat: Constructing Immigrants, Citizens, and the Nation.* 2nd ed. Redwood City, CA: Stanford University Press.

Chinchilla, Norma, Nora Hamilton, and James Loucky. 1993. "Central Americans in Los Angeles: An Immigrant Community in Transition." *In the Barrios: Latinos and the Underclass Debate.* Edited by Joan Moore and Raquel Pinderhughes. New York: Russell Sage Foundation.

Chishti, Muzaffar, Sarah Pierce, and Jessica Bolter. 2017. "The Obama Record on Deportations: Deporter in Chief or Not?" Migration Policy Institute. www.migrationpolicy.org/article/obama-record-deportations-deporter-chief-or-not.

Christensen, Dusty. 2021. "Joshua Garcia Prevails in Holyoke Mayor's Race." *Daily Hampshire Gazette*. November 2.

Citrin, Jack, Donald Green, and David Sears. 1990. "White Reactions to Black Candidates: When Does Race Matter?" *Public Opinion Quarterly* 54, no. 1: 74–96.

Clayton, Janet. 1985. "Alatorre Garners 60% of the Vote to Win L.A. City Council Seat." *Los Angeles Times*. December 11. https://www.latimes.com/archives/la-xpm-1985-12-11-mn-986-story.html.

CNN. 2000. "100,000 March in Miami in Protest over Elian." *CNN News*. April 30.

Coalition for Humane Immigrant Rights (CHIRLA). N.d. "Mission & History." CHIRLA. https://www.chirla.org/who-we-are/about-us/mission-history.

Colburn, David R., and Lance deHaven-Smith. 1999. *Government in the Sunshine State: Florida Since Statehood*. Gainesville: University Press of Florida.

Cole, Caroline L. 2001. "Lawrence Mayoral Race: Sullivan Follows Brother's Path." *Boston Globe*. November 17.

Collingwood, Loren, and Benjamin Gonzalez O'Brien. 2019. *Sanctuary Cities: The Politics of Refuge*. New York: Oxford University Press.

Collins, Sheila D. 1986. *The Rainbow Challenge: The Jackson Campaign and the Future of U.S. Politics*. New York: Monthly Review.

Conyers, James E., and Walter L. Wallace. 1976. *Black Elected Officials: A Study of Black Americans Holding Governmental Office*. New York: Russell Sage Foundation.

Córdova, Teresa. 1999. "Harold Washington and the Rise of Latino Electoral Politics in Chicago, 1982–1987." In *Chicano Politics and Society in the Late Twentieth Century*. Edited by David Montejano. Austin: University of Texas Press.

Cox, Kenneth R., and A. Mair. 1988. "Locality and Community in the Politics of Local Economic Development." *Annals of the Association of American Geographers* 78, no. 2: 307–325.

———. 1989. "Urban Growth Machines and the Politics of Local Economic Development." *International Journal for Urban and Regional Research* 13, no. 1: 137–146.

Coy, Cissie. 2017. *Dennis Chavez: The First Hispanic US Senator*. Houston, TX: Arte Publico Press.

Crocker, R. 2000. "La Raza to the Top." *Coast Weekly*. October 5.

Cruz, Jill L., and Melinda S. Molina. 2009. *National Study on the Status of Latinas in the Legal Profession*. Washington, DC: Hispanic National Bar Association.

Cruz, Jose E. 1998. *Identity and Power: Puerto Rican Politics and the Challenge of Ethnicity*. Philadelphia: Temple University Press.

Dahl, Robert. 1961. *Who Governs? Democracy and Power in an American City*. New Haven, CT: Yale University Press.

Dahlburg, John-Thor. 2001. "Backed by Cuban Americans, Diaz Wins Miami Mayor's Race." *Los Angeles Times*. November 14.

216 References

Dallek, Robert. 1998. "Taking the Long View on Alarcón's Victory." *Los Angeles Times*. July 15.

Damora, David F. 2015. "It's the Economy Stupid? Not So Fast: The Impact of the Latino Vote on the 2012 Presidential Election in Nevada." In *Latinos and the 2012 Election: The New Face of the American Voter*. Edited by Gabriel R. Sanchez. East Lansing: Michigan State University Press.

Daniels, Cletus E. 1995. "Cesar Chavez and the Unionization of California Farmworkers." In *Working People of California*. Edited by Daniel Cornford. Berkeley: University of California Press.

Date, S. V. 2002. "Cuban Americans' Clout in Legislature Growing." *Palm Beach Post*. May 1.

Davidson, Bruce. 2000. "Mayoral Race Ready for Lift Off." *San Antonio Express News*. November 23.

———. 2001a. "Garza Says Timing Bad for Term-Limit Changes." *San Antonio Express News*. August 11.

———. 2001b. "Garza's Task Will Be to Sell Better Jobs." *San Antonio Express News*. June 3.

———. 2007. "A Conversation with Julian Castro." *San Antonio Express News*. June 24.

———. 2009. "Mayor Making Right Moves in CPS Ordeal." *San Antonio Express News*. December 16.

Davidson, Chandler. 1972. *Biracial Politics: Conflict and Coalition in the Metropolitan South*. Baton Rouge: Louisiana State University Press.

Davidson, Chandler, and Bernard Grofman, eds. 1994. *Quiet Revolution in the South: The Impact of the Voting Rights Act, 1965–1990*. Princeton, NJ: Princeton University Press.

Davidson, Charles 1990. *Race and Class in New Mexico*. Princeton, NJ: Princeton University Press.

Davila, Vianna. 2012. "Both Sides Rail over Planned Streetcars." *San Antonio Express News*. November 29.

Davis, Mike. 1992. "Chicano (and Landlord) Power! Is Bell Gardens' Not-Quite-Grassroots Revolt the Future of L.A.'s Working-Class Immigrant Suburbs?" *LA Weekly*, January 10–16.

De la Garza, Rodolfo O. 1992. "From Rhetoric to Reality: Latinos and the 1988 Election in Review." In *From Rhetoric to Reality: Latino Politics in the 1988 Elections*. Edited by Rodolfo O. de la Garza and Louis DeSipio. Boulder, CO: Westview.

De la Garza, Rodolfo O., and Louis DeSipio. 1997. "Save the Baby, Change the Bathwater, and Scrub the Tub: Latino Electoral Participation After Twenty Years of Voting Rights Act Coverage." In *Pursuing Power: Latinos and the Political System*. Edited by F. Chris Garcia. Notre Dame, IN: University of Notre Dame Press.

———, eds. 1999. *Awash in the Mainstream: Latino Politics in the 1996 Elections*. Boulder, CO: Westview.

De la Garza, Rodolfo O., and David Vaughan. 1985. "The Political Socialization of Chicano Elites: A Generational Approach." In *The Mexican American*

Experience: An Interdisciplinary Anthology. Edited by Rodolfo O. de la Garza, Frank D. Bean, Charles M. Bonjean, Ricardo Romo, and Rodolfo Alvarez. Austin: University of Texas Press.

"Delano Population." US Census Bureau. 2020 American Community Survey Office (2022). www.census.gov/.

De León, Arnoldo. 1989. *Ethnicity in the Sunbelt: A History of Mexican Americans in Houston.* Houston: Mexican American Studies.

De Los Angeles Torres, Maria. 1991. "The Commission on Latino Affairs: A Case Study of Community Empowerment." In *Harold Washington and the Neighborhoods: Progressive City Government in Chicago, 1983–1987.* Edited by Pierre Clavel and Wim Wiewel. New Brunswick, NJ: Rutgers University Press.

———. 1999. *In the Land of Mirrors: Cuban Exile Politics in the United States.* Ann Arbor: University of Michigan Press.

Dearman, Eleanor. 2020. "Racism and the Aug. 3 Shooting: One Year Later, El Paso Reflects on the Hate Behind the Attack." *El Paso Times.* July 29.

DeForge, Jeanette, and Dennis Hohenberger. 2021. "Holyoke Voters Elect Joshua Garcia as 1st Latino Mayor." *Masslive.* November 2. https://www.masslive.com/politics/2021/11/holyoke-voters-elect-joshua-garcia-as-1st-latino-mayor.html.

Desilver, Drew. 2021. "With Fewer State Governments Divided by Party Than in Years Past, GOP Has Edge in Redistricting." Pew Research Center. March 4. https://www.pewresearch.org/fact-tank/2021/03/04/with-fewer-state-governments-divided-by-party-than-in-years-past-gop-has-edge-in-redistricting.

DeSipio, Louis. 1996. *Counting on the Latino Vote: Latinos as a New Electorate.* Charlottesville: University of Virginia Press.

Dey, Sneha, and Karen Brooks Harper. 2022. "Transgender Texas Kids Are Terrified After Governor Orders That Parents Be Investigated for Child Abuse." *Texas Tribune.* February 28.

Diaz, Manny. 2013. *Miami Transformed: Rebuilding America One Neighborhood at a Time.* Philadelphia: University of Pennsylvania Press.

Diehl, Kemper, and Jan Jarboe. 1985. *Cisneros: Portrait of a New American.* San Antonio, TX: Corona.

District Profile. 2021. *Texas House District 104.* June 21, https://wrm.capitol.texas.gov/fyiwebdocs/PDF/house/dist104/profile.pdf.

Dominguez, Jaime. 2015. "Machine Matters: The Politics of Immigrant Integration in the Chicago Metro Area." In *Unsettled Americans: Metropolitan Context and Civil Leadership for Immigrant Integration.* Edited by John Mollenkopf and Manuel Pastor. Ithaca, NY: Cornell University Press.

Dominquez, Jorge I. 1999. "U.S.-Latin American Relations During the Cold War and Its Aftermath." In *The United States and Latin America: The New Agenda.* Edited by Victor Bulmer-Thomas and James Dunkerly. Cambridge, MA: Institute of Latin American Studies, University of London, and David Rockefeller Center for Latin American Studies, Harvard University.

Domínquez-Villegas, Rodrigo, Nick Gonzalez, Angela Gutierrez, Kassandra Hernandez, Michael Herndon, Ana Oaxaca, Michael Rios, Marcel Roman, Tye Rush, and Daisy Vera. 2021. "Vote Choice of Latino Voters in the Presidential

218   References

Election." UCLA Latino Policy & Politics Institute. January 19. https://latino.ucla.edu/research/latino-voters-in-2020-election.

Donato, Ruben. 1987. "In Struggle: Mexican Americans in the Pajaro Valley Schools, 1900–1979." PhD diss., Stanford University, Stanford, CA.

Drier, Peter, Regina Freer, Robert Gottlieb, and Mark Vallianatos. 2006. "Movement Mayor: Can Antonio Villaraigosa Change Los Angeles?" *Dissent* 53, no. 3 (summer): 45–52.

Duany, Jorge. 1998. "Reconstructing Racial Identity: Ethnicity, Color, and Class Among Dominicans in the United States and Puerto Rico." *Latin American Perspectives* 25, no. 3 (May): 148–149.

Duffin, Erin. 2021. "High School Dropout Rate of Hispanic Students U.S. from 1975 to 2019." Statista. https://www.statista.com/statistics/260345/high-school-dropout-rate-of-hispanic-students-in-the-us.

Dye, T. R. 2001. *Who's Running America: The Bush Restoration.* New York: Pearson College Div.

Eaton, T. 2013. "Celia Israel Likely Won't Face Primary Challenger." *Austin American-Statesman.* November 21.

Edsall, Thomas B. 2001. "A Political Fight to Define the Future: Latinos at Odds over California's Two New Democratic Congressional Districts." *Washington Post.* October 31.

El Paso Herald-Post. 1970. "Mrs. Chacon Is Sworn In." *El Paso Herald-Post.* April 29.

Endersby, James W., and Charles E. Menifield. 2000. "Representation, Ethnicity, and Congress: Black and Hispanic Representatives and Constituencies." In *Black and Multiracial Politics in America.* Edited by Yvette M. Alex-Assensoh and Lawrence J. Hanks. New York: New York University Press.

Endersby, James W., and Byron E. Price. 2001. "Hispanic Representation in State and Local Governments." Paper presented at the Western Political Science Association, Las Vegas, Nevada, March 15–17.

Epstein, R., and J. Medina. 2021. "Did the 2020 Census Undercount the Hispanic Population?" *New York Times.* April 28.

Equis Research. 2021. "2020 Post-Mortem (Part One): Portrait of a Persuadable Latino." April 1. Equis Research. https://equisresearch.medium.com/2020-post-mortem-part-one-16221adbd2f3.

Escobar, Veronica. 2017. "TX-16 Veronica Escobar for Congress." Veronica Escobar Democrat for Congress. https://veronicaescobar.com.

Escutia, Martha, and Gloria Romero. 2001. "MALDEF's Lawsuit Is Racially Divisive." *Los Angeles Times.* November 1.

Estrada, Leobardo F., F. Chris Garcia, Reynaldo Flores Macias, and Lionel Maldonado. 1988. "Chicanos in the United States: A History of Exploitation." In *Latinos and the Political System.* Edited by F. Chris Garcia. Notre Dame, IN: University of Notre Dame Press.

Eulau, Heinz, and John C. Wahlke. 1978. *The Politics of Representation: Continuities in Theory and Practice.* Beverly Hills, CA: Sage.

Evans, Marissa. 2018. "2018 Was the Year of the Woman in Texas. Candidates Say It's 'Not a One-Time Deal.'" *Texas Tribune.* November 11.

Fagen, Richard R., Richard A. Brody, and T. J. O'Leary. 1968. *Cubans in Exile: Disaffection and Revolution.* Palo Alto, CA: Stanford University Press.

Fainstein, Susan S., Norman L. Fainstein, Richard C. Hill, Dennis R. Judd, and Michael P. Smith, eds. 1983. *Restructuring the City: The Political Economy of Urban Redevelopment.* New York: Longman.

Falcon, Angelo. 1988. "Black and Latino Politics in New York City: Race and Ethnicity in a Changing Urban Context." *New Community* 14, no. 3 (spring): 370–384.

———. 1992. "Puerto Ricans and the 1988 Election in New York City." In *From Rhetoric to Reality: Latino Politics in the 1988 Elections.* Edited by Rodolfo O. de la Garza and Louis DeSipio. Boulder, CO: Westview.

———. 1996. "Puerto Ricans and the 1992 Presidential Election in New York." In *Ethnic Ironies: Latino Politics in the 1992 Elections.* Edited by Rodolfo O. de la Garza and Louis DeSipio. Boulder, CO: Westview.

———. 1999. "Beyond La Macarena? New York City Puerto Rican, Dominican, and South American Voters in the 1996 Election." In *Awash in the Mainstream: Latino Politics in the 1996 Elections.* Edited by Rodolfo O. de la Garza and Louis DeSipio. Boulder, CO: Westview.

———. 2001. "Census 2000 Misreporting of Latino Subgroups." LatinoJustice PRLDEF. https://www.latinojustice.org/en/latinojusticeopina.

———. 2002. "Another Response to Gregory Rodriguez." Unpublished letter. May 21.

———. 2003. "Pues, at Least We Had Hillary: Latino New York, the 2000 Election, and the Limits of Party Loyalty." In *Muted Voices: Latinos and the 2000 Elections.* Edited by Rodolfo O. de la Garza, Louis DeSipio, Robert Y. Shapiro, Manuel Avalos, Matt A. Barreto, Angelo Falcon, and Luis Ricardo Fraga. Lanham, MD: Rowman & Littlefield Publishers.

Fears, Darryl. 2002. "A Diverse—and Divided—Black Community: As Foreign-Born Population Grows, Nationality Trumps Skin Color." *Washington Post.* February 24.

File, Thom. 2017. "Voting in America: A Look at the 2016 Presidential Election." US Census Bureau. May 10. https://www.census.gov/newsroom/blogs/random-samplings/2017/05/voting_in_america.html.

Filindra, Alexandra, and Shanna Pearson-Merkowitz. 2013. "Research Note: Stopping the Enforcement 'Tide': Descriptive Representation, Latino Institutional Empowerment, and State-Level Immigration Policy." *Politics and Policy* 41, no. 60: 814–832.

Finnegan, Michael. 2001. "Latinos Blast Rep. Berman in Map Fight: Redistricting; Protesters Say Proposed Boundary Changes, Which the Congressman Backs, Dilute Their Power." *Los Angeles Times.* September 7.

Fitzgerald, B. 2003. "Reflections on a Glass Ceiling." *New York Times.* August 10.

Flores, Aileen B. 2018. "Veronica Escobar on Path to Make Latina, Texas History After Congress Primary Victory." *El Paso Times.* March 9.

Flores, Antonio, and Mark Hugo Lopez. 2018. "Key Facts About Latinos in the 2018 Midterm Elections." Pew Research Center. October 15. https://www.pewresearch.org/fact-tank/2018/10/15/key-facts-about-latinos-in-the-2018-midterm-elections.

220 References

Flores, Henry. 2002. "Mayor Ed Garza of San Antonio, Texas: A Cisneros Legacy." Paper presented at the Western Political Science Association, Long Beach, California, March 22–24.

Flores, Matt. 2002. "Most Bexar Lawmakers Claim Wins." *San Antonio Express News*. March 14.

Flores, William V. 1992. "Chicano Empowerment and the Politics of At-Large Elections in California: A Tale of Two Cities." In *Chicano Empowerment and Chicano Scholarship: Proceedings of the National Association of Chicano Studies Conference 17th Annual Conference, Berkeley*. Edited by Mary Romero and Cordelia Candelaria. Los Angeles, CA: National Association of Chicano Studies.

Flores, William V., with Rina Benmayor, eds. 1997. "Constructing Cultural Citizenship." In *Latino Cultural Citizenship: Claiming Identity, Space, and Rights*. Boston: Beacon Press.

Flores-Gonzalez, Nilda, and Elena R. Gutierrez. 2010. "Taking the Public Square: The National Struggle for Immigrant Rights." In *¡Marcha! Latino Chicago and the Immigrant Rights Movement*. Edited by Amalia Pallares and Nilda Flores-Gonzalez. Urbana: University of Illinois Press.

Flynn, Ken. 2003. "Worthy Women." *El Paso Times*. March 21.

Fraga, Luis Ricardo. 1992. "Prototype from the Midwest: Latinos in Illinois." In *From Rhetoric to Reality: Latino Politics in the 1988 Elections*. Edited by Rodolfo O. de la Garza and Louis DeSipio. Boulder, CO: Westview.

Fraga, Luis Ricardo, Valerie Martinez-Ebers, Linda Lopez, and Ricardo Ramirez. 2008. "Representing Gender and Ethnicity: Strategic Intersectionality." In *Legislative Women: Getting Elected, Getting Ahead*. Edited by Beth Reingold. Boulder, CO: Lynne Rienner.

Frank, Larry, and Kent Wong. 2004. "Dynamic Political Mobilization: The Los Angeles County Federation of Labor." *Journal of Labor and Society* 8, no. 2: 123–252.

Galarza, Ernesto. 1964. *Merchants of Labor: The Mexican Bracero Story*. Charlotte, NC: McNalley and Loftin.

Gamboa, Suzanne. 2021. "Over Half of Eligible Latinos Voted in 2020—a Historic First." *NBC News*. May 11.

Gamboa, Suzanne, and Anita Hassan. 2020. "'Years in the Making': Established Latino Groups Helped Biden in Arizona, Nevada." *NBC News*. November 13. https://www.nbcnews.com/news/latino/years-making-established-latino-groups -helped-biden-arizona-nevada-n1246864.

García Bedolla, Lisa, and Christian Hosam. 2021. *Latino Politics*. 3rd ed. Medford, MA: Polity Press.

Garcia, F. Chris. 1974. *La Causa Politica: A Chicano Politics Reader*. Notre Dame, IN: University of Notre Dame Press.

Garcia, F. Chris, and Rodolfo O. de la Garza. 1977. *The Chicano Political Experience: Three Perspectives*. North Scituate, MA: Duxbury.

Garcia, F. Chris, and Gabriel R. Sanchez. 2008. *Hispanics and the U.S. Political System: Moving into the Mainstream*. Upper Saddle River, NJ: Pearson/Prentice Hall.

Garcia, Gilbert. 2019. "No Clear Contenders for Joaquin Castro's Congressional Seat." *San Antonio Express News*. March 20.

Garcia, Ignacio M. 1989. *United We Win: The Rise and Fall of La Raza Unida Party*. Tucson: University of Arizona Press.

———. 1997. *Chicanismo: The Forging of a Militant Ethos Among Mexican Americans*. Tucson: University of Arizona Press.

———. 2000. *Viva Kennedy: Mexican Americans in Search of Camelot*. College Station: Texas A&M University Press.

Garcia, John A. 2003. *Latino Politics in America: Community, Culture, and Interests*. Lanham, MD: Rowman & Littlefield.

———. 2017. *Latino Politics in America: Community, Culture, and Interests*. 3rd ed. Lanham, MD: Rowman & Littlefield.

Garcia, Juan R., and Thomas Gelsinon. 1997. *Mexican Americans in the 1990s: Politics, Policies, and Perceptions*. Tucson: University of Arizona Press.

García, María Cristina. 1996. *Havana USA*. Berkeley: University of California Press.

Garcia, Mario T. 1989. *Mexican Americans: Leadership, Ideology, and Identity, 1930–1960*. New Haven, CT: Yale University Press.

———. 1994. *Memories of Chicano History: The Life and Narrative of Bert Corona*. Berkeley: University of California Press.

Garcia-Navarro, Lulu. 2021. "Latino Voters Are Leaving the Democratic Party." NPR. July 11. https://www.npr.org/2021/07/11/1014967344/latino-voters-are -leaving-the-democratic-party.

Gay, Claudine. 2001. *The Effect of Minority Districts and Minority Representation on Political Participation in California*. San Francisco: Public Policy Institute of California.

Gee, Robert W. 2001. "Easy Smile, Confident Stride Hide New Mayor's Story of Struggle." *Austin American-Statesman*. November 7.

Georges, Eugenia. 1984a. "Dominican Diaspora: Putting Down Roots?" *Hispanic Monitor* 1, no. 2: 6.

———. 1984b. *New Immigrants and the Political Process: Dominicans in New York*. New York: Research Program in Inter-American Affairs.

Geron, Kim. 1998. "The Political Incorporation of Latinos: Symbolic or Substantive Changes at the Local Level?" PhD diss., University of California, Riverside.

———. 2005. *Latino Political Power*. Boulder, CO: Lynne Rienner Publications.

Gimpel, James G., and Karen Kaufman. 2001. *Impossible Dream or Distant Reality? Republican Efforts to Attract Latino Voters*. Backgrounder. Washington, DC: Center for Immigration Studies.

Gold, Mateo. 2001. "Villaraigosa Lets Others Court Latinos." *Los Angeles Times*. June 2.

Golden, Ryan. 2022. "California's $15 Minimum Wage Begins This Year. Debate on the Next Increase Has Already Begun." *HRDive*. February 24. https://www .hrdive.com/news/californias-15-minimum-wage-begins-this-year-debate-on -the-next-increase/619111.

Goldsmith, Annie. 2020. "The 2020 Election Had the Highest Voter Turnout in Modern History." *New York Times*. November 7.

GoLocalProv News Team. 2021. "Providence Passes New Budget with Fanfare, New Programs, and Ignores Old Liabilities." *GoLocalProv*. July 19.

www.golocalprov.com/news/providence-passed-a-new-budget-with-fanfare-new-programs-and-ignores-old-li.

Gomez, A. 2019 "Another Election Surprise: Many Hispanics Backed Trump." *USA Today*. November 9.

Gomez Quiñones, Juan. 1990. *Chicano Politics: Reality and Promise, 1940–1990*. Albuquerque: University of New Mexico Press.

———. 1994. *Mexican American Labor, 1790–1990*. Albuquerque: University of New Mexico Press.

Gonzales, Manuel G. 1999. *Mexicanos: A History of Mexicans in the United States*. Bloomington: Indiana University Press.

Gonzalez, Juan. 2000. *Harvest of Empire: A History of Latinos in America*. New York: Penguin.

Gonzalez-Barrera, Ana. 2017. "Why Mexican Lawful Immigrants Have Not Naturalized." Pew Research Center. June 29. https://www.pewresearch.org/hispanic/2017/06/29/why-mexican-lawful-immigrants-have-not-naturalized.

Gonzalez-Pando, Miguel. 1998. *The Cuban Americans*. Westport, CT: Greenwood Press.

Goodman, Adam. 2020. *The Deportation Machine: America's Long History of Expelling Immigrants*. Princeton, NJ: Princeton University Press.

Gottlieb, Catherine. 1993. "Pomona: A Voting Change Shifts Political Power." *Los Angeles Times*. July 26.

Gould, Elise, Daniel Perez, and Valerie Wilson. 2020. "Latinx Workers—Particularly Women—Face Devastating Job Losses in the COVID-19 Recession." Economic Policy Institute. August 20. https://www.epi.org/publication/latinx-workers-covid.

Gould, William B., IV. 1993. *A Primer on American Labor Law*. 3rd ed. Cambridge, MA: MIT Press.

Graham, Pamela M. 1998. "The Politics of Incorporation: Dominicans in New York." *Latino Studies Journal* 9, no. 3 (fall): 39–64.

Gramlich, John. 2020. "What the 2020 Electorate Looks Like by Party, Race and Ethnicity, Age, Education and Religion." Pew Research Center. October 26. https://www.pewresearch.org/fact-tank/2020/10/26/what-the-2020-electorate-looks-like-by-party-race-and-ethnicity-age-education-and-religion.

Greenhouse, Steven. 2001. "At the End, Labor Made Little Effort for Green." *New York Times*. November 8.

Grenier, Guillermo J., and Max J. Castro. 1998. "The Emergence of an Adversarial Relation: Black-Cuban Relations in Miami, 1959–1998." In *Research in Urban Policy: Solving Urban Problems in Urban Areas Characterized by Fragmentation and Division*. Edited by Fred W. Bala and Milan J. Dluchy. Stamford, CT: JAI Press.

———. 2001. "Blacks and Cubans in Miami: The Negative Consequences of the Cuban Enclave on Ethnic Relations." In *Governing American Cities: Interethnic Coalitions, Competition, and Conflict*. Edited by Michael Jones-Correa. New York: Russell Sage Foundation.

Grenier, Guillermo J., Fabiana Invernizzi, Linda Salup, and Jorge Schmidt. 1994. "Los Bravos de la Politica: Politics and Cubans in Miami." In *Barrio Ballots:*

Latino Politics in the 1990 Elections. Edited by Rodolfo O. de la Garza, Martha Menchaca, and Louis DeSipio. Boulder, CO: Westview.

Griswold del Castillo, Richard. 1990. *The Treaty of Guadalupe Hidalgo: A Legacy of Conflict*. Norman: University of Oklahoma Press.

Griswold del Castillo, Richard, and Arnoldo De León. 1996. *North to Aztlán: A History of Mexican Americans in the United States*. New York: Twayne.

Grofman, Bernard, and Chandler Davidson, eds. 1992. *Controversies in Minority Voting: The Voting Right Act in Perspective*. Washington, DC: Brookings Institution.

Guerin-Gonzales, Camille. 1994. *Mexican Workers and American Dreams: Immigration, Repatriation, and California Farm Labor, 1900–1939*. New Brunswick, NJ: Rutgers University Press.

Guerra, Fernando J. 1991. "The Emergence of Ethnic Officeholders in California." In *Racial and Ethnic Politics in California*. Edited by Bryan O. Jackson and Michael B. Preston. Berkeley, CA: Institute of Governmental Studies Press.

Guerra, Fernando J., and Brianne Gilbert. 2013. *Los Angeles Votes 2013: Mayoral General Election Exit Poll*. Los Angeles: Thomas and Dorothy Leavey Center for the Study of Los Angeles, Loyola Marymount University.

Guinier, Lani. 1994. *The Tyranny of the Majority: Fundamental Fairness in Representative Democracy*. New York: Free Press.

———. 1995. "The Representation of Minority Interests." In *Classifying by Race*. Edited by Paul E. Peterson. Princeton, NJ: Princeton University Press.

Gulasekaram, Pratheepan, and E. Karthick Ramakrishnan. 2015. *The New Immigration Federalism*. New York: Cambridge University Press.

Gurwitz, Jonathan. 2005. "Hardberger Machine Ran at Full Throttle." *San Antonio Express News*. June 12.

Gutierrez, Angela, Angela X. Ocampo, Matt A. Barreto, and Gary Segura. 2019. "How Racial Threat and Anger Mobilized Latino Voters in the Trump Era." *Political Research Quarterly* 72, no. 4: 960–975.

Gutiérrez, David G. 1995. *Walls and Mirrors: Mexican Americans, Mexican Immigrants, and the Politics of Ethnicity*. Berkeley: University of California Press.

Gutierrez, Jose Angel, and Rebecca E. Dean. 2000. "Chicanas in Texas Politics." JSRI Occasional Paper 66. Julian Samora Research Institute. October.

Guzman, Betsy. 2001. "The Hispanic Population: Census 2002 Brief." Report C2KBR/01-3. Washington, DC: US Census Bureau.

Haley, Grace, and Sarah Bryner. 2021. "Which Women Can Run? The Fundraising Gap in the 2020 Elections' Competitive Primaries." OpenSecrets. June 9. https://www.opensecrets.org/news/reports/2020-gender-race.

Hamilton, Nora, and Norma Stoltz Chinchilla. 1991. "Central American Migration: A Framework for Analysis." *Latin American Research Review* 26, no. 1: 75–110.

Hanks, Lawrence J. 1987. *The Struggle for Black Political Empowerment in Three Georgia Counties*. Knoxville: University of Tennessee Press.

Hardy-Fanta, Carol. 1993. *Latina Politics, Latino Politics: Gender, Culture, and Political Participation in Boston*. Philadelphia: Temple University Press.

Harris County Elections Division 2016. https://files.harrisvotes.com/harrisvotes/prd/HISTORY/20161108/cumulative/cumulative.pdf.

224 References

Harris County Elections Division 2018. https://files.harrisvotes.com/harrisvotes/prd/HISTORY/20181106/cumulative/cumulative.pdf.

Heins, Marjorie. 1972. *Strictly Ghetto Property*. Berkeley, CA: Ramparts.

Hendricks, David. 2012. "'Yes' Vote Gives S.A. New Image." *San Antonio Express News*. November 21.

Henry, Charles P. 1980. "Black-Chicano Coalitions: Possibilities and Problems." *Western Journal of Black Studies* 4: 202–232.

Henry, Daja E. 2020. "'Long Time Coming': Latino Voters Help Flip Arizona, Tighten Key Races." *Cronkite News*. November 4. https://cronkitenews.azpbs.org/2020/11/04/long-time-coming-latino-voters-help-flip-arizona-tighten-key-races.

Hernández, Ramona, and Francisco L. Rivera-Batiz. 2003. "Dominicans in the United States: A Socioeconomic Profile 2000." Dominican Research Monograph, CUNY Dominican Studies Institute. CUNY Academic Works. https://academicworks.cuny.edu/cgi/viewcontent.cgi?article=1008&context=dsi_pubs.

Hernandez-Gomes, Carlos. 2001. "Latino Leadership: Population Grows, but Political Power Lags." *Chicago Reporter* (September/October).

Hero, Rodney. 1992. *Latinos and the U.S. Political System: Two-Tiered Pluralism*. Philadelphia: Temple University Press.

———. 1997. "Latinos and Politics in Denver and Pueblo, Colorado: Differences, Explanations, and the 'Steady-State' of the Struggle for Equality." In *Racial Politics in American Cities*. Edited by Rufus P. Browning, Dale R. Marshall, and David H. Tabb. 2nd ed. New York: Longman.

Hero, Rodney, and Kathleen M. Beatty. 1989. "The Election of Federico Peña as Mayor of Denver: Analysis and Implications." *Social Science Quarterly* 70, no. 2 (June): 300–310.

Hero, Rodney, F. Chris Garcia, John Garcia, and Harry Pachon. 2000. "Latino Participation, Partisanship, and Office Holding." *PS: Political Science and Politics* 23, no. 3 (September): 529–534.

Hero, Rodney, and Caroline Tolbert. 1995. "Latinos and Substantive Representation in the U.S. House of Representatives: Direct, Indirect, or Nonexistent?" *American Journal of Political Science* 39 (August): 240–261.

———. 1999. "Dealing with Diversity: Racial/Ethnic Context and Policy Change." Paper presented at the annual meeting of the Western Political Science Association, Seattle, Washington, March 25–27.

Hiawassee, Georgia Population 2020. *World Population Review*. 2022, https://worldpopulationreview.com/us-cities/hiawassee-ga-population.

Hickey, Jennifer G. 2003. "No Monopoly on Ethnicity." www.insightmag.com.

Hicks, Nolan. 2011. "New Map Avoids a Democrat Face-Off." *San Antonio Express News*. November 14.

Highton, Benjamin. 2004. "White Voters and African American Candidates for Congress." *Political Behavior* 26, no. 1: 1–25.

Hill, Kevin V., and Dario Moreno. 2005. "Battleground Florida." In *Muted Voices: Latinos and the 2000 Elections*. Edited by Rodolfo O. de la Garza and Louis DeSipio. Lanham, MD: Rowman & Littlefield.

Hill, Kim Quaile, and Kenneth R. Mladenka. *Texas Government: Politics and Economics*. 4th ed. Belmont, CA: Wadsworth.

Hirsch, Arnold R. 2001. "Harold Washington of Chicago and 'Dutch' Morial of New Orleans." In *African American Mayors: Race, Politics, and the American City*. Edited by David R. Colburn and Jeffrey S. Adler. Chicago: University of Illinois Press.

"Hispanic American Senators." N.d. US Senate. https://www.senate.gov/senators /hispanic-american-senators.htm.

Holbrook, Stett. 1999. "Land Plan Nixed: LAFCO Rejects Proposal for Watsonville Annexation." *Santa Cruz Sentinel*. August 4.

Holmes, Jack E. 1967. *Politics in New Mexico*. Albuquerque: University of New Mexico Press.

Hood, Lucy. 2001. "Garza Outlines Goals if He's Elected Mayor—Race with Bannwolf Likely Will Be Heated." *San Antonio Express News*. January 8.

Hooks, Christopher, R. G. Ratcliffe, and Andrea Zelinski. 2021. "2021: The Best and Worst Legislators." *Texas Monthly*. July 1. https://www.texasmonthly .com/news-politics/2021-the-best-and-worst-legislators.

Hoschchild, Jennifer, and John Mollenkopf, eds. 2011. *Bringing Outsiders In: Transatlantic Perspectives on Immigration Political Incorporation*. Ithaca, NY: Cornell University Press.

Houston Chronicle. 2020. "Garcia's Experience in Public, Political Sectors Brings a Vital Perspective to the U.S. House." *Houston Chronicle*. September 30: A22.

Howard, John. 2012. "Term Limits: A Saga of Irony and Miscues." *Capitol Weekly*. June 2. https://capitolweekly.net/term-limits-a-saga-of-irony-and-miscues.

Howe, Amy. 2021. "Court Upholds Arizona Voting Restrictions, Limits Cases Under Voting Rights Act." *Scotus Blog*. July 1. https://www.scotusblog.com/2021/07 /court-upholds-arizona-voting-restrictions-limits-cases-under-voting-rights.act.

Hrenchir, Tim. 2018. "Michelle De La Isla Becomes Topeka's First Hispanic Mayor." *Topeka Capital-Journal*. January 8. https://www.cjonline.com/story /news/local/2018/01/08/michelle-de-la-isla-becomes-topeka-s-first-hispanic -mayor/16083488007.

Hughes, Melanie M. 2013. "The Intersection of Gender and Minority Status in National Legislature: The Minority Women Legislative Index." *Legislative Studies Quarterly* 38, no. 4: 489–516.

Hunner, Jon. 2001. "Preserving Hispanic Lifeways in New Mexico." *Public Historian* 23, no. 4.

Hussar, B., J. Zhang, S. Hein, K. Wang, A. Roberts, A. J. Cui, M. Smith, F. Bullock Mann, A. Barmer, and R. Dilig. 2020. *The Condition of Education*. Washington, DC: National Center for Education Statistics.

Industrial Areas Foundation. N.d. "About IAF." www.industrialareasfoundation.org.

Ingram, David. 2000. *Group Rights: Reconciling Equality and Difference*. Lawrence: University Press of Kansas.

Israel, Emma, and Jeanne Batalova. 2020. "Mexican Immigrants in the United States." Migration Policy Institute. November 5. https://www.migrationpolicy .org/article/mexican-immigrants-united-states-2019.

226 References

Izigsohn, Jose, Carlos D. Cabral, Esther Hernandez Medina, and Obed Vazquez. 1999. "Mapping Dominican Transnationalism: Narrow and Broad Transnational Practices." *Ethnic and Racial Studies* 22, no. 2 (March): 316–339.

Jacobs, Paul. 1990. "California Elections/Proposition 140: Initiative Cuts More Than Term of Office." *Los Angeles Times*. October 28.

Jacobson, Louis. 2015. "How Will the Rapidly Growing Hispanic Population Affect Politics and Policy?" National Conference of State Legislatures. June 1. https://www.ncsl.org/bookstore/state-legislatures-magazine/the-hispanic -dynamic.aspx.

Jennings, James. 1977. *Puerto Rican Politics in New York City*. Washington, DC: University Press of America.

———. 1992. *The Politics of Black Empowerment: The Transformation of Black Activism in Urban America*. Detroit, MI: Wayne State University Press.

———, ed. 1994. *Blacks, Latinos, and Asians in Urban America: Status and Prospects for Politics and Activism*. Westport, CT: Praeger.

Jennings, James, and Monte Rivera. 1984. *Puerto Rican Politics in Urban America*. Westport, CT: Greenwood Press.

Jervis, Rick. 2012. "San Antonio Mayor Says Education Is Key for Latinos." *USA Today*. October 15. http://api.durangoherald.com/amp/45612-san-antonio-mayor -says-education-is-key-for-latinos.

Jimenez, Francisco, Alma M. Garcia, and Richard A. Garcia. 2007. *Ethnic Community Builders: Mexican Americans in Search for Justice and Power the Struggle for Citizenship Rights in San Jose*. Lanham, MD: Alta Mira Press.

Johnson, David R., John A. Booth, and Richard J. Harris, eds. 1983. *The Politics of San Antonio: Community, Progress, and Power*. Lincoln: University of Nebraska Press.

Joint Center for Political and Economic Studies. 2001. "Number of Black Elected Officials in the United States by State and Office, January 1999." www.joint center.org.

Jones, Nicholas, Rachel Marks, Roberto Ramirez, and Merarys Rios-Vargas. 2021. "2020 Census Illuminates Racial and Ethnic Composition of the Country." US Census Bureau. August 12. https://www.census.gov/library/stories/2021/08 /improved-race-ethnicity-measures-reveal-united-states-population-much -more-multiracial.html.

Jones-Correa, Michael. 2001. "Under Two Flags: Duel Nationality in Latin America and Its Consequences for Naturalization in the United States." *International Migration Review* 35, no. 4 (winter): 997–1029.

Jordan, Howard. 1997. "Dominicans in New York: Getting a Slice of the Apple." *NACLA Report of the Americas* 30, no. 5 (March/April): 37–42.

Juenke, Eric Gonzalez and Anna Christina Sampaio. 2010. "Deracialization and Latino Politics." *Political Research Quarterly* 63.1 (March): 43–54.

Keck, Benjamin. 1990. "New Judges Vows No More 'Circus' Acts." *El Paso Times*. November 7.

———. 1991. "A Master of People Power." *El Paso Times*. June 26.

Keiser, Richard A. 1990. "The Rise of a Biracial Coalition in Philadelphia." In *Racial Politics in American Cities*. Edited by Rufus P. Browning, Dale R. Marshall, and David H. Tabb. New York: Longman.

Krebs, Timothy B., and David B. Holian. 2007. "Competitive Positioning, Deracialization, and Attack Speech: A Study of Negative Campaigning in the 2001 Los Angeles Mayoral Election." *American Politics Research* 35, no. 1 (January): 123–149.

Kerr, Brinck, and Will Miller. 1997. "Latino Representation: It's Direct and Indirect." *American Journal of Political Science* 41, no. 3 (July): 1066–1071.

Kerr, J. 2014. "Israel Wins House District 50 Runoff Election." *Daily Texan*. January 2. https://thedailytexan.com/2014/01/29/israel-wins-house-district-50-runoff-election.

Kinghorn, Austin. 2005. "Commissioner Garcia Seeks a Second Term." *Baytown Sun*. December 3.

Kleist, Trina. 2000. "Old Foes, New Trust: North-South Cooperation Proved Vital to Approval of Watsonville School Site." *Santa Cruz County Sentinel*. March 19.

Koidin, Michelle. 2004. "City's Image Seen Taking Beating in Mayor-Manager Fight—Dispute Has One Former S.A. Leader Asking, 'Hey Guys Who's in Charge Here?'" *San Antonio Express News*. August 29.

Kousser, J. Morgan. 1999. *Colorblind Injustice: Minority Voting Rights and the Undoing of the Second Reconstruction*. Chapel Hill: University of North Carolina Press.

———. 2001. "The Role of Cross-Over Districts in a Fair Redistricting: Lessons from the 1990s." In *California Senate Redistricting Plan*. Submitted July 31 by MALDEF and WCVI.

Krebs, Timothy, and David Holian. 2007. "Competitive Positioning, Deracialization, and Attack Speech: A Study of Negative Campaigning in the 2001 Los Angeles Mayoral Election." *American Politics Research* 35, no. 1: 123–149.

Kripalani, Jasmine. 2003. "Many Broward Latino Residents Still Participate in Their Home Countries' Elections but Ignore Local Politics." *Miami Herald*. September 28.

Krogstad, Jens Manuel. 2020. "Most Cuban American Voters Identify as Republican in 2020." Pew Research Center. October 2. https://www.pewresearch.org/fact-tank/2020/10/02/most-cuban-american-voters-identify-as-republican-in-2020.

Krogstad, Jens Manuel, and Mark Hugo Lopez. 2016. "Hillary Clinton Won Latino Vote but Fell Below 2012 Support for Obama." Pew Research Center. November 29. https://www.pewresearch.org/fact-tank/2016/11/29/hillary-clinton-wins-latino-vote-but-falls-below-2012-support-for-obama.

———. 2020. "Hispanic Voters Say Economy, Health Care and COVID-19 Are Top Issues in 2020 Presidential Election." Pew Research Center. September 11. https://www.pewresearch.org/us-politics-vote-5.

Krogstad, Jens Manuel, Mark Hugo Lopez, Gustavo Lopez, Jeffrey S. Passel, and Eileen Patten. 2016. "Looking Back to 2014: Latino Voter Turnout Rate Falls to Record Low." Pew Research Center. January 19. https://www.pewresearch

228 References

.org/hispanic/2016/01/19/looking-back-to-2014-latino-voter-turnout-rate-falls
-to-record-low.

Krogstad, Jens Manuel, and Luis Noe-Bustamante. 2021. "Key Facts About U.S. Latinos for National Hispanic Heritage Month." Pew Research Center. September 27. https://www.diversityined.com/blog/2021/09/key-facts-about-u-s-latinos -for-national-hispanic-heritage-month/.

Krogstad, Jens Manuel, and Jeffrey S. Passel. 2014. "Those from Mexico Will Benefit the Most from Obama's Executive Action." Pew Research Center. November 20. https://www.pewresearch.org/fact-tank/2014/11/20/those-from-mexico-will -benefit-most-from-obamas-executive-action.

KXTV Staff. 2015. "Military Academy Coming to San Joaquin County." ABC10.com. June 5. https://www.abc10.com/article/news/local/stockton/military-academy -coming-to-san-joaquin-county/103-181911901.

Lai, James S. 2000. "Asian Pacific Americans and the Pan-ethnic Question." In *Minority Politics at the Millennium*. Edited by Richard A. Keiser and Katherine Underwood. New York: Garland.

Lamagdeleine, Izz Scott. 2021. "What Is Gender-Affirming Medical Care for Transgender Children? Here's What You Need to Know." *Texas Tribune*. August 4. https://www.texastribune.org/2021/08/04/gender-affirming-care-transgender -texas.

Latino Decisions. 2016. "Lies, Damn Lies, and Exit Polls." Latino Decisions. November 10. https://latinodecisions.com/blog/lies-damn-lies-and-exit-polls.

———. 2020. "Latino Voters in the 2020 Election National Survey Results." Latino Decisions. November 5. https://www.unidosus.org/publications/2096-latino -voters-in-the-2020-election-national-survey-results.

Latinos Issues Forum. 1998. "The Latino Vote 1998." Latinos Issues Forum. May. https://www.worldcat.org/title/latino-vote-1998-the-new-margin-of-victory /oclc/39574786?

Lawless, Jennifer, and Richard Fox. 2005. *It Takes a Candidate: Why Women Don't Run for Office*. New York: Cambridge University Press.

Leech, Gary. 2000. "Plan Colombia: A Closer Look." *Colombia Report*. Information Network of the Americas. https://reliefweb.int/report/colombia/plan-colombia -closer-look.

Leighley, Jan E. 2001. *Strength in Numbers? The Political Mobilization of Racial and Ethnic Minorities*. Princeton, NJ: Princeton University Press.

Lemus, Frank. 1973. *The National Roster of Spanish Surnamed Elected Officials*. Los Angeles: Atzlan Production.

Levitt, Peggy. 2001. *The Transnational Villagers*. Berkeley: University of California Press.

Levitz, Eric. 2021. "David Shor on Why Trump Was Good for the GOP and How Dems Can Win in 2022." *New York*. March 3. https://nymag.com/intelligencer /2021/03/david-shor-2020-democrats-autopsy-hispanic-vote-midterms-trump -gop.html.

Levy, Jacques E. 1975. *Cesar Chavez: Autobiography of La Causa*. New York: W. W. Norton.

Lewis Mumford Center for Comparative Urban and Regional Research. 2001. "The New Latinos: Who They Are and Where They Are" (September 10). http://mumford.albany.edu/census/HispanicPop/HspReport/HspReportPage1.html.

Libertad. 1994. "40th Anniversary of the Attack on Congress." National Committee to Free Puerto Rican Prisoners of War and Political Prisoners. www.etext.org/Politics/Autonome.Forum/Political.Prisoners/Puerto.Rico/libertad.spring94.

Lilley, Sandra. 2013. "How U.S. Latinos Feel About Undocumented Immigration." El Colegio de la Frontera Norte. October 4. https://observatoriocolef.org/articulos/how-u-s-latinos-feel-about-undocumented-immigration.

Limon, Elvia. 2021. "Gov. Greg Abbott Signs Off on Texas' New Political Maps, Which Protect GOP Majorities While Diluting Voices of Voters of Color." *Texas Tribune*. October 25. https://www.texastribune.org/2021/10/25/2021-texas-redistricting-explained.

Lineberry, Robert L. 1977. *Equality in Urban Policy: The Distribution of Minority Public Services*. Sage Publications 39. New York: Sage Library of Social Research.

Livingston, Michael. 2018. "A Changing Electorate Has Pushed Republicans Out of This Assembly District." *Los Angeles Times*. July 1. https://www.latimes.com/politics/la-pol-ca-76th-district-20180701-story.html.

Lockhart, P. R. 2019. "How Shelby County v. Holder Upended Voting Rights in America." *Vox*. June 25. https://www.vox.com/policy-and-politics/2019/6/25/18701277/shelby-county-v-holder-anniversary-voting-rights-suppression-congress.

Logan, John R. 2001. "The New Latinos: Who They Are, Where They Are." Lewis Mumford Center. September 10. http://mumford.albany.edu/census/HispanicPop/HspReport/MumfordReport.pdf.

Logan, John, and Harvey Molotch. 1987. *Urban Fortunes: The Political Economy of Place*. Berkeley: University of California Press.

Long, Trish. 2005. "Whatever." *El Paso Times*. March 24.

Lopez, Mark Hugo, Jens Manuel Krogstad, and Jeffrey S. Passel. 2021. "Who Is Hispanic?" Pew Research Center. September 23. https://www.pewresearch.org/fact-tank/2021/09/23/who-is-hispanic.

Lopez, Mark Hugo, Jeffrey Passel, and Molly Rohal. 2015. "Modern Immigration Wave Brings 59 Million U.S., Driving Population Growth and Change Through 2065." Pew Research Center. September 28. https://espas.secure.europarl.europa.eu/orbis/sites/default/files/generated/document/en/Modern-immigration-wave_REPORT.pdf.

Lopez, Mark Hugo, and Paul Taylor. 2012. "Latino Voters in the 2012 Election." Pew Research Center. November 7. https://www.pewresearch.org/hispanic/2012/11/07/latino-voters-in-the-2012-election.

Lopez, Robert J. 1994. "Campaign's Bitter Roots Run Deep." *Los Angeles Times*. April 10.

Los Angeles County Economic Development Corporation (LAEDC). 2017. *An Economic Profile of the Latino Community in Los Angeles County*. Los Angeles,

CA: LAEDC. https://laedc.org/wp-content/uploads/2017/02/LAEDC_2017 -Forecast_20170222a.pdf.

Los Angeles Times. 1994. Exit poll. November 10. https://www.latimes.com /archives/la-xpm-1994-11-10-me-61453-story.html?

———. 1996. Exit poll. November 5. https://ca-times.brightspotcdn.com/08/c3 /82a8919e4b098f2301898b647ed1/43120439.pdf.

———. 2001. Exit poll 460. June 5. https://ropercenter.cornell.edu/ipoll/study?doi =10.25940/ROPER-31093134.

Los Angeles Times/CNN. 1998. Exit poll. June 2. https://www.cnn.com/ALLPOLITICS /1998/06/03/exit.poll/.

Louie, Miriam Ching Yoon. 2001. *Sweatshop Warriors: Immigrant Women Take on the Global Factory.* Cambridge, MA: South End.

Lucas, Isidro. 1984. "Puerto Rican Politics in Chicago." In *Puerto Rican Politics in Urban America.* Edited by James Jennings and Monte Rivera. Westport, CT: Greenwood Press.

Magana, Lisa, and Cesar Silva. 2021. *Empowered Latinos Transforming Arizona Politics.* Tucson: University of Arizona Press.

Man, Anthony. 2021. "Broward and Palm Beach Counties Have Few Hispanic Elected Officials Despite Growing Population. That May Be Starting to Change." *Sun Sentinel.* March 6. https://www.sun-sentinel.com/news/politics /elections/fl-ne-few-hispanic-elected-officials-broward-palm-beach-20210306 -tnpot22acfdaro4jc3hwgansge-story.html.

Manning, Jennifer E. 2022. "Membership of the 117th Congress: A Profile." Congressional Research Service. Updated August 8. https://crsreports.congress.gov /product/pdf/R/R46705.

Manzano, Sylvia, and Arturo Vega. 2013. "'I Don't See Color, I Just Vote for the Best Candidate': The Persistence of Ethnically Polarized Voting." In *The Roots of Latino Urban Agency.* Edited by Sharon A. Navarro and Rodolfo Rosales. Denton: University of North Texas.

Marquez, Benjamin. 1985. *Power and Politics in a Mexican Barrio: A Study of Mobilization Efforts and Community Power in El Paso.* New York: University Press of America.

———. 1993. *LULAC: The Evolution of a Mexican American Political Organization.* Austin: University of Texas Press.

Marrable, Manning. 2004. "Globalization and Racialization." *Znet.* August 13. https://zcomm.org/znetarticle/globalization-and-racialization-by-manning -marable.

Marrero, Pilar. N.d. "187. Gil Cedillo and the Fight to Return Driver's Licenses to Undocumented Immigrants." KQED. https://www.kcet.org/shows/187 /clip/gil-cedillo-and-the-fight-to-return-drivers-licenses-to-undocumented -immigrants.

Martinez, Oscar J. 1980. *The Chicanos of El Paso: An Assessment of Progress.* Southwestern Studies Monograph 59. El Paso: Texas Western Press.

Mason, Melanie. 2015. "The Woman Behind California's End-of-Life Law." *Los Angeles Times.* October 7. https://www.latimes.com/local/politics/la-me-pol -sac-eggman-assisted-suicide-20151007-story.html.

Matos Rodríguez, Félix V. 2003. "Puerto Rican Politics in New York City: A Conversation with Roberto Ramirez." *Centro: Journal of the Center for Puerto Rican Studies* 15, no. 1 (spring): 196–211.

McCormick, Joseph P., and Charles E. Jones. 1993. "The Conceptualization of Deracialization." In *Dilemmas of Black Politics: Issues of Leadership and Strategy.* Edited by Georgia A. Persons. New York: HarperCollins.

McGhee, Eric, Jennifer Paluch, and Vicki Hsieh. 2021. "Redistricting Opens New Opportunities for Communities of Color." Public Policy Institute of California. October 13. https://www.ppic.org/blog/redistricting-opens-new-opportunities-for-communities-of-color.

Medoff, Peter, and Holly Sklar. 1994. *Streets of Hope: The Fall and Rise of an Urban Neighborhood.* Boston: South End.

Meier, Kenneth J., J. L. Polinard, and Robert D. Wrinkle. 2000. "Michael Giles and Mancur Olson Meet Vincent Ostrom: Jurisdiction Size and Latino Representation." *Social Science Quarterly* 81, no. 1 (March): 123–135.

Menchaca, Martha. 1995. *The Mexican Outsiders: A Community History of Marginalization and Discrimination in California.* Austin: University of Texas Press.

Mendez, Lys. 2021. "Latino Voters Were Decisive in 2020 Presidential Election." *UCLA Newsroom.* January 19. https://newsroom.ucla.edu/releases/latino-vote-analysis-2020-presidential-election.

Mendez, Maria. 2018. "Candidates, Advocates Tout 'Latina Movement' in Texas 2018." *Austin American-Statesman.* September 29. https://www.statesman.com/story/news/politics/elections/2018/09/29/candidates-advocates-tout-latina-movement-in-texas-us-elections/9736584007.

Menifield, Charles E. 2001a. "Hispanic Representation in State and Local Governments." In *Representation of Minority Groups in the U.S.: Implications for the Twenty-First Century.* Edited by Charles E. Menifield. Lanham, MD: Austin and Winfield.

———. 2001b. "Minority Representation in the Twenty-First Century: An Introduction." In *Representation of Minority Groups in the U.S.: Implications for the Twenty-First Century.* Edited by Charles E. Menifield. Lanham, MD: Austin and Winfield.

MetNews Staff Writer. 2001. "Ex-Wilson Appointee, Ousted by Voters, Named to Monterey Court." *Metropolitan News-Enterprise.* October 3. http://www.metnews.com/articles/2001/judg100301.htm.

Metz, David H., and Katherine Tate. 1996. "The Color of Urban Campaigns." In *Classifying by Race.* Edited by Paul Peterson. Princeton, NJ: Princeton University Press.

Mexican American Legal Defense and Education Fund (MALDEF). N.d. "Our History," MALDEF. https://www.maldef.org/our-history.

———. 2001. "Voting Rights." MALDEF. https://www.maldef.org/court-cases/voting-rights/.

Migration Policy Institute (MPI). N.d. "Migration Information Source." MPI. www.migrationinformation.org/USfocus.

Milanese, Marisa. 2001. "Man on a Fast Track." *Stanford Magazine.* September/October. https://stanfordmag.org/contents/man-on-a-fast-track.

232 References

Miles, Jack. 1992. "Blacks vs. Browns." *Atlantic Monthly*. October 1.

Milkman, Ruth. 2011. "LA's Past America's Future? The 2006 Immigrant Rights Protests and Their Antecedents." In *Rallying for Immigrant Rights: The Fight for Inclusion in 21st Century America*. Edited by K. Voss and I. Bloemraad. Berkeley: University of California Press.

Milkman, Ruth, with Kent Wong. 2000. "Organizing Immigrants: Case Studies from Southern California." In *Rekindling the Movement: Labor's Quest for Relevance in the 21st Century*. Edited by Lowell Turner, Harry C. Katz, and Richard W. Hurd. Ithaca, NY: Cornell University Press.

Millard, E. 2019. "2019 Women in Business Awards: Maria Regan Gonzalez, Mayor of Richfield." *Minneapolis/St. Paul Business Journal*. May 22. https://www .bizjournals.com/twincities/news/2019/05/22/2019-women-in-business-awards -maria-regan-gonzalez.html.

Miller, Gary J. 1981. *Cities by Contract: The Politics of Municipal Incorporation*. Cambridge, MA: MIT Press.

Miller, Ronald F. 1987. "Our Town: Salinas, California." Oral History. April. Salinas Public Library, Special Collections Reference Room.

Mohl, Raymond A. 1989. "Ethnic Politics in Miami, 1960–1986." In *Essays on Ethnicity, Race, and the Urban South*. Edited by Randell M. Miller and George E. Pozzetta. Boca Raton: Florida Atlanta University Press.

Mollenkopf, John. 1997. "New York: The Great Anomaly." In *Racial Politics in American Cities*. Edited by Rufus P. Browning, Dale R. Marshall, and David H. Tabb. 2nd ed. New York: Longman.

Molony, J. 2013. "Garcia Wins District. 6 Special Election." *Dear Park Broadcaster*. March 7.

Montejano, David. 1987. *Anglos and Mexicans in the Making of Texas, 1837–1986*. Austin: University of Texas Press.

Moore, C. 2013. "Celia Israel Runs for District 50 with a Long History of Public Service." *Austin Monitor*. October 4. https://www.austinmonitor.com/stories /2013/10/celia-israel-runs-for-district-50-with-a-long-history-of-public-service.

Morales, Ed. 2004. "Brown Like Me?" *Nation*. February 19. https://www.thenation .com/article/archive/brown-me.

Morales, Iris. 1998. "Palante, Siempre Palante!" In *The Puerto Rican Movement: Voices from the Diaspora*. Edited by Andrés Torres and José E. Velázquez. Philadelphia: Temple University Press.

Morales-Doyle, Sean. 2021. "Reversing the Supreme Court's Latest Blow to Voting Rights." Brennan Center for Justice. July 16. https://www.brennancenter.org /our-work/analysis-opinion/reversing-supreme-courts-latest-blow-voting-rights.

Moreno, Dario, Kevin Hill, and Lourdes Cue. 2001. "Racial and Partisan Voting in a Tri-ethnic City: The 1996 Dade County Mayoral Election." *Journal of Urban Affairs* 23, no. 3–4: 291–307. https://www.tandfonline.com/doi/abs/10.1111 /0735-2166.00090.

Moreno, Dario, and Maria Ilcheva. 2018. "Carlos Gimenez's Conservative Reforms in Miami-Dade County." In *Latino Mayors*. Edited by Marion Orr and Domingo Morel. Philadelphia: Temple University Press.

Moreno, Dario, and Christopher L. Warren. 1992. "The Conservative Enclave: Cubans in Florida." In *From Rhetoric to Reality: Latino Politics in the 1988 Elections.* Edited by Rodolfo O. de la Garza and Louis DeSipio. Boulder, CO: Westview.

———. 1996. "Cuban Americans in Miami Politics: Understanding the Cuban Model." In *The Politics of Minority Coalitions: Race, Ethnicity, and Shared Uncertainties.* Edited by Wilbur C. Rich. Westport, CT: Praeger.

———. 1997. "The Cuban Model: Political Empowerment in Miami." In *Pursuing Power: Latinos in the Political System.* Edited by F. Chris Garcia. Notre Dame, IN: Notre Dame University Press.

Moret, Louis F. 1998. "The Latino Political Agenda in Southern California Municipalities." DPA diss., University of La Verne, California.

Moritz, John C. 2022. "USA Today's Women of the Year 2022." *Corpus Christi Caller Times.* March 13.

Morris, Mike. 2012. "Redistricting Testimony Yields (Some) Political Intrigue." *Houston Chronicle.* November 16.

Morse, Janice M. 2000. "Determining Sample Size." *Qualitative Health Research* 10, no. 1 (January 1): 3–5.

Munoz, Carlos, Jr. 1989. *Youth, Identity, and Power: The Chicano Movement.* London: Verso.

Munoz, Carlos, Jr., and Charles Henry. 1990. "Coalition Politics in San Antonio and Denver: The Cisneros and Peña Mayoral Campaigns." In *Racial Politics in American Cities.* Edited by Rufus Browning, Dale Marshall, and David Tabb. New York: Longman.

Murguia, Janet. 2020. "Latino and Black Americans Are Allies in Fight for Racial Justice." *The Hill.* June 12. https://thehill.com/opinion/civil-rights/502465-latinos -allies-are-fighting-for-social-and-economic-justice.

Murphy, Patricia. 2018. "Happy New Year, Republicans! It's All Downhill Now." *Texarkana Gazette.* December 31. https://www.texarkanagazette.com/news /2018/dec/31/happy-new-year-republicans-its-all-downhill-now.

Myrdal, Gunnar. 1944. *An American Dilemma: The Negro Problem and Modern Democracy.* New York: Harper.

Narea, Nicole. 2020. "Hispanic Voters Helped Decide the Election—and Not Just in Miami-Dade." *Vox.* November 4. https://www.vox.com/21549607/latino-hispanic -vote-2020-trump-biden-arizona-florida.

National Association of Latino Elected and Appointed Officials (NALEO). 1994. *National Roster of Hispanic Elected Officials.* Los Angeles, CA: NALEO Educational Fund.

———. 1996. *National Roster of Latino Elected Officials.* Los Angeles, CA: NALEO Educational Fund.

———. 2000a. *2000 Latino: Election Handbook.* Los Angeles, CA: NALEO Educational Fund.

———. 2000b. *2000 National Directory of Latino Elected Officials.* Los Angeles, CA: NALEO Educational Fund.

———. 2001a. *National Directory of Latino Elected Officials.* Los Angeles, CA: NALEO Educational Fund.

234 *References*

———. 2001b. "Research Brief: The Growth of Latinos in the Nation's Congressional Districts: The 2000 Census and Latino Political Empowerment" (June). Los Angeles, CA: NALEO Educational Fund.

———. 2002. *National Directory of Latino Elected Officials*. Los Angeles, CA: NALEO Education Fund. http://www.naleo.org/civic_education.htm.

———. 2003. *National Directory of Latino Elected Officials*. Los Angeles, CA: NALEO Educational Fund.

———. 2004. "Latinos Win Big on Election Night." Press release. NALEO. November 3.

———. 2010. *National Directory of Latino Elected Officials*. Los Angeles, CA: NALEO Educational Fund.

———. 2020. *National Directory of Latino Elected Leaders*. Los Angeles, CA: NALEO Education Fund.

———. 2021. *National Directory of Latino Elected Leaders*. Los Angeles, CA: NALEO Education Fund.

———. 2022. *National Directory of Latino Elected Leaders*. Los Angeles, CA: NALEO Education Fund.

National Civic League. 1996. *Communities and the Voting Rights Act: A Guide to Compliance in These Changing Times*. Denver: National Civic League.

National Conference of State Legislatures (NCSL). 2021a. "Undocumented Student Tuition: Overview." NCSL. June 9. www.ncsl.org/research/education /undocumented-student-tuition-overview.aspx.

———. 2021b. "States Offering Driver's Licenses to Immigrants." NCSL. August 9. https://www.ncsl.org/research/immigration/states-offering-driver-s-licenses -to-immigrants.aspx.

National School Boards Association (NSBA). 2018. "Today's School Boards and Their Priorities for Tomorrow." NSBA. https://www.nsba.org/-/media /NSBA/File/nsba-todays-school-boards-and-their-priorities-for-tomorrow -2018-survey.pdf.

Navarro, Armando. 1995. *Mexican American Youth Organization: Avant-Garde of the Chicano Movement in Texas*. Austin: University of Texas Press.

———. 1998. *The Cristal Experiment: A Chicano Struggle for Community Control*. Madison: University of Wisconsin Press.

———. 2000. *La Raza Unida Party: A Chicano Challenge to the U.S. Two-Party Dictatorship*. Philadelphia: Temple University Press.

Navarro, Carlos, and Rodolfo Acuña. 1990. "In Search of Community: A Comparative Essay on Mexicans in Los Angeles and San Antonio." In *Twentieth Century Los Angeles: Power, Promotion, and Social Conflict*. Edited by Norman Klein and Martin Schiesl. Claremont, CA: Regina.

Navarro, Sharon A. 2015. "The Latino Mayors: San Antonio Politics and Policies." Research Report 52. Julian Samora Research Institute. https://jsri.msu.edu /publications/research-reports/355.

———. 2018. "Latinas and the Texas Judiciary." In *Race, Gender, Sexuality, and the Politics of the American Judiciary*. Edited by Samantha L. Hernandez and Sharon A. Navarro. Cambridge: Cambridge University Press.

Navarro, Sharon A., Samantha L. Hernandez, and Leslie A. Navarro, ed. 2016. *Latinas in American Politics: Changing and Embracing Political Tradition*. MD: Lexington Press.

Needham, Jerry. 2001. "S.A. Weighs No-Hotel PGA Plan." *San Antonio Express News*. November 15.

Nelson, Albert J. 1991. *Emerging Influentials in State Legislatures: Women, Blacks, and Hispanics*. New York: Praeger.

———. 1996. *Democrats Under Siege in the Sunbelt Megastates: California, Florida, and Texas*. Westport, CT: Praeger.

Nevins, Joseph. 2002. *Operation Gatekeeper: The Rise of the "Illegal Alien" and the Making of the U.S.-Mexico Boundary*. New York: Routledge Press.

Ngai, Mae. 2014. *Impossible Subjects: Illegal Aliens and the Making of Modern America*. Princeton, NJ: Princeton University Press.

Noe-Bustamante, Luis, Abby Budiman, and Mark Hugo Lopez. 2020. "Where Latinos Have the Most Eligible Voters in the 2020 Election." Pew Research Center. January 31. https://www.pewresearch.org/fact-tank/2020/01/31/where-latinos -have-the-most-eligible-voters-in-the-2020-election.

Noe-Bustamante, Luis, Mark Hugo Lopez, and Jens Manuel Krogstad. 2020. "U.S. Hispanic Population Surpassed 60 Million in 2019, but Growth Has Slowed." Pew Research Center. July 7. https://www.pewresearch.org/fact-tank/2020/07 /07/u-s-hispanic-population-surpassed-60-million-in-2019-but-growth-has -slowed.

Noe-Bustamante, Luis, Lauren Mora, and Mark Hugo Lopez. 2020. "About One-in-Four U.S. Hispanics Have Heard the Term Latinx, but Just 3% Use It." Pew Research Center. August 11. https://www.pewresearch.org/hispanic/wp-content /uploads/sites/5/2020/08/PHGMD_2020.08.11_Latinx_FINAL.pdf.

Nowicki, Dan. 2010. "Arizona Immigration Law Ripples Though History, U.S. Politics." *Arizona Republic*. July 25.

Ocasio Rivera, Juan Antonio. 2012. "Our Resistance: An Interview with Rafael Cancel Miranda." *NACLA Report of the Americas* 45, no. 3: 75–78.

Office of Connecticut State Representative Felipe Reinoso. 2001. Representative Reinoso Elected New President of the Association of Peruvian Organizations. Press release. May 31.

Office of the Press Secretary. 2016. "Fact Sheet: Obama Administration Efforts That have Expanded Opportunities for the Hispanic Community." *White House, President Barack H. Obama*. May 5.

Oliver, J. Eric. 2001. *Democracy in Suburbia*. Princeton, NJ: Princeton University Press.

Oliver, J. Eric, and Tali Mendelberg. 2000. "Reconsidering the Environmental Determination of White Racial Attitudes." *American Journal of Political Science* 44, no. 3: 574–589.

Omi, Michael, and Howard Winant. 1994. *Racial Formation in the United States: From the 1960s to the 1990s*. 2nd ed. New York: Routledge.

Ong, Paul, Edna Bonacich, and Lucie Cheng. 1994. "The Political Economy of Capitalist Restructuring and New Asian Immigration." In *The New Asian Immigration*

236 References

in Los Angeles and Global Restructuring. Edited by Paul Ong, Edna Bonacich, and Lucie Cheng. Philadelphia: Temple University Press.

Orey, Byron D'Andra. 2006. "Deracialization or Racialization: The Making of a Black Mayor in Jackson, Mississippi." *Politics and Policy* 3, no. 4: 814–836.

Orr, Marion, and Domingo Morel, eds. 2018. *Latino Mayors: Political Change in the Postindustrial City.* Philadelphia: Temple University Press.

Orr, Marion, Domingo Morel, and Emily Farris. 2018. "Managing Fiscal Stress in Providence: The Election and Governance of Mayor Angel Taveras." In *Latino Mayors.* Editors Marion Orr and Domingo Morel. Philadelphia. Philadelphia: Temple University Press.

Ortiz, Paul. 2018. *An African American and Latinx History of the United States.* Boston, MA: Beacon Press Books.

Ortiz-Wythe, Bianca, Christa M. Kelleher, Fabian Torres-Ardila. 2019. "Latino Political Leadership in Massachusetts: 2019." Gastón Institute Publications. ScholarWorks. https://scholarworks.umb.edu/gaston_pubs/243/?utm_source =scholarworks.umb.edu%2Fgaston_pubs%2F243&utm_medium=PDF&utm _campaign=PDFCoverPages.

Otarola, Miguel. 2018. "Richfield Elects Maria Regan Gonzalez, the First Latina Mayor in the State." *Star Tribune.* November 7.

"Our Campaigns—TX District 20 Race." 2012. Our Campaigns. November 6. www.ourcampaigns.com.

"Our Campaigns—TX State House 125-D Primary Race." 2002. Our Campaigns. May 12. www.ourcampaigns.com.

Pachon, Harry P., and Louis DeSipio. 1990. "Latino Legislators and Latino Caucuses." Working Paper 11. UP/SSRC Committee for Public Policy Research on Contemporary Hispanic Issues. Center for Mexican American Studies, University of Texas, Austin.

Pachon, Harry P., Lupe Sanchez, and Dennis Falcon. 1999. "California Latino Politics and the 1996 Elections: From Potential to Reality." In *Awash in the Mainstream: Latino Politics in the 1996 Elections.* Edited by Rodolfo O. de la Garza and Louis DeSipio. Boulder, CO: Westview.

Pack, William. 2001a. "City Issues Fail to Excite Voters—Proposition 3 Draws Most Controversy." *San Antonio Express News.* November 4.

———. 2001b. "Council Delays Aquifer Tax Vote—Memo Proposes Ending Breaks." *San Antonio Express News.* October 5.

———. 2001c. "Council Says No Golf, No Deal—Evaluation of Environmental Studies Required for PGA Site." *San Antonio Express News.* July 15.

———. 2001d. "Mayor, Panel to Mull Term Limit Vote—the Public Can Voice Opinions During Hearing." *San Antonio Express News.* July 29.

Padilla, Felix M. 1985. *Latino Ethnic Consciousness: The Case of Mexican Americans and Puerto Ricans in Chicago.* Notre Dame, IN: University of Notre Dame Press.

———. 1987. *Puerto Rican Chicago.* Notre Dame, IN: University of Notre Dame Press.

Pallares, Amalia, and Nilda Flores-Gonzalez, eds. 2010. *¡Marcha! Latino Chicago and the Immigrant Rights Movement*. Urbana: University of Illinois Press.

Pantoja, Adrian D., Ricardo Ramirez, and Gary M. Segura. 2001. "Citizens by Choice, Voters by Necessity: Patterns in Political Mobilization by Naturalized Latinos." *Political Research Quarterly* 54, no. 4 (December): 729–750.

Pantoja, Adrian D., and Gary M. Segura. 2000. "Citizens by Choice, Voters by Necessity: Patterns in Political Mobilization by Naturalized Latinos." Paper presented at the annual meeting of the Western Political Science Association, San Jose, California, March 24–26.

Pardo, Mary. 1998. *Mexican American Women Activists: Identity and Resistance in Two Los Angeles Communities*. Philadelphia: Temple University Press.

Passel, Jeffery. 2002. "New Estimates of the Undocumented Population." Migration Information Source. May 22.

Passel, Jeffrey S., and D'Vera Cohn. 2014. "Unauthorized Immigrant Totals Rise in 7 States, Fall in 14." Pew Research Center. November 18. https://www.pewresearch.org/hispanic/2014/11/18/unauthorized-immigrant-totals-rise-in-7-states-fall-in-14.

Passel, Jeffrey S., Mark Hugo Lopez, and D'Vera Cohn. 2022. "U.S. Hispanic Population Continued Its Geographic Spread in the 2010s." Pew Research Center. February 3. https://www.pewresearch.org/fact-tank/2022/02/03/u-s-hispanic-population-continued-its-geographic-spread-in-the-2010s/.

Patoski, Joe Nick. 2002. "Water Hazards." *Texas Monthly*. November 29.

Patterson, Mitchell. 2018. "Lavelle vs. Sturgeon: A Key Race You Ought to Watch." *The Review*. November 6. https://udreview.com/lavelle-vs-sturgeon-a-key-race-you-ought-to-watch.

Paxton, Pamela, and S. Kunovich. 2003. "Women's Political Representation: The Importance of Ideology." *Social Forces* 82, no. 1: 87–113.

Pazniokas, Mark. 2001. "Perez's Crowning Moment Is at Hand." *Hartford Courant*. December 4.

Perez y Gonzalez, Maria E. 2000. *Puerto Ricans in the United States*. Westport, CT: Greenwood Press.

Perez, Elida S. 2021. "Two Years Later, Prosecution of Walmart Shooting Suspect Faces Ongoing Delays." *El Paso Matters*. August 3. https://elpasomatters.org/2021/08/03/two-years-later-prosecution-of-walmart-shooting-suspect-faces-ongoing-delays.

Perry, R. K., ed. *21st Century Urban Race Politics: Representing Minorities as Universal Interests*. Bingley, UK: Emerald Group Publishing.

Peterson, Paul. 1981. *City Limits*. Chicago: University of Chicago Press.

Pew Hispanic Center. 2002. *The Latino Population and the Latino Electorate: The Numbers Differ*. Washington, DC: Pew Hispanic Research Center.

———. 2004a. "The 2002 National Survey of Latinos." Pew Hispanic Center. January 7. https://www.pewresearch.org/wp-content/uploads/sites/5/reports/39.pdf.

———. 2004b. "The 2004 National Survey of Latinos: Politics and Civic Participation." Pew Research Center. July 22. https://www.pewresearch.org/hispanic

/2004/07/22/pew-hispanic-centerkaiser-family-foundation-2004-national-survey-of-latinos.

Pew Research Center Staff. 2017. "Looking Back: The Obama Administration." Pew Research Center. February 23. https://www.pewresearch.org/hispanic/2017/02/23/looking-back-the-obama-administration.

Phillips, Christian Dyogi. 2021. *Nowhere to Run: Race, Gender and Immigration in American Elections*. Oxford: Oxford University Press.

Pinderhughes, Dianne M. 1997. "An Examination of Chicago Politics for Evidence of Political Incorporation and Representation." In *Racial Politics in American Cities*. Edited by Rufus Browning, Dale R. Marshall, and David H. Tabb. 2nd ed. New York: Longman.

Pitkin, Hanna. 1967. *The Concept of Representation*. Berkeley: University of California Press.

Pitnick, R. 1998. "Outside In: Latino Political Clout on the Rise in Salinas Mayoral Race." *Coast Weekly Online*. October 15.

Piven, Francis F., and Richard A. Cloward. 1977. *Poor People's Movements: Why They Succeed, How They Fail*. New York: Vintage.

Pizarro, Max. 2020. "Diaz Loses in Perth Amboy." *Insider NJ*. December 18. https://www.insidernj.com/diaz-loses-perth-amboy.

Pla, George L., and David R. Ayon. 2018. *Power Shift: How Latinos in California Transformed Politics in America*. Berkeley, CA: Berkeley Public Policy Press.

Planas, Roque. 2015. "A Tiny Rural Town Just Elected an All-Latino City Council." *Huffington Post*. December 1. https://www.huffpost.com/entry/latino-city-council-idaho_n_565cd443e4b08e945fec5701.

Polinard, Jerry L., Robert D. Wrinkle, Tomas Longoria, and Norman E. Binder. 1994. *Electoral Structure and Urban Policy: The Impact on Mexican American Communities*. Armonk, NY: M. E. Sharpe.

Puerto Rican Legal Defense and Education Fund (PRLDEF). 2002. "Redistricting Latino Communities: Turning Our Numbers into Political Power?" *Política Social*. Newsletter of the PRLDEP Institute for Puerto Rican Policy.

Porter, Eduardo. 2001. "Up to 8.5 Million Immigrants Believed to Be in the U.S. Illegally." *Wall Street Journal*. August 14.

Powell, Barbara. 2004. "'It's a Big Deal for Us'—Toyota Plant Begins Rising—Officials Watch as Assembly Plant's First Post Is Planted." *San Antonio Express News*. November 16.

Prendez, Linda. 2001. "Castro Unveils Political Goals—More Public Input One Priority." *San Antonio Express News*. June 13.

Purdom, Todd S. 2001. "Hahn Wins Los Angeles Mayor's Race." *New York Times*. June 6.

Ramakrishnan, S. Karthick, and Thomas J. Espenshade. 2001. "Immigrant Incorporation and Political Participation in the United States." *International Migration Review* 35, no. 3 (fall): 870–895.

Ramirez, Roberto R., and G. P. de la Cruz. 2002. *The Hispanic Population in the United States*. Current Population Reports. US Census Bureau. Washington, DC: US Government Printing Office.

Ramos, Henry A. J. 1998. *American GI Forum: In Pursuit of the Dream, 1948–1983*. Houston, TX: Arte Público Press.

Reed, Adolph, Jr. 1995. "Demobilization in the New Black Political Regime: Ideological Capitulation and Radical Failure in the Post-segregation Era." In *The Bubbling Cauldron: Race, Ethnicity, and the Urban Crisis*. Edited by Michael P. Smith and Joe R. Feagin. Minneapolis: University of Minnesota Press.

Regalado, Jaime. 1988. "Latino Representation in Los Angeles." In *Latino Empowerment: Progress, Problems, and Prospects*. Edited by Roberto E. Villarreal, Norma G. Hernandez, and Howard D. Neighbor. New York: Greenwood Press.

———. 1998. "Minority Political Incorporation in Los Angeles: A Broader Consideration." In *Racial and Ethnic Politics in California*. Edited by Michael B. Preston, Bruce E. Cain, and Sandra Bass. Berkeley, CA: Institute of Government Studies Press.

Regalado, Jaime, and Gloria Martinez. 1991. "Reapportionment and Coalition Building: A Case Study of Informal Barriers to Latino Empowerment in Los Angeles County." In *Latinos and Political Coalitions: Political Empowerment in the 1990s*. Edited by Roberto E. Villarreal and Norma G. Hernandez. New York: Praeger.

Reid, Stuart. 1987. *Working with Statistics: An Introduction to Quantitative Methods for Social Scientists*. Totowa, NJ: Rowman & Littlefield.

Renner, T., and V. de Santis. 1993. "Contemporary Patterns and Trends in Municipal Government Structures." In *Municipal Yearbook*. Washington, DC: International City Managers' Association.

Reny, Tyler, Bryan Wilcox-Archuleta, and Vanessa Cruz Nichols. 2019. "Threat, Mobilization, and Latino Voting in the 2018 Election." *The Forum* 16, no. 4 (February 27).

Reuter, Theodore. 1995. *The Politics of Race: African Americans and the Political System*. New York: M. E. Sharpe.

Reynoso, Felipe. 2001. "Representeative Reinoso Elected New President of the Assocation of Peruvian Organizations." Press Release, Office of Connecticut State Representative Felipe Reinoso 130th Assembly District. D-Bridgeport, (May 31).

Rivard, Robert. 2004. "Let the Games Begin: Spectacle Pits Garza Against Brechtel." *San Antonio Express News*. August 29.

Rodriguez, Gregory. 1996. "The Browning of California: Proposition 187 Backfires." *New Republic* 215, no. 10.

———. 2002a. "Latinos: No Longer Society's Victims." *Los Angeles Times*. May 12.

———. 2002b. "Where the Minorities Rule." *New York Times*. February 10.

Rodriguez, Ken. 2004a. "Castro Ventures North, Makes Pitch For Conservatives' Votes." *San Antonio Express News*. March 21.

———. 2004b. "Hardberger Announces Mayoral Bid, Heads Out to Sea in a Boat." *San Antonio Express News*. April 28.

———. 2004c. "Schubert Rises, Castro Falls in the Collapse of PGA Village." *San Antonio Express News*. June 4.

240 References

———. 2004d. "Timing May Be Right for City Hall 'Outsider' like Hardberger." *San Antonio Express News*. December 1.

Rodriguez, Lori. 2001. "Sanchez's Mayoral Bid Targets Disparate Voters." *Houston Chronicle*. October 7.

Rodriguez, Rebecca. 2005a. "Hardberger Opens Wallet to Fight Back." *San Antonio Express News*. April 30.

———. 2005b. "Mayoral Foes Set Sights on Prize." *San Antonio Express News*. May 9.

———. 2005c. "Politics Did Make Strange Bedfellows." *San Antonio Express News*. June 9.

Rodriguez, Victor M. 2005. *Latino Politics in the United States: Race, Ethnicity, Class and Gender in the Mexican American and Puerto Rican Experience*. Dubuque, IA: Kendall Hunt Publishing.

Romo, David. 2001. "Running with Ray: Is El Paso's Next Mayor a Caballero?" *Texas Observer*. April 27.

"Ros-Lehtinen, Ileana." N.d. History, Art, and Archives, United States House of Representatives. https://history.house.gov/People/Detail/20624#biography.

Rosales, Rodolfo. 2000. *The Illusion of Inclusion: The Untold Political Story of San Antonio*. Austin: University of Texas Press.

Rosentiel, Tom. 2008. "Inside Obama's Sweeping Victory." Pew Research Center. November 5. https://www.pewresearch.org/2008/11/05/inside-obamas-sweeping-victory.

Ross, Karl, Jay Weaver, and Oscar Corral. 2001. "Cuban American Vote Lifts Diaz to Miami Mayor's Post." *Miami Herald*. November 14.

Rott, Nathan. 2015. "A Tiny Town in Idaho Welcomes the State's First All-Latino City Council." NPR. December 24. https://www.npr.org/2015/12/24/460959623/small-town-set-to-swear-in-idahos-first-all-latino-city-council.

Ruiz, Vicki L. 1987. *Cannery Women, Cannery Lives: Mexican Women, Unionization, and the California Food Processing Industry, 1930–1950*. Albuquerque: University of New Mexico Press.

Russell, Jan Jarboe. 2009a. "Councilman Shone in Nuclear Debate." *San Antonio Express News*. December 27.

———. 2009b. "DeBerry-Mejia Not Giving Up on Public Service." *San Antonio Express News*. July 19.

Ruthhart, Bill, and Juan Perez Jr. 2015. "Garcia Winning Latino Vote, but Emanuel Has Hold on Sizable Portion." *Chicago Tribune*. April 2. https://www.chicagotribune.com/politics/ct-chicago-mayor-race-latino-vote-met-20150401-story.html.

Sailer, Steve. 2001. "Analysis: Mexican-Americans and the Vote." United Press International. July 24.

Sampaio, Anna. 2002. "Transforming Chicana/o and Latina/o Politics: Globalization and the Formation of Transnational Resistance in the United States and Chiapas." In *Transnational Latina/o Communities: Politics, Processes, and Cultures*. Edited by Carlos G. Velez-Ibanez and Anna Sampaio, with Manolo González-Estay. Lanham, MD: Rowman & Littlefield.

References 241

———. 2015. *Terrorizing Latino/a Immigrants: Race, Gender, and Immigration Politics in the Age of Security.* Philadelphia: Temple University Press.

San Antonio Express News. 2001. "Garza's Easy Victory Offers Hope for Unity- Although the Campaign was Negative the Results Offer Hope That the City can Work on a Collective Vision." *San Antonio Express News.* May 7.

———. 2003. "Report of the Mayor's Committee on Integrity and Trust in Local Government." *San Antonio Express News.* January 31.

———. 2020. "Mayor Must Outrun This Speeding Train." *San Antonio Express News.* October 12.

Sánchez Korrol, Virginia E. 1994. *From Colonia to Community: The History of Puerto Ricans in New York City.* Berkeley: University of California Press.

Sanchez, George J. 1993. *Becoming Mexican American: Ethnicity, Culture, and Identity in Chicano Los Angeles, 1900–1945.* Oxford: Oxford University Press.

Sánchez, José R. 1996. "Puerto Rican Politics in New York: Beyond 'Secondhand' Theory." In *Latinos in New York: Communities in Transition.* Edited by Gabriel Haslip-Vera and Sherrie L. Baver. Notre Dame, IN: University of Notre Dame Press.

Sanders, Heywood T. 1979. "Government Structure in American Cities." In *The Municipal Yearbook.* Washington, DC: International City Managers' Association.

———. 2018. "Mayoral Politics and Policies in a Divided City: Latino Mayors in San Antonio." In *Latino Mayors: Political Change in the Postindustrial City.* Edited by Marion Orr and Domingo Morel. Philadelphia: Temple University Press.

Santa Ana, Otto. 2012. "Arizona's Provincial Responses to Its Global Immigration Challenges: Introduction to Arizona Firestorm." In *Arizona Firestorm Immigration Realities, National Media, and Provincial Politics.* Edited by Otto Santa Ana, Celeste González de Bustamante, and Celeste Gonzalez De Bustamante. Lanham, MD: Rowman & Littlefield.

Saunders, P. 2021. "This Small Town in North Georgia Loves Its First LGBTQ Mayor." *Project Q Atlanta.* September 22.

Schaeffer, Katherine. 2021. "Racial, Ethnic Diversity Increases Yet Again with the 117th Congress." Pew Research Center. January 28. https://www.pewresearch .org/the-u-s-house-of-representatives-convenes-117th-congress-swears-in-new -members.

Schaper, David. 2011. "A Look at Iowa's First Majority Hispanic Town." NPR. October 10. https://www.npr.org/2011/10/10/141150607/west-liberty-is-iowas -first-majority-hispanic-town.

Schiffrin, Andrew. 1984. "The Story of Measure J—Santa Cruz County's Growth Management Program." *Regional Exchange: A Quarterly Publication of People for Open Space* (February).

Schor, Elana, and David Crary. 2020. "AP VoteCast: Trump Wins White Evangelicals, Catholics Split." *Associated Press.* November 6. https://apnews.com/article /votecast-trump-wins-white-evangelicals-d0cb249ea7eae29187a21a702dc 84706.

242 References

Schwartz, M. 2002. "Outgoing City Controller Gets Round of Applause." *Houston Chronicle*. December 26.

Scott, Steve. 2000. "Competing for the New Majority Vote." *California Journal* 41, no. 1 (January): 16–23.

Sears, David O., Jim Sidanius, and Lawrence Bobo, eds. 2000. *Racialized Politics: The Debate About Racism in America*. Chicago: University of Chicago Press.

Segura, Gary M., Dennis Falcon, and Harry Pachon. 1997. "Dynamics of Latino Partisanship in California, Immigration, Issue Salience, and Their Implications." *Harvard Journal of Hispanic Policy* 10: 62–80.

Sekul, Joseph D. 1983. "Communities Organized for Public Service: Citizen Power and Public Policy in San Antonio." In *The Politics of San Antonio: Community, Progress, and Power*. Edited by David R. Johnson, John A. Booth, and Richard J. Harris. Lincoln: University of Nebraska Press.

Sena, Gilbert Louis. 1973. "The Politics of New Mexico, 1960–1972." Master's thesis, California State University, Fullerton.

Serwer, Adam. 2021. "Texas Pays the Price of the Culture War." *The Atlantic*. February 22. https://www.theatlantic.com/ideas/archive/2021/02/texas-pays-price-culture-war/618107.

Shaw, Randy. 2011. "Building the Labor-Clergy-Immigrant Alliance." In *Rallying for Immigrant Rights: The Fight for Inclusion in 21st Century America*. Edited by Kim Voss, and Irene Bloemraad. Oakland: University of California Press.

"Shelby County v. Holder." 2018. Brennan Center for Justice. August 4. https://www.brennancenter.org/our-work/court-cases/shelby-county-v-holder.

Shiau, Ellen. 2018. "Coalition Building in Los Angeles: The Administration of Mayor Antonio Villaraigosa." In *Latino Mayors: Political Change in the Postindustrial City*. Edited by Marion Orr and Domingo Morel. Philadelphia: Temple University Press.

Shockley, John Staples. 1974. *Chicano Revolt in a Texas Town*. Notre Dame, IN: University of Notre Dame Press.

Sierra, Christine Marie. 2000. "Hispanics and the Political Process." In *Hispanics in the United States: An Agenda for the Twenty-First Century*. Edited by Pastora San Juan Cafferty and David W. Engstrom. New Brunswick, NJ: Transaction.

Sierra, Christine Marie, and Adaljiza Sosa Riddell. 1994. "Chicanas as Political Actors: Rare Literature, Complex Practice." In *The Challenge to Racial Stratification: National Political Science Review*. Edited by Matthew Holden Jr. New Brunswick, NJ: Transaction.

Simpson, Dick. 2006. "From Daley to Daley: Chicago Politics, 1955–2006." Great Cities Institute Publication Number GCP-06-03. College of Liberal Arts and Sciences. University of Illinois at Chicago.

Skelton, George. 2001. "Latino Impact Felt Through Labor Movement." *Los Angeles Times*. June 14.

Smetanka, Mary Jane. 2008. "Richfield, the State's Oldest Suburb." *Star Tribune*. February 11.

Smith, Adam C. 2003. "Alex Penelas Confronts a Tough Critic: His Own Party." *St. Petersburg Times*. August 31.

Smith, Michelle R. 2011. "New Providence Mayor Angel Tavares Sworn In." *Boston.com*. January 3. http://archive.boston.com/news/education/k_12/articles /2011/01/03/new_providence_mayor_angel_taveras_sworn_in.

Smith, Robert C. 1990a. "From Insurgency Toward Inclusion: The Jackson Campaigns of 1984 and 1988." In *The Social and Political Implications of the 1984 Jesse Jackson Presidential Campaign*. Edited by Lorenzo Morris. New York: Praeger.

———. 1990b. "Recent Elections and Black Politics: The Maturation or Death of Black Politics?" *PS: Political Science and Politics* 22 (June): 160–162.

Sonenshein, Raphael J. 1993. *Politics in Black and White: Race and Power in Los Angeles*. Princeton, NJ: Princeton University Press.

———. 1997. "Post Incorporation Politics in Los Angeles." In *Racial Politics in American Cities*. Edited by Rufus P. Browning, Dale R. Marshall, and David H. Tabb. 2nd ed. New York: Longman.

Sonneland, Holly K. 2020. "Chart: How U.S. Latinos Voted in the 2020 Presidential Election." *CNN News*. November 5. https://www.cnn.com/election/2016/results /exit-polls/national/president.

Sonneland, Holly, and Nicki Fleischner. 2016. "Chart: How U.S. Latinos Voted in the 2016 Presidential Election." AS/COA. November 10. https://www.as-coa .org/articles/chart-how-us-latinos-voted-2016-presidential-election.

Sosa Riddell, Adaljiza. 1974. "Chicanas and el Movimiento." *Aztlán* 5: 155–165.

Sosa Riddell, Adaljiza, and Robert Aguallo Jr. 1979. "A Case of Chicano Politics: Parlier, California." *Aztlán* 9: 1–22.

Southwest Voter Registration Education Project (SVREP). N.d. "History." SVREP. https://www.svrep.org/history.

———. 1984. *Analysis of the Hispanic Vote in 1984 Presidential Elections*. San Antonio, TX: Southwest Voter Registration Education Project.

Starks, Robert T., and Michael B. Preston. 1990. "Harold Washington and the Politics of Reform in Chicago, 1983–1987." In *Racial Politics in American Cities*. Edited by Rufus P. Browning, Dale R. Marshall, and David H. Tabb. New York: Longman.

State of California. 2001. "Labor Market Information, Directory of California Local Area Wages: Wages from 1998–2000." CCOIS Surveys.

State of California, Employment Development Department. 2002a. "Labor Force Data for Sub-county Areas." Department of Employment Development. February 21.

———. 2002b. "Revised Historical City and County Population Estimates 1991– 2000 with 1990 and 2000 Census Counts." Department of Finance. March.

Statista Research Department. 2021. "Percentage Distribution of Population in the United States in 2016 and 2060, by Race and Hispanic Origin." https://www .statista.com/statistics/270272/percentage-of-us-population-by-ethnicities/.

Stepnick, Alex, Guillermo Grenier, Max Castro, and Marvin Dunn. 1993. *This Land Is Our Land: Immigrants and Power in Miami*. Berkeley: University of California Press.

Stewart, Katherine. 2022. "The Democratic Party Is Shedding Latino Voters Here's Why." *New Republic*. May 11. https://newrepublic.com/article/166406/democrats -losing-latino-voters-2022.

244   References

Stille, Alexander. 2001. "Prospecting for Truth in the Ore of Memory." *New York Times*. March 19.

Stinchcombe, Arthur L. 1987. *Constructing Social Theories*. Chicago: University of Chicago Press.

Stinson, Roddy. 2004. "Who Is the Mayor of San Antonio, Ed Garza or Nelson Wolff?" *San Antonio Express News*. January 13.

Stone, Clarence N. 1989. *Regime Politics: Governing Atlanta, 1946–1989*. Lawrence: University Press of Kansas.

Stone, Clarence N., and Heywood Saunders, eds. 1987. *Politics of Urban Development*. Lawrence: University Press of Kansas.

Stroud, Scott. 2011. "SA2020 Provides Castro's Leadership Moment." *San Antonio Express News*. February 16. https://www.mysanantonio.com/news/news_columnists/scott_stroud/article/SA2020-provides-Castro-s-leadership-moment-1015380.php.

Suárez-Orozco, Marcelo M., and Mariela M. Páez. 2002. Introduction to *Latinos Remaking America*. Edited by M. M. Suárez-Orozco and M. M. Páez. Berkeley: University of California Press.

Suh, Michael. 2012. "Pew Research Center's Exit Poll Analysis on the 2012 Election." Pew Research Center. November 7. https://www.pewresearch.org/2012/11/07/pew-research-centers-exit-poll-analysis-on-the-2012-election.

Suro, Roberto. 1998. *Strangers Among Us: How Latino Immigration Is Transforming America*. New York: Alfred A. Knopf.

———. 2002. "Counting the Other Hispanics: How Many Colombians, Dominicans, Ecuadorians, Guatemalans, and Salvadorans Are There in the U.S.?" Washington, DC: Pew Hispanic Center.

Suro, Roberto, Richard Fry, and Jeffrey S. Passel. 2005. "Hispanics and the 2004 Election: Population, Electorate, and Voters." Washington, DC: Pew Hispanic Center.

Svitek, Patrick. 2017. "El Paso County Judge Veronica Escobar Begins Campaign for Congress." *Texas Tribune*. August 25. https://www.texastribune.org/2017/08/25/el-paso-county-judge-veronica-escobar-announce-congressional-campaign.

Swain, Carol M. 1993. *Black Faces, Black Interests: The Representation of African Americans in Congress*. Cambridge, MA: Harvard University Press.

Sziarto, Kristin M., and Helga Leitner. 2010. "Immigrants Riding for Justice: Space-Time and Emotions in the Construction of a Counterpublic." *Political Geography* 29: 381–391.

Takash, Paula Cruz. 1990. "A Crisis of Democracy: Community Responses to the Latinization of a California Town Dependent on Immigrant Labor." PhD diss., University of California, Berkeley.

———. 1993. "Breaking Barriers to Representation: Chicana/Latina Elected Officials in California." *Urban Anthropology* 22, no. 3–4 (fall–winter): 325–360.

Takash, Paula Cruz, and Joaquin Avila. 1989. "Latino Political Participation in Rural California." Working Paper 8 (February), Working Group on Farm Labor and Rural Poverty. Davis: California Institute for Rural Studies.

Taladrid, Stephania. 2020. "Deconstructing the 2020 Latino Vote." *New Yorker*. December 31. https://www.newyorker.com/news/news-desk/deconstructing-the-2020-latino-vote.

———. 2021. "Lina Hidalgo's Political Rise." *New Yorker*. June 28. https://www.newyorker.com/news/us-journal/lina-hidalgos-political-rise.

Taylor, D. 2021. "The Nevada Turnaround." In *Immigration Matters: Movements, Visions, and Strategies for a Progressive Future*. Edited by R. Milkman, D. Bhargava, and P. Lewis. New York: New Press.

Taylor, Ronald B. 1975. *Chavez and the Farm Workers*. Boston: Beacon.

"Tejano Politics." N.d. *Handbook of Texas Online*. https://www.tshaonline.org/handbook/entries/tejano-politics.

Texas Civil Liberties Union. 1938. "San Antonio: The Cradle of Texas Liberty and Its Coffin?" Document 13. http://efaidnbmnnnibpcajpcglclefindmkaj/https://history.illinoisstate.edu/downloads/journals/spring05.pdf.

"Information for Rep. Joaquin Castro." 2011. Texas Legislature Online, 82nd Legislature. https://capitol.texas.gov/Members/MemberInfo.aspx?Leg=82&Chamber=H&Code=A2495.

Texas Secretary of State. *November 4, 2004 Election Archives*. https://www.sos.state.tx.us/elections/earlyvoting/2004/index.shtml.

"Texas State Directory." 2018. *Texas State Directory*. January 1.

Theis, Michael. 2014. "Austin Ranks Among Most LGBT-Friendly U.S. Cities," *Austin Business Journal*. May 28. https://www.bizjournals.com/austin/news/2014/05/28/austin-ranks-among-most-lgbt-friendly-u-scities.html.

Therrien, Melissa, and Roberto R. Ramirez. 2001. "The Hispanic Population in the United States: Population, Characteristics." Report P30-535 (March). Current Population Reports, US Census Bureau. Washington, DC.

Thomas, Ken. 2012. "Democrats Creating 2016 White House Buzz." Associate Press New Service. September 5.

Tocqueville, Alexis de. 1956. *Democracy in America*. New York: Mentor/Penguin.

Tolbert, Caroline, and Rodney Hero. 1996. "Race/Ethnicity and Direct Democracy: An Analysis of California's Illegal Immigrant Initiative." *Journal of Politics* 58, no. 3 (August): 806–818.

Tomas Rivera Policy Institute (TRPI). 2001. "2001 Post-election Analysis: LA Mayoral Race." TRPI. wwww.trpi.org/Mayoral2001.html.

Torres, Andrés, and Jose E. Velázquez, eds. 1998. *The Puerto Rican Movement: Voices from the Diaspora*. Philadelphia: Temple University Press.

Towns Co Content Specialist. 2019. "Mayor Ordiales Named 'Elected Official of the Year' by GMC." Towns.fetchyournews.com. https://towns.fetchyournews.com/2019/12/08/hiawassee-mayor-ordiales-elected-official-year-georgia-mountian-regional-commission.

Travis, Toni-Michelle. 1990. "Boston: The Unfinished Agenda." In *Racial Politics in American Cities*. Edited by Rufus P. Browning, Dale R. Marshall, and David H. Tabb. New York: Longman.

Trejo, Jennifer. 2001. "WCVI Analysis Shows Split Among Non-Hispanic White Voters." *La Prensa* 12, no. 51 (June 24): 1a.

246　References

Tribune News Service. 2020. "Alex Padilla Becomes California's First Latino US Senator, Replacing Kamala Harris." Tribune Content Agency. December 22. https://tribunecontentagency.com/tns_articles/alex-padilla-becomes-californias -first-latino-us-senator-replacing-kamala-harris.

Underwood, Katherine. 1997a. "Ethnicity Is Not Enough: Latino-Led Multiracial Coalitions in Los Angeles." *Urban Affairs Review* 33, no. 1 (September): 3.

————. 1997b. "Pioneering Minority Representation: Edward Roybal and the Los Angeles City Council, 1949–1962." *Pacific Historical Review* 66, no. 3 (August): 399–425.

United Farm Workers of America (UFW). N.d. "The Rise of the UFW." UFW. www.ufw.org/the-rise-of-the-ufw.

Ura, Alexa and Carla Astudillo. 2021. "In 2021, White Men are Still Overrepresented in the Texas Legislature." *Texas Tribune.* January 11.

Ura, Alexa. 2021. "Gov. Greg Abbott Signs Texas Voting Bill into Law Overcoming Democratic Quorum Breaks." *Texas Tribune.* September 7. https://www.texas tribune.org/2021/09/01/texas-voting-bill-greg-abbott.

US Bureau of Labor Statistics (BLS). 2021. "The Employment Situation—January 2021." Press release. BLS. February 5. https://www.bls.gov/news.release /archives/empsit_02052021.pdf.

US Census Bureau. 1960. "Census of Population and Housing Summary." Washington, DC: US Government Printing Office.

————. 1970. "Census of Population and Housing Summary." Washington, DC: US Government Printing Office.

————. 1980. "Census of Population and Housing Summary." Washington, DC: US Government Printing Office.

————. 1990. "Census of Population and Housing Summary." Washington, DC: US Government Printing Office.

————. 1992. "Popularly Elected Officials: Census of Governments." Washington, DC: US Government Printing Office.

————. 1997. Current Population Survey (March). Washington, DC: US Government Printing Office.

————. 1999. Current Population Survey (March). Washington, DC: US Government Printing Office.

————. 2000a. "Census 2000 Summary File 1." Miami-Dade County, Florida. Washington, DC: US Government Printing Office.

————. 2000b. "Household Income, Per Capita Income, and Persons Below Poverty." Census of Population and Housing, Demographic Profile. Washington, DC: US Government Printing Office.

————. 2000c. "Voting and Registration in the Election of November 1998." Washington, DC: US Government Printing Office.

————. 2001a. "The Hispanic Population in the United States: Population Characteristics, March 2000." Current Population Survey. Washington, DC: US Government Printing Office.

————. 2001b. "The Hispanic Population: 2000, Percent of Population for One or More Races." Washington, DC: US Government Printing Office.

References   247

———. 2002. "Voting and Registration in the Election of November 2000: Population Characteristics." Current Population Survey. Washington, DC: US Government Printing Office.

———. 2004. "We the People: Hispanics in the United States: Census 2000 Special Reports." Washington, DC: US Government Printing Office.

———. 2010. U.S. Census Bureau. https://www.census.gov/data.html.

———. 2020. *American Community Survey 5-year Estimates.* www.censusreporter .org/profiles/79500US2701410-hennepin-county-bloominton-richfield-cities -puma-mn.

———. 2020a. "Race and Ethnicity Miami Dade County 2020." US Census Bureau. https://data.census.gov/cedsci/profile?g=0500000US12086.

———. 2020b. "Top 50 Cities in the U.S. by Population and Rank." Washington, DC: US Government Printing Office.

———. 2020c. "Decennial Census of Population and Housing." US Census Bureau https://www.census.gov/programs-surveys/decennial-census.html.

———. 2020. "P2 Hispanic or Latino, and Not Hispanic or Latino by Race." 2020 Census State Redistricting Data (Public Law 94-171) Summary file. Census. www.census.gov/.

———. 2021a. "About the Hispanic Population and It's Origin." Washington, DC: US Government Printing Office.

———. 2021b. *Hispanic Heritage Month 2021.* Washington, DC: US Government Printing Office.

US Centers for Disease Control and Prevention (CDC). 2021. "Risk for COVID-19 Infection, Hospitalization, and Death by Race/Ethnicity." CDC. https://www .cdc.gov/coronavirus/2019-ncov/covid-data/investigations-discovery/hospital ization-death-by-race-ethnicity.html.

US Department of Justice (DOJ). N.d. "About Language Minorities Voting Rights." DOJ. www.usdoj.gov/crt/voting/sec_203/activ_203.htm.

———. N.d.b. "Hispanic Americans in Congress, 1822–1995." LOC. http://lcweb .loc.gov/rr/hispanic/congress/geog.html.

Vaca, Nicolás C. 2004. *The Presumed Alliance: The Unspoken Conflict Between Latinos and Blacks and What It Means for America.* New York: HarperCollins.

Valdes, Daniel T. 1971. *A Political History of New Mexico, Stressing New Sources, Offering Startling New Interpretations.* Vol. 1: *Political Growth.* N.p.: n.p.

Valle, Victor M., and Rodolfo D. Torres. 2000. *Latino Metropolis.* Globalization and Community Series 7. Minneapolis: University of Minnesota Press.

Vargas, Arturo. 1999–2000. "A Decade in Review." *Harvard Journal of Hispanic Policy* 11: 3–7.

Velázquez, José E. 1998. "Coming Full Circle: The Puerto Rican Socialist Party, U.S. Branch." In *The Puerto Rican Movement: Voices from the Diaspora.* Edited by Andrés Torres and José E. Velázquez. Philadelphia: Temple University Press.

Vespa, Jonathan, David M. Armstrong, and Lauren Medina. 2020. "Demographic Turning Points for the United States. Population Projections for 2020 to 2060." Report Number P25-1144. US Census. February. https://www.census.gov /library/publications/2020/demo/p25-1144.html.

248   References

Vigil, Maurillo E. 1987. *Hispanics in American Politics: The Search for Political Power*. New York: University Press of America.

———. 1996. *Hispanics in Congress: A Historical and Political Survey*. New York: University Press of America.

———. 1997. "Hispanics in the 103rd Congress: The 1990 Census, Reapportionment, Redistricting, and the 1992 Election." *In Pursuing Power: Latinos and the Political System*. Edited by F. Chris Garcia. Notre Dame, IN: University of Notre Dame Press.

———. 2000. "The Ethnic Organization as an Instrument of Political and Social Change: MALDEF, a Case Study." In *En Aquel Entonces: Readings in Mexican American History*. Edited by Manuel G. Gonzales and Cynthia M. Gonzales. Bloomington: Indiana University Press.

Vignor, Neil. 2020. "Carlos Gimenez Ousts Incumbent Democrat in South Florida House Seat." *New York Times*. November 4.

Villarejo, Don, David Lighthall, Daniel Williams, Ann Souter, and Richard Minds. 2000. *Suffering in Silence: A Report on the Health of California's Agricultural Workers*. Davis: California Institute for Rural Studies.

Villarreal, Roberto E., Norma G. Hernandez, and Howard D. Neighbor, eds. 1988. *Latino Empowerment: Progress, Problems, and Prospects*. Westport, CT: Greenwood Press.

Voss, Kim, and Bloemraad, Irene. 2011. *Rallying for Immigrant Rights: The Fight for Inclusion in 21st Century America*. Edited by Kim Voss and Irene Bloemraad. Berkeley: University of California Press.

Voter News Service. 2000. "VNS Election Day Exit Polls, November 8." Inter-university Consortium for Political and Social Research, Stanford University.

Brennan Center for Justice. 2013. "Voting Laws Roundup 2013." Brennan Center for Justice. Updated August 6 https://www.brennancenter.org/sites/default /files/analysis/Voting_Laws_Roundup_2013.pdf.

———. 2021. "Voting Laws Roundup: October 2021." Brennan Center for Justice. https://www.brennancenter.org/our-work/research-reports/voting-laws-roundup -october-2021.

Walker, Mark. 2012. "Election: Chavez Ahead in 76th Assembly District Race, Hodges Second." *San Diego Union-Tribune*. June 6. Available from News-Bank: Access World News–Historical and Current: https://infoweb-newsbank -com.libweb.lib.utsa.edu/apps/news/document-view?p=WORLDNEWS& docref=news/13F42742EB0D31C8.

Wallace, Jeremy. 2017. "Green Endorses Garcia for Seat in Congress." *Houston Chronicle*. December 2: A6.

Wallace, Sophia J. 2014. "Papers Please: State-Level Anti-immigrant Legislation in the Wake of Arizona's SB 1070." *Political Science Quarterly* 129, no. 2 (summer): 261–291.

Warren, Christopher L., and Dario V. Moreno. 2003. "Power Without a Program: Hispanic Incorporation in Miami." In *Racial Politics in American Cities*. Edited by Rufus P. Browning, Dale R. Marshall, and David H. Tabb. 3rd ed. New York: Longman.

Washington Post, Henry J. Kaiser Family Foundation (KFF), and Harvard University. 2000. "National Survey on Latinos in America." KFF. April 29. www.kff.org /other/poll-finding/national-survey-on-latinos-in-america.

Webb, Eric. 2017. "How Liberal Is Austin?" *Austin American-Statesman*. August 7. https://www.statesman.com/story/news/2017/02/17/how-liberal-is-austin /10402757007.

Weiss, Eric M. 2001. "Call Him Señor Alcalde: Perez Sweeps to Overwhelming Victory as First Hispanic Mayor." *Hartford Courant*. November 7.

Welch, Susan, and John R. Hibbing. 1988. "Hispanic Representation in the U.S. Congress." In *Latinos and the Political System*. Edited by F. Chris Garcia. Notre Dame, IN: University of Notre Dame Press.

Welch, William M. 2005. "Issues, Not Race, Elected San Antonio's New Mayor." *U.S.A. Today*. June 6.

Wells, Miriam J. 1996. *Strawberry Fields: Politics, Class, and Work in California Agriculture*. Ithaca, NY: Cornell University Press.

Westad, Odd Arne. 2005. *The Global Cold War: Third World Interventions and the Making of Our Times*. New York: Cambridge University Press.

Whitby, Kenny J. 1997. *The Color of Representation: Congressional Behavior and Black Interests*. Ann Arbor: University of Michigan Press.

William C. Velásquez Institute. 1997. "The 1996 California Latino Vote." Special issue of *Southwest Voter Research Notes* 10, no. 2 (spring).

———. 2000a. *Special Edition: The 2000 Latino Vote in California* 1, no. 3 (winter).

———. 2000b. *Special Edition: The 2000 Latino Vote in Texas* 1, no. 4 (winter).

———. 2000c. *U.S. Latinos Cast Record Number of Votes*. Press release. November 15.

———. 2002. Texas Exit Poll (November). www.wcvi.org.

———. 2004a. "More Than 7.6 Million Latinos Vote in Presidential Race." Press release. November 4.

———. 2004b. "The 2004 WCVI National Latino Election Day Exit Poll." St Mary's University. www.wcvi.org.

Williams, John. 2001. "Ground Effort Put Brown over Top." *Houston Chronicle*. December 3.

Williams, Melissa S. 1998. *Voice, Trust, and Memory: Marginalized Groups and the Failings of Liberal Representation*. Princeton, NJ: Princeton University Press.

Williamson, Abigail Fisher. 2018. *Welcoming New American? Local Governments and Immigrant Incorporation*. Chicago: University of Chicago Press.

Willon, Phil, and Patrick McGreevy. 2020. "Alex Padilla Becomes California's First Latino US Senator, Replacing Kamala Harris." *Tribune News Service*. December 22.

Willis, Eliza, and Janet A. Seiz. 2020. "All Latinos Don't Vote the Same Way— Their Place of Origin Matters." *The Conversation*. March 17. https://the conversation.com/all-latinos-dont-vote-the-same-way-their-place-of-origin -matters-133600.

Wilson, Robert H. 1997. *Public Policy and Community*. Austin: University of Texas Press.

250 References

World Population Review. 2020. "Hispanic Population by State." World Population Review. https://worldpopulationreview.com/state-rankings/hispanic-population -by-state.

World Staff. 2020. "Meet the Young Latino Voters of 'Every 30 Seconds.'" *The World*. June 11. https://théworld.org/stories/2020-06-10/meet-young-latino-voters -every-30-seconds.

Yardley, Jim. 2002a. "Democrats Pick Novice in Texas Race for Governor." *New York Times*. March 13.

———. 2002b. "The 2002 Elections: Races for Governor; in Texas, Republican Who Inherited Top Job Is the Winner Outright." *New York Times*. November 6.

Zars, Belle. 2001. "Ed Garza Takes the Pot: The Mayor Is San Antonio's New Favorite Son." *Texas Observer Online*. September 28. https://www.texasobserver .org/438-ed-garza-takes-the-pot-the-mayor-is-san-antonios-new-favorite-son.

Zepeda-Millan, Chris. 2017. *Latino Mass Mobilization: Immigration, Racialization and Activism*. Cambridge: Cambridge University Press.

Zucker, Norman L., and Naomi Flink Zucker. 1996. *Desperate Crossing: Seeking Refuge in America*. New York: M. E. Sharpe.

Index

AB 540 (California), 86
ACA. *See* Affordable Care Act
Acosta, Ralph, 51
Adams, Eric, 79
Affordable Care Act (ACA), 91
AFL-CIO. *See* American Federation of Labor–Congress of Industrial Organizations
African Americans: Blacks as, 3, 16n21, 45, 52–53, 80, 113–114, 131, 131*tab*, 156*tab*; on civil rights, 130; on Cubans, 130; Dominicans and, 61; elected offices and numbers of, 7; Latino coalitions with, 13, 159; Latino opposition to, 130–132, 138, 152; in Los Angeles, 152–153; in Miami-Dade County, 130–132, 138; 1960s protests by, 21; racial exclusion on, 98; Texas poll tax and, 28; VRA (1965) for, 88; White liberals and, 53, 80, 130, 152, 154, 200
Alabama, 87, 114
Alarcón, Richard, 155
Alatorre, Richard, 32–33, 152–155, 158
Alfonso, Manny, 133
Alianza Federal de Pueblos Libres, 30
La Alianza Hispano-Americana, 27
Alinksy, Saul, 141
Alinsky, Saul, 25
Almanzan, Alicia, 185
Alonzo, Roberto, 177

Alvarado, Carol, 174
Alvarez, Carlos, 137
American Federation of Labor–Congress of Industrial Organizations (AFL-CIO), 82
American GI Forum, 22–23, 27, 30
Anaya, Toney, 47
Anglos: bloc-votes by, 148; California and elites as, 34–35; in Crystal City, Texas, 27–28; GGL as, 140–142; on Mexican Americans, 32; in New Mexico, 24, 113; as non-Latino, 3; political and economic domination by, 5; in Southwest US, 57. *See also* Whites
Anti-immigrant backlash, 207; in Cold War dynamic, 23; Gutiérrez, Luis V. on, 74; Illegal Immigration Relief Act as, 86; Latino politics on, 81; in 1960s, 64–65; of 1990s, 64–65, 67–68, 83; by Republican Party, 73, 81–82, 84–86; after September 11, 2001, 71, 82–83; in 2000s, 82
Anti-Latino backlash, 64–65, 92–93
Antipoverty programs, 13, 37–38, 60
Apodaca, Jerry, 47
Argentina, 139, 179–181, 183, 190, 192
Arizona: diversity in, 117; Hispanics and state exit polls of, 16n24; Latino population growth in, 100, 101*tab*; Latino vote in, 9, 112; Latinos and

251

Index

elected offices in, 122–123, 123*tab*; Propositions 100 and 200 in, 83; racial profiling in, 86, 106–107; SB 1070 in, 86, 106–107, 107*tab*

Arpaio, Joe, 106

Asian Americans, 1, 206; for Fong, 136; Hawaii for, 121; Latinos as, 3; in liberal-progressive coalition, 49, 51, 53; population growth of, 99; racial exclusion on, 98; on 2001 Los Angeles race, 156*tab*

Askew, Reubin, 132

ASPIRA, 37

Asylum seekers, 81, 89, 93

At-large elections: challenges against, 115, 141; for Cisneros, 47; cities and, 142, 183–184, 203; district election structure and, 44, 54–55, 114–115, 135–136, 153–155, 196–198, 203; history of, 67, 113–115; legal challenges against, 54–55, 135; as minorities election roadblock, 44, 67, 113–115

August 29th Movement, 33–34

Austin, Texas, 30, 116, 150, 171, 175–178

Avila, Joaquin, 54

Ayuntamiento (self government), 139–140

Badillo, Herman, 37–38, 46–47, 52

Balido, Nelson, 150

Ballot harvesting, 89

Bannwolf, Tim, 144

Bass, Karen, 159, 162

Bautista, Maria, 54

Becerra, Xavier, 155–156, 158–159, 168

Berrios, Jose, 45

Berriozábal, Maria, 143

Bias, 6, 115–116

Biden, Joseph R.: diverse cabinet of, 168; on Garcetti, 162; on ICE and police, 83; Latinos for, 8–9, 106, 138, 168; Puerto Ricans for, 107; voting rights restrictions on, 88

Bilingual issues, 4–5, 48, 71, 114

Blacks: as African heritage, 3, 16*n*21; on Chicago, 45; for Dinkins, 52–53; Latinos as, 3; Miami population growth of, 131*tab*; on police brutality,

80, 131; on 2001 Los Angeles race, 156*tab*; for VRA, 88, 113–114. *See also* African Americans

Bloc-votes: of Anglos, 148; by Asian Americans, 136; of Cubans, 134–136, 139; of Latinos, 9, 67, 134, 196; as not racialized, 147–148

Bloomberg, Michael, 77

Blunt, Jeffrey, 150

Border Protection Anti-Terrorism and Illegal Immigration Control Act (2005), 81–82, 84–85

Bosch, Juan, 59

Boston, 49, 51, 58

Bracero Program, 22–23, 29, 64, 103

Bradley, Tom, 152–153

Bratton, William, 159

Brechtel, Terry, 146

Briones, Dolores, 172–173

Broward County, 139

Brown, Lee, 77

Browning, Rufus, 11, 13, 17, 56, 69, 125, 129

Bush, George W., 71–72, 76–77, 82–83, 89, 92, 182

Byrne, Jane, 49

Caba, Helmin, 78

Caballero, Raymond, 173

Cadava, Geraldo, 110

California: Anglo elites in, 34–35; anti-immigrant backlash in, 82; Delano of, 29, 183, 185, 200; on driver's licenses, 87, 90; Hispanics and state exit polls of, 16*n*24; Los Angeles County in, 55–56, 101*tab*, 122–123, 123*tab*, 130, 161; LRUP party in, 32; minimum wage in, 202; Parlier of, 34–35; Pomona of, 55; Proposition 187 of, 65–67, 86; protests in, 33–34; Salinas of, 33, 55; state term limits in, 181–182; voter racialization in, 196; Wilson of, 66. *See also* East Los Angeles; Los Angeles

California Latinos: elected offices for, 122–123, 123*tab*; Latinas and Southern, 171; Latinas in State Legislature as, 181–183; population growth of, 100, 101*tab*; vote for, 10

Californio, 3

Campaign School, 180, 192*n*66
Candidate credibility, 118
CANF. *See* Cuban American National Foundation
Cardenas, Tony, 119–120*tab*, 155–156, 158
Cardona, Miguel, 168
CARES. *See* Coronavirus Aid, Relief, and Economic Security Act
Caribbeans, 3, 16*n*21, 20–21
Carollo, Joe, 132
Carter, Jimmy, 36, 75, 154
Caruso, Rick, 162
CASA. *See* Centro de Acción Social Autónoma—Hermandad General de Trabajadores
Castile, Philando, 188
Castro, Fidel, 73, 110, 185
Castro, Joaquin, 120*tab*, 146, 150–151
Castro, Julián, 91, 129–130, 146–151, 200
Cedillo, Gil, 52
Central Americans, 21, 62–63, 100, 102, 111, 111*tab*
Centro de Acción Social Autónoma—Hermandad General de Trabajadores (CASA), 33
Chacón, Alicia Rosencrans, 172
Chavez, Cesar, 26, 29–30
Chavez, Dennis, 23–24
Chicago: Democratic machine in, 50; Gutiérrez, Luis V., of, 74; Latino population growth in, 101*tab*; Latinos and elected offices in, 122–123, 123*tab*; political machine of, 45, 49–50, 64; PRLDEF, MALDEF, Blacks, Republicans on, 45; Puerto Ricans in, 37–38; redistricting electoral boundaries in, 50; Washington in, 49–50, 136
Chicanos: definition of, 3; education protests by, 33; elected office protests for, 35; in 1960s, 28–35; on police brutality, 33; underrepresentation of, 34, 34*tab*
Los Cinco, 27–28
Cisneros, Henry, 47, 129, 140, 142–151
Citizens Organized for Public Service (COPS), 141–143, 145, 203–204
Citizenship status: for African Americans, 7; of Central Americans,

62; Cubans on, 132; Latino differences as, 4; Latino politics for, 81; Latinos without, 100, 102; Mexicans on, 103; undocumented immigrants and, 74, 81, 102, 105; on voting, 82, 102, 105
Civil rights: African Americans on, 130; Farmworker movement and, 29; Latino goal as, 4; in 1950s, 98; 1960s for Latino, 5–6, 21, 98; Puerto Ricans on, 44–45; Roybal on, 25; VRA (1965) and, 113–114
Civil Rights Act (1964), 24
Civil workforce composition, 56–57
Class interests, 201–203, 206–207
Clinton, Bill, 9, 76, 89, 138
Clinton, Hillary, 8, 89, 92, 106, 112
Coalition for Humane Immigrant Rights of Los Angeles, 62
Coalition politics, 33, 44–45, 196; with African Americans, 13, 159; Asian Americans in liberal-progressive, 49, 51, 53; Democrat allies in, 200; minorities and Whites for, 13; as multiracial, 49–51, 67, 124; for political incorporation, 12–13, 129, 199–200; Rainbow Coalition in, 51–53, 67; for Roybal, 25–26; in urban and suburban districts, 198
Cockrell, Lila, 143
Cold War dynamic, 19, 21–23, 36
Colombians, 2, 63–64, 107–108, 139
Colorado, 16*n*24, 30, 47, 58, 80, 100
El Comité—Movimiento de Izquierda Nacional Puertorriqueño, 38–39
Committee for Barrio Betterment, 31, 141, 146
Community Service Organization (CSO), 25–27
Congressional Hispanic Caucus, 46, 184
Connecticut, 63, 80, 86–87
Constituent benefits, 11; interest group protests and, 12; interest responsiveness for, 129; political agendas as, 195, 197, 203–204; as political objective, 4–5, 12; political representation as, 7, 10
Contreras, Miguel, 157–158
COPS. *See* Citizens Organized for Public Service

254 Index

Cornejo, Juan, 28
Cornyn, John, 111
Coronavirus Aid, Relief, and Economic Security (CARES) Act, 184, 192n83
Corrada, Baltasar, 46–47
Cortes, Eddie, 141
Covid-19: on economy, 109, 112, 206; Latino health care concerns on, 112, 206; research limits from, 14–15; Vasquez, V., on, 183–185
CPS. *See* Current Population Survey
Crime, 157, 201; fear of, 32, 107, 198; LEOs on, 11, 56; Trump and, 108
Crusade for Justice, 30
Crusius, Patrick Wood, 108–109
Crystal City, Texas, 27–28, 31, 34–36, 170
CSO. *See* Community Service Organization
Cuban American National Foundation (CANF), 48
Cubans, 77, 185–186; on African Americans, 130; anti-immigrant backlash by, 73; bloc-votes by, 134–136, 139; as business power brokers, 202; on citizenship status, 132; on Democratic Party, 111, 137; first-generation politics by, 131–132, 136; Miami dominant role by, 12, 129–130, 133, 138–139, 151; on naturalization, 48; Operation Peter Pan for, 134; origin numbers as, 100; political struggles of, 2; redistricting electoral boundaries by, 45, 48; as reference, 4; in Republican Party, 48–49, 110, 137; in South Florida, 48–49, 130, 134; for Trump, 107, 110; US policy favoring, 21, 205; on voter turnout, 132–133; without White liberals, 130, 200; Whites on, 48
Current Population Survey (CPS), 106
Cutting, Bronson, 24

DACA. *See* Deferred Action for Childhood Arrivals
Daley, Richard M., 49–50
Deferred Action for Childhood Arrivals (DACA), 87, 90, 92–94
Delano, California, 29, 183, 185, 200
Delaware, 87, 179–181

Democratic Party, 136–137; in Chicago, 50; coalition politics with, 200; MAPA on, 23; in New Mexico, 24; percentage registration of, 138; political machines as, 36, 45, 141, 199; UFW and, 29; Viva Kennedy clubs on, 26–27, 39; as White, 36
Democratic Party minorities: Central Americans as, 111, 111*tab*; Cubans and, 111, 137; Dominicans and, 60; Latinos as, 5, 8–9, 67, 72–73, 109, 122; Latinos influencing, 52, 111*tab*; Latinos rejecting, 110–111; Mexican Americans as, 23, 111, 111*tab*; Native Americans as, 200; Puerto Ricans and, 36, 111, 111*tab*
Department of Homeland Security (DHS), 83, 93, 168
Deracialization, 198
Descriptive representation, 10, 124*tab*, 197
Development, Relief, and Education for Alien Minors (DREAM) Act, 74, 84, 87, 90
DHS. *See* Department of Homeland Security
Diaz, Grace, 79
Diaz, Manny, 133–134
Diaz, Manuel, 63
Diaz, Wilda, 77–78
Díaz-Balart, Lincoln, 73, 135
Díaz-Balart, Mario, 73, 135
Dinkins, David, 52–53
Discrimination: American GI Forum on, 22–23, 27, 30; on Crystal City cheerleaders, 31; ending of, 29, 207; Fair Employment Bill on, 24; Latinos overturning, 12; legacy of, 6; in politics, 20–21; for poverty, 57; in schools, 15
District election structure: expansion of Latino, 196; Latino-majority districts in, 197–198; Latinos creating, 54–55, 115; legal challenge on, 153–155; in Miami, 135–136; policy formation in, 203; political power in, 114–115; in Texas, 44. *See also* At-large elections
Diversity: LGBT+ and, 1, 67, 169; state level lacking, 117; in US House and Senate, 117–118, 119–120*tab*, 120–121

Doggett, Lloyd, 150
Dominicans, 2, 38–39, 59–62, 78–79, 100
DREAM. *See* Development, Relief, and Education for Alien Minors Act
Driver's licenses, 87, 90
Dukakis, Michael, 52
Duran, Alfredo, 131–132
Durazo, Maria Elena, 161
Durbin, Dick, 84, 90

East Los Angeles, 158; incorporation bid by, 32–33, 75, 151–153; Mothers of, 58; Roybal in, 25; Roybal-Allard of, 74; undocumented immigrants in, 32–33; Villaraigosa of, 159
Economics: Anglos dominating, 5; Covid-19 on, 109, 112, 206; Cuban power brokers in, 202; globalization on, 19–20; of Latino workforce, 100–101; Latinos on, 81, 90, 112; LEOs on, 11; middle-class increases in, 202, 206–207; politics for, 98
Education, 21; Alabama on immigrant, 87; Castro, Julián, and, 149–150; Chacón on, 172; Chicano protests on, 33; discrimination in, 15; Dominicans on New York, 38–39, 60, 78–79; González, J., on, 177–181, 183, 187, 190, 201; Head Start programs for, 91; immigrants and in-state tuition, 83, 86–87; inequalities, 6; Latinos and elected offices in, 7*tab*, 122–124, 123*tab*; of LEOs, 201; Miami politics in, 132; Sturgeon and, 179–181, 183, 190, 192; Villaraigosa on, 160; for voting experience, 104–105
Eggman, Susan Talamantes, 181–183, 187, 190, 192
El Paso, Texas: immigration into, 25, 65; Latinas in, 10, 172–173, 175; Latinos in, 23; La Mujer Obrera in, 58–59; racist massacre in, 108
Elected offices. *See specific subjects*
Electoral strategy, 12
Electorate: Arizona Latino, 107*tab*; Florida Latino, 108*tab*; Latina and state percentage of, 169*tab*; Latino party affiliation in, 111*tab*; Latino percentage of, 8–9, 101*tab*; Latino

turnout of, 105*tab*; Latino UC Congress members, 119–120*tab*; LEO numbers in, 7*tab*, 8*tab*, 123*tab*; LEOs and descriptive, 124*tab*; Los Angeles mayor, 156*tab*; Miami-Dade County Latino, 131*tab*; states with Chicano, 34*tab*
Elorza, Jorge O., 80
Employment: economics of Latino, 100–101; inequalities, 6; low wages in, 22, 26, 29–30; political incorporation and, 201–202; politics for, 98
Enhanced Border Security and Visa Entry Reform Act (2002), 83
Environmental issues, 11, 75, 145, 159, 201
Equal opportunity, 4, 6, 43, 195–196
Escobar, Veronica, 10, 120*tab*, 173–174
Espaillat, Adriano, 61, 78–79
Ethnic groups, definition of, 2, 99
Exclusion: challenges to, 43; interest group strategy for, 12; of Latinos, 7, 13, 78, 129; of minorities, 11, 98

Fair Employment Practice Bill (1944), 24
Falcon, Angelo, 45
Farm Labor Organizing Committee (FLOC), 51
Farmworkers: from Caribbean and Latin America, 20; Chavez, C., organizing, 26, 29–30; for civil rights, 29; on low wages, 22, 26, 29–30; UFW for California, 33–34
Ferré, Maurice, 63, 133
Ferrer, Fernando, 77
Figueroa, Liz, 62
Firebaugh, Marco Antonio, 86
First-generation politics, 102–104, 131–132, 136
FLOC. *See* Farm Labor Organizing Committee
Florida: Cuban dominance and Miami, 12, 129–130, 133, 138–139, 151; Hispanics and state exit polls of, 16*n*24; Latino electorate in, 108*tab*; Latino political power in, 139; Latino population growth in, 100; Martinez, Mel, of, 72; for Republicans, 107; Ros-Lehtinen of, 73; single-member districts in, 48, 130, 135

256 Index

Florida cities: Broward County as, 139; Palm Beach County as, 139; South Florida and, 48–49, 107, 130, 134, 136. *See also* Miami-Dade County
Floyd, George, 13
Fong, Matt, 136
Foreign policy (US), 19, 21, 48, 86
Formal representation, 196–197

Gallego, Pete, 144
Gallegos, Mario, 174
Garcetti, Eric, 130, 158, 160, 162
Garcia, Hector, 22
Garcia, Jesus (Chuy), 50, 74
Garcia, Joshua, 201
Garcia, Robert, 73
Garcia, Sylvia, 10, 120*tab*, 174
Garza, Ed, 77, 129, 144–146, 148
de la Garza, E. "Kika," 46–47
Garza v. County of Los Angeles, 54–55
Garza v. Smith, 44
Gatti, John, 141
Gender-fluid and hybrid identities, 4
Georgia, 9, 185–187, 193*n*97
Gerrymandered districts, 44; challenges on, 48, 113, 154; in large cities, 185; in Los Angeles, 151–152; redistricting and bias, 115; *Rucho v. Common Cause* supporting, 116–117; in Texas, 116, 125
GGL. *See* Good Government League
GI Forum, of America, 22–23, 27, 30
Gimenez, Carlos, 137–138
Giuliani, Rudolph, 53
Globalization, 19–20
Gomez v. City of Watsonville, 54–55
Gonzales, Rodolfo (Corky), 30
Gonzales, Ron, 77
Gonzalez, Charlie, 150–151
Gonzalez, Elian, 133, 136–137
González, Henry B., 23, 25, 46–47, 151
González, Jessica, 177–181, 183, 187, 190, 201
Good Government League (GGL), 140–143
Goode, Wilson, 51
Gore, Al, 71, 136–137
Governors: Latinos as, 2, 75–76, 79, 169*tab*; Latinos running for, 23, 31, 80

Green, Gene, 174
Greuel, Wendy, 160
Grisham, Michelle Lujan, 76
Guatemalans, 62, 79–80
Guerrero, Lina, 171
Guns, 172, 189
Gutierrez, Ana Sol, 62–63
Gutierrez, Luis, 50, 64
Gutiérrez, Luis V., 74
Guzman, Isabel, 168

Hahn, James, 77, 156–157, 156*tab*, 159
Hardberger, Phil, 147–149
Harris, Kamala, 10, 161
Hart-Cellar Act, 64
Hartford, Connecticut, 53, 80–81
Hawaii, 86–87, 117, 121, 181
Health care, 3, 16, 110; Covid-19 and, 14–15, 109, 112, 183–185, 206; Latinos gaining, 91; Latinos on, 112, 182, 188, 205; Latinos without, 38, 65–66; reform for, 86, 89
Hermanas en la Lucha, 58
Hernandez, Mike, 155
The Hispanic Republican (Cadava), 110
Hispanics: Arizona exit polls and, 16*n*24; Miami population growth of, 131*tab*; New Mexico governors as, 9, 47; in state exit polls, 16*n*24; term use, 3–4, 16*n*7, 204; on 2001 Los Angeles race, 156*tab*
History: of at-large elections, 67, 113–115; of Latina politics, 167, 205; of Latino politics, 15–16, 20–21, 97–98, 109, 112–113, 162, 195; of Los Angeles and Latinos, 151–152; of Mexican Americans, 20, 22, 151–152; of New Mexico, 24; in San Antonio, 139–140, 144; of Southwest US, 40, 98, 101–102, 113; of Spanish and Mexican settlers, 2, 16*n*3; of US and Latino politics, 20–21, 97–98, 109, 112–113, 162, 195; US judicial branch in, 170
Homeland politics, national-origin and, 4
Homeland Security Act (2002), 83
Housing, 91, 98
Houston, Texas, 44, 67, 77, 94, 116, 174; Latino population in, 101*tab*, 123*tab*, 163

Huerta, Dolores, 29, 160
Huffman, Joan, 116

IAF. *See* Industrial Areas Foundation
ICE. *See* Immigration and Customs Enforcement
Idaho, 75, 77, 85, 185
Ideological beliefs, 4
Illegal Immigration Reform and Immigrant Responsibility Act (IIRIRA), 66
Illegal Immigration Relief Act, 86
Illinois, 16n24, 100. *See also* Chicago
Immigrant Workers Freedom Rides, 84
Immigration: AFL-CIO for, 82; asylum seekers as, 81, 89, 93; Bush on, 82–83, 89; CASA on, 33; into El Paso, Texas, 25, 65; in-state tuition and, 83, 86–87; Latino politics on, 81–86; Latinos on, 5, 89; police and, 83, 93; political participation and, 7; unauthorized numbers in, 102–103. *See also* Anti-immigrant backlash
Immigration and Customs Enforcement (ICE), 83, 93
Immigration and Naturalization Service (INS), 65–67
Immigration legislation: California AB 540 as pro, 86; DACA for, 87, 90, 92–94; DREAM Act and, 74, 84, 87, 90; Hart-Cellar Act for, 64; McCain-Kennedy Bill on, 84; Obama and, 89–92
Immigration Reform and Control Act (IRCA), 65, 67, 82
Independents, 111, 111*tab*, 206; Diaz, Manny, in, 133–134; percentage registration of, 138
Indigenous peoples, 2–3
Industrial Areas Foundation (IAF), 25–26
INS. *See* Immigration and Naturalization Service
Institute for Puerto Rican Policy, 45
Interest group strategy, 12
Interest responsiveness, 129
Iowa, 185
IRCA. *See* Immigration Reform and Control Act
de la Isla, Michelle, 78

Israel, Celia, 175–177, 180–181, 183, 187, 191
Itliong, Larry, 29

Jackson, Jesse, 51–52
Johnson, Lyndon B., 22, 64, 113–114
Jones, Andrieus A., 24

Katz, Richard, 155
Kennedy, John F., 27, 48, 182
King, Mel, 51
Koch, Ed, 37, 52–53

La Fuerza Unida, 58
La Mujer Obrera, 58–59
Labor organizations. *See* Unions
Land struggles, in US Southwest, 30, 33–34, 140
Lara, Ricardo, 161
Latin Americans, 20–21
Latina locations: in California State Legislature, 181–183; in El Paso, 10, 172–173, 175; in Georgia, 185–187; in Idaho, 185; in Iowa, 185; in Los Angeles, 154; in New Jersey, 172; in New York, 79; in Texas, 58–59, 170, 172–175; in Texas Legislature, 175–179; in US Senate and House of Representatives, 169*tab*
Latina people: Berriozábal as, 143; Diaz, W., as, 77–78; González, J., as, 177–181, 183, 187, 190, 201; Grisham as, 76; de la Isla, Michelle, as, 78; Israel on, 176–177; Martinez, S., as, 76; Ros-Lehtinen as, 73, 134–135, 171; Roybal-Allard as, 74, 119–120*tab*, 155, 171; Sotomayer as, 89, 91, 170
Latinas, 14; boycott and strike by, 58–59; challenges for, 161–162, 190; Covid-19 on, 109; as eldest daughter matriarch, 189; elected official increase of, 72, 124*tab*, 125; history of politics and, 167, 205; LEO increase among, 72; LGBT+ protections and, 1, 169, 178–179, 183, 185, 201, 205; at local level, 183–190; in 1960s, 170; political offices and 1970s, 170–171; political roles for, 57–58, 67; underrepresentation of, 168; unions

and, 170; watchdogs on Latino politics, 59

Latino, definition of, 3, 16n7, 204. *See also specific subjects*

Latino community: Latinos for benefits and, 2; LEOs on, 14, 195, 197, 201, 206; police reforms with, 80

Latino elected officials (LEOs): city influence by, 1; on crime, 11, 56; on education, 7tab, 122–124, 123tab; education level of, 201; on environment, 11; Latina increase in, 72; on Latino community, 14, 195, 197, 201, 206; as liberal, 53, 80, 200–201; NALEO and, 46–47, 67, 118, 167–168, 171, 190n4; in national offices, 1; in 1990s, 73, 121; numbers of, 6–7, 7tab; research on, 14–15; state percentages of, 1, 7–8, 8tab, 72–73, 123; 2000s increase for, 72, 94–95; in 2020s, 121; visibility of, 197

Latino politics, definition of, 1, 3. *See also specific subjects*

Latino Voting Rights Project, 45

Latino-majority districts, 197–198

Latinx, 4, 16n7, 81–82, 84–85, 204

League of United Latin American Citizens (LULAC), 27, 30, 54, 140

Lebron, Lolita, 36

Legal challenge list: *Garza v. County of Los Angeles*, 54–55; *Garza v. Smith*, 44; *Gomez v. City of Watsonville*, 54–55; *Plyler v. Doe*, 66; *Roe v. Wade*, 191n48; *Rucho v. Common Cause*, 116–117; *Shelby v. Holder*, 116

Legal challenges, 196; on at-large elections, 54–55, 135; on district election structure, 153–154; for elected offices, 6; on gerrymandering, 48, 113, 154; for new districts, 153–155; political incorporation through, 12; political reform through, 45; on Proposition 187, 65–67, 86; on redistricting electoral boundaries, 12; rules changed by, 43; VRA for, 115–116

de Leon, Kevin, 162

LEOs. *See* Latino elected officials

LGBT+ protections: diversity politics for LGBTQ, 1, 67, 169; Eggman on, 181–183, 187, 190, 192; for gender-fluid and hybrid identities, 4; González, J., on, 177–181, 183, 187, 190, 201; Israel on, 177; Latinas and, 1, 169, 178–179, 183, 185, 201, 205

Linares, Guillermo, 60–61, 78–79

Lindsay, John, 37

Lindsey, Gilbert, 152–153

Linguistic minorities, 6

Local level: at-large elections at city, 142, 183–184, 203; coalition politics in city, 198; gerrymandered large cities at, 185; Latinas at, 183–190; Latino politics at, 2, 7tab, 76–78, 122–123; limits or accomplishments at, 13, 129; National League of Cities and, 46; in Northeast, 78–81, 121; political machines at, 198; redistricting electoral boundaries at, 155, 161

Longoria, Felix, 22

Lopez, Henry, 23

Lopez, Linda, 170

Lopez, Vito, 79

Lora, Federico, 39

Los Angeles, 163; African Americans in, 152–153; city council elections in, 160–161; gerrymandered districts in, 151–152; history of Latinos and, 151–152; Latinas in, 154; Latino wins and 1990s, 155–156; Latinos and 2000s wins in, 156, 156tab, 158; mayor results in, 156tab; political machine of, 154, 157–158; unions and Latinos, 157–158

Los Angeles County, 55–56; Latino population growth in, 101tab, 130; Latinos and elected offices in, 122–123, 123tab, 161

LRUP. *See* La Raza Unida Party

Ludlow, Martin, 159

LULAC. *See* League of United Latin American Citizens

Majority-minority district, 117, 124–125, 168, 172–173, 196

Malapportionment, 44

MALDEF. *See* Mexican American Legal Defense and Education Fund

MAPA. *See* Mexican American Political Association
Marshall, Dale, 11, 13, 17, 56, 69, 125, 129
Martin, Trayvon, 188
Martinez, Joe, 138
Martinez, Marty, 56, 75, 172
Martinez, Mel, 72
Martinez, Miguel, 78–79
Martinez, Nury, 161
Martinez, Raul, 132
Martinez, Susana, 9, 76
Massachusetts, 79, 81
Masto, Catherine Marie Cortez, 9–10, 120*tab*, 121, 168, 169*tab*
Masvidal, Raul, 133
Matos, Sabina, 79
MAYO. *See* Mexican American Youth Organization
Mayorkas, Alejandro, 168
Mayors: as county mayor, 137–138; Latinos as, 76–78; 2001 Los Angeles race and, 156*tab*
McCain, John, 8, 84, 89, 112
McCain-Kennedy Bill, 84
McCarren-Nixon Internal Security Act (1950), 23
Melendez, Isabel, 79
Melendez, Robert, 49
Mendez, Olga, 170–171
Menendez, Katherine, 170
Mexican American Legal Defense and Education Fund (MALDEF), 43–45, 47, 54, 68
Mexican American locations: in Los Angeles County, 32, 55–56; Parlier with elected, 34–35; San Antonio and politics of, 139–151; in Southwest US, 2, 22–24, 29, 45–46, 75–76, 205
Mexican American Political Association (MAPA), 23
Mexican American Youth Organization (MAYO), 31, 45, 141
Mexican Americans: Anglos on, 32; CSO for, 25–27; definition of, 3; on Democratic Party, 23, 111, 111*tab*; history of, 20, 22, 151–152; on Jackson, 51–52; in mass deportation, 23; 1960s Chicano movement as, 28–35; political leaders as, 23–24;

SVREP for, 45–46; Texas poll tax and, 28; voter turnout by, 25, 45–46, 103–104
Mexican-American War (1846), 24, 30, 113
Mexicans: Bracero Program and, 22–23, 29, 64, 103; CASA for undocumented, 33; mass deportation of, 23; on naturalization, 102–104; in 1940s, 25; in 1950s, 27, 64; from poverty, 25, 64; as reference, 4; in San Antonio, 129–130; settler history of, 2, 16*n*3; as Tejano and Californio, 3; Trump on, 93, 108; undocumented immigrants as, 103; on US citizenship status, 103; US left by, 104
Mexico, 20, 100
Miami-Dade County: African Americans in, 130–132, 138; Cubans dominating, 12, 129–130, 133, 138–139, 151; district election structure in, 135–136; education politics in, 132; Ferré in, 63, 133; Miami county mayor in, 137–138; population growth in, 131*tab*; to Trump, 9, 108, 108*tab*
Midwest, 1, 9, 46, 185, 187–188
Midwest Voter Registration Education Project, 45
Militant confrontations, by Puerto Ricans, 36–39
Millennial Latinos, 200–201
Minnesota, 187–188
Minorities: for antipoverty programs, 13, 37–38, 60; at-large elections against, 44, 67, 113–115; coalition politics in Whites and, 13; elected office underrepresentation for, 6, 207; exclusion of, 11, 98; group mobilization of, 129; political power and, 11; South Americans as, 63; voting strength of, 44
Minutemen, 83–84
Mixed-race people, 3
Molina, Gloria, 75, 143, 153–155, 158, 160
Montenegro, Ruth Bermudez, 170
Morales, Dan, 75–76
Mothers of East Los Angeles, 58
Movimiento Pro Independencia, 38–39

Mucarsel-Powell, Debbie, 138
Multilingual election materials, 44
Multimember districts, 44
Multiracial coalition politics, 49–51, 67, 124
Munguia, Ruben, 142
Murtaugh, Brian, 61
Musquiz, Virginia, 170
Mutual aid association, 66

NAACP. *See* National Association for the Advancement of Colored People
NALEO. *See* National Association of Latino Elected and Appointed Officials
Napolitano, Grace, 171
National Association for the Advancement of Colored People (NAACP), 43
National Association of Hispanic County Officials, 46
National Association of Latino Elected and Appointed Officials (NALEO), 46–47, 67, 118, 167–168, 171, 190*n*4
National Coalition for Fair Immigration Laws and Practices, 33
National Congress for Puerto Rican Rights, 45
National League of Cities, 46
National Puerto Rican Coalition, 44–45
Native Americans, 53; as Democrats, 200; languages and, 114; for office, 55, 114, 121, 200; percentage of, 181, 187; racial exclusion on, 98; in US House, 121
Nativism, 64
Naturalization: Central Americans and, 62, 102; CSO for, 26; Cubans on, 48; INS and, 65–67; Latinos on, 46, 66–67, 82, 85; Mexicans on, 102–104; NALEO for, 46; Proposition 187 and, 65–67, 86
Nevada: Hispanics and state exit polls of, 16*n*24; Latino population growth in, 100; Latino vote in, 9–10; Masto of, 9–10, 120*tab*, 121, 168, 169*tab*; Salt Lake City of, 1; Sandoval of, 9, 76
New Jersey, 16*n*24, 49, 77–78, 100, 172
New Mexico: Anglos in, 24, 113; Chavez, D., of, 23–24; Chicano

movement in, 30; Democratic Party in, 24; Hispanic governors of, 9, 47; Hispanics and state exit polls of, 16*n*24; history of, 24; Jones, A., of, 24; Latino population growth in, 100; Latino vote in, 9, 20; Latinos and elected offices in, 122; Richardson in, 76
New York: Dominicans in, 38–39, 60, 78–79; Latinas in, 79; Latino population growth in, 100, 101*tab*; Latinos and elected offices in, 122–123, 123*tab*; political machine of, 36, 45; PRLDEF on, 45; Puerto Ricans in, 37–39, 79; redistricting and state of, 61; undocumented immigrants in, 59–60
New York elected representatives: Garcia, R., as, 73; Jackson as, 51–52; Linares as, 60–61, 78–79; Serrano, José E., as, 73; Velázquez, N., and, 73–74, 171
Nicaraguans, 62–63, 74–75, 107–108, 139
1940s: Latinos and politics in, 15, 20, 23–24, 39; Mexicans in, 25; Puerto Ricans in, 35–36; social justice in, 22; Whites through, 140
1950s: anticommunist hysteria in, 22–23; Chavez, C., in, 26; civil rights in, 98; Latinos in, 15, 21, 25, 113; Mexicans in, 27, 64; Puerto Ricans in, 35–36, 38
1960s: African American protests in, 21; anti-immigrant backlash of, 64–65; Central Americans in, 62; Chicano movement in, 28–35; civil rights in, 5–6, 21, 98; Latinas and political offices in, 170; Latino civil rights in, 5–6, 21, 98; Latino politics in, 19–20, 39–40, 43, 121; Puerto Rican militants in, 36–39
1970s: Central Americans in, 62; Cuban politics in, 48; elected office lack in, 34, 34*tab*, 67, 121; Latinas and political offices in, 170–171; for multilingual election materials, 44; New York Puerto Ricans in, 38
1980s: Central Americans in, 62; Cuban politics in, 48; Dominican

Index **261**

community in, 60–61; Latino breakthroughs in, 47, 73, 121, 154–155; Latino majority populations in, 54–57; multiracial coalition politics in, 49–51; Rainbow Coalition of, 51–53, 67; redistricting electoral boundaries in, 45, 48; undocumented immigrants and, 65

1990s: anti-immigrant backlash of, 64–65, 67–68, 83; Dominican community in, 60–61; Latina elected officials in, 171; Latino majority populations in, 54–57, 68; Latinos and Los Angeles wins in, 155–156; LEOs in, 73, 121; redistricting electoral boundaries in, 38, 155, 171; undocumented immigrants in, 65–67; US census in, 171

Nirenberg, Ron, 130

Nixon, Richard, 23, 110, 175, 182

Nonconfrontational political evolution, 12

Non-Latino-majority districts, 197

Nonpartisan offices, 198–200

North American Free Trade Agreement, 59

Northeast US, 52, 78–81, 111, 121

Obama, Barack H.: on Arizona anti-immigrant law, 86; Castro, Julián, for, 130, 150; DACA by, 87, 90, 92–94; on ICE and police, 83; immigration and, 89–92; Latinos for, 8, 85–86, 89–92, 112; on Solis, 75; state voting restrictions on, 88

Ocasio-Cortez, Alexandria, 10, 75, 119–120*tab*

O'Neill, Tip, 198

Operation Bootstrap, 35–36

Operation Peter Pan, 134

Ordiales, Liz, 185–187

O'Rourke, Beto, 10, 173

Pacheco, Nick, 158

Padilla, Alex, 10, 120*tab*, 121, 155–156, 158, 161

Padilla, Gilbert, 25

Padin, Evelyn, 170

Paez, Mariela, 3

Palin, Sarah, 8

Palm Beach County, 139

Pantoja, Antonia, 37

Parks, Bernard, 157, 159

Parlier, California, 34–35

Party affiliation, 111*tab*; Latino differences as, 4; Puerto Rican Socialist Party and, 38–39; racialization or, 136, 195; Young Lords Party and, 38, 45

PASSO. *See* Political Association of Spanish-Speaking Organizations

Patriot Act (2001), 83

Peña, Federico, 47, 80

Penelas, Alex, 135–137

Pennsylvania, 86

Pepper, Claude, 134

Perez, Eddie, 80

Pérez, Myrna, 170

Perez, Thomas, 91

Perry, Rick, 75–76

Personal Responsibility and Work Opportunity Act (Welfare Act), 66

Peruvian-Americans, 63, 139

Petro-Eschler, Victoria, 1

Philadelphia, 51, 78, 101*tab*, 123

Pitkin, Hanna, 196–197

Pluralism, 6, 98

Plyler v. Doe, 66

Polanco, Richard, 154, 156, 158

Police: Blacks on brutality and, 80, 131; Chicanos on brutality and, 33; community and reforms with, 80; as elected or representational position, 35, 57, 157, 159, 203; ICE and, 83; immigration and, 83, 93; monitoring board on, 176; political activities and interference by, 44; Puerto Ricans on brutality and, 37; on White nationalist manifesto, 108–109

Policymakers: district election structure and, 203; Latino politics and, 101; Latinos becoming, 2; political incorporation and, 203–204

Political activities: discrimination in, 20–21; district election structure and power of, 114–115; for employment or housing, 98; Florida with Latino power, 139; guns and, 172, 189; Latina roles in, 57–58, 67; Mexican

262 Index

Americans leading, 23–24; police interference on, 44; racism limiting, 13, 98; winning strategies for, 197

Political activities commentary: Eggman on, 181–183, 187, 190, 192; González, J., on, 177–178; Regan Gonzalez on, 187–190, 200–201; Sturgeon on, 179–181, 183, 190, 192; Vasquez, V., on, 183–185

Political agendas, 195, 197, 203–204

Political Association of Spanish-Speaking Organizations (PASSO), 27

Political boundaries, 4, 45

Political incorporation: as biracial, 200; class interests and, 201–203; coalition politics for, 12–13, 129, 199–200; definition of, 11–12; East Los Angeles bid for, 32–33, 75, 151–153; Latinos in, 12; pathways for, 12–14; policy benefits and, 203–204

Political machines: of Chicago, 45, 49–50, 64; as Democratic Party, 36, 45, 141, 199; of Latinos, 199–200; as local, 198–199; of Los Angeles, 154, 157–158; of New York City, 36, 45; Puerto Rican alternative to, 39, 45; of San Antonio, 140–141

Political objectives, 4–5, 12

Political power: Latino struggles for, 15, 21, 43; Latinos and, 11–12; minorities and, 11; racism limiting, 13, 98

Political representation, definition of, 7, 10

Politics: Anglos dominating, 5; definition of, 3; Latino representation in, 2–3; Latinos and 1940s, 15, 20, 23–24, 39

Poll taxes, 28, 104, 113

Polls, on elections, 16n24, 106

Pomona, California, 55

Population growth, 98, 101–102, 109; Arizona with Latino, 100, 101tab; of Asian Americans, 99; CPS on, 106; of Hiawassee, Georgia, 193n97; Latino empowerment as majority, 54–57; for Latino politics, 97; in Miami-Dade County, 131tab; 1980s Latino, 54–57; 1990s Latino, 54–57, 68; in San Fernando Valley, 155; US House of Representatives and, 115; US states and Latino, 100, 101tab

Poverty: Mexicans escaping, 25, 64; stratification and discrimination for, 57

Presidential elections, 26–27, 39, 112

PRLDEF. See Puerto Rican Legal Defense and Education Fund

Proposition 187, 65–67, 86

Proposition 200 (Arizona), 83

Proposition 300 (Arizona), 83

Protests, 196; August 29th Movement for, 33–34; in California, 33–34; for Chicano elected offices, 35; for elected offices, 6; interest group strategy with demands and, 12; by Latin Americans, 21; 1960s with African American, 21; for political incorporation, 12

Puedes, Sal Si, 26

Puerto Rican elected officials: Diaz, W., as, 77–78; Ferré as, 63, 133; Serrano, José E., as, 73; Velázquez, N., as, 73–74, 171

Puerto Rican Legal Defense and Education Fund (PRLDEF), 45

Puerto Rican Revolutionary Workers Organization, 38

Puerto Rican Socialist Party, 38–39

Puerto Ricans, 4, 205; for Biden, 107; in Chicago, 37–38; with citizenship, 102; on civil rights, 44–45; for Democrats, 36, 111, 111tab; of Hartford, 53; human capital transfers of, 20; independence for, 36, 38–39, 50; for Jackson, 51; militant confrontations by, 36–39; in New York, 37–39, 79; in 1940s, 35–36; in 1950s, 35–36, 38; in 1960s, 36–37; 1970s New York and, 38; origin numbers and, 100; on police brutality, 37; political machine alternative in, 39, 45; political struggles of, 2, 21; underrepresentation of, 38

Puy, Alejandro, 1

Racialization: bloc-votes without, 147–148; in California, 196; cross-racial support deemphasizing, 198; definition of, 4; deracialization and, 198; of Latinos, 2, 4; party vote or, 136, 195; of South Florida, 136

Index   263

Racism: American GI Forum on, 22–23, 27, 30; on Asian Americans, 98; Hahn using, 157; Minutemen and, 83–84; on Native Americans, 98; political incorporation or, 200; political limitations from, 13, 98
Racism locations: Arizona racial profiling as, 86, 106–107; Crusius and El Paso, 108–109; in South Florida, 130; in Texas, 75–76
Raimondo, Gina, 80
Rainbow Coalition, 51–53, 67
Ramos, Tim, 78
Rangel, Irma, 171
La Raza Unida Party (LRUP), 31–33, 152
Reagan, Ronald, 48–49, 65, 89
Reboso, Manolo, 48, 131–132
Redistricting electoral boundaries: bias in, 115–116; in Chicago, 50; by Cubans, 45, 48; gerrymandering and bias in, 115; for Latino-majority districts, 197–198; Latinos for, 4; lawsuits for, 12; at local level, 155, 161; by New York state, 61; in 1980s, 45, 48; in 1990s, 38, 155, 171; Republicans on, 116; US census for, 115
Regalado, Tomas, 134
Regan Gonzalez, Maria, 187–190, 200–201
Reid, Harry, 76
Reid, Rory, 76
Reinoso, Felipe, 63
Religion, Latino politics and, 84, 93, 109–110
Rendell, Ed, 51
Rendon, Anthony, 161
Representation types, 196–197
Republican Party: anti-immigrant legislation and, 73, 81–82, 84–86; on Chicago, 45; Cubans in, 48–49, 110, 137; Latino Protestant evangelicals for, 110; Latinos against, 49; Latinos for, 5, 72–73, 107, 110–111, 122; Latinos on, 8, 94, 111*tab*; New Mexico Anglos in, 24; percentage registration of, 138; on redistricting electoral boundaries, 116; South Florida for, 107

Reyes, Ben, 174
Reyes, Ed, 158
Reyes, Rico, 176
Reyes, Silvestre, 65
Reyna, Arthur, 150
Reyna, Diana, 79
Rhode Island, 79–80
Richards, Ann, 175–176
Richardson, Bill, 76
Riordan, Richard, 158–159
Rios, Oscar, 55
Rizzo, Frank, 51
Robaina, Julio, 137–138
Rodriguez, Steve, 153
Roe v. Wade, 191*n*48
Romero, Gloria, 52
Romney, Mitt, 8, 90, 112
de la Rosa, Carmen, 79
Rosales, Rodolfo, 148
Ros-Lehtinen, Ileana, 73, 134–135, 171
Ross, Fred, 25–26
Roybal, Edward, 23, 34, 74, 151–153, 155; CSO by, 25–27; NALEO by, 46–47
Roybal-Allard, Lucille, 74, 119–120*tab*, 155, 171
Rucho v. Common Cause, 116–117
Ruiz, Raul, 32, 119–120*tab*

Salazar, Kenneth, 72, 91
Salazar, Maria Elvira, 138
Salazar, Ruben, 33
Salinas, California, 33, 55
Salt Lake City population, 1
Salvadorans, 2, 62–63, 100
San Antonio, 162–163; history in, 139–140, 144; Mexican American politics in, 139–151; Mexicans in, 129–130; political machine of, 140–141; single-member districts in, 142
Sanchez, John, 76
Sanchez, Linda, 171
Sanchez, Loretta, 171
Sanchez, Orlando, 77
Sanchez, Tony, 75–76
Sandoval, Brian, 9, 76
Sanguinetti, Evelyn, 9
SB 1070. *See* Support Our Law Enforcement and Safe Neighborhoods Act

264 *Index*

Schubert, Carroll, 147–148
Segarra, Pedro, 80
Segregated society: in Crystal City, Texas, 27–28; González, H., on, 23, 25, 46–47, 151; Latinos in, 195–196; on soldiers, 22
Seguin, Juan, 140
Self government. *See Ayuntamiento*
Sensenbrenner, James, 81–82, 84–85
September 11, 2001, 71, 82–83
Serrano, José E., 73
Serrano, Jose M., 171
Shalala, Donna, 138
Shelby v. Holder, 116
Sheppard, Jade Chang, 176
Shor, David, 110
Silva, Cristina D., 170
Single-member districts: in Florida, 48, 130, 135; for inclusion, 6, 12; San Antonio adopting, 142; in Texas, 44
Snyder, Art, 153
Social advancement inequalities, 6
Social media, Latinx in, 4, 16*n*7, 84–85, 204
Solarz, Stephen J., 171
Solis, Hilda, 74–75, 91, 171–172
Soto, Cynthia, 64
Sotomayer, Sonia, 89, 91, 170
South Americans, 63, 100, 111, 111*tab*, 139
South Florida, 48–49, 107, 130, 134, 136
Southeast US, 9, 121, 185–187, 193*n*97
Southwest US: Anglos in, 57; at-large elections influencing, 113; history of, 40, 98, 101–102, 113; land struggles in, 30, 33–34, 140; Latinos and elected offices in, 20, 27–29, 40, 121–122, 200; Mexican Americans in, 2, 22–24, 29, 45–46, 75–76, 205; 1970s and Latino elected office lack in, 34, 34*tab*; nonpartisan offices in, 199–200; SVREP in, 45–46; Tejanos and Californios in, 3; unions in, 26
Southwest Voter Registration Education Project (SVREP), 45–46
Spanish settlers, 2–3, 16*n*3
State level: Chicano electorate at, 34*tab*; Delaware legislators at, 179–181; diversity lack at, 117; Latina percentage at, 169*tab*; Latinas at

California, 181–183; Latino politics at, 2, 122, 175–183; LEO numbers at, 1, 7–8, 8*tab*, 72–73, 123; "right-to-work" at, 29–30
Strama, Mark, 176
Strikes, by farmworkers, 22, 26, 29–30, 58–59. *See also* Unions
Sturgeon, Laura Viviana, 179–181, 183, 190, 192
Suarez, Francis, 134
Suarez, Xavier, 133, 135
Suarez-Orozco, Marcelo, 3
Substantive representation, 197
Support Our Law Enforcement and Safe Neighborhoods Act (SB 1070), 86, 106–107, 107*tab*
SVREP. *See* Southwest Voter Registration Education Project
Symbolic representation, 10–11, 197

Tabb, David, 11, 13, 17, 56, 69, 125, 129
Tammany Hall political machine, 36
Tancredo, Tom, 82
Tavares, Angel, 80
Taylor, Ivy, 130
Teamsters Union, 28
Teele, Arthur, 136
Tejano, 3
Telles, Raymond, 23, 25
Tenayucca, Emma, 170
Term limits, 145, 158, 171, 181–182
Texas, 24; Bush, G. W., of, 71–72; Cisneros of, 47, 129, 140, 142–151; district election structure in, 44; gerrymandering in, 116, 125; Hispanics and state exit polls of, 16*n*24; Jackson in, 52; Mexican poverty and Texas, 25; poll tax in, 28; racism in, 75–76; segregated society in, 27–28; single-member districts in, 44. *See also* Houston; San Antonio
Texas cities: Crystal City as, 27–28, 31, 34–36, 170; El Paso as, 10, 23, 25, 58, 65, 108, 172–173, 175. *See also* Houston; San Antonio
Texas Latinos: elected offices for, 122–123, 123*tab*; Latina boycott and strike as, 58–59; Latinas as, 170, 172–175; Latino legislators as, 175–

179; population growth in, 100, 101*tab*; vote by, 10, 112; voting rights and, 104

Texas Legislature, Latinas in, 175–179

Texas Monthly, 191*n*61

Texas organizations: FLOC and, 51; LRUP party and, 31–33, 152; MALDEF on election laws and, 44; MAYO and, 31, 141; SVREP and, 45–46

Tijerina, Pete, 43

Tijerina, Reies López, 30

Torres, Art, 152, 154–155

Torres, Peter, 141

Torres, Ritchie, 73

Traffic congestion, 11

Trujillo, Rafael L., 59

Trump, Donald, 89; as anti-Latino, 92–93; Colombians for, 107–108; crime and, 108; Cubans for, 107, 110; on DACA, 93–94; on ICE and police, 83; Latinos on, 8–9, 90–94, 110–112, 138, 168; on Mexicans, 93, 108; Miami-Dade County for, 9, 108, 108*tab*; Nicaraguans and Venezuelans for, 107–108; on undocumented immigrants, 94; Whites for, 109–110

Tuerk, Matt, 78

287(g) Program, 83

2000s: anti-immigrant backlash in, 82; Immigrant Workers Freedom Rides in, 84; Latino politics increase in, 71; Latino Voting Rights Project in, 45; Latinos and Los Angeles wins in, 156, 156*tab*, 158; Latinos and US census of, 61; LEO increase in, 72, 94–95; undocumented immigrants in, 82, 84–86

2001 Los Angeles race, 156*tab*

2020 Latino elected officials, 6–7, 7*tab*

2020s: Latino voting patterns in, 107–109; LEOs in, 121; US census in, 99–100

UFW. *See* United Farm Workers

Underrepresentation: of Chicanos, 34, 34*tab*; of Latinas, 168; of Latinos, 2, 5–6, 46, 53, 94, 98, 103; of minorities, 6, 207; of people of color, 80; of Puerto Ricans, 38

Undocumented immigrants: Arizona on, 106; assistance for, 86–87; CASA for Mexican, 33; as Central Americans, 62; citizenship and, 74, 81, 102, 105; DACA for, 87, 90, 92–94; DREAM Act for, 74, 84, 87, 90; in East Los Angeles, 32–33; as Mexicans, 103; in New York City, 59–60; 1980s actions on, 65; 1990s actions on, 65–67; numbers of, 5, 23, 81, 100, 104; Trump on, 94; 2000s actions on, 82, 84–86; without voting rights, 104

Unemployment, 59–60

Union groups: AFL-CIO as, 82; Teamsters, 28; UFW as, 22, 26, 29, 33, 54

Union people: Caba and, 78; Chavez, C., as, 26, 29–30; Jackson and, 52; Martinez, J., and, 138; Solis and, 74–75; Valentin and, 37–38; Vasquez, V., in, 183–185; for Villaraigosa, 157, 159

Unions, 23; Latinas and, 170; Los Angeles Latinos and, 157–158; "right-to-work" states and, 29–30; strikes by, 22, 26, 29–30, 58–59; for voting experience, 104–105. *See also* Farmworkers

United Farm Workers (UFW), 22, 26, 29, 33, 54

United States (US): Caribbeans and, 21; Central Americans and intervention by, 21; Cold War dynamic of, 22; Congressional Hispanic Caucus of, 46; Cubans favored by, 21, 205; Cubans on foreign policy and, 48; history of Latino politics, 15–16, 20–21, 97–98, 109, 112–113, 162, 195; human capital transfers to, 20; Latino percentage in, 10; Latino politics in, 5; Latinos and political system of, 1; Mexicans leaving, 104; New Mexico annexation by, 2; Operation Bootstrap by, 35–36; on Proposition 187, 65–67, 86; with two-tiered pluralism, 6

US. *See* United States

US census: CPS of, 106; Latinos in 2000, 61; in 1990, 171; for redistricting, 115; in 2020, 99–100

US Constitution, 66, 86, 114–116

266 Index

US Department of Justice, 114, 142, 154
US foreign policy, 19, 21, 48, 86
US House of Representatives: diversity in, 117–118, 119–120*tab*, 120–121; Latinas in, 169tab; Latino numbers in, 7*tab*, 72–73; Lebron and, 36; Native Americans in, 121; population determining, 115; Solis in, 74–75; Velázquez, Nydia M. in, 73–74, 171
US judicial branch, Sotomayer of, 89, 91, 170
US Senate: diversity in, 117–118, 119–120*tab*, 120–121; Latinas in, 169tab; Latino numbers in, 7*tab*, 72; Melendez, R., and, 49

Valdermoros, Ana, 1
Valdés, Jorge (George), 132, 135
Valentin, Gilberto Gerena, 37–38
del Valle, Miguel, 50
VanDeWalle, Mike, 176
Vasquez, Kendrys, 79
Vasquez, Veronica, 183–185
Velasco, Pete, 29
Velásquez, William C., 45–46, 144–145
Velázquez, Nydia M., 73–74, 171
Velez, Ramon, 37–38
Venezuelans, 107–108, 139
Vera Cruz, Philip, 29
Villalobos, Javier, 78
Villaraigosa, Antonio, 77, 130, 136, 156–160, 156*tab*
Viva Kennedy clubs, 26–27, 39
Voter turnout: age and registration on, 101–102; COPS for, 141–143, 145, 203–204; by CSO, 26; Democrat registration for, 138; education for, 104–105; as low, 152–153; naturalization for, 46, 66–67, 82, 85; polls and, 106; in presidential elections, 112; SVREP for, 46; Texas poll tax on, 28; in 2020, 107–109; unions for, 104–105; after Watsonville legal challenge, 55
Voter turnout groups: Arizona exit polls and Hispanic, 16*n*24; California and Latino, 10; Cubans in, 132–133; Latino youth in, 103; by Latinos, 90–91, 103, 105–107, 105*tab*, 157, 159, 163, 195; by Mexican Americans, 25,

45–46, 103–104; of minorities, 44; by Whites, 153, 159
Voting rights: Arizona restricting, 83; attacks or expansions on, 88–89; ballot harvesting and, 89; citizenship for, 82, 102, 105; *Gomez v. City of Watsonville* on, 54–55; majority-minority district for, 117, 124–125, 168, 172–173, 196; poll taxes on, 28, 104, 113; PRLDEF on, 45; registration for, 85, 104; restrictions on, 195; September 11, 2001, on, 71; Texas tightening, 191*n*60; undocumented immigrants without, 104
Voting Rights Act (VRA) (1965), 6; for African Americans, 88, 113–114; Alabama against, 114; at-large voting and, 54–55; Civil rights movement for, 113–114; current need for, 195–196; dilution attempts on, 49; for Latinos, 88; for legal challenges, 115–116; to Texas, 44
Voting Rights Act (VRA) (1975), 104
Voting Rights Act (VRA) (1982), 44

Walters, Rita, 153
Washington, Harold, 49–50, 136
Weddington, Sarah, 175–176, 191*n*48
Welfare Act. *See* Personal Responsibility and Work Opportunity Act
West US, 198–199
Whitacre, Veronica Vela, 78
White liberals: African Americans and, 53, 80, 130, 152, 154, 200; Asian Americans with, 49, 51, 53; on Cubans, 130; Cubans without, 130, 200; Latinos and, 53, 80, 200–201
Whites: bias to, 6; coalition politics in minorities and, 13; on Cubans, 48; Democratic Party as, 36; for Dinkins, 52–53; Latinos as, 3; Miami population growth of, 131*tab*; through 1940s1940s, 140; as non-Latino, 3; Perry for, 75–76; police on manifesto and, 108–109; as privileged, 6; Salt Lake City population of, 1; for Trump, 109–110; on 2001 Los Angeles race, 156*tab*; voter turnout by, 153, 159. *See also* Anglos

Whitmire, Kathryn, 174
William C. Velásquez Institute, 46, 145
Williams, Melissa, 207
Wilson, Pete, 66
Wisconsin, 1, 9

Xenophobia, 64

Ya Es Hora! Campaign, 85
Young Lords Party, 38, 45

Zaffirini, Judy, 171
Zapata, Juan C., 63–64

About the Book

This new, fully revised edition of *Latino Political Power* reflects a diverse community evolving in its ethnic, racial, and sexual identities, as well as in its voting behavior and party affiliations.

Sharon A. Navarro and Kim Geron map the transformation of Latino political power from the 1960s to the present. Comprehensive and accessible, their analysis of the complex processes of political incorporation, representation, and inclusion at all levels of government is based on the most current data available.

With an entirely new chapter on Latinas as candidates and as elected officials in 2021–2022, discussion of the latest voting-rights cases, and rich case studies throughout, this up-to-date text will provide readers with a solid understanding—and appreciation—of Latino political power today.

Sharon A. Navarro is professor of political science at the University of Texas at San Antonio. **Kim Geron** is professor emeritus of political science at California State University East Bay.